Prophetic Drama
in the Old Testament

PROPHETIC DRAMA
IN THE
OLD TESTAMENT

David Stacey

EPWORTH PRESS

British Library Cataloguing in Publication Data
Stacey, W. D.
Prophetic drama in the Old Testament.
1. Bible. O. T. Prophecies. Interpretation, etc
I. Title
221.15

ISBN 0–7162–0470–3

First published 1990
by Epworth Press
Room 195, 1 Central Buildings,
Westminster, London SW1

Phototypeset at Input Typesetting Ltd
London SW19 8DR
Printed and bound in Great Britain
by Dotesios Printers Ltd, Trowbridge, Wiltshire.

Contents

Preface

The story of this book began many years ago in a seminar in the Department of Theology in the University of Bristol. Strictly it was an Old Testament seminar, but a colleague from the study of religion, the late Revd Fred Welbourn, shared it with me. His wide experience in Africa and his knowledge of anthropology greatly enriched the discussion and set me thinking about the inner meaning of 'prophetic symbolism', as it was commonly called. At the same time, the Revd. Professor Kenneth Grayston suggested that it was time I embarked on a doctoral thesis; this provided a further stimulus. A Ph.D. dissertation, however, is one thing, and a book is quite another; and the present work would never have seen the light of day if I had not had the advantage of a few periods of study leave. I am more than grateful to the Divinity School of Duke University, North Carolina and to its Dean, the Revd Dr Dennis Campbell, for inviting me to serve as Visiting Professor on three different occasions. With the help of Duke's excellent library, most of this work was done.

I acknowledge a very large debt to the Revd Professor George Anderson of Edinburgh, who was my first teacher of Old Testament and Hebrew, then briefly a senior colleague, and has been a guide and encourager throughout the whole of my teaching life. He generously gave his time to read this typescript and he suggested many improvements. My wife, Professor Morna Hooker, also read the typescript and made innumerable suggestions; that simple formula must suffice to cover a debt that goes beyond expression. In recording my gratitude I also register the hope that the imperfections that undoubtedly remain will be attributed directly to me and not to those who went out of their way to help me.

Cambridge, 1990   David Stacey

Abbreviations

AB	The Anchor Bible, New York
AJSL	*American Journal of Semitic Languages and Literatures*, Chicago
ATD	Das Alte Testament Deutsch, Göttingen
BA	*Biblical Archeologist*, Ann Arbor, Michigan
BBC	*Broadman Bible Commentary*, London
Bib	*Biblica*, Rome
BJRL	*Bulletin of the John Rylands Library*, Manchester
BTB	*Biblical Theology Bulletin*, New York
BTFT	*Bijdragen: Tijdschrift voor Filosofie en Theologie*, Amsterdam
BZAW	*Beihefte zur Zeitschrift für die alttestamentliche Wissenschaft*, Berlin
CB	The Century Bible, Edinburgh
CBC	The Cambridge Bible Commentary, Cambridge
CBQ	*Catholic Biblical Quarterly*, Washington
CurrTM	*Currents in Theology and Mission*, Chicago
CBSC	The Cambridge Bible for Schools and Colleges, Cambridge
DSB	The Daily Study Bible, Edinburgh
ERE	*Encyclopaedia of Religion and Ethics*, Edinburgh
ET	English Translation
EVQ	*The Evangelical Quarterly*, Exeter
ExpTim	*The Expository Times*, Edinburgh
HDB	*Hastings' Dictionary of the Bible*, Edinburgh 1905
HTR	*Harvard Theological Review*, Cambridge, Mass.
HUCA	*Hebrew Union College Annual*, Cincinnati, Ohio
IB	*The Interpreter's Bible*, New York and Nashville
IBS	*Irish Biblical Studies*, Belfast
ICC	The International Critical Commentary, Edinburgh and New York
IDB	*The Interpreter's Dictionary of the Bible*, New York and Nashville 1962
Int	*Interpretation*, Richmond, Virginia
JB	Jerusalem Bible
JBC	*Jerome Bible Commentary*, edited by R.E. Brown, J.A. Fitzmyer and R.E. Murphy, London 1968
JBL	*Journal of Biblical Literature*, Philadelphia
JNES	*Journal of Near Eastern Studies*, Chicago
JSOT	*Journal for the Study of the Old Testament*
JSOTS	Journal for the Study of the Old Testament, Supplement Series
JTS	*Journal of Theological Studies*, Oxford
MT	Massoretic Text

NBC	*The New Bible Commentary* edited by F. Davidson, A.M. Stibbs and K.F. Kevan, London 1953
NBCR	*The New Bible Commentary Revised* edited by D. Guthrie and J.A. Motyer, London 1970
NBD	*New Bible Dictionary* edited by J.D. Douglas, London 1962
NCB	New Century Bible, Grand Rapids and London
NEB	New English Bible
NIC	The New International Commentary, Grand Rapids, Michigan
NRT	*Nouvelle Revue Théologique*, Heverlee, Belgium
ONC	New Clarendon Bible, Oxford
OTL	Old Testament Library, London
PC	*Peake's Commentary on the Bible* edited by Matthew Black and H.H. Rowley, London and Edinburgh 1963
PEQ	*Palestine Exploration Quarterly*
PEFQS	*Palestine Exploration Fund Quarterly Statement*
RB	*Revue Biblique*, Paris and Rome
REB	Revised English Bible
ResQ	*Restoration Quarterly*, Abilene, Texas
RelSRev	*Religious Studies Review*, Ontario
RevScRel	*Revue de sciences religieuses*, Paris
RHPR	*Revue d'Histoire et de Philosophie Religieuses*, Strasbourg
RSV	Revised Standard Version of the Bible
RV	Revised Version of the Bible
SBL	Society for Biblical Literature
SBT	Studies in Biblical Theology, London
SJT	*Scottish Journal of Theology*, Edinburgh
StBTh	*Studia Biblica et Theologica*, Pasadena, California
StTh	*Studia Theologica*, Lund
TBC	The Torch Bible Commentaries, London
TC	Tyndale Commentaries
TU	Texte und Untersuchungen zur Geschichte der altchristlichen Literatur, Berlin
TWNT	*Theologisches Wörterbuch zum Neuen Testament*, Stuttgart
TIR	*The Iliff Review*, Denver
VT	*Vetus Testamentum*, Leiden
WBC	Word Biblical Commentary, Waco, Texas
WC	Westminster Commentaries, London
ZAW	*Zeitschrift für die alttestamentliche Wissenschaft*, Berlin

· I ·

BACKGROUND

1 · Introduction

Every student of the Old Testament is familiar with those narratives which speak of prophets performing strange, dramatic actions, apparently to support and clarify their message. Ahijah tore his cloak into twelve pieces and gave ten to Jeroboam, at the same time affirming that Jeroboam would gain possession of ten of the tribes that formed Solomon's empire (I Kings 11.29–31). Zedekiah made horns of iron in order to support his contention that Ahab, with Jehoshaphat's help, would overwhelm the Syrians (I Kings 22.11). Isaiah walked around naked, or almost naked, to depict the plight of those who would be carried away captive by Assyria (Isa. 20). Jeremiah broke a pot to signify the doom of the city (Jer. 19.1–13). There are more than forty examples of such behaviour in the Old Testament; the purpose of this book is to examine them.

Despite the fact that the narratives pose intriguing problems, interest in the subject among Old Testament scholars has been limited. H.W. Robinson produced a much-quoted article in 1927.[1] Three books appeared in Holland in the next two decades.[2] Georg Fohrer wrote an article in 1952 followed by a book in 1953.[3] Recently, Samuel Amsler has produced a short work in French discussing the main texts under very general headings.[4] Commentaries include brief notes on the individual narratives, but only rarely does a commentator think it necessary to provide an overall account of the phenomenon or even

---

[1] 'Prophetic Symbolism' in *Old Testament Essays*, 1927.

[2] A. van den Born, *De Symbolische Handelingen der Oud-Testamentische Profeten*, 1935, and *Profetie Metterdaad*, 1947; A.W. Groenman, *Het Karakter van de Symbolische Handelingen der Oud-Testamentische Profeten*, 1942.

[3] 'Die Gattung der Berichte über symbolische Handlungen der Propheten', *ZAW* 64, 1952; *Die symbolischen Handlungen der Propheten*, 1953, second edition 1968.

[4] *Les Actes des Prophètes*, 1985.

an extended discussion of the examples that occur in the book on which he is commenting. Many articles occur in journals, but they are usually concerned with individual texts; we can read a great deal about Shear-jashub or Ezekiel's dumbness, but relatively little about prophetic drama as a whole. It is fair to say, then, that discussion of the subject has been muted. Almost everyone who writes at length about the prophets mentions dramatic action in passing, but most tend to assume that any questions raised have a simple answer. Much time is given to consideration of the prophet's word, but a page or two is usually sufficient to dispose of the prophet's actions. Judgments made by H.W. Robinson sixty years ago seem sound enough to stand today, despite the enormous advances that have been made in the study of Israel's cultic practice, the meaning of ritual and drama, the relevant literary problems, and so on.

A brief summary of the subject area as it is commonly understood would be as follows. Prophets normally declaimed oracles, but sometimes, in order to make their message more impressive, they performed dramatic actions to accompany the oracle. The oracles and the dramatic actions pointed to future events, and, once the word had been spoken and the action performed, the fulfilment must inevitably come to pass. This idea of actions inevitably bringing about fulfilment suggests a magical procedure and indeed prophetic drama does have the appearance of magic, but the theology is Yahwist. The prophet is not coercing the deity but submitting to his will. This explanation suffices for most actions. Some, however, particularly those of Ezekiel, are so complex and occasionally so indelicate that it is necessary to ask whether they were ever performed at all.

Almost every detail in this summary requires closer examination, and this book is an attempt to provide it. The aim will be to establish an account of prophetic drama which gives a reasonable explanation of all the data.

There is more than one way to examine these actions. They could be the subject of historical enquiry. Did these events actually happen as the narratives state? Some of them sound improbable, some even distasteful. Did prophets actually do these things? Van den Born and Groenman were particularly interested in this kind of question. Again, it is possible to be less concerned with the historical element and to concentrate on the record and its literary form. This is Fohrer's method and his work is very significant. As befits a form critic, he is more concerned with the shape of the narrative as it has come down to us, than with the phenomenon that is being described. Fohrer carried out a form-critical analysis of thirty-two narratives and reached the conclusion that the typical narrative consists of, first, a command to the prophet to carry out the action, then the account of him carrying it out, and finally some explanation of its meaning. This method is very revealing, but it tells us little about why the prophetic action was thought to be peculiarly potent or how the action was understood by contemporaries. Moreover the method has the unfortunate side effect of separating those dramatic actions that are narrated in Fohrer's typical form from all the other dramatic actions performed by various people in Israel, including non-prophets, and presumably sharing, in some measure, in the dynamic of prophetic actions, though they are actually described in all kinds of ways and forms.

It is also possible to examine the actions in terms of comparative anthropology. Dramatic action figures in the cults and activities of people and tribes all over the world and in every period of history. Can something be learned about prophetic behaviour in Israel by comparing it with pitcher-breaking or robe-tearing or foundation-stone-laying in other fields? Fohrer gives examples of such parallels, but he also recognizes the dangers of proceeding too far in this direction. The tendency to assume that similar actions had similar meanings characterized the anthropology of long ago. Certain elemental actions, the shedding of blood, for example, may give rise to profound and universal reactions, and this is a proper area for study, but even these reactions are overlaid by peculiar, cultural interpretations; so the gain from the comparison may not be great. Moreover, few if any of the prophetic dramas come, as dramas, in the category of elemental actions such as blood-shedding.

These methods are not totally separable. They meet and inform each other. We shall often need to discuss what actually happened, especially in Chapter 15, and we shall make frequent reference to the literary form of the narratives, but our main concern will be with the dramatic actions themselves and how they were understood both by contemporaries and later editors. It may be assumed that, within the total religious context and the theological traditions of ancient Israel, the prophetic actions were understood in a peculiar way; it is that way of understanding that we shall try to unravel.

The undertaking is not without its dangers. In the first place, discussion of how an action is understood demands the question: understood by whom? The prophet may have one intention, but the onlookers may infer that intention incorrectly. And a distinction must be made between the inferences of sophisticated observers, familiar with the prophet's message and its theological context, and those of the common people whom we must suppose to have been unsophisticated, not to say downright superstitious, in their religious understanding. We must also distinguish between the understanding – we should say the understandings – of the original actors, the onlookers, the disciples who compiled the records, the subsequent editors, and those who read the records as part of their Holy Scripture. Added to that, there is every reason to suppose that understanding changed through the centuries. The way in which the earliest stories were recorded influenced the way in which later actions were understood, and when finally all the stories, of all dates and situations, came together in the canon, the overall understanding would change again.

Redaction criticism has taught us the importance of editors. More recently canonical criticism has taught us the importance of the context in which the text was preserved. We need to be aware from the beginning that the only data we possess regarding prophetic drama come to us from the pages of 'Holy Scripture'. We who study the text today may try not to allow our own confessional attitudes to influence our historical methods improperly, we may struggle for some kind of 'procedural neutrality'; but we may be sure that those who gave us the Bible did no such thing. All those texts about the prophets were preserved by editors who believed that God was addressing Israel through them. That belief, that reverence for the text, was passed on to later generations; and the emergence of a canon of Hebrew Scriptures accentuated the reverential aura that surrounded the ancient writings. We need constantly to remind ourselves that it is not the acts of the prophets that we are observing but narratives relating to those acts which have been preserved and passed on by a devout community. That, however, is no loss. The beliefs and attitudes of the prophets themselves are only part of the data; the beliefs and attitudes of those who preserved and used the Old Testament are equally important and much more accessible. To suppose, therefore, that a simple and universal 'explanation' of prophetic drama is there to be discovered is a great error. This does not make the present enquiry useless, but it complicates the undertaking and imposes limits on our expectations.

Secondly, there is the philosophical problem of the relation of action to meaning. What is the precise force of the word 'meaning' when it is predicated of a piece of dramatic action? Words can, with some difficulty, be given meanings; concepts can, with much greater difficulty, be given meanings; but what of actions when no words are spoken at all? What, in our own society, is the meaning of a kiss, a bow, a swift, dramatic exit? These questions are not unanswerable, but they suggest further complications. The kiss and the bow have explicit meanings for us, warmth and intimacy for the kiss, respect and loyalty for the bow. We need, however, to beware of over-confidence when trying to define explicit meanings for actions of a similar kind that took place in ancient Israel. And this problem is as nothing compared to the problem of giving meaning, not to general, but to particular actions. It is one thing to talk about the meaning of mourning rites, quite another to speak of the meaning of the action of one particular prophet on one particular day. Explanations of actions of this kind will need to be tentative, and never precise, dogmatic and final. This factor puts a further constraint on our expectations.

Thirdly, we need to be aware of the danger of speculation when there is no way of putting speculations to the test. Anthropologists have long been aware that it is necessary to observe what people do for a very long time before it is wise to speculate on how they think. Here the biblical student is in difficulty, but he does have the advantage of a large amount of written text. While this text does not give a formal account of the meaning of prophetic drama, it does provide oblique evidence from which conclusions can be drawn. We can study the record, the background of the incident, the precise actions of the prophet, the reactions of the onlookers and the apparent consequences. We can study the way the record has been preserved and modified. We can study any accompanying words spoken by the prophet and the relation of the incident to the total message of the prophet. We can study analogous actions from other areas of Israel's life. We can consider the theological ambience of the incident, what might and might not be reasonably implied by such a man at such a time. We can even make sparing use of comparative material. From all these things we can draw inferences and construct some account of meaning.

A question arises over the category of incidents to be investigated. The involvement of a prophet is crucial, but what other criteria are there? Should the enquiry be limited to *deliberate* actions? But some incidents that were treated as significant happened by accident. Should the enquiry be limited to actual *incidents*, whether deliberate or accidental? But sometimes a prophet discovered significance in a

situation that was not properly an incident at all. Jeremiah found
significance in the everyday work of a potter (Jer. 18.1–12). Even
beyond this, prophets seem to find significance in their *imagination*,
as they reflect on common objects or happenings (Jer. 25.15–29; Ezek.
2.8–3.3). Should these reflections be included, as if the subject matter
of them had actually taken place? There is an obvious difficulty here.
The broadest possible category is desirable if the aim is to discover
how Hebrews thought about significant action, but space imposes
limits. This book, however, will range more widely than is customary
in the discussion of this topic.

Questions of method raise further problems; by no means the least
of these has to do with the attitude of the investigator. The worst
mistake that can be made is to regard our language, our thought forms,
our mental map, our social constructs as norms, and to discuss Hebrew
ideas in terms of how they depart from these norms. This is an
error well-known to historians, anthropologists and many others. An
interesting article showing the parallel problems of biblical interpreters
and anthropologists occurs in an issue of *Current Anthropology*.[5] The
Watsons point out that the first principle of anthropological enquiry
is to seek understanding in context, as distinct from 'pre-understanding'.[6] No enquirer is free from pre-understanding, so the task is not
to seek some extra-terrestrial, neutral point from which a culture can
be observed objectively, but to recognize the difficulty and pursue the
enquiry in terms of question and answer between one culture and
another. It may be impossible completely to penetrate the other
culture, but, equally, it is not true that we can understand only what
is within our own horizon. Disciplined imagination is necessary and
valuable. The Watsons adduce a quotation from Gadamer that puts
this point nicely, 'imagination (Phantasie) is not an undisciplined
rambling, but rather a creative force which enables one to find the
questions worth asking in the new context.'[7]

[5] Maria-Barbara Watson-Franke and Lawrence C. Watson, 'Understanding Anthropology: a Philosophical Reminder', *Current Anthropology* 16, 1975, pp. 247–62.

[6] Many investigators use the term 'ethnocentricity', e.g., 'There is a real danger that
the investigator will fall prey to ethnocentricity and evaluate more highly what to him
is more familiar or intelligible or "rational" ' (Overholt, 'Prophecy: the Problem',
p. 57). Overholt deals with the whole matter in *Prophecy in Cross-Cultural Perspective*,
1986.

[7] Watson-Franke and Watson, 'Understanding Anthropology', p. 251. The quotation
is from H.G. Gadamer, 'Die Universalität des hermeneutischen Problems' in *Kleine
Schriften I: Philosophie, Hermeneutik*, 1967. It has to be said, however, that not even this

As far as interpretation of the Scriptures is concerned, the problem of pre-understanding may express itself in various ways. One is that of confessional bias. The Bible is a sacred book for most of those who are interested in the present topic; it provides the authentic account of the way of salvation; it is the Word of God. Anthropologists burrowing into the mysteries of ancient lore have no such considerations. What they uncover may be interesting, important, unique, but, on the other hand, it may be none of these things; and, if it is not, the anthropologist is under no compulsion to make it so. The student of the Bible may feel that he is not so free. His approach may be governed by the *a priori* notion that the material must be positive, because it is material for the theologian and for preaching. Here the student is in danger.[8] Of course, nobody comes to the text free of bias. Indeed, it might be argued that the supposition that a scholar of any kind can be free from bias is itself a bias. Nevertheless a conscious attempt to let the text speak for itself and not to order the investigation in the way most positive for confessional interpretation is demanded. The work should proceed on the assumption that the prophets deserve the most careful scrutiny, but that there is no reason to suppose that their words and actions will always prove relevant or positive or comprehensible.

A further example of pre-understanding is seen in the confidence that everything in Scripture *can* be explained, that obscurities have only to be noted and analysed for their mysteries to be resolved. There seems to be an assumption that, perhaps providentially, we always have enough material to make a reasonable analysis, that we are capable of understanding it thoroughly, that we are astute enough to translate it into our own language and thought forms, and that this process will give us a satisfactory account of the meaning of the material. All these assumptions are open to question. Too great a desire for clarity and too confident a belief that it can be supplied may have much the same effect as confessional bias. If the approach is such

---

eminently reasonable proposition goes without challenge. The first of the comments published immediately after the Watsons' article finds it dated and boring. The writer, Morris Freilich, is a structuralist who is interested, not in discrete cultures, but in the psychic unity of mankind and in the universal structures created by it (p. 254).

[8] Of course it can be argued that a study of this kind is propaedeutic for theology. The more deeply we penetrate the mind of the biblical writers, the better prepared we shall be to understand Scripture for ourselves.

as to serve a predetermined end, whether faith or lucidity, the material may be wrongly read.

Pre-understanding can also prevent us from seeing the logic of another culture. It is reasonable to assume that the Hebrews were as mentally alert and as systematic as we are, though their notion of system may differ from ours; and it is dangerous to assume that, because system, as we understand it, is not evident in the texts, it is non-existent, or, even worse, that the people concerned were not capable of systematic or coherent thought. Anthropologists of a previous generation wrote about 'pre-logical mentality'.[9] We are a little wiser now. The people being investigated may be extremely logical, but the logic may operate on a different plane from our own, and so it may be missed by the modern scholar.[10] Lévi-Strauss sees in primitive thought the same demand for order, the same search for definitions and classifications as prompts the modern scientist.[11] He supplies two interesting examples of this in *The Savage Mind*.[12] In the first instance, early travellers in South America assumed that the classification of animals made by the Indians was worthless because it was different from their own. In fact, as was recognized later, the native classification possessed a range and subtlety far in advance of anything the visitors could provide. In the second case, the archaeologist H.C. Conklin found himself confused when he tried to

[9] L. Lévy-Bruhl, *How Natives Think* (with its lofty French title, *Les Fonctions Mentales dans les Sociétés Inférieures*), 1910, ET 1926. Lévy-Bruhl had considerable influence in Old Testament circles in his day.

[10] A comment from Nur Yalman in his article on 'Magic' in the *International Encyclopedia of the Social Sciences*, edited by David L. Sills, 1968, vol. 9, p. 525, is worth quoting in full. 'The process of understanding the minds of others is partly a matter of insight and freedom from prejudice, and although the discipline of anthropology has gone far in this direction, there is much room for improvement. In any case, the objective and respectful attempt to understand the inner logic in what superficially appears meaningless or illogical cannot be taken for granted. But the further question must also be raised of whether the linked or orderly system of ideas presented to us is really that of the native, or whether the order is artificially imposed on the phenomena by the mind of the anthropological observer. This issue is a difficult one, resting near the precipice of metaphysics, but its difficulty does not prevent the observation that the heuristic assumption of "system" in primitive ideologies has proved to be very fruitful. The claim regarding the systematic nature of primitive ideas is always open to further verification, but as yet no anthropologist has been able to sustain an argument based on the senselessness or illogicality of primitive beliefs.'

[11] *The Savage Mind*, pp. 9f.

[12] Ibid., pp. 44 and 55.

understand the colour definition of the Philippines in terms of the system with which he was familiar. Confusion vanished when his informants, instead of using names, actually compared one colour with another. There emerged a perfectly coherent system. The Bible clearly demands of us the same positive approach. The aim must be to search for a schema by which prophetic actions can be understood. This schema is unlikely to be obvious to aliens like ourselves, and it will require of us a certain amount of cultural divestment in order to grasp it. We need constantly to remind ourselves that the Old Testament can be understood only within its own ambience.

Equally it would be folly not to make use of all we know of the Old Testament context, for plainly prophetic drama cannot be understood apart from the whole complex of Hebrew thought. Yet there has been a tendency to ignore this fact and to treat prophetic dramas as curious and occasional incidents, not deeply rooted in Hebrew culture. To see the dramatic actions as cultural oddities belonging only to the prophetic calling, and so to detach them from other symbolic actions must lead to misinterpretation. It follows that the task of the investigator is to examine certain broad areas of Hebrew thought in an attempt to grasp the structure, the logic, the categories, so that the place of prophetic drama within those areas becomes apparent and the meaning of the actions can be more readily understood.

It is trite, however, to affirm that the Old Testament must be interpreted *from within* without recognizing the difficulties. The most obvious lies in the language. James Barr has shown that the wide currency of generalizations about Hebrew being 'dynamic' and 'concrete' indicates that the language barrier is far from being overcome.[13] Language is related to corporate experience, and translation, even when brilliantly carried out, rarely gets down to that experience. It is right to translate *šĕmĕš* by 'sun', but the Hebrew experience of sun involves impressions that are not implied when a Briton uses the word. Another difficulty lies in the difference between Hebrew social structure and our own, another concerns climate, another experience of the natural order, another life expectancy, and so on. All these determine the way in which life is lived, thought about and written about. The differences between the two worlds, theirs and ours, are so radical that it is reasonable to expect that the Hebrew understanding

---

[13] *The Semantics of Biblical Language*, pp. 10ff., 30f. Lévi-Strauss makes a similar point over a wider field (*Savage Mind*, pp. 1f).

of even the most basic matters will be different from our own. We have no reason to suppose, for example, that a society which lacked books, archives, newspapers, museums and written records would have the same attitude to the past as we have. Nor that a society which had made little progress in the field of empirical science would have the same approach to questions of sequence and causation as we have. That is not to say that we are right and they were wrong, still less that we are wise and they were foolish. Our map of knowledge is simply larger than theirs and different from theirs. Moving from one world to the other requires patience. There is much un-learning, as well as much learning to be done.

Finally there is the danger of trying to build too complicated a structure on too small a base. This is illustrated by a monumental book on Hebraic thought, Johs. Pedersen's *Israel*.[14] Pedersen's fault, other than following too closely in the wake of Lévy-Bruhl, is in constructing too elaborate a system on too little evidence. Pedersen assumes that there is a correlation between the structure of Hebrew language and the structure of Hebrew thought. James Barr, in *The Semantics of Biblical Language*, is able to show that this apparently reasonable hypothesis is so full of contradictions that it must be rejected entirely.[15] Pedersen also propounds the view that the human person is essentially a 'soul', a centre of vital energy from which all human processes, physical and mental, radiate, and into which all human experiences are gathered. This simple, undifferentiated totality, represented by the word 'soul', provides the key to the understanding of the Hebrew person. 'The biblical evidence simply does not confirm his theory', comments Brevard Childs, and Old Testament scholars line up to agree with him.[16] Imposing a schema on the material is an ever-present danger in Old Testament studies; the schema, if it is to be useful, must grow out of the evidence and not be imposed upon it. At this point we are on the edge of a philosophical debate. In the last resort, there is no such thing as a schema that grows out of the evidence. All schemata are mental constructs. Does that mean that they are also impositions? However this argument goes, it must be granted that there is a difference between a scholar who strives

---

[14] *Israel, its Life and Culture*, ET I (I–II), 1926 and II (III–IV), 1940.

[15] *Semantics*, pp. 33–45, 89–96, 181–4.

[16] *Memory and Tradition in Israel*, p. 29. See also the criticism of Pedersen's idea of the 'soul' in the article by Peter Addinall, 'The Soul in Pedersen's *Israel*'.

to express the order inherent in the material and the scholar with a thesis to prove.

This chapter has been largely about difficulties and dangers. It is necessary to note them, but they do not invalidate the enquiry. The Hebrews, like the people of every other society that has ever been, experienced reality on two levels. There was the historical level, represented by the actual things that happened, the events, situations, conditions that determined the circumstances under which they had to live; and there was the cultural level, the word, the drama, the ritual, which they manufactured, which stood over against the historical, and which enabled them to report, comprehend, endure, celebrate, anticipate, and even, in a measure, control the historical level. This is the world in which we are moving. Prophetic actions stand over against some historical reality. In the simplest instance that means that the prophetic action stands over against an event which it prefigures. It is the relationship between the action and that other reality that is the concern of this book. The material is there to be studied. There need be no doubt that, as far as the Hebrew was concerned, there was a certain rationale to it, and it is incumbent upon us to try to divine what that rationale was.

2 · Terminology

A question arises over terminology. There is unfortunately no Hebrew word that specifically relates to the prophetic acts with which we are concerned. Three words occur, none of them more than occasionally, *'ôṯ*, *môpēṯ*, and *māšāl*. All have wider senses that have nothing to do with the prophets. The first is commonly translated in the LXX by σημεῖον, which is translated into English by 'sign'. The second appears in the LXX as τέρας, and in English as 'wonder'. The third is usually rendered by παραβολή, sometimes by παροιμία, giving us 'parable' and 'proverb'. None of these translations is exact.[1]

To speak generally, *'ôṯ* is a means whereby some entity of great significance, but not immediately and fully apprehensible, is made concrete and accessible. Sabbath and circumcision are signs or tokens in this sense (Gen. 17.11; Ex. 31.13,17; Ezek. 20.12,20). They express and actualize the covenant in concrete ways. At the same time, these rites are an intrinsic part of the covenant; they are not external indicators that can be scrapped when their usefulness is over.

This notion also applies in relation to history. Yahweh's activity in history is something every Israelite, including those who live in times of apostasy and disaster, must savour to the full. There is a reference to a sign upon the hands (described as an *'ôṯ*) and a memorial between the eyes recalling the exodus event, in the account of the festival of unleavened bread, though it is not clear exactly what the words mean

---

[1] In the Bible as a whole *'ôṯ* occurs seventy-nine times; *môpēṯ* occurs thirty-six times, about half of them involving a close link with *'ôṯ*; *māšāl* occurs as a noun thirty-nine times. Much work has been done on this subject, particularly by Keller (*Das Wort OTH*) and Rengstorf (article on σημεῖον in *TWNT*). See also Eichrodt, *Theology II*, pp. 162ff., and Jacob, *Theology*, pp. 223ff.

(Ex. 13.9).[2] Naturally, in later Judaism, they were connected with the scrolls and phylacteries worn on arm and forehead, but this cannot have been the original meaning. Whatever they were, their purpose was to recall the past and make it existentially present. The sign apparently acts as a *zikkārôn*, a memorial; similarly in Josh. 4.6f., *'ôt* is clearly related to *zikkārôn*. In later times Israelites will see the stones by the Jordan and will recognize them, not simply as a reminder, but as a manifestation of a great event which is ever-present in Israel's history.

Future events equally can be experienced through signs. The man of God tells Eli that his sons, Hophni and Phinehas, will die on the same day and this misfortune will be a token of a greater misfortune. The shock and desolation will introduce Eli to the greater shock of the total humiliation of Israel – though in point of fact, Eli did not survive the first news (I Sam. 2.34). Similarly, Jeremiah in Egypt expects a terrible doom to visit the apostate Jews there; not one of them will survive. The sign will be that Pharaoh Hophra will meet the same fate as Zedekiah, personal misfortune again being the indicator of much greater misfortune to follow (Jer. 44.29f.).

Allied to this usage is the sense that carries the idea of proof. When Gideon is visited by an angel, he asks for a sign that will prove the identity of his visitor; his offering is then consumed by spontaneously kindled fire. From one point of view this is a preliminary revelation of the power that will fight for Gideon, from another it is simply an answer to his request for verification of his call (Judg. 6.17). Deut. 13.1ff. finds it necessary to warn against prophets of other cults who attempt to establish their credibility in a similar way. The *'ôt* was commonly thought to validate words that were not otherwise capable of proof. Samuel made a rather extravagant promise to Saul when he came looking for his asses, and the narrator seems to think that no reasonable man would believe such a promise, so a complicated sign is provided. Unlike some of the others, this sign is completely artificial in its form, but it establishes Samuel's authority in that the fulfilment of the immediate prophecies validates the larger and more distant prophecy. A similar usage is found in the story of Rahab and the spies in Josh. 2.12ff., though the details are lacking. Rahab asks for a

---

[2] It is possible that the sign alludes to practices that were *not* current in Israel; the sense may be that the festival of unleavened bread takes the place in Israel of tattoo marks on the hands or badges worn on the forehead in other cults. S.R. Driver seems to imply this (*Exodus*, pp. 107f.; see also Noth, *Exodus*, p. 101).

promise and a sign that her family will be spared; a simple word would not be reliable, but a word with a sign would be. Two stories of Isaiah provide well-known examples of this usage. In Isa. 7.10–17 Isaiah has just prophesied that the Syro-Ephraimite confederacy will break down, that Ahaz and Jerusalem will be safe. This seems extravagant, so he – the text says Yahweh – offers to confirm the prophecy by a sign.[3] Ahaz can ask for anything, which shows that a sign can be completely artificial, but he refuses, so Isaiah himself chooses a sign which is anything but artificial; it involves an event which is basic to the security of the royal house. When the birth of the child takes place, the prophecy begins to be actualized, and as birth and deliverance are both part of the same prophecy, the deliverance is likewise set on its way. In the other example, II Kings 20.8–11, similar ideas are operating, though the sign is artificial only. Hezekiah is ill; Isaiah prophesies his death and then retracts the prophecy and tells the king that he will live for fifteen years more. Hezekiah wants proof, so Isaiah asks him how he would like the sun's shadow to behave. What Hezekiah asks happens against all reason; the movement of the shadow and the recovery of the king, joined together in the word of the prophet, both evidence the power of Yahweh.

A common use of 'ôṯ, very close to the one we have just been discussing, is for something that indicates an aspect of Yahweh's nature commonly affirmed, but not always evident. The author of Ps. 86 seems not to doubt that Yahweh is gracious and merciful, but he wants that grace to appear in some evidential way (v. 17). This is not the usual situation. Normally the sign appears first to convince the witnesses that the facts are as prophesied. In Ps. 86.17 the writer is already convinced, but he would like a sign just the same. In Job 21.29 the word almost means evidence, and a number of references describe signs of Yahweh's sovereign, but hidden, power (Num. 14.11; Deut. 4.34; Ps. 65.8; Isa. 19.20; 66.19). This is nowhere more clear than in the account of events leading to the exodus. References to the plagues and the wonders of the exodus, in fact, supply the standard usage of the word (Ex. 8.23; 10.1f.; Num. 14.22; Deut. 6.22; 7.19; 11.3; 26.8; 29.2f.; 34.11; Jer. 32.20f.; Pss. 78.43; 105.27; 135.9; Neh. 9.10).

Perhaps the most interesting example of the word from our point of view is II Kings 19.29. Judah is suffering at the hands of the

---

[3] 'The purpose of a "sign" is to produce or increase faith in those who experience it or who learn about it from reliable witnesses' (Willis, 'The Meaning of Is. 7.14 and its Application to Mt. 1.23', p. 4).

Assyrians, and Isaiah comes forth with an oracle about eventual restoration. The sign given is that the people will live for a season or two on corn that is self-sown. This normally happens in an agricultural community if war breaks up the cycle of sowing and reaping, but Isaiah represents it as a sign that a remnant will endure to take root again and bear fruit. There is a certain similarity between Isaiah's way of thinking in this instance and Jeremiah's reflection on the potter at work. Both men are living in critical situations; both feel themselves called to give oracles; both hold that Yahweh is continually breaking into history and will do so again; both see themselves, their words, their thoughts, their actions, their signs as the means whereby Yahweh's purpose begins its course in history; both, therefore, expect to see signs of the advent of Yahweh in what happens around them; and both, in fact, do so. The 'ôṯ and the prophetic reflection – and, therefore, we presume, the prophetic action – come close together at this point. Both rest on the ability of the prophet to recognize ways in which God's hidden purpose shows itself in subtle revelations.

Despite this similarity, the cases in which the word 'ôṯ is used explicitly of prophetic actions are few. There are, at the most, four. In Isa. 8.18 the prophet and his children are described as signs, which means that the actions of Isa. 7.3 and 8.1–4 are, by inference, signs; Isaiah's representation of the plight of the prisoner of war (Isa. 20.1–5), and Ezekiel's mock siege of Jerusalem (Ezek. 4.1–3) are two further examples.

Half the occurrences of môp̄ēṯ link the word directly with 'ôṯ, but there are differences of emphasis.[4] It seems clear that môp̄ēṯ is used to describe people and events only, whereas 'ôṯ is used for objects as well, but perhaps this is not very significant. It is fair to say that môp̄ēṯ usually means something extraordinary and 'ôṯ can often mean something mundane, though, in referring to the plagues of Egypt, both words

---

[4] The psalmist himself is a wonder in Ps. 71.7, though it is not clear in what way. The high priest and his colleagues are a wonder in Zech. 3.8. The distinction made by Driver, which H.W. Robinson quotes with approval, is that môp̄ēṯ is 'an occurrence regarded merely as something extraordinary', whereas 'ôṯ is 'something, ordinary or extraordinary, as the case may be, regarded as significant of a truth beyond itself, or impressed with a divine purpose' (Driver, *Deuteronomy* p. 75; Robinson, *Inspiration*, p. 37). It is hard to believe that Driver had considered all the usages and even harder to understand how Robinson, who had already investigated prophetic symbolism, could have endorsed it. There are eighteen occurrences when môp̄ēṯ appears to be synonymous with 'ôṯ and there are several occasions when môp̄ēṯ describes a prophetic action.

have the sense of the extraordinary. Occasionally *môpēt* implies the ominous, whereas, in this respect, *'ôt* is neutral.

The incident in I Kings 13.1–10, where the word *môpēt* is used, is not far removed from a prophetic action, though interpretation is difficult because of the form of the narrative and the fact that it is plainly an insertion. An unknown man of God denounces Jeroboam and the altar at Bethel and prophesies the destruction of the syncretistic northern cult. He announces, as a *môpēt*, that an accident will happen to the altar. The accident happens at once, but it is not until three centuries later that the prophecy is fulfilled (II Kings 23.16–18). Into the story is inserted a detail about Jeroboam – he points at the man to have him arrested and finds his arm paralysed – which has the effect of confusing the picture. Nevertheless it is legitimate to say that, in the final redaction of the Deuteronomistic history, I Kings 13.1–10 is set out as an anticipation of II Kings 23.15–20, that the former is recounted in terms of a *môpēt*, and the latter as the fulfilment of it.

Finally we note those prophetic actions where *môpēt* is used. Isaiah and his children are wonders as well as signs (Isa. 8.18); so too is the prophet's scandalous appearance in 20.1–5. The other examples are all from Ezekiel. Ezekiel's dramatic representation of the inhabitant of Jerusalem packing his bags and leaving for exile is twice called a *môpēt* (12.6,11). The prophet himself, when he fails to mourn his wife's death, is a *môpēt* (24.24); and when he recovers his speech after the fall of Jerusalem, he is to be a *môpēt* to the people (24.27).

The majority of prophetic dramas are not described either as *'ôt* or as *môpēt*. Nevertheless, a few parallels between the meaning of *'ôt* and *môpēt* and the thought world of prophetic actions are worth noting. First, although the primary usage of the terms is in relation to the exodus, they seem to be part of the prophetic trade in Deut 13.1f. (cf. Ps. 74.9). Secondly, both prophetic action and signs and wonders display a similar diversity. There is no clearly defined procedure in either case; artificial actions and natural incidents given significance by interpretation occur in both categories; both involve specially gifted persons, either to act or to explain;[5] both are usually accompanied by words; both include some examples that are momentary and others that are of long duration or permanent; audiences occur in both and their function is not constant in either; both involve objects sometimes but not always. Such variety is daunting to anyone who is looking for

[5] Keller, *Das Wort OTH*, pp. 11ff.

a tight definition in either case, but it strengthens the contention that the principle of consistency, which makes definition possible, lies, not in the thing that happens, but in the way that it is thought about. Thirdly, there is similarity in thought structure. In both cases there are two factors, a hidden reality and a manifest indicator of it; in both cases the relationship between the two depends upon the conception of a single reality that has two modes, one hidden, one revealed; in both cases the indicators exhibit a part of what they signify. In neither case is the man of God an initiator; he is simply the one to whom the hidden reality is revealed.

The third word to consider is *māšāl*.[6] Broadly speaking, the word has two senses, the more common one denoting a shrewd statement or epigram, usually expressed in figurative language, the other denoting a practical example of a universal truth. To take the second one first, Deut. 28.37 asserts that apostate Israel will suffer such miseries that she will be a *māšāl* to the surrounding peoples. The truth is that God is righteous and punishes the unfaithful, and Israel's sufferings provide a practical example of this truth.[7] In Ezek. 14.8 *māšāl* is used as a near synonym for *'ôt*; both mean a visible proof of the dynamic nature of the wrath of God. This element in the meaning of *māšāl* provides a pointer to the interpretation of some prophetic actions, even though the term *māšāl* is not used to describe them. The relationship of truth to proof is not chronological. One is a permanent reality, the other a temporary expression of it. The truth is durative, the proof is punctual. This factor is relevant to prophetic actions which often actualize a reality that is not itself bounded by time and space. Hosea's marriage is an example.

In the other sense, that of shrewd statement or epigram, the *māšāl* has a number of different forms: the short epigram, of which there are many examples both within Proverbs and without, the longer proverbial statement, the figurative speech, the dirge, and the lengthy recital. It is not immediately obvious how the notion of resemblance

---

[6] The root means 'to resemble', and the verb occurs several times in passive forms in this sense (Job 30.19; Pss. 28.1; 49.12 [13 Heb.]; 49.20 [21 Heb.]; 143.7; Isa. 14.10); a nominal form with the same sense occurs in Job 41.33 [25 Heb.]. Noun forms, however, are not so patently linked with the idea of resemblance. For an illuminating and modern treatment of the term, see Polk, 'Paradigms, Parables and Mesalim'. Polk takes his examples from Ezekiel and stresses the performative aspect of the term.

[7] See also I Kings 9.7; II Chron. 7.20; Pss. 44.14 [15 Heb.]; 69.11 [12 Heb.]; Jer. 24.9.

operates in every case. Part of the explanation is that the *māšāl* often takes the form of a simile or metaphor and so always represents one reality by another. In such a case the simile is not so much a literary artifice as a drawing together of two entities, so that one becomes a revelation and interpretation of the other. In the *māšāl* of Ezek. 24, the words of Ezekiel bring together the cauldron and Jerusalem; what happens to one also happens to the other.[8]

The most common term in English for the phenomenon we are discussing is 'prophetic symbolism', perhaps because it was the first to be used.[9] In favour of 'symbol' it can be said that symbols are normally supposed to participate directly in what they represent, and we shall discover before long that prophetic action and the reality to which it relates participate in each other. It would help the argument if we could rule out, from the beginning, the idea that the prophets were 'merely acting'. (The word 'mere' tends to crop up wherever symbolism is under discussion and it rarely helps the argument.) Unfortunately there is a general lack of precision in usage which weakens the point being made.

A more substantial point is that symbols do more than convey information, and this is a reason why the more commonplace 'sign' is not satisfactory. An action intended simply to announce that the city would fall could well be called a sign, but an action intended to arouse the same anguish, the same shocked horror as the disaster itself is more than a simple sign. Isaiah walking naked and barefoot (Isa. 20), Jeremiah breaking his earthen flask (Jer. 19), Ezekiel lying on his side

---

[8] On the basis of Ezek. 24, A.R. Johnson has suggested that *māšāl* is the most appropriate word for prophetic action (*Cultic Prophet*, pp. 40f.; *Sacral Kingship*, pp. 88, 101, 134; see also Godbey, 'The Hebrew Masal' p. 89.

[9] Robinson speaks of 'prophetic symbolism' in his essay of 1927 ('Prophetic Symbolism'). Buzy had already made use of the word 'symboles' (*Les Symboles*, so too Regnier, 'Le Réalisme'). Some turn 'symbol' into an adjective, and so 'symbolic acts', or 'symbolischen Handlungen' in German, or 'symbolische handelingen' in Dutch. Not everyone is satisfied. Lods, writing in the same volume as Robinson, uses inverted commas, 'les actes dits "symboliques" des prophètes' ('Le Rôle', p. 59). Pedersen also used inverted commas (*Israel II*, p. 112). Uncertainty about the appropriateness of the word 'symbol' probably explains Lods' later preference for 'prophetic act' (*The Prophets*, pp. 54ff.; so too Bowker, 'Prophetic Action' and Amsler, 'Les Prophètes et la Communication par les Actes'). Guillaume confuses the matter by using 'symbolic action' and 'acted sign' interchangeably (*Prophecy and Divination*). R.B.Y. Scott prefers 'sign', but 'prophetic symbolism' is the most common term. There are still more options, 'symbolic act' (Greenberg), 'symbolic action' (Holladay), and 'Zeichenhandlung' (Zimmerli).

(Ezek. 4.4–8), were not simply passing on information. They were provoking, as they believed under divine compulsion, the same disquiet, fear and remorse that the further acts of God would create when they eventually came to pass. In the common understanding of the terms, symbols have an inner, compelling power that signs lack. Symbols communicate through the senses to the unconscious and the response is profound, not entirely rational nor volitional. Signs are often trivial, communicating simply with the conscious intelligence and requiring only a superficial response. A sign is all that is necessary to make a person stand in the right queue at a railway station, but something more is necessary to make him leave home and enlist as a soldier. If railway officials need to be proficient with signs, recruiting officers need to understand symbols.

There is, however, much to be said against the traditional term. First, one has to consider the technical meanings of 'symbol'. Mathematicians, musicians, poets, artists, philosophers, psychologists and others make use of the word and there is enormous diversity between the usages. Secondly, to discuss prophetic action in the biblical context without prejudice we need ideally a neutral term, a term that will not bring with it into the biblical world the sophisticated overtones of another culture. 'Symbol' is certainly not that. Thirdly, symbols, because they probe deeply into human consciousness, cannot be easily contrived. They need to make use of archetypal elements that are, in some sense, natural and universal. Some prophetic actions employ such elements, but the majority do not. Most are contrived for one, particular occasion. This leads to a fourth point. Symbols are essentially multi-vocal; they stimulate the unconscious; they appeal to the imagination. One never fully grasps the meaning of a symbol. Prophetic actions, however, are uni-vocal; there is no make-of-it-what-you-will element.[10] It is true that, as a means of communication, some of them are extraordinarily abstruse, but abstruseness is not the same as imprecision. Ezekiel, the most abstruse of prophets, had a precise message. His methods puzzle us, but we should not conclude that Ezekiel was deliberately acting in an elusive and mysterious way.

It therefore seems best to reject both symbol and sign as the standard term for prophetic action. In this book we have opted for the word

[10] It is true that, again and again, prophetic actions were reinterpreted by later editors, not because the meaning of the action was thought to be open-ended, but for the opposite reason: because the editor wanted to present the action as specifically meaningful to his own generation.

'drama'.[11] Often it may not be a drama in the strict sense, but usually some kind of dramatic action is either performed or conceived. We shall not follow this option slavishly; 'acts' and 'actions' will often appear, even the word 'sign', when it seems more appropriate. We shall use the word 'reality' for the other element in the pairing, that is, the event or truth or condition to which the prophetic drama relates or draws attention. Happily these terms do not predispose us to accept one predetermined account of the chronological relationship between them. The drama can represent the past, the present, the imminent and even the distant future without difficulty. That is a very important factor with regard to the dramatic actions performed by the prophets.

---

[11] Watts argues vigorously for the propriety of using the term 'drama' in relation to the Old Testament cult and the prophetic vision. Unfortunately he does not mention prophetic actions (*Isaiah 1–33*, pp. xlv–l). In everyday usage, the relation of the drama to reality in the world at large is a deep and engaging subject. See the seminal study by Erich Auerbach, *Mimesis: The Representation of Reality in Western Literature*.

3 · Conventional Actions

Every society has its repertoire of conventional signs and actions. When people meet for the first time, they shake hands. Brides wear white and wedding guests wear flowers. Anyone who doubts the importance of conventional actions needs to keep clear of parliament, the law courts, the armed services, royal occasions, the universities, the Cup Final, the Olympic Games, the Kremlin, the last night of the Proms, even the local Scout troop.

Conventional actions are distinguished from natural, spontaneous actions by their formality and artificiality. The origin of conventional actions may be found in natural behaviour – and some, like shaking the fist to convey anger, may fall somewhere between the two – but it is useful to preserve the distinction between the natural and the conventional. This book is largely concerned with contrived and artificial acts, so it is appropriate to look for parallels among conventional forms rather than among natural responses. Conventional forms, however, are usually manufactured over many generations and endlessly repeated, whereas prophetic acts are almost always contrived for, and carried out on, one occasion only; so the parallel is by no means perfect. Nevertheless the way in which conventional actions convey meaning is interesting and relevant.

Discussion of meaning in this context carries us into deep water. Presumably, when the conventional actions were first used, the meaning was evident in the act. Kneeling before a superior meant putting oneself deliberately in a vulnerable position in order to affirm submission. It is not always easy, however, to trace that kind of meaning in conventional acts, and in practice people of a later day tend to rely heavily on the social programme in order to 'do the right thing'. Investigators of biblical culture are, therefore, at some disadvantage; explanations are rare and inference is almost the only means available to them.

Hebrew life was rich in expressive actions. Moses removed his shoes at the burning bush (Ex. 3.5) and Joshua did the same at Jericho (Josh. 5.15). When Solomon prayed, he went down on his knees (I Kings 8.54; II Chron. 6.13) or spread out his hands (I Kings 8.22). Moses spread out his hands in Ex. 9.29. Perhaps at one time the people who performed these actions knew why they did so, but their reasons are now lost.[1] All we can say is that it was done because acting in that way was commonly regarded as acting reverently. It is interesting to note that a momentary action, kneeling, represents a permanent disposition, submission; the punctual represents the durative.

The case is rather different with mourning. The wearing of sackcloth corresponds with the period of acute grief. It is a means of expressing, and coming to terms with, an unwelcome condition. Jacob tore his clothes and put on sackcloth and mourned his son for many days (Gen. 37.34). The messenger from the battlefield at Aphek tore his clothes and put earth on his head before bringing the bad news to Shiloh (I Sam. 4.12). So too did the messenger who brought David the news of the death of Saul and Jonathan (II Sam. 1.2). David himself mourned Abner in a similar way (II Sam. 3.3). The inhabitants of Jabesh-gilead mourned Saul by fasting for seven days (I Sam. 31.13). These are all deliberate actions. No doubt there was an element of doing what was normally done, but the references do not suggest actions performed in a perfunctory way. The prescribed behaviour was also appropriate behaviour. Sitting in squalor was a conventional sign of misery, but both the squalor and the misery were real. The actions may have been psychologically therapeutic, but it is hard to believe that they were carried out pragmatically, to achieve an end. They were carried out to express a grief that, being real, seemed to demand outward expression.[2]

A person of substance wrapped a garment around someone in need as a sign that he was prepared to give the other protection (Ruth 3.9;

---

[1] Gaster (*Myth, Legend and Custom in the Old Testament*, p. 231) provides a choice of explanations for the removing of shoes at holy places, and it would not be difficult to add to his list.

[2] For mourning rites in Israel, see Kennett, *Ancient Hebrew Social Life and Custom as indicated in Law, Narrative and Metaphor*; Ehrlich, *Die Kultsymbolik im Alten Testament und im nachbiblischen Judentum*; de Vaux, *Ancient Israel: Its Life and Institutions*.

I Kings 19.19; Ezek. 16.8). A man made a contract with a slave who had served six years and did not want his freedom by boring through his ear and so putting their relationship on a new and permanent basis (Ex. 21.6; Deut. 15.16f.). These actions were acknowledged as socially effective.[3] The boring had no mechanical efficacy. One could not gain servants by holding them still and boring their ears. This was first an agreement; then came the boring, the public confirmation.

Other similar conventional actions were the use of salt in covenant making (Num. 18.19; II Chron. 13.5), the intimate touch that seals the vow (Gen. 24.2,9; 47.29; Ezra 10.19; Ezek. 17.18), the careful use of right and left hands in blessing (Gen. 48.14,17), the washing of hands to symbolize innocence (Deut.21.6f.), taking off the sandal and spitting in the face as a sign of repudiation (Deut. 25.9), eating meals to affirm a bond (Gen. 26.26–31; 27.19; II Sam. 3.17–21), and so on. In all these cases the actions bear witness to a condition that exists apart from the actions themselves. One exception may be Gen. 27, where there seems to be no blessing apart from the action; Isaac's intention miscarries, but what he has done is irretrievable. This certainly underlines the importance of the physical act, but it does not mean that it is inherently effective. Isaac's intention was clear; the physical act expressed it. Intention and act together create the irreversible situation.[4] That is evidence for the importance of the whole process, but not proof that the act is sufficient by itself. Consequently this example hardly disturbs the thesis that conventional acts do not create new conditions but bear witness to and stabilize conditions that are already in being.

There are a number of references to opening the mouth as a means of insulting someone (Job 16.10; Pss. 22.13; 35.21; Isa. 57.4; Lam. 2.16; 3.46). The verb used in three of these references is fairly neutral, but the others sound more aggressive, and in every case the verb is followed by the preposition ʿal, meaning 'against', with a hostile

---

[3] One can only guess at the rationale behind the boring of ears. According to S.R. Driver, 'The ear, as the organ of hearing, is naturally that of obedience as well; and its attachment (Deut. 15.17) to the door of the house would signify the perpetual attachment of the slave to that particular household' (*Exodus*, p. 211). Noth has something similar to say, 'the piercing of it was understood as a removal of its integrity and thus the original freedom of hearing' (*Exodus*, p. 178). The point is not that these guesses are right but that they concentrate attention on the fact that the Hebrews accepted the action as both representing and giving social validity to a new state of affairs.

[4] Thiselton argues that blessings were not irreversible. See 'The Supposed Power of Words in the Biblical Writings'.

sense. How can opening the mouth initiate or express an act of aggression? One can simply guess that the mouth was regarded as something of a weapon. Animals used it for slaughter. Human beings used it to issue powerful words. Bitter, poisonous matter was vomited from it. A gaping mouth was, therefore, probably understood as a weapon to convey some evil force against another individual. Poking out the tongue made it even more direct (Isa. 57.4). The action expresses an attitude of mind which exists before the action takes place, but more than that, the action seems to be a way in which the aggressive intent is projected out towards its target. It seems to require both verbal expression and actual physical violence to complete it. The full series would be: malevolent attitude, insulting action, insulting word, violent action. No doubt prudence often dictated that the series should not run its full course. In this case the conventional action is both expressive and effective. It takes over an evil intention, strengthens it, and conveys it on its way.[5]

A more spontaneous action is Saul's grand gesture in cutting up two oxen and sending the pieces around the villages as a demonstration of what would happen to the oxen of any who failed to rally to his standard (I Sam. 11.7).[6] It was not necessary for Saul to carve up oxen to make himself understood, because the message was simple and clear. The action was exemplary, but conditional. Other oxen will end up like these unless the owners take up arms. There is a hypothetical series: Saul's violent intention, the sign of dismembered oxen, inappropriate cowardice on the part of Hebrew farmers, more dismembered oxen. But note that the full series can be intercepted; it is, therefore, wrong to think of the act as necessarily effective. A horrible example of the same line of thought seems to be present in Judg. 19–20. The Levite from Ephraim was outraged by the behaviour of the men of Gibeah, who had ravished and apparently killed his concubine, when he and the unfortunate woman were guests in Gibeah. The action of carving up the body of the concubine into twelve pieces and sending the pieces round the territory of Israel is rather obscure, though the consequence was a mission of revenge against Gibeah, attended by much slaughter. It is easy to infer the series: thirst for revenge, bloodthirsty action, bloodthirsty consequence, but there is not enough

---

[5] A more complex example of 'body language' is found in Prov. 6.12f., but the sense is not clear enough to help.

[6] There is a similar but less dramatic gesture in Neh. 5.13.

evidence to be sure that this is right. If it is, the force of the action is much the same as in the previous example.

An interesting question arises with the covenant sealing in Gen. 15, especially in relation to the interpretation offered in Jer. 34.18. Genesis 15 can be read in two ways. It can be said that, in making a covenant, the contracting parties pass between the halves of a dismembered animal and so are joined together, embraced, as it were, within the animal's body. If that is correct, it provides another example of a dramatic action which both expresses and gives force to a relationship that has just been established. But Jer. 34.18 implies an entirely different explanation, particularly if the text is emended by the addition of the word 'like', as many commentators suggest and as the RSV has accepted. 'The men who transgressed my covenant . . . I will make *like* the calf which they cut in two and passed between its parts.' This brings the story more in line with I Sam. 11 and a similar analysis would apply. The original intention of the participants would be, first, to enter into a covenant with the partner, and second, to enact a punishment if the partner failed.

After his comprehensive defeat of the Canaanite alliance in Josh. 10, Joshua found himself with five Amorite kings as his captives. He brought them out of the cave where they were being guarded and caused his commanders to put their feet on the kings' necks. As a punishment this amounted to little, for the kings were soon hanged; as a means of humiliation it counted for much. Joshua wants his ascendency to continue into the future, so the ascendency needs to be both expressed and extended. Joshua declares that, if his commanders were brave and trusting, Yahweh would give them further victories. So the action stands between two victories, one that it demonstrates and seals, and one that it helps to promote.

Another significant incident from the Joshua narrative comes in Josh. 8.18–26. Joshua is encamped before Ai. He manages to lure the defenders out of the city by counterfeiting a retreat, and then, at the crucial moment, he holds up his javelin and points it at the city. The Israelites turn to attack, the defenders are cut off, and the city falls. Pointing the javelin may have been a military signal, but it was more than that. In the first place, Yahweh commanded the action and promised victory (v. 18). Secondly, according to the narrative, the javelin was pointed at the city throughout the whole day's slaughter (v. 26). Thirdly, parallels occur in Ex. 17.8–13 and II Kings 13.14–17, both of which suggest significant actions and both of which must be

discussed later. Fourthly, pointing a weapon against an enemy is, of
all the actions to be considered, the one most widely regarded as
significant beyond any functional purpose. Anthropologists produce
parallels from all over the world. Here, however, the action is
significant because Yahweh first required the sign, then through it
brought the victory. The series now begins with a divine intention,
then comes the significant action, and finally the victory. This gives
the appearance of an essentially effective action, but it is not what it
seems. The effective force is the divine intention; the action with the
javelin is the means used by Yahweh to bring about the intended
victory.

Another similar narrative occurs in Ex. 17.8–13, in which God is
not mentioned directly. It is the well-known story of Moses bringing
about a victory for Israel over Amalek by holding his staff above his
head all day. It might be argued that, in this narrative, Moses' action
was responsible for the victory, but it is more reasonable to see a
theological explanation here and to conclude that the staff, called the
staff of God in Ex. 4.20 and 17.9, was effective simply because it was
being used in pursuance of God's will. The editorial comment in
vv. 14–16 and Yahweh's promise to obliterate Amalek confirm that
this was the view of later generations.

The use of the rod in this last incident raises the question of how
important physical objects are in the narratives being investigated.
The notion that objects can be charged with mysterious potency is
widespread in societies ancient and modern. The mandrakes of Gen.
30.14–16 provide one biblical example; they had some force as an
aphrodisiac. No similar explanation will suffice, however, for the
incident with the rods of fresh poplar in the latter part of the same
chapter (Gen. 30.25–43). Jacob and Laban had made a deal that gave
Jacob all the speckled and spotted goats and the black lambs. Laban
deceitfully tried to remove the speckled and spotted before Jacob
could claim them, so Jacob replied with what looks like a piece of
imitative magic. He took poplar rods, peeled them in stripes, and left
them around for the goats to see when they were mating. The result
was large numbers of speckled and spotted kids. The power to achieve
this result rested, not in the poplar rods themselves, nor in the action
of peeling them, but in the pattern made on the rods. The rationale
of this incident, therefore, stands somewhere between the notion of
the dynamic object (the mandrakes) and the notion of the effective
action (Joshua pointing his javelin) in which the object is relatively

unimportant. The mandrake incident is almost isolated in the Bible, while dramatic actions have parallels everywhere.

This list of conventional actions is by no means complete, but it does suggest some tentative conclusions. Significant actions occur across the whole range of human life. They are both formal and informal, public and private, with and without spontaneous variations. They are carried out by charismatic figures or by ordinary folk. Some occur only once, others are repeated again and again. Some have an obvious meaning, others are obscure. In some cases the action focusses in a moment of time; others imply an enduring situation. In some the action is expressive of a situation already in existence; in others it anticipates a situation yet to come; in some cases it does both. Whatever conclusion an action anticipates, it can be forestalled, and it is never right to speak of essentially effective actions. Often the effectiveness rests in God who requires the action as well as the fulfilment. Finally, though the notion that objects have inherent potency is not entirely absent from the Old Testament, the explanation of dramatic actions does not lie in that direction. It follows that there cannot be a simple, homogeneous category of significant acts, which suggests that prophetic dramas, when we come to them, will defeat any attempt to confine them within a single definition or one inclusive category.

4 · Cultic Actions

No account of how dramatic action was understood can be satisfactory if it is not informed by evidence from the cult, for dramatic action in the world at large must have been decoded in terms of similar action within the cultic programme. Moreover the argument, inaugurated by Hölscher seventy-five years ago, continued by Mowinckel and strongly supported in Britain by Aubrey Johnson, that some parts of the prophetic movement were deeply involved in the cult, has now been widely accepted.[1] If the cult provides the working context of some prophets, it may safely be said that it provides the conceptual framework for all.[2] The contention, if it could be sustained, that dancing, drama, and processions at the festivals were thought to have a 'magical effect' on nature and history would inevitably lead to the presumption that prophetic dramas were likewise regarded as instrumentally effective.[3] In point of fact, the argument here advances a different thesis; it is that prophetic drama was thought to express and introduce divine action but not, of itself, to cause anything. This thesis, however, would simply float in mid-air if it could not be shown that it was consistent with the way the cult was understood.

Dancing

A good place to begin is with the sacred dance. Dancing in the Old Testament is not done simply for exercise or for aesthetic reasons; it is done as an act of celebration. The Old Testament yields evidence

---

[1] Hölscher, *Die Profeten*, pp. 143f.; Mowinckel, *Psalmenstudien III: Kultsprophetie und prophetische Psalmen*; Johnson, *Cultic Prophet*. Fohrer, however, refused to be convinced. See 'Remarks on Modern Interpretation of the Prophets'.

[2] Kapelrud, 'Cult and Prophetic Words'.

[3] Porteous, 'Prophet and Priest in Israel'.

of processional dances (II Sam. 6.5), dancing at sacrifices (Ex. 32.6,19), dancing in a state of prophetic trance (I Sam. 10.5f.), festival dances (Judg. 21.16–24), victory dances (Ex. 15.20f.), and perhaps other kinds as well.[4] Dancing is so widespread in connexion with ritual that this is scarcely surprising.[5] One example is the dance that follows a victory. In Ex. 15.20, Miriam and all the women of Israel danced with timbrels to celebrate the victory at the Red Sea. If this verse is read historically, the dance is a reaction to the deliverance, but if it is read cultically, it may be either a reaction to the past or a celebratory anticipation of a deliverance in the future.[6] In Judg. 11.34, when Jephthah comes home from his victory over the Ammonites, his daughter comes to meet him with timbrels and with dances, celebrating and extending his triumph. Similarly in I Sam. 18.6, when David and Saul returned from their victories over the Philistines, the women came dancing out of the cities to meet them (cf. I Sam. 21.11; 29.5).

These are all dances related to historical events. There are others where the 'victory' may be simply an acknowledgement of the victorious character of Yahweh. Psalm 149 is a comprehensive shout of praise that includes a call to dance, but no specific deliverance is referred to; the purpose of the dance is to affirm that Yahweh's nature and activity call for constant, triumphal celebration. So too with Ps. 150. Psalm 30 suggests that the deliverance to be celebrated with dancing is personal, probably recovery from a severe illness. The dancing before the golden calf in Ex. 32.19 also belongs in this context. The bull image derives from the fertility cults of Canaan, but in v. 4 the historical element has been introduced, and the bull is now said to represent the gods that have brought the people up out of the land of Egypt. The theology changes, it seems, but the dance goes on.

David's dance before the Ark in II Sam. 6 was a dance of wild abandon. The most probable meaning of the Hebrew verb suggests violent whirling and rotating, and Michal was disgusted because,

---

[4] See Ehrlich, *Die Kultsymbolik im Alten Testament und im nachbiblischen Judentum*. Ehrlich finds evidence for seven kinds of dance in the Old Testament and early Judaism: processional dances, dances around a holy object, ecstatic dances, dances at festivals, war dances, nuptial dances and funeral dances, though there is no Old Testament evidence for the last two. Note also Oesterley, *The Sacred Dance*.

[5] Dancing was well established in the cults of Canaan before the arrival of the Hebrews. See, for example, the behaviour of Jezebel's prophets on Mount Carmel in I Kings 18.

[6] For the contention that the dance of Miriam belongs to the regular celebration of the Passover, see Pedersen, *Israel II*, pp. 406ff.

either by accident or design, David had exposed himself. 'With all his might' in v. 14 implies that David had driven himself to his physical limit (cf. v. 16); and when the Chronicler came to tell the story, he watered it down and used a verb for dancing much more reminiscent of children at play than of vigorous men with a serious task in hand (I Chron. 15.29). After the dance was over, David blessed the people in the name of the Lord; he would have blessed his own household particularly, but Michal resisted him. Then comes the comment, 'Michal the daughter of Saul had no child unto the day of her death'. There can hardly be any doubt that the blessing that David could have offered Michal was conception.[7] The culmination of the whole event was the release of Yahweh's creative energy. In the previous examples the victory came first and the dance followed and extended it; here the dance comes first and the divine activity was expected to follow. It is reasonable, therefore, to see the dance of Miriam and the dance of David as parallel cases, one following the event it celebrated, the other preceding it, though in the second case the coldness of Michal frustrates the creative purpose.

Another example is found in the story of the young women of Shiloh (Judg. 21). The occasion is the autumn vintage festival, 'the yearly feast of the Lord', though the Canaanite influence is strong. The young women begin a dance that provides the men of Benjamin with an opportunity for carrying them off as sexual partners. The dance is a necessary part of the cult; it stimulates the participants, facilitates physical contact and reaches its climax in the supreme act of blessing and fertilizing. Theologically the rite can be read in two ways. In Canaanite terms the dancers stimulate Baal and his consort to release their fertilizing power and so to ensure that the earth is renewed in the spring. In Yahwist terms the dance is the means whereby the divine act of renewing the earth expresses itself cultically. In both cases the dance is necessary. Mowinckel, speaking generally, suggests that dancing is 'an expression of, and a means to produce, that feeling of strength which guarantees fertility, victory, success in hunting, and daily bread; it is "work", "cult" '.[8]

Even this brief look at the place of dancing in the life of Israel reveals several points of interest. The dance is a significant and broadly mimetic action that stands over against some other reality, usually, in

---

[7] Porter, 'II Sam. vi and Psalm cxxxii', pp. 165f.

[8] Mowinckel, *Psalms I*, p. 10.

Israel, an act of Yahweh. Dance and reality are parts of one whole. The reality may be a continuing factory in history, in which case the dance actualizes what is for ever true; more commonly in Israel, the reality relates to a specific historical occasion. The greatest error we can make is to disconnect the dance from the reality and say that it is 'mere celebration'. By dancing, the women, who have not been involved in the battle, participate in the total event and give it greater 'presence'. The victory that is thoroughly 'worked through' is a more substantial and more effective victory than one that passes unregarded.[9] The dance may precede the reality it celebrates, or follow it, or give temporary expression to a reality that is permanent. This ambiguity regarding the chronological relation between the two elements, the dance and the reality, means that questions about a causal relationship between the two should not be asked. It seems truer to the Hebrew understanding to see both elements together as part of a single integrated reality; Yahweh acts in both. Israel responds to Yahweh's prompting, in the one case by fighting a battle, in the other by working in the cult to prepare for the battle or to celebrate its outcome. Yahweh is always dynamic; Israel, ideally at least, always compliant. These points have some importance in relation to prophetic drama.

Processions

Consideration of dancing leads naturally to the consideration of processions. There is plenty of evidence of processions in the psalter, though it is not easy to form a clear idea of exactly what took place.

[9] This presumably is what A.S. Herbert means when he talks about the dance that, 'sought to strengthen the spirit of victory in the life of Israel' (*Worship in Ancient Israel*, p. 23). In another context, Pedersen speaks of the dance that is able to 'strengthen the blessing that gives fertility to the crops and to man' (*Israel II*, p. 421). See also van der Leeuw, *Religion in Essence and Manifestation*, pp. 373ff. In his chapter on 'Service', van der Leeuw carries the discussion much further. He contends that, among many primitive peoples, dancers represent the gods themselves and re-enact the triumph. We are here very close to prophetic ecstasy, for both are means of entering into and releasing the power of the deity. Yahwism set its own limits on what could be achieved in this way, but it never proscribed either the dance or the ecstasy. Even so sober a writer as Kraus quotes van der Leeuw with approval and continues, 'Ecstatic dancing set power in motion, expressed it and brought it into contact with the spirit world. These rites were taken over unaltered into the worship of Yahweh' (Kraus, *Worship*, p. 174). See also Ehrlich, *Kultsymbolik*, pp. 35f.

No one has taken this challenge more seriously than Mowinckel. He has been much criticized, but even those who are in disagreement with him recognize the importance of his work.[10] Mowinckel gathers up the evidence to establish a single, cultic procession, on the Babylonian model, which begins outside the temple precincts and ends with the ark installed in glory.

In I Sam. 6 the ark, which had been seized by the Philistines, was returned to Kiriath-jearim. II Sam. 6 takes up the story from there – it is clear from I Chron. 13.6 that Baale-judah (II Sam. 6.2) is the same place as Kiriath-jearim (I Sam. 7.1). David brings the ark as far as the house of Obed-edom, and then, when the prosperity of Obed-edom had persuaded him that the time was propitious, right up to Zion. To this must be added the narrative in I Kings 8, which deals with the entrance of the ark into the newly built temple. The fact that the latter event took place in the seventh month, 'at the feast' (v. 2), opens up the question of how far we are dealing with a once-for-all historical event and how far with a ritual procession which took place as a regular feature of the liturgy of the autumn festival. It is not difficult to read II Sam. 6 and I Kings 8 as historicized versions of an annual rite.[11]

From the psalms, particularly from Pss. 24, 68, 118 and 132, it is possible to rewrite the story cultically. The ark, which represents the presence of Yahweh (Num. 10.35), lies away from its proper place, so Israel is temporarily in a state of humiliation. Psalm 132, which Weiser regards as 'part of the festal liturgy of the feast of the dedication of the Jerusalem temple', is concerned with the restoration of the ark to the place where it can be the centre of worship for all Israel.[12] Porter points out that in both I Sam. 7.1 and II Sam. 6.3 the ark rests in the house of Abinadab 'in the hill'. Evidence from Babylon and Ras Shamra suggests that their great festivals began with the deity imprisoned in or on a mountain. So, argues Porter, Ps. 132.6 refers to the search for the ark which, on the day of the festival, is hidden.[13] The liturgy, therefore, reflects the narrative of I Sam. 4, in which the ark

[10] See both *Psalmenstudien* and *Psalms*. Also Kraus, *Worship*, pp. 206ff.; Johnson, 'Hebrew Conceptions of Kingship', p. 223; R. de Vaux, *Ancient Israel*, pp. 502ff.; Weiser, *Psalms*, pp. 62ff.

[11] John Gray, *I & II Kings*, pp. 207f.; Mowinckel, *Psalms I*, pp. 127, 175; *Psalms II*, pp. 237ff.

[12] *Psalms* p. 779; cf. Anderson, *Psalms 2*, p. 879.

[13] Porter, 'II Samuel vi and Psalm cxxxii', pp. 169ff.

fell into the hands of the Philistines.[14] So Ps. 132 begins with David, in the midst of affliction, vowing that he will find 'a place for the Lord', which means a place for the ark.

The ark is discovered in a place that represents the historical Kiriath-jearim, David's trials and intentions are recalled, and the qualifications of those who are fit to follow after him are rehearsed (Ps. 24.3–6). Psalm 68 deals with the setting up of the procession. Verses 25–7 give the details. Singers lead the way; girls follow playing instruments; all the tribes are represented. Aubrey Johnson has set to work on vv. 28f. and, by means of a series of emendations, most of them involving simply the rearrangement of the consonantal text of the Hebrew, has produced a version that is more clearly related to the occasion.[15] Henton Davies takes up his suggestion and combines it with the contention that the word translated 'strength' in 68.28 actually refers to the ark. The verse then reads as a direction indicating the place of the ark in the procession.[16] This is simply hypothesis, but it has to be remembered that the general evidence for a procession is strong and the verses do need emendation. Johnson and Davies would claim to be tidying up the text, not introducing something new.

The road that the procession takes is steep. The threshing-floor of Araunah the Jebusite occupied the highest point on the ridge, so that even the move from the city of David to the site later to be occupied by the temple would have involved an ascent. This gives rise to the notion of 'going up' to the house of the Lord and perhaps to the title at the head of Pss. 120–34. The route must have been recognized as a *via sacra*. Isa. 35.8–10 make better sense if there was, in fact, an ascending 'way of holiness' to Mount Zion, and Ps. 84.5 has greater force if the faithful bear in their hearts the memory of an actual 'high way' to the sanctuary.[17] At the gates of the temple the procession halts

[14] Throughout this discussion cross-currents from the debate about kingship affect the argument. Some scholars contend that, because the ark is displaced and Israel humiliated, the king himself must be in straitened circumstances, and this is indeed the case in Ps. 118 where the king is surrounded by enemies and on the verge of death (see especially vv. 10–12, 18). Israel's festival thus follows the Babylonian pattern in which the king is dethroned and symbolically assaulted. See Engnell, *Kingship*, pp. 17, 35.

[15] Johnson, *Sacral Kingship*, pp. 83–5.

[16] Henton Davies, 'The Ark in the Psalms', pp. 56ff.

[17] In the historical narrative the journey was broken at the house of Obed-edom and there may have been stations on the cultic route. Porter argues for a 'cultic pause' on the ascent ('II Sam. vi and Psalm cxxxii', pp. 171f.).

to work through the entrance formula. Dwellers in open cities do not understand the significance of gates. The wall creates an enclave, secure against intrusion and defilement, and the gate is crucial, for every passage, in or out, affects the nature of the enclave. This explains the 'gates of righteousness' in Ps. 118.19. Admission is only for the right people, so qualifications have to be tested at the gate. Psalm 24.7–10 gives details of the dialogue. This psalm speaks about ascending the hill of the Lord, and the last four verses suggest an entrance formula in the grand style, a formula to be used when Yahweh, represented, we may assume, by the ark, reached the gates of the temple. This is the cultic version of what must have been a common secular incident. The leader of the procession twice asks for the gates to be opened for the King of glory to enter, and twice he is asked to say who the King of glory is. The replies stress the prowess of the warrior deity, 'mighty in battle', the Lord of hosts. Several verses in Ps. 118 suggest that it too was an entry psalm belonging to a festal liturgy, the purpose of which was to celebrate Yahweh's victories (vv. 19–24). The gates open and the procession moves inside, receiving the priestly blessing as it does so (Ps. 118.26). The climax comes within the temple area as the procession approaches the altar (Ps. 118.27). Unfortunately at this point the text is obscure. The object of the imperative in the second line of v. 27 does not mean 'sacrifice', as the RV suggests, but rather 'festal gathering'. 'Bind the sacrifice' is, therefore, wrong, but it is not at all clear what a right translation would be.[18] The instruction probably has to do with drawing up the procession for the final act. Commentators have long thought, on the basis of the LXX, that the rest of the line is concerned with 'foliage' and not with 'cords'. This interpretation owes a little to the post-exilic festival (Lev. 23.40) and the Mishnah, but it is a reasonable resolution of a difficult problem.[19] The climax comes, therefore, with the procession marching round the altar, singing and waving palm branches to honour Yahweh, the victorious king who has now returned to his temple in state. The constant theme of the liturgy is Yahweh's triumph. Sinai is recalled and the march through the desert (Ps. 68.7f.). Unspecified victories are noted (Pss. 68.11–14; 118.10–14) and others anticipated (Ps. 68.19–23). All other features

---

[18] 'Join in the dance with festal boughs' is Johnson's suggestion (*Sacral Kingship*, pp. 127f).

[19] This interpretation goes back at least to Cheyne, *Psalms*, pp. 316f. See, too, Kirkpatrick, *Psalms*, pp. 699f. and *Mishnah*, Sukkah, 4.5.

of these particular psalms can be seen in relation to this central idea.

A number of factors in this account of the great procession have a bearing on prophetic drama. First, there is the sense of compulsion that activates the celebration. Yahweh's presence in Zion is fundamental to Israel's existence; consequently the ceremonial is not incidental to the life of the community but constitutive of it.

Secondly, the procession is an *activity*. Its purpose was largely fulfilled in the actions of the worshippers. Substances, such as blood, and objects, such as the ark, had their place in Israel's cult, and the ark is particularly important here, but nothing takes away from the significance of the people carrying out, with spontaneous enthusiasm, a carefully contrived programme of action.

Thirdly, the procession is the cultic aspect of Yahweh's victorious coming to Zion; it naturally evidences his power, and the power shows itself in blessing for the people (Ps. 132.15).[20] Blessing is no abstract matter; it means fertility, harvest, food, safety, and victory and security for the king (Ps. 132.11,18). There are other examples of processions accompanying acts of divine power. In the Jericho story the power worked destructively. Marching round the town marked out the area in which the power was to act.[21] Nehemiah organized a procession that was to have exactly the opposite effect (Neh. 12). There can hardly be any doubt that Ps. 48 also relates to a procession, perhaps to the one under discussion, and that its purpose was to strengthen the defences of the city. If God did not intend to defend the city, the procession would, of course, be useless, but when God wills to defend the city, the cultic action is the means he wills to express his power at that particular time and place.

Fourthly, the procession reveals an interesting ambivalence regarding time and causation. There has been much discussion about whether the victories referred to in the psalms are to be understood as historical, eschatological, or cultic. The psalms we have examined give grounds for all three. There are references back to Sinai, to the conquest, to the taking of Jerusalem and the ascent of the ark. There are references to the future, to the permanent establishment of David's dynasty and David's throne. There are also references to the present, to the blessing and victory that is being worked out now. No interpretation is adequate

---

[20] Mowinckel, *Psalms I*, p. 173.

[21] Van der Leeuw, *Religion*, p. 377; Gaster, *Myth, Legend and Custom in the Old Testament*, pp. 411ff., 747.

if any one of these aspects is ruled out. It is idle to ask which of the
three is primary, because each reflects and interprets the others.
Yahweh's victorious activity is many-sided and timeless. Consequently
the attempt to press upon the material an analysis in terms of before
and after, cause and effect, is to misrepresent the world of thought.
This has considerable bearing on prophetic drama.

Cultic Drama

There are grounds for believing that Israel's cult made use of drama,
though the direct evidence is slight, which leads, as one would expect,
to controversy regarding the validity of the indirect evidence. Broadly
speaking, there are two lines of argument. Some scholars, who display
a bias towards the mythological, see the autumn festival as a cultic
drama culminating in the enthronement of Yahweh, thus bringing
about a 'reinvigoration' of the cycle of the year.[22] Others, less willing
to see foreign influence at work in Israel's cult, see the festival as a
renewal of the covenant, less dramatic in form and similar to the
ceremony that Joshua carried out at Shechem in Josh. 24.[23] The lines
of battle, however, are not always clear. Mowinckel, who is criticized
for being the inspiration of some of the more extravagant theories, is,
in fact, far less extreme than many of his Scandinavian colleagues and
is often to be found criticizing them.[24] Eichrodt, on the other hand, who
is notably moderate, shows considerable interest in the enthronement
theme.[25] To some extent the passing of the years has brought a
mellowing of attitudes. John D.W. Watts makes a balanced comment
on the matter in his commentary on *Isaiah*.[26] The argument in favour
of some form of cultic drama is persuasive and it can be briefly
summarized.

---

[22] The word is used by Gaster, *Thespis*, p. 17.

[23] Haldar accepts the idea of Yahweh's cultic death with equanimity (*Cult Prophets*,
pp. 131f.; *Nahum*, pp. 145f., 154), whereas de Vaux denies that there was a New Year
festival in Israel in Old Testament times at all (*Ancient Israel*, pp. 502ff.).

[24] To some extent the suspicion directed against Mowinckel is due to the fact that he
was largely responsible for bringing a modern anthropological approach to the study of
the Bible. For his criticisms of Scandinavian colleagues see *He that Cometh*, pp. 27,
457ff. and *Psalms I*, pp. 50, 58. He also has some measured words to say about the
British 'myth and ritual' school (*Psalms II*, p. 241). For his reply to some of his own
critics, see *Psalms II*, pp. 228ff.

[25] *Theology I*, pp. 123ff.

[26] *Isaiah 1–33*, pp. xlv–xlvii.

There is a wealth of comparative material. The cults of the ancient Near East made extensive use of ritual drama. 'All cult is drama', says van der Leeuw, and the researches of Mowinckel, Engnell and Gaster, to name only three, provide all the supporting evidence necessary.[27] The contention that there was no ritual drama in Israel means that the cult was distinguished from all others, not simply by historical experience and theology, but by means of expression as well. Indeed, it implies that Israelites in their festivals participated in a kind of Protestant 'service of the Word' that would have been alien, not simply to the general context, but to the rest of the religion of Israel as we know it from the Old Testament. This is so improbable that one suspects that the nub of the objection is not to drama as such but to the content of the particular drama that some of the comparative scholars propose.

Unfortunately, while the Psalter gives plenty of evidence of the libretto of temple worship, it provides little information about the accompanying activity. There must have been action, if for no other reason than that words of such vigour invariably break into action. In Deuteronomy and the Priestly writings there is some evidence regarding the conduct of temple rituals, but details of the great corporate celebrations, into which the psalms properly fit, are lacking. We read phrases such as 'holy convocation', 'keep the feast', 'rejoice before the Lord', and we can only make inferences about what they mean. But inferences must be made, and dramatic activity is the most probable inference of all.

In addition there are certain detailed arguments from the Psalter and it is only necessary to refer to one or two examples.[28] In Ps. 48 Yahweh is acclaimed for a triumph that takes place in the temple and which affects the kings of surrounding nations. In v. 9 the worshippers both hear and see something related to this triumph. The next line is usually translated, 'We have thought on thy steadfast love, O God', but the primary meaning of the verb in question is not 'to think'; it has to do with acknowledging a resemblance or striking a comparison. Consequently the right translation is something that follows on from the hearing and seeing, such as, 'we have enacted or made a representation of' your steadfast love. Similarly in Ps. 66.5 the

[27] *Religion*, p. 376; see too Ringgren, *Israelite Religion*, pp. 183ff. and Weiser, *Psalms*, p. 28.

[28] Much work has been done in this area by Aubrey Johnson; see *Sacral Kingship in Ancient Israel*.

congregation is invited to see what God has done within the context of worship, and this time the divine triumph has to do with the exodus. Again in Ps. 46.8 the congregation is able to behold the works of Yahweh, which involve establishing peace, not only among the nations, but throughout the natural order. From such references one can infer a dramatic ritual in which the majesty of Yahweh is both proclaimed in words and expressed in actions.

These arguments suggest that the real question is not whether there was cultic drama in Israel but what form the drama took. Some hypotheses in this area arouse more controversy than others. The more controversial theories are (a) that the death and rebirth of Yahweh were dramatized in the cult, (b) that a sacred marriage between Yahweh and his consort was enacted, (c) that Yahweh was dramatically enthroned for the succeeding year, and (d) that the king personated Yahweh in some or all of these rites.[29] It is not profitable to discuss any of these because hotly contested theories provide poor evidence for hypotheses in another sphere. There is, however, one element in the complex that is not quite so problematic and which provides a useful analogy for prophetic action; that element is the ritual combat.

Combat is a constant motif in mythology, perhaps because some of man's most intense experiences are connected with fighting, perhaps because the rise and fall of the year suggest an unending struggle between fecundity and barrenness, perhaps because tribal history is full of battles, perhaps even because of the dramatic opportunities the battle motif provides. The basic plot of the drama is the three-act sequence of conflict, defeat almost to the point of finality, and victory at the eleventh hour. Whether the participants are light and darkness, rain and drought, the righteous and the wicked, the new year and the

---

[29] It is interesting to note that Mowinckel eventually came to the point of rejecting theories (a), (b), and (d) (*Psalms I*, p. 243; *He that Cometh*, pp. 82–6, 457–9). Opposition from other quarters is not difficult to find: Frankfort, *Kingship*, p. 342; G.W. Anderson, 'Hebrew Religion', p. 300; Rowley, *Worship*, pp. 188–90. Support is found in Haldar, *Cult Prophets*, pp. 112f., 128f.; *Nahum*, pp. 145f., 154; Widengren, 'Early Hebrew Myths and their Interpretation', p. 191; Oesterley, 'Early Hebrew Festival Rituals', pp. 123ff. The annual enthronement of Yahweh is much more readily accepted, no doubt because the theory does not necessarily imply a previous dethronement. See Mowinckel, *Psalmenstudien II; Psalms I*, Ch. 5; Pedersen, *Israel II*, p. 440; Johnson, 'The Rôle of the King in the Jerusalem Cultus', pp. 85f.; Porter, 'II Sam. vi and Psalm cxxxii', p. 173. But note the continued opposition of de Vaux (*Ancient Israel*, pp. 504–6) and, to a less extent, Kraus (*Worship*, pp. 205–8).

old, the king and his enemies, life and death, or the gods and the demons, the dramatic force and the relevance to human experience remain the same.[30] It is, therefore, reasonable to look for evidence of this plot in the Psalter. Enmity, despair and salvation recur constantly. On one side is the righteous worshipper putting his faith in Yahweh and in Zion; on the other are the adversaries, described as the wicked, workers of iniquity, enemies, scorners, etc. In psalm after psalm there is a clash; the righteous one is tried to the point of despair; then suddenly comes release and salvation.[31] The question is what kind of drama accompanied these psalms and how it was understood.

Several psalms suggest a rite in which the military successes of the past year are represented and future victories anticipated (e.g. 47,48). It may even have begun with a ritual humiliation of the king.[32] In view of the Hebrew concern with history, it is reasonable to suppose that such a rite replaced the naturalistic and seasonal rites of Israel's neighbours, but by no means all references to conflict are to be understood in military terms. Sometimes the conflict takes on cosmic dimensions. Psalm 68, for example, which we have already discussed, begins with a confrontation between Yahweh and his enemies, then alludes to Israel's progress through the desert, the overcoming of summer drought, the establishment of justice, and victory over enemies; it concludes with what appears to be a cultic celebration of cosmic victory. In the middle, in v. 20, in a line in which the sense is none too clear, the idea of salvation is parallelled by a phrase which apparently refers to escape from death.[33] Other psalms carry the message in a more personal way, for example Ps. 18 and those psalms in which personal deliverance appears to take place between one verse and another, sometimes known as 'certainty of a hearing'

---

[30] Lévi-Strauss has made much of this simple fact in expounding his structuralist approach to mythology. See 'The Structural Study of Myth'.

[31] See Brueggemann, 'From Hurt to Joy, from Death to Life'; Westermann, *The Praise of God in the Psalms*.

[32] This case is argued in detail by Johnson in *Sacral Kingship*, particularly pp. 77ff. Babylonian parallels to the humiliation of the king are discussed by Frankfort (*Kingship*, p. 320), Pritchard (*ANET*, p. 334), and Mowinckel (*He that Cometh*, p. 41).

[33] The Hebrew literally means, 'to Yahweh are the escapes for death'. Given that 'escape from death' is the most reasonable translation (as RSV, REB), it remains doubtful how we are to interpret 'death'. If, as Dahood suggests, it is an allusion to captivity in Egypt (*Psalms II*, p. 144), then it surely indicates the exodus, not as a single historical event, but as a paradigm of escapes from disasters of all kinds.

psalms.[34] It is well known that the Babylonian Creation Epic recounts a battle between Marduk and Tiamat, and one naturally asks whether the battle motif in the Psalter extends to the struggle with chaos in creation.[35] Psalm 74.12–17 is quite precise. By breaking the heads of the dragons God establishes land and sea, day and night, summer and winter. All this is preceded by a lament bewailing the fact that God's enemies are spreading destruction in the holy place. Psalm 89.9f. also alludes to Yahweh's lordship over the turbulent sea, the destruction of Rahab, a female monster representing chaos, and the scattering of all other enemies; these triumphs are brought into conjunction with the psalmist's present painful state. Psalm 46 depicts a God, so firmly in control of creation and created beings, that perfect confidence is possible for his people. Whatever uncertainties there may be here, the one sure and recurrent theme is the victory brought about by Yahweh over every kind of enemy, a victory which is perceived as present to the worshipper.

Some of the comments made about processions can be repeated here. There can be no doubt of the importance of these dramatic rituals, nor of the enthusiasm with which they were carried out. The celebration is an essential dimension of the salvation. Note, too, that the celebration is transparent and expressive, not esoteric. The references to the worshippers dancing, singing, and waving branches show that the triumph is real and immediate to the participants. It is *out of Zion* that the salvation of Israel comes, no matter what the problem (Ps. 14.7). This conclusion holds good whether the salvation is related primarily to the historical, as with Weiser, or the mythological, as with Mowinckel.[36] It is also true that the drama of combat transcends time. It is not a past battle that is being celebrated in the psalms we have quoted, still less a future battle the outcome of which is being determined by some act of effective magic. Rather it is all the conflicts of the created order drawn together in one comprehensive encounter. The whole cosmic war focusses in a single time and place, and victory is remembered, celebrated, promoted, and anticipated, all at the same time. When this factor is understood, the apparent muddle of motifs in such psalms as 18 presents no problem. Because Yahweh is the source of all victories, each victory participates in all

[34] In Ps. 6, compare vv. 1–7 with vv. 8–10; similarly Ps. 13.1–4 and 5f.; Ps. 28.1–5 and 6–9; Ps. 31.1–20 and 21–4; Ps. 56.1–11 and 12f.

[35] Pritchard, *ANET*, pp. 60ff.

[36] Weiser, *Psalms*, p. 28; Mowinckel, *Psalms I*, pp. 165f., 182.

the others, and the cultic victory looks back to the creation and on to the last things and out to the natural order, as well as to historical encounters, past, present, and to come.[37]

Much of the discussion of this matter has been beggared by the assumption that, if cultic actions worked effectively to overcome the evil powers that threatened the life of the people, they must have the undesirable character of magic. This by no means follows, as we shall see when we come to Chapter 16. Cultic actions are necessary but not sufficient; they are effective, but it is not accurate to speak of them having instrumental force. A more subtle relationship between the drama and the thing dramatized is called for. This is both a guide and a warning, for our aim is to construct a pattern of thought that will give an adequate account of prophetic action and yet avoid the confusion with what is commonly called instrumental magic.

Sacrifice

The relation of sacrifice to prophetic drama was treated by H.W. Robinson in an article in 1942.[38] Sacrifice has two quite different aspects: on one hand it is a dramatic and expressive action, which Robinson describes as 'representative realism', on the other it involves the manipulation of a most potent substance, namely blood. In the former case the relevance of the sacrificial procedure to prophetic action is comparatively easy to work out; in the second there is a point of contrast rather than comparison. Material objects, cloaks, girdles, bows, arrows, horns, yokes, slates, tiles, pots, and so on figure in the prophetic narratives, but none of them appears to be potent in the way that blood is potent; they are simply the furniture, the properties of the action. Blood is potent *in itself*. There are other points of contrast. Prophetic dramas are usually performed once, sacrifice is repeated endlessly; prophetic dramas are often uncomplicated actions, sacrifice, due to its long history and numerous accretions, is complex; prophetic dramas often have a simple and direct reference to what they signify, but no such clarity is possible with sacrifice. It is, in any case, dangerous to talk about the meaning of sacrifice, because whatever meaning it had changed throughout history and, without

---

[37] Johnson, *Sacral Kingship*, pp. 131–6.
[38] 'Hebrew Sacrifice and Prophetic Symbolism'.

any doubt, the rite was variously interpreted within Israel at any one time.[39]

The two kinds of sacrifice, the peace offering and the whole burnt offering, are equally dramatic, but they represent different things.[40] The peace offering concludes with a meal at which the carcase is consumed by the worshipper and his guests, Yahweh already having received the kidneys and the fat (Lev. 3; 7.11-4). This action conjures up the meal symbolism found throughout the Bible. The meal is constitutive of the community, for the meal was the way in which the Hebrew's sense of belonging to the family was declared and secured, and the family unit had great social importance. The individual is protected by the family, disciplined by it, given status and identity by it. To have no family was so great a disaster that artificial means had to be devised to ensure that the disconnected were joined to another family.[41] Expulsion from the family was the worst possible disaster. It meant often, not simply loneliness, but death.[42] Moreover the food itself, particularly in a sacrificial meal, strengthens this symbolism. A single animal is divided between the participants and so they are united in sharing in the one carcase.

In the peace offering the worshippers form a community of which Yahweh is the head, and as head, he receives the choicest share. Between them they consume the animal that has been offered, and so the community they form is affirmed and strengthened. Just as, in the normal family, privileges follow from membership of the community, so it is believed that Yahweh's protection will follow on from the community meal that has been shared. As with the other cultic actions

[39] This is a point of which Rowley was no doubt aware when he wrote his essay on 'The Meaning of Sacrifice in the Old Testament'. He refers (pp. 76ff.) to the various possible approaches: sacrifice as a means to communion (Robertson Smith), sacrifice as a gift (E.B. Tylor), sacrifice as the release of vital energy (E.O. James). These factors alone make it clear that 'meaning' in any complete sense is out of the question. See also G.B. Gray, *Sacrifice*, pp. 2f.; Oesterley, *Sacrifice*, pp. 11ff.; de Vaux, *Sacrifice*, pp. 3ff.

[40] Lev. 1 gives the procedure for the burnt offering and Lev. 3 for the peace offering, though references to sacrifice are scattered throughout the Old Testament.

[41] Orphans and widows appear frequently in Deuteronomy in this connection (10.18; 16.11; 24.17f.; 26.12f.; 27.19). Protection of the widow was one of the functions of the institution of levirate marriage (Deut. 25.5-10). For the importance of the *bêt āb* in the Hebrew social structure, see Parts VI and VII on Social Structure in N.K. Gottwald, *The Tribes of Yahweh*, especially pp. 285-92; also Wright, *The Biblical Doctrine of Man in Society*; Shedd, *Man in Community*; Chamberlayne, *Man in Society*.

[42] The Priestly Code makes frequent use of expulsion from the community as a serious punishment (Ex. 12.15; 30.33; 31.14; Num. 15.30; Lev. 17.10 etc.).

we have examined, there is no simple causative relationship between the action and the benefits. The community of Yahweh exists before the sacrifice and the meal demonstrates and fortifies it; the two elements are two aspects of a reality that is empowered by Yahweh in every part.

In the holocaust there is no meal and the significant action is the immolation of the animal in the altar fire to the glory of Yahweh. The animal is given up totally and unreservedly. The victim was, of necessity, precious to the worshipper; it was an animal from the flock that existed to supply the worshipper's own needs (Lev. 1.3); it must be 'without spot and without blemish', precisely the kind of animal one would want to keep for oneself. The victim is presented in the temple and the worshipper lays his hands on its head. This action, which also has a place in the ritual of the peace offering, raises several problems, but its meaning here is relatively clear.[43] Laying on of hands establishes a representational link between the worshipper and the animal thus specified. It identifies the animal as the gift of one particular worshipper. The animal is part of his wealth and so part of his total identity, for a man's flocks and herds as well as his family represent who he is. In the offering of the representative part the whole is presented to Yahweh in a complete and essentially irreversible act of homage. Once again the holocaust does not create the relationship; the homage already existed; the function of the sacrifice is to give explicit and dramatic expression to a state of affairs that belongs to past, present and future.

The Temple

Quite apart from the rites that took place within it, the temple itself provides an example of Hebrew thinking. The presence of Yahweh is seen as having two aspects, local and universal, earthly and heavenly,

---

[43] The problems are (a) that the action of laying hands on a person or a beast occurs in various contexts fulfilling various functions, (b) that several different Hebrew verbs are used, (c) that the different Hebrew verbs do not entirely correlate with the different contexts and functions, and (d) that, in the ceremonial area, where *sāmak* is used consistently as a technical term, a simple explanation is impossible because of important differences between the peace offering, the holocaust, and the expulsion of the goat for Azazel, in all of which laying on of hands occurs. Theories abound. See de Vaux, *Israel*, p. 416; *Sacrifice*, p. 28; Sansom, 'Laying on of Hands in the Old Testament'. The interpretation given above is minimal. Even so, it cannot apply to Lev. 16. 21, but we are discussing sacrifice and not the Azazel rite.

expressible and inexpressible. From one point of view the temple was a practical necessity. The capital city needed a shrine and the Jebusite tradition could not be abandoned. But more significant than these factors were the Sinai traditions which came in with some of the conquering tribes and ultimately became the possession of all Israel. The central theme of these traditions was the presence of Yahweh in majesty, a presence which could be seen and heard on a particular mountain. The probable location of the original Sinai makes it unlikely that the sacred mountain was volcanic, but some of the evidence is so impressive that it is necessary to suppose that traditions from another mountain east of Aqabah have been mingled with those of Sinai.[44] A mountain where the presence of Yahweh was evident is essential to the story. After the settlement, the notion of 'the God of Israel' takes its place beside 'the God of Sinai', and the need for a place of meeting with God, a new Sinai within the land of Israel, becomes paramount. It must be a mountain for obvious reasons.[45] According to Deuteronomy, Zion was chosen by God before it was captured, before there was a Hebrew shrine there, and before the ark was installed; indeed, while Israel was still in the wilderness (12.13f.; 16.2, 5–7; 26.2). So three strands are drawn together: the historical and geographical Sinai is given presence in Israel; Yahweh's possession of the land is given formal, cultic expression; and the people of Israel are provided with a place of worship.[46] The link with Sinai is not the least of these three. The fire and smoke of the altar recalled the desert traditions; the annual renewal of the covenant on Mount Zion recapitulated the Sinaitic theophany; and the ark with its contents provided a physical reminder.

[44] In view of the facts that (a) in later traditions the mountain of God had two names, (b) that – as is now almost universally acknowledged – the settlement involved different groups coming from different areas with different cultic traditions, and (c) that the volcanic references are more easily traced to the J source and the non-volcanic to E, this conclusion is more than probable.

[45] Ancient cosmologies seem to regard mountains as the abode of the gods and the sea as the abode of monsters. Besides Sinai and Zion one must set Zaphon of Ras Shamra and the ziggurats, or artificial hills, of Babylon. See Kraus, *Worship*, pp. 201f.; de Vaux, *Israel*, pp. 279ff.; Wright, 'The Temple in Palestine-Syria' p. 180; Clements, *God and Temple*, pp. 2f.; G.B. Gray, *Sacrifice*, pp. 151f.; Engnell, 'The Book of Psalms', p. 93; Albright, *Archaeology*, pp. 150ff.; Brandon, *Creation Legends*, pp. 18ff.

[46] Von Rad, 'The Promised Land and Yahweh's Land in the Hexateuch', pp. 87f. That this factor represents a borrowing from Canaanite mythology is asserted by Clements (*God and Temple*, pp. 47ff., 55) but denied by von Rad ('The Promised Land', pp. 88f).

The function of the temple in relation to Yahweh himself has been understood in various ways. It has been said that the temple provides him with an earthly home to correspond with his home in the heavens, but the notion of a 'home' hardly does justice to the Hebrew imagination. The presence of Yahweh is dynamic rather than static, and it is the experience of theophany rather than the idea of permanent residence that gives the temple its character. Again it is tempting to look back to the volcanic mountain and wonder how much this understanding of priorities owes to a place that, though permanently awesome, from time to time displays its unique character in displays of incomparable power. Yahweh's presence in the temple does not conflict either with his universal presence or with the idea of occasional crises when his power breaks out in specific acts of judgment and salvation.

This notion of presence, local, particular, occasional and concrete over against a presence that is universal, permanent and unchanging is a useful preparation for what we shall discover when we come to the prophets. The two presences are not in contradiction; they are different aspects of the same reality. What *is* sometimes *happens*; what is eternally true sometimes reveals itself; the invisible reality becomes the visible event. So in the prophetic context, particular actions express divine dispositions and once-for-all performances express permanent conditions. This idea is more relevant to some prophetic dramas than to others, but it does illuminate some of the more difficult.

Further light is thrown on this comparison by consideration of the so-called cosmic significance of the temple.[47] The argument for the hypothesis begins with Ugaritic and Babylonian parallels and the surely quite reasonable attempt to show that Hebrew tradition was influenced by them. The conclusion is, to quote Clements, 'that the temple was a microcosm of the macrocosm, so that the building gave visual expression to the belief in Yahweh's dominion over the world and all natural forces'.[48] This leads to the notion of the temple as the centre of the earth, the point where two worlds meet, where worshippers ascend and Yahweh descends so that there can be an encounter. The temple is the place of theophany, of salvation, of

[47] Different scholars pursue this theme with varying degrees of enthusiasm, but the conclusions of Wright (*Archaeology*, p. 144; 'Temple', pp. 170ff., Kraus (*Worship*, pp. 201f.), and Clements (*God and Temple*, pp. 9, 54, 65ff., 73) seem moderate and unassailable, despite de Vaux's dissent (*Israel*, pp. 328f.).

[48] *God and Temple*, p. 67.

acclamation, and these terms are both specific and universal. The presence is not simply local and momentary. The salvation applies not simply to the cultic day but to creation, to exodus, to the eschatological triumph and to all the deliverances in between. The acclamation is not simply the present company's tribute but the praise of the whole created order. Prophetic dramas often display the same features: huge events are focussed in brief actions; a nation in mourning is seen in a single man; a rotten garment means apostate generations. This is how the 'microcosm of the macrocosm' works out in the prophetic field. The link between the one and the other is conceived to be so strong that it is hardly proper to think of two linked elements at all. Rather there is a single reality that is at once universal and precise.

5 · Reliving the Past

A major concern of this study is the relation betwen prophetic action and historical events. That raises the old problem of what prophecy actually is. A few generations ago it was assumed that a simple, linear understanding of time could be inferred from the Bible. The prophet, so it was supposed, stood at the mid-point of a line, able to look backwards to the great, saving events of the past, but, in a purely human capacity, unable to look forwards. To God, however, the future was not hidden, and from time to time he revealed to the prophet what lay in his purpose; the prophet was thus able to foretell what would come to pass, even in the very distant future.[1] In the course of time protests were made against this account of prophetic function; it was too mechanical, too supernatural, and it did not stand up to the closest scrutiny. The relevance of prophetic oracles in any precise way to the far distant future, once doubted, is soon disproved, so a new account of prophecy was introduced with the slogan, 'forth-telling, not foretelling'.[2] It was now assumed that the prophet looked deeply into the affairs of his day and at the lessons of the past and to the nature of Yahweh; then he was able to proclaim, his fallible human nature doubtless charged by the Spirit, what the outcome of the contemporary situation would be. Skinner writes, 'The canonical prophets were a minority of chosen individuals who read the signs of the times with a clearer insight into the character of Yahweh and the principles of His government than their contemporaries, and who perceived that it was His purpose to bring Israel's national existence

---

[1] See, for example, A.B. Davidson, *Old Testament Prophecy*, pp. 151ff. and Sanday, *Inspiration*.

[2] R.H. Charles appears to have been the originator of this catchphrase (*Daniel*, p. xxvi).

to an end.'[3] Neither of these accounts of prophecy is satisfactory; but if we heed what was said in the previous chapter about the relation of cultic activity to time sequence, the problem begins to take on a different aspect.

Again we refer to the cult. At first appearance cult and prophecy face in opposite directions, the cult looking to the past and prophecy to the future; but a careful study of time in the cult shows that a common understanding of time sequence is implicit in them both. Both prophecy and cult were concerned with history. Whatever mythic elements existed in Israel's cult, from the time of the early monarchy onwards there was a definite trend away from the mythical and towards the historical. In the end that trend became dominant. Mowinckel, whose willingness to establish bridges between Israel's cult and those of her neighbours is not open to question, is clear on this point. To the Canaanite mythology Israel brings historical experience, and the Hebrew cult is thus concerned with the celebration of historical events, not simply with the representation of mythic drama.[4]

The Passover record and the Psalter (Pss. 44, 66, 78, 81, 105, 106, 107, 114, 135, 136) reveal that an essential element in cultic celebration was the reliving of the great events of Israel's history. It is common to speak of recapitulating or actualizing the past, but these terms are not free from the notion of linear sequence and, as far as possible, that notion ought to be avoided. Weiser comes nearer to the point when he tries to reduce all to a single moment. 'God's presence in the holy place also implies that his entire redemptive work in history is simultaneously present, and through the ritual act performed in the cult, exercises its influence upon the cult community.' Not only the past but the future disappears. 'Here, too, we find the root of the eschatological way of thinking peculiar to the Old Testament, which bridges the gap between periods and localities, and concentrates the

---

[3] Skinner, *Prophecy and Religion*, p. 187.

[4] Mowinckel, *Psalms I*, pp. 139f. How did the change come about? Did the myth come to embrace historical traditions (Mowinckel), or did the historical material recast the myth for its own ends (von Rad)? Von Rad's view is set out in 'The Form-Critical Problem of the Hexateuch', particularly pp. 20ff. He is followed by Ringgren who suggests that 'mythologization of history' would be more accurate than the common 'historicization of myth' (*Israelite Religion*, p. 115). The priority of the history would thus be established. Mowinckel's last word in response is to be seen in Note xxiii of *Psalms II*. The difference between the positions is not great. See too Mowinckel, *Psalms I*, p. 167.

whole range of events in the single moment of the cultic act, so that the past, the present and the future coincide and Israel together with the whole world and all the nations are summoned to be witnesses of these events.'[5] Van Rad points out that the cultic event was 'the one and only "time" in the full sense of the word, for it alone was furnished with content in the truest sense of the term'.[6] Once this is established, the notion of reliving the past is more easily understood. In the supreme cultic moment, all Israel's history is present and the worshipper groans in slavery, escapes through the waters, and dances on the shore. Whatever divine power was made known in the original event is made known in the celebration.[7]

The cultic process illustrates the Hebrew attitude to time, but it would be wrong to infer that the telescoping of past, present and future was simply a cultic technique. B.S. Childs, in his study of Hebrew memory, criticizes the views of Weiser because he limits the experience of saving power to a cultic act.[8] The significant factor is not the technique, cultic or otherwise, but the nature of the events themselves and the notions of time and deity that go with it. Events, whether past, present or future, were regarded as centres of power. The power derived from the one who brought the event into being. The word of the event, the event itself, the memory of the event, the celebration of the event, are all charged with the force of the initiator. Everyone who is exposed to the event in any way is affected by its power; hence all the rejoicing in the historical psalms. In theory all events contain a 'charge' of this kind; in most cases the 'charge' is soon spent because the initiators are insignificant, but it is quite otherwise with events that Yahweh initiates. The 'charge' of the exodus is inexhaustible. That is what von Rad means when he describes the historical events by which Yahweh founded the community of Israel as 'absolute'.[9] They are in a class of their own because their energy is never spent.[10] On this view, the complete event takes little

[5] Weiser, *Psalms*, p. 44; Mowinckel, *Psalms I*, p. 187.

[6] Von Rad, *Theology II*, p. 102.

[7] Kraus, *Worship*, p. 9; Ringgren, *Faith of Psalmists*, pp. 99f.; Jacob, *Theology*, p. 191.

[8] Childs, *Memory and Tradition*, pp. 61ff.

[9] Von Rad, *Theology II*, pp. 103f.

[10] Everson examines eighteen occurrences of the term 'Day of Yahweh' in the prophets and concludes that some of the 'Days' are past, some near at hand, and some future. The 'Day' is not, therefore, a single, universal, future event, but a series of particular acts of judgment and salvation. See 'The Days of Yahweh'.

account of the passage of time. It embraces actual event and all representations of it and is thus permanently contemporary.[11] This factor became the cornerstone of Israel's worship. Yahweh's creative energy was continually being released in Israel; the real agent in the cultic drama and even in the simple act of remembering was not the priest or the worshipper but Yahweh.[12]

This understanding of history is relevant and positive. Of course one cannot claim that a refined faith in Yahweh as the God of history, in the sense we are now discussing it, was universal in Israel. The complaints of the prophets make that clear. The discussion in this chapter, however, is concerned with modes of thought rather than with theology, and modes of thought are more pervasive than theological conviction. No doubt each of these influenced the other, but the Hebrew understanding of time was not dependent on Yahwist orthodoxy. It is also necessary to recognize that the Old Testament reveals other approaches to history, some of them more in line with the linear view.[13] Nevertheless there is enough evidence to show that it is a serious error to suppose that Israel's understanding of time can be interpreted purely in terms of a linear view.

There is no better example to illustrate this point than the festival of the Passover. The Old Testament contains plenty of material relating to the Passover. There is the quasi-historical account of the founding of the feast in Ex. 12, brief references in the various liturgical calendars (Ex. 23.15; 34.18,25; Lev. 23.5–8), the longer account in Deut. 16 which introduces new features, a priestly narrative in Num. 9.1–14, another priestly version in Num. 28.16–25, and Ezekiel's anticipation in Ezek. 45.21–4. Besides these there is more historical material in Josh. 5.10–12 and II Kings 23.21–3, and priestly histories in II Chron. 30, 35.1–19 and Ezra 6.19–22. From all this we can deduce that the feast underwent many changes within the biblical period, so that only very loosely can we speak about 'the Passover'. The origin of the Passover proper and its relation to the feast of unleavened bread is a puzzle. There appears to have been an amalgamation between two spring festivals, a nomadic sacrifice to

[11] See Snaith's discussion of 'vertical time' in an article in which he defends himself against Barr's criticisms ('Time in the Old Testament', p. 191.).

[12] The effectiveness of cultic drama in liberating new forces and changing situations is discussed by Mowinckel (*Psalms I*, pp. 119f., 129f., 138, 169f.), Kraus (*Worship*, pp. 8f., 14f., 39), Porter ('II Samuel vi', p. 169), etc.

[13] Barr, *Old and New*, p. 70.

secure fecundity for the flocks and an agrarian celebration to mark the beginning of the barley harvest. Whatever its origin, the Passover came to have a peculiar force in Israel due to the link that was made between the ancient spring celebrations and the events of the exodus. How this link was forged is not difficult to imagine. If the exodus took place in spring, the celebration of it would coincide with the spring festivals. So 'historicization' would take place naturally by a kind of inevitable association.

If the Passover is considered as a whole, then, when the historicizing process had been completed, the entire festival was understood to represent dramatically the last night of Israel in Egypt.[14] It is called *zikkārôn* in Ex. 12.14 and 13.9 and, as Ex. 12.42 makes clear, the emphasis is on reliving the experiences of the fateful night. It is an open question as to how much of the drama was drawn from supposed records of the event and how much Passover observance in later years actually gave rise to quasi-historical traditions about the fateful night. It is best to regard the historical as one aspect of the reality and the ritual as another and so to see both as different media in which the divine will to save Israel expresses itself.

Examination of the details supports this general impression. The appointed time in the month of Abib, when the Passover is eaten, is held to be the very night on which the Israelites left Egypt (Ex. 13.4; 23.15; 34.18; Deut. 16.1). The feast is nocturnal because those escaping ate their last meal in the middle of the night (Ex. 12.42). The celebrants dressed as the escaping captives dressed, with girdles drawn tight, sandals on their feet, and staves at hand for the journey (Ex. 12.11). They ate in haste because the departure was sudden (Ex. 12.11; Deut. 16.3). Unleavened bread had a place in the Passover itself quite apart from the related feast of that name. In the general haste there was no time to allow the bread to rise. So on the journey into freedom the Israelites had to eat this 'bread of affliction' (Ex. 12.8,39; Deut. 16.3). Equally the bitter herbs of Ex. 12.8 and Num. 9.11 suggest that there was no time or opportunity for picking cultivated vegetables. The common herbs of the desert were the only seasoning available. It is notable that these allusions come from sources of different dates, which strengthens the impression that the Passover

---

[14] This is one of Pedersen's points. He sees the Passover legend as a mythical account of Yahweh's continual exploits on behalf of his people, and argues that the force lies in the total impact rather than in particular details. See *Israel II*, pp. 407, 411, 728, 731, 736f.

was understood from earliest times as a dramatic re-enactment of the escape from Egypt and that later tradition built on this and extended the application.[15] Year by year the worshippers repeated liturgically what the captives were reckoned to have done functionally.

Not all the material is explicable on this theory. The painting of the blood on the lintels (Ex. 12.7,22f.) and the roasting of the animal whole so that no bone is broken (Ex. 12.8f., including 12.10 in the LXX; 12.46; Num. 9.12) present problems. It is true that painting the blood on the doorposts is given a functional explanation in Ex. 12.23, but the immense significance of blood in the Old Testament world precludes acceptance of the contention that the blood in this case was a mere indicator to guide 'the destroyer'. On the contrary, blood had apotropaic force on its own.[16] Similarly, eating the animal without breaking its bones, a detail not easily drawn from a historical narrative, is probably an imitative ritual, in which the worshippers express the deeply felt wish that their community will be preserved intact.[17] The historical narrative is assimilating points that have a cultic origin. It is hardly surprising that a rite as complex as the Passover defies explanation in terms of a single historical drama. What is striking is the determination, proved to be entirely effective, to make a rite that had a previous existence as a spring festival, and that contained important elements of a non-historical character, into a single drama apparently dependent solely upon a historical event.

One notable element in the Passover material is the stress on the continuation of the rite annually for ever. Over and beyond the normal instructions in the calendars, this feast is enjoined to the people of Israel throughout all generations (Ex. 12.14,17,42). An explanation, in historical terms, must be given by every parent to his children to ensure that both the drama and its legend should continue intact (Ex. 12.24–7; 13.5,8–10,14). The reason is that the rite was held to be essential for the identity of Israel as a nation. Corporate sharing in a disaster followed by deliverance is one of the most powerful ways of

[15] Pedersen, *Israel II*, pp. 384ff.; de Vaux, *Ancient Israel*, pp. 492f.; *Sacrifice*, p. 21.

[16] There are two conceptions of power mixed up here, both relevant to prophetic drama, but one supplying a point of comparison, the other a point of contrast. The use of blood as an element in the dramatic action, when it is the action itself that is potent and not the substance used, accords well with the use of material things in the narratives of prophetic dramas. The implication that the blood had inherent potency of its own is a negative point. Material things do not usually have this quality in the prophetic stories. See Chapter 14 below.

[17] De Vaux, *Sacrifice*, p. 9.

achieving a communal bond. Through the Passover, experienced 'contemporaneously', all Israel is bound together by the sense of having been saved. The loyalty of the Israelites both to the community and to Yahweh himself is strengthened. As Pedersen points out, 'It is the participation in this historical event which decides whether or not one belongs to Israel.'[18] The development of the liturgy simply strengthened the notion of solidarity. Whether the feast took place in family units at local shrines or in the neighbourhood of the temple afer the Deuteronomic reform, the community element is clear and inescapable. The necessity of the feast is, therefore, undeniable. This was no 'mere memorial'. Eating the feast was the means of experiencing Yahweh's saving activity and discovering present deliverance within the saved community.

The relevance of all this to prophecy is not difficult to establish; it points us towards a fairly complex understanding of time. If an event can be encountered in its dramatic representation, then it can be so encountered before it happens, just as easily as afterwards. In this case, the representations will be prophetic oracles and dramatic action rather than remembrance and cultic drama, but the power of the event will be experienced in just the same way. If remembering the redemptive acts of God brings solace, anticipating them brings hope. To say that cult and prophecy face different ways is not the whole truth. Both are concerned with Yahweh's saving acts; both enable contemporary Israel to enter into the divine salvation in the here and now. In this regard cultic action and prophetic oracle fulfil a similar purpose.

---

[18] Pedersen, *Israel II*, p. 409; cf. pp. 397f.; Kraus, *Worship*, p. 46.

6 · Prophets and Prophetic Drama

The fact that so much material exists in the background, particularly in the cult, seems to suggest that prophetic drama does not constitute a category of its own; it simply indicates significant acts done by people who happen to be regarded as prophets. Various questions arise. Was the Old Testament prophet a clearly defined figure? Was there something in the way that he performed his dramatic actions that marked them off from other significant actions? And, to begin at the other end, is it possible to define a discrete category of prophetic dramas in Scripture? Let us take the points in that order.

In what sense was the prophet a clearly defined figure? It would be idle to deny that this is a very complicated question; indeed, it embraces a number of different questions. What did the term 'prophet' indicate in the centuries before the exile? How did the post-exilic editors use the term? In what way or ways do modern investigators understand prophecy? Is the prophet to be defined in terms of behaviour – one who declaims oracles and adopts a particular lifestyle – or in theological terms – one who, in humble submission, mediated the word of God?[1] There is the further question of when prophecy began and when it ended. At the root of these questions lies the problem of the link between the various kinds of people called prophets in the Bible, particularly between the classical writing prophets and the rest.[2]

---

[1] 'The prophet is essentially a man who knows himself to be under orders to do that which Yahweh wants done . . . Through the prophet, as through none other, the will of Yahweh is done', writes H.W. Robinson (*Inspiration*, p. 185). So it may seem to a twentieth-century theist, but that kind of definition operates best with very considerable hindsight.

[2] The number of different kinds of prophecy is bafflingly large. There are the ecstatic bands of I Sam. 10 and 19.18–24; the royal advisors, Gad and Nathan; the sycophantic

One fact has to be recognized. The editors who preserved the oracles, particularly the post-exilic editors, were in a very different position from the contemporary onlookers. The latter could observe prophetic behaviour and hear the oracles, but they never knew whether the word could be trusted. The editors, however, were able to apply the Deuteronomic test (Deut. 18.22) and ensure that certain prophets were given due honour and that their oracles were preserved and extended and reapplied. The result was that the great figures who, in their own day, might well have been regarded as most unusual prophets, if prophets at all, became, in the course of time, accepted as the true examples of the phenomenon. So there came about a semantic shift. Originally the bands of I Sam. 10 and 19 and those who followed in their wake, good and bad, were known as prophets and the great figures were oddities and outsiders, fitting uneasily into the category; but, by the time the canon was completed, the designation 'prophet' had been so much associated with the great figures and endowed with so much dignity that it is all the other kinds of prophet that seem out of place.

In this study we want to be as comprehensive as we can. We are interested in everyone who purports to convey a divine message and who, in the process, performs dramatic actions. It does not matter for our purposes whether the message was true, or even whether it was sincere, for bogus performances can reveal how the process was supposed to operate.

From one point of view, there is no beginning and no end to the phenomenon of prophecy, since something like it appears, in one form or another, in all societies; but we are concerned only with the Hebrew tradition and with the movement that gave us the classical 'writing prophets'. Some want to trace this tradition back to Moses; he is called a prophet (Deut. 18.15,18; 34.10f.; Hos. 12.13), he mediated God's word, and he did signs and wonders.[3] From one point of view Moses

---

cheer-leaders led by Zedekiah; the solitary Micaiah ben Imiah; the heroic, mysterious Elijah; Elisha and his company; classic figures to whom books are attributed and others, like Hananiah, who were in direct contention with them. There were true prophets and false prophets, sincere and insincere (these categories do not always coincide); prophets who addressed the court and prophets who addressed the nation. Prophets were sometimes revered (Num. 11.29; 12.6; Deut. 18.15; Amos 3.7; Jer. 25.4) and sometimes put down as deceivers (Deut. 13.1–5; 18.20–2; Isa. 9.15; 28.7; Micah 3.5). It is small wonder that Amos' ambiguous protest in 7. 14f. has given rise to so much discussion.

[3] Num. 12.6ff. might be mentioned here; it makes Moses rather more than a prophet.

is a prophet *par excellence*. But Moses is a figure on his own; it is not
appropriate to treat him as a member of the category of prophets.
Consequently his actions may be discussed in Chapter 3, but not in
Section II. The same argument might tell against Samuel, though he,
too, is called a prophet (I Sam. 3.20; cf. the difficult verse, 9.9), and
he is recorded as presiding over a group of ecstatic prophets (I Sam.
19.20). Samuel was a charismatic figure, but he was many other things
as well. One story relating to Samuel is included in our list because it
is an interesting example of the genre and because it is not stretching
definitions to say that Samuel, in regard to this incident, is acting in a
prophetic capacity. The end of prophecy is also indefinite; post-exilic
prophets do exist, but by this time the phenomenon was evidently
dying out, and those who were preserving the texts of Hebrew religion
found fewer and fewer prophetic oracles worthy of their attention.[4]

Prophets were not born to their task like priests, and it seems
unlikely that they were admitted to prophetic status by consecration,
ordination or any such ceremony.[5] It is true that there are one or two
references to the anointing of prophets (I Kings 19.16; Ps. 105.15),
but not enough to establish the notion of a widespread ceremony of
appointment. Individual prophets or groups of prophets may have
had their own methods of initiation, but there is little evidence that
the prophetic character was thus conveyed.[6] The prophet is defined,
in the first place, by his gifts. There is, of course, what may be called
a 'prophetic life-style'. Commonly, especially in early times, it involved
membership of a guild and participation in the ecstatic activities of
the group. It involved a particular dress (I Kings 19.19; II Kings 1.8;
Zech. 13.4), and possibly also stigmata (I Kings 20.35ff.; Zech. 13.6)
and a tonsure (II Kings 2.23f.).[7] Most of all it involved proclaiming

---

[4] John Barton points out that, as early as the exile, Hebrew tradition was identifying
a group who were to be known as 'the prophets'. Thereafter, though occasional
individuals might still claim to stand in the true prophetic succession, there was a clear
sense that prophecy was a phenomenon of the past (*Oracles of God*, pp. 5f.).

[5] Brockington, 'The Lord Shewed Me: the Correlation of Natural and Spiritual in
Prophetic Experience'.

[6] The possible exception is the appointment of Elisha in I Kings 19. Elijah is ordered
to anoint Elisha but, in fact, he wraps him in the prophetic cloak. This incident is an
excellent example of a prophetic drama, but it cannot be regarded as a demonstration
of the standard or correct procedure for appointing a prophet.

[7] The single reference to the tonsure looks insecure, but both Lindblom and John
Gray are convinced by it for different reasons. Lindblom points out that individual
characteristics are very rarely mentioned in biblical stories and that, therefore, the

oracles, either to individuals, possibly for reward (I Sam. 9.8), or to the nation. In the latter case the oracles may have been unsought or, alternatively, the prophet might be employed at court precisely for his oracles. It is not entirely clear whether prophets ever became professionals in the sense that they made their living at court, or in the temple, by fulfilling prophetic functions. It is certain, however, that the term 'profession' is inappropriate and misleading when pre-exilic prophecy is concerned. As M.J. Buss remarks, 'The prophetic role should therefore be described in terms of a certain kind of activity, not in terms of a full-time or exclusive profession.'[8] Part of that activity was to stand in judgment over kings and priests alike.

The ability to deliver oracles that, over a period of time, proved themselves to be worthy of notice is the root of the whole matter. The qualification, 'worthy of notice' is crucial. There were many in ancient Israel who belonged to prophetic guilds, dressed in prophetic garb, took part in prophetic performances, and mouthed words taken to be divine oracles, and yet who perished leaving not a trace behind them.[9] We know something about Zedekiah and Hananiah, largely because of their opponents, but we know little about all the others who, through the pre-exilic period, functioned in a similar way. The classical prophets delivered oracles that were worthy of notice, which raises the question whether this was the only factor that distinguished them from other prophets. Were the great figures so different that they must be regarded as a separate category altogether, and not even be called prophets?[10] Or were they examples of the same phenomenon, but so gifted that they departed far from the prophetic norm; so far, in fact,

---

reference to Elisha's baldness must relate to his being a prophet. (*Prophecy*, p. 68). Gray says that Elisha's head must have been covered and that the taunt was based on inference from the fact that Elisha was a prophet (*Kings*, p. 480). It is possible that I Kings 20.41 indicates a tonsure rather than scars.

[8] Buss, 'The Social Psychology of Prophecy', p. 5.

[9] The effectiveness of the Deuteronomic test of prophecy speaks for itself (Deut. 18.22). Later generations took no pains to preserve oracles that time proved to be vacuous.

[10] See John Barton, *Oracles of God*, pp. 272f. Barton contends that the great figures were not prophets, but lone geniuses who made use of the prophetic style in order to gain a hearing. He is almost persuaded to call them simply 'laymen'. Carroll would prefer 'poets' ('Poets not Prophets'). See also, E.W. Heaton, *The Old Testament Prophets*, ch. 2; and Auld, 'Prophets through the Looking Glass' and 'Prophets and Prophecy in Jeremiah and Kings', where he argues that the honorific use of the term 'prophet' was post-exilic.

that they were often in conflict with the common prophets? This is a large question. The classical prophets may have dissociated themselves from local prophetic groups because of their corruption, and later tradition may have emphasized the distinction. Nevertheless there are common features: the style and the overt purpose are recognizably the same. It is fair to conclude that a working definition of a prophet and the deliniation of a viable category are possible, particularly as regards those whose work has survived.[11] The dramas that we consider were performed by men who were recognized, not only in their day but in later times, to be prophets.

Secondly, how does prophetic drama differ from all the other dramatic actions that took place in the life of Israel? There are several features that assist a definition. In the first place, and very obviously, it was carried out by peculiarly gifted people called prophets. Prophetic acts partake of the mysterious potency that is associated with prophecy in general. The study of significant acts in Israel suggests that the person who carries them out is all-important. There is little evidence that the action depends upon an impersonal technique, secret, subtle, difficult or whatever. On the contrary, the actions are usually straightforward and their effectiveness – however effectiveness is reckoned – derives from the dynamic nature of the person who carries them out.[12] Moses, Joshua and Saul had the power that was given to leaders. The priests, carrying out their significant acts in the cult, were in a different category, but they had access to a power that made their actions effective. The prophets are a third category. Not priests, not charismatic leaders, not sacral kings, they none the less acted effectively. When they spoke or acted they achieved a result that was beyond the capacity of ordinary men. It is interesting that, by the time the

[11] Recently there has been much discussion of the social role of the prophet and definitions have been set out in sociological terms. The writers owe much to the work of Max Weber. See Lang, *Monotheism and the Prophetic Minority*; Overholt, 'Prophecy: the Problem of Cross-Cultural Comparison' and *Prophecy in Cross-Cultural Perspective*; Wilson, *Prophecy and Society* and *Sociological Approaches*; Long, 'Prophetic Authority' and 'Social Dimensions'; Petersen, *The Roles of Israel's Prophets* and 'The Prophetic Process Reconsidered'. Cf. the critical note struck by Hobbs, 'The Search for Prophetic Consciousness'.

[12] It is common to suppose that the effectiveness of the prophet was judged in terms of his ability to cause things to happen. Zedekiah, in I Kings 22, was simply attempting to bring about a victory for Ahab. It is contended here that this explanation is oversimple. The prophets were undoubtedly regarded as effective figures, but the precise nature of this effectiveness needs closer analysis. See below Chapter 17.

monarchy is established, kings tend to resign to prophets a special area of activity corresponding to the cultic area resigned to the priests. Ahab and Jehoshaphat apparently have to rely upon prophets. It is out of the question that they should attempt a dramatic display themselves.

This leads to an important observation before we have even thought of prophetic drama. The prophet was *himself* a symbol. By his very presence in society he represented the immanence, the power, and the unpredictability of the divine word. Of the prophets as statesmen or counsellors or strategists or demagogues, very little is known. What they were in themselves appears to have been of no great importance to those who preserved the Old Testament for us. But as potential speakers of the word of God, they had immense significance. Like Ahijah's cloak, Isaiah's children and Jeremiah's pot, they represented something far beyond what they were in themselves. This is one reason why the classical prophets always appear to be relatively free of institutional ties.[13] Essentially they are free men, but bound absolutely by their prophetic vocation.

Secondly, prophetic drama was usually performed at the specific behest of Yahweh. This is so much an essential element that Fohrer takes the *Befehl* as one of the constitutive elements of the true form. As a matter of fact, a specific divine command does not appear in the drama stories that are recounted in the Deuteronomic history; nevertheless the sense of divine compulsion is strong. The records never treat the actions as bright ideas thought up by the prophets themselves. Time-serving prophets like Zedekiah and Hananiah claimed divine inspiration as readily as Jeremiah and Ezekiel; they may have been sincere in believing that they were inspired, and evidently they convinced many others beside themselves.

Thirdly, prophetic actions were single actions, taking place once for all. They were not like the acts of social convention or cultic practice that were repeated over and over again by different people. That is not to say that prophetic actions were more significant, but they were more noteworthy. One could become used to cultic practice, however much one respected it and acknowledged its effectiveness. It can hardly have grasped the attention every time as the prophetic act would.[14]

[13] Wolff, 'Prophets and Institutions in the Old Testament'.

[14] This, in effect, is Groenman's point when he talks of prophetic action being consciously chosen and consciously symbolical (*Het Karakter*, p. 9).

Fourthly, the prophetic act was deliberate and artificial. It was contrived for one particular situation and, therefore, could relate to it perfectly. The cultic action is necessarily generalized. It is a universal means of expiation and, therefore, relates only partially to one particular sin. It is a universal means of seeking victory and, therefore, relates only partially to one particular enemy. Something similar can be said about conventional actions. But the prophet is free from the universal and can relate to the circumstances precisely.

Fifthly, prophetic actions were usually, but not always, accompanied by an oracle or supplied with an explanation which brought out whatever meaning may not have been obvious in the act itself. Dramas which have no oracle and no explanation are rare. Often, particularly in Ezekiel, the explanation is included in the instruction to perform the sign. It is difficult, of course, to know whether the explanation belonged to the incident itself or simply to the literary record. No doubt scribes and editors elaborated and expanded some of the explanations, but, equally, the fact that there was an explanation, either for the public or, at least, for the prophet himself, seems to be implicit in the dramatic action from the beginning. This is an important feature. The inference is that, unlike some cultic and conventional acts where the meaning was undefined, the prophetic act had a specific and finite meaning.

Prophetic actions must, therefore, be seen as a class by themselves. They were specific actions with a specific purpose, carried out by a peculiar kind of person, who believed himself to be, and was generally acknowledged to be, called by God, perhaps even from the womb (Jer. 1.5), to this special service.

So we come to the third question. Within the prophetic corpus, how does one isolate that which can be reasonably described as prophetic *drama*? This, as Regnier pointed out more than half a century ago, is no easy matter.[15] Regnier's point is that one either determines a particular approach to prophetic drama and then adopts a definition that ties in with that particular approach, which means in effect that the evidence is programmed to suit the theory, or one adopts a comprehensive approach, in which case the category becomes uncontrollable. Buzy, for example, dealt only with acts or visions which presage future events. Van den Born considers only those actions that can be regarded as historical. This means passing over

[15] Regnier, 'Le Réalisme'.

very important material in Ezekiel. One might consider only deliberate and positive actions initiated by prophets, but this would rule out three widely recognized dramas in Jer. 16 where the prophet is inactive and much other valuable material as well.

An obvious way of defining and limiting the category is to concentrate, not on the actions themselves, but on the records, and to apply form critical methods to them. This is what Fohrer has done.[16] His method has its advantages, but also its limitations, and it is particularly inappropriate for the objectives pursued here. In the first place, as Fohrer recognizes, the three main elements (command, account, explanation) are not always present. In the early prophetic narratives, the command from Yahweh to perform the action hardly appears at all, and in Ezekiel, more often than not, command and explanation are entangled together and an account of the action being performed is lacking. In such circumstances the decision what to include and what to leave out cannot follow the formula and it must appear arbitrary. Secondly, Fohrer agrees that other elements break into the stories. These occasional features are often as important as the definitive ones, and any tidy arrangement that excludes them or makes them appear marginal would not help the understanding of the whole phenomenon. Thirdly, study of the literary form of a narrative tends to exclude detailed study of the content. Our concern is with the mentality that gives rise to the action, and far less with the shape of the narrative that records it. Fourthly, the selection of the thirty-two passages effectively cuts off prophetic drama from those other actions that we have been discussing in the last few chapters. It should not be assumed *a priori* that prophetic drama represents a distinct and isolated feature of Hebrew thought. The evidence points in the opposite direction. Fohrer considers that the specific call of Yahweh provides the only occasion of the true prophetic act, but such an argument is dangerously circular.[17] It is better for us to be concerned with all prophetic actions, whether they include divine commands or not. Only when the whole range is surveyed is it possible for the most interesting and important examples within it to be recognized and understood.

Of course it is possible to throw off all limits and maintain that there is a continuum in the prophetic programme ranging from contrived

---

[16] Fohrer, 'Die Gattung der Berichte', p. 94; *Die Handlungen*, p. 18; *Introduction*, p. 356.

[17] 'Die Gattung der Berichte', p. 105.

actions, through unexpected experiences, observations, actions which are only conceived, and images described in words, to oracles expressed in graphic metaphor. All involve, in some way, the symbol-making process, and it could be said that the relation between the dramatic element and the reality to which it relates is the same in all cases. Any reduction of the field is, therefore, artificial. One can see the force of this argument. It is unlikely that an explanation of prophetic drama will appear that has no bearing on prophetic oracles. Nevertheless some limitation must be accepted and it is reasonable to suppose that a study of drama of one kind or another will shed light on other forms of prophetic expression.

At the risk of losing clarity and definition, therefore, we must be ready to consider every prophetic action that goes beyond the functional and that is reckoned to signify something beyond itself. Selection is still necessary, and it may still at times seem arbitrary, but the intention is to be as inclusive as possible.

In the first place, we shall be concerned with actions and not with oracles. No doubt oracles stand in the same relation to events as dramas, but if the enquiry were extended in that direction, it would be extended out of sight. In most cases the action is devised and performed by the prophet himself, and he alone understands its full meaning. There are one or two instances, however, where somebody else acts and the prophet infers a meaning from the action. Instances of this kind are included in the list because the way in which they are described suggests that they have the same force as actions deliberately performed by the prophet. If the real agent in both action and interpretation is held to be Yahweh, it matters little whose hands are physically engaged in the act. This leads to the question of visions. If Jer. 18 is included because Jeremiah reflected on an actual potter, what about Amos 7, where Amos reflected, equally forcefully, on a plague of locusts which was seen only in a vision? The answer must be that, if we were to include all the visions, we should over-extend the list. Nevertheless some passages are included where the significant action is conceived rather than carried out, because these passages illustrate, better than others, the important fact that we are not dealing with actions that are effective in themselves. A further refinement concerns actions which were intended but are not actually described. Micah 1.8, for example, has to be included, because, though there is no evidence that Micah actually did these things, they represent prophetic actions that stand over against an actual state of affairs, just like the more obvious examples. Inevitably arbitrary decisions have to be made about what constitutes an action.

The second criterion is that the action must be significant. It must stand over against some important reality, event or state of affairs with which it is positively linked. That means ignoring a group of potent and dramatic actions which appear in the stories of Elijah and Elisha: Elijah stretches himself three times on the son of the widow of Zarephath and the child revives (I Kings 17.21); Elijah divides the Jordan by striking it with his cloak (II Kings 2.8); Elisha also divides the Jordan (II Kings 2.14); he has salt poured into a spring to cure the water (II Kings 2.19–22); he stretches himself over the Shunammite's son and he revives (II Kings 4.34–7); he puts meal into a stew to take away its noxious quality (II Kings 4.38–41); he causes Naaman to wash himself seven times in the Jordan to be cured (II Kings 5.11–14); he makes an axehead float (II Kings 6.5–7); Isaiah manipulates a shadow to prove to Hezekiah that he will recover (II Kings 20.8–11; Isa. 38.7f.,22).

The line between these actions and those we call prophetic drama is a fine one, but there are good reasons for dismissing them. In the first place, some of these actions may be simply functional. Putting meal in a sour stew may be the action of a man who is shrewder than his companions. Secondly, in some cases, the prophet appears to be under no great constraint; he is acting to suit his own convenience or to do a favour to someone. Thirdly, the issues are relatively trivial; they concern the taste of a stew rather than the fate of an empire. Fourthly, and most importantly, these actions are largely self-contained. They do not stand over against a great event or state of affairs which they proclaim or evidence or prefigure. In this sense, they are not *significant*. Elijah's stretching himself upon the widow's son may signify the return of life to the child and Naaman's bathing may signify his cure, but it remains that the scope of the drama is an incident in an individual's life; there is no pointer to a reality on a larger scale.

Of course these actions have a place on the map of Hebrew thought, as do the actions of Zedekiah, Hananiah, Jehoiakim and others; and of course the editorial history of these narratives is important. Ideally one would want to give a comprehensive account of all dramatic behaviour in Israel and all reflection thereon; but limitations have to be accepted. It is evident that the category 'prophetic actions' is not homogeneous and that, by the criteria indicated above, certain prophetic actions can be distinguished that represent an understanding of reality, and the prophet's relations thereto, which is especially interesting and informative. Actions in this category deserve study on their own.

The result of these qualifications is a list of some forty-eight passages or incidents that fall to consideration. This is a long list by the standards of other authors. Van den Born lists thirty-two references in *Profetie Metterdaad*, and Groenman speaks of thirty-one, though he does not actually treat that number. Fohrer gives a precise list of thirty-two accounts.[18] Although the totals are close, the lists are by no means identical; all the scholars concerned provide their own limiting criteria; only about twenty are common to all.

Another feature of prophetic drama that must never be overlooked lies in the fact that the prophets knew nothing of professional detachment; they were, or wished to be thought to be, totally involved in their work. Often it seems that they experience the reality, the actuality of Yahweh's will, first in their own persons.[19] Jeremiah is broken long before the people whose fate he sees so clearly are broken. As a true representative, he takes the ills of the people first upon himself, even though, personally, he is not guilty of the sins which have brought this doom upon them.[20] Von Rad argues that this representative element belongs only to Jeremiah and Ezekiel, that, 'in the case of the earlier symbolic acts, the sign was something exterior to the soul and spirit of the prophet concerned'.[21] The actions of Isaiah and Hosea, however, show the same involvement, and the oracles of the early prophets were certainly not exterior to the 'soul and spirit' of the prophet concerned.[22] On the contrary, 'the prophet threw his whole self into his prophecy, and made not his lips alone, but his whole personality, in some cases his whole family, the vehicle of the

---

[18] Van den Born, *Profetie Metterdaad*, p. 14f.; Groenman, *Het Karakter*, p. 8; Fohrer, *Die Handlungen*, p. 17.

[19] Fohrer, 'Die Gattung der Berichte', p. 93; van den Born, *Profetie Metterdaad*, p. 80; Fraser, 'Symbolic Acts', pp. 45f.; Polk, *The Prophetic Persona*, p. 81; Polk's whole argument, though concerned specifically with Jeremiah, is relevant to the issue of the prophet's involvement in his task. See too Holladay, *Jeremiah 1–25*, pp. 472f.

[20] See Blank, 'The Prophet as Paradigm'.

[21] Von Rad, *Theology II*, pp. 274f.

[22] The deep involvement of Hosea in his prophetic vocation can hardly be gainsaid. Many writers refer to it, none more perceptively than Vogels in an article with the rather obscure title, ' "Osée-Gomer" *car* et *comme* "Yahweh-Israel" '.

divine "word" '.[23] Moreover, it is wrong to make a fundamental distinction between actions and oracles at this point. Nonetheless, von Rad is raising an important point. The Old Testament does bear witness to a change of emphasis from the powerful man of God who retains some sense of independence – Elijah – to the servant figure who is completely taken up into Yahweh's will – Jeremiah. This confirms the contention that the class of prophetic actions is not homogeneous. Prophetic actions may together be distinguished from other significant actions, but there are important differences within the category.

If the prophet is so deeply involved in his message, if his private life is ordered by it, if his oracles are fulfilled in himself, then a question is raised about his non-prophetic activity. Is it possible to separate particular, deliberate actions and give them a significance that his other actions did not have? 'Nothing that happens to the prophet in his personal life is without a deep, esoteric significance. Hosea in his marriage, Jeremiah in his celibacy, Ezekiel in the death of his wife, see so many Words uttering the divine compassion or shadowing forth the divine purpose.'[24] Must we assume, then, that empires tottered every time Jeremiah broke a cup? The short answer seems to be yes. In early times, the prophet was thought to be so closely in touch with the unseen powers that they were constantly showing themselves through him and to him. This is why Samuel is able to turn a pure accident against Saul (I Sam. 15.27f.). In later times, although the theological account of the relationship of prophet to Yahweh changed, this element remained constant. The slightest action, or even thought, of the great prophets might be of universal significance.

We must, however, credit the Hebrews with common sense and, therefore, we must presume that it is possible to make a distinction between significant prophetic dramas and what one might call the neutral actions of a prophet, just as it is between his oracles and his everyday conversation. The prophet knew himself to be not only a mouthpiece but a man. In early times, the man became the mouthpiece when the spirit of Yahweh came upon him in ecstasy (I Sam. 10.10), and the same idiom is preserved throughout the prophetic period,

[23] Rowley, 'The Nature of Prophecy', p. 28, citing the view expounded by L.H. Brockington in 'The Lord Shewed Me'.

[24] Knight, *Hebrew Prophetic Consciousness*, p. 51. Lods makes the same point, even implying that the prophet reflected the future in his private life without knowing it (*The Prophets and the Rise of Judaism*, p. 55.).

though some books make more use of it than others.[25] Through the spirit, the prophet is able to say '*kōh 'āmar Yhwh*', and this very formula implies that there were occasions when the prophet spoke but Yahweh did not speak. One has to distinguish, therefore, between the permanent factors in prophecy, the charismatic person, the call, the commitment to the prophetic way of life, and the occasional factors, trance or ecstasy, 'the invasion of the spirit', the sense of compulsion to deliver a specific oracle or perform a specific action. Dramas are usually carried out in a deliberate, almost a ceremonial way. There is little room for doubt in the onlooker's mind that the prophet is doing something out of the ordinary. On this ground, Jeremiah's action with the earthen flask in ch.19 is clearly distinguishable from domestic accidents, and the same applies to dramatic acts with less definition. Jeremiah saw the potter at work and it was, for him, a sign. Presumably he also saw the baker at work and it was not. The reason is that the baker did not stir his mind, did not suggest to him notions that grew in force till they manifested themselves as divine realities. The prophet himself distinguished between his own words and actions and those that he felt constrained to speak or perform in the service of Yahweh. In the former case, the effective energy was merely his own; in the latter it was Yahweh's.

In actual fact this distinction is one which the modern reader scarcely has to make. The *obiter dicta* of the prophets simply are not recorded. The sifting has already been done and what meets us in the prophetic books is not prophetic small talk or prophetic opinion but oracles and acts which were impressive at the time and which were held by Hebrew tradition to be of such weight that they needed to be preserved. From these considerations it follows that prophetic dramas can reasonably be distinguished from significant actions performed by those who were not prophets and from insignificant actions, postulated rather than reported, by those who were. In that way a clear category of prophetic drama can be established.

It is wrong to conclude a passage on the prophetic differentia without some reference to the complex issue of false and unfulfilled prophecy.[26] False prophets are of different kinds. There are godly

---

[25] Ezekiel is often overwhelmed by the spirit (Ezek. 2.2; 3.12, 14.24; etc.), though the idea is missing from Jeremiah.

[26] I Kings 22 speaks of four hundred prophets who look very much like time-servers and who certainly gave the two kings bad advice; it also relates that Micaiah ben Imlah, plainly recognized as an honest prophet, prophesied a lie (v. 15) and immediately

prophets, often proved right, who are occasionally proved wrong. There are godly prophets whom Yahweh deliberately uses to prophesy falsely in order to mislead. There were genuinely misguided prophets who thought they had the word of God, but who were proved to be wrong. There were doubtless time-serving liars and deceivers who knew themselves to be such. There were those who, though in general lying prophets, occasionally spoke the truth. Strictly speaking, therefore, it is more correct to speak of false prophecy than of false prophets, though, by the time the prophetic narratives had reached canonical form, certain figures had been clearly characterized as true prophets, though they occasionally made mistakes, and others as false.[27] The tragedy of false prophecy was that it could not easily be recognized as such. All too often the liars were believed and the faithful repudiated.

Fundamentally false prophecy was that given by one who was not speaking the word of Yahweh, but who was simply addressing his own words to the situation. However impressive the outward phenomena, the divine power was lacking. Naturally it was important for Hebrews to be able to tell empty prophecies from those divinely given, but it was not easy. Our apprehension of the problem is distorted by the fact that history, tradition, and indeed, the formation of the canon have settled the question for us. Maybe Hananiah spoke

---

thereafter prophesied the opposite. The curious story of I Kings 13.11–32 preserves the notion that those recognized as prophets are capable of lying as well as prophesying the truth. Jeremiah is under constant attack from prophets regarded by him and proved by events to be false (Jer. 5.30f.; 6.30; 8.10; 14.13–16; 23.11, 21f.; 27–28; 29.8f.). The term 'false prophets' is ambiguous and, as Carroll says, facile ('Poets not Prophets'). It can refer to those who untruthfully pretend to have received a word from God. Alternatively it can refer to those who were proved to be consistently wrong; by the nature of the case, their oracles were rarely preserved. We must assume, however, that this latter group included both those who thought they were being truthful and time-serving rogues such as those referred to in Micah 3.5–11. It must also be noted that even the most noble prophets were sometimes wrong (see Carroll, *When Prophecy Failed*). The way in which prophecy was dealt with in later times does not help to clarify this matter. By the time the post-exilic editors were at work some figures had been shown to be largely accurate and profoundly influential; their oracles were properly treated with the greatest respect. We cannot be sure, however, that the tradition was entirely just to the others.

[27] It has often been noted that there is no Hebrew word for false prophet. The LXX invented ψευδοπροφήτης and used the word on about ten occasions, almost all of which are in Jeremiah. Cf. Rimbach, 'Prophets in Conflict'.

volumes of oracles; maybe his disciples preserved them; but time has proved them worthless. Time, however, has canonized Jeremiah. So it is easy for us, but it was not easy at the time. The only test was to wait and see – an ironic situation, for, by that time, the truth or falsehood of the prophecy would hardly matter. Nevertheless that is how the test of prophecy operated according to Deut. 18.22 and Jer. 28.9, and the only crumb of comfort was that a prophet who had been wrong once might reasonably be treated with suspicion next time.

The whole matter is well illustrated by the account of Ahab and Jehoshaphat's council of war in I Kings 22. Ahab asked the advice of four hundred prophets. It is not clear to what extent the prophets were devoted to Yahweh. Jehoshaphat's question in v. 7 and Zedekiah's formula in v. 11 both suggest that they claim to be Yahwists. Whatever the truth, they prophesied what Ahab wanted to hear. No doubt the performance was adequate technically, maybe they even believed what they were saying, but Jehoshaphat was not impressed. 'Is there no other prophet of the Lord?' he asks. Micaiah is sent for. The court prophets, challenged and offended, improved their act. To the word they added the drama, straining every nerve to envisage and proclaim a victory for Ahab. They failed, not through want of trying, probably not because they were consciously practising deception, but simply, according to Hebrew belief, because Yahweh had not given them the word. Micaiah comes and he too prophesies victory, but it is obvious to everyone present that he is simply giving his own word. It may be the word of a true prophet, but it is useless because not even a true prophet can, of himself, create victory. Micaiah is rebuked and commanded to speak the truth *in the name of the Lord*, and he prophesies disaster. This time, because the spirit of God is thought to be in him, his word is taken as true. For good measure Micaiah explains how his court rivals had gone wrong. Yahweh had sent a lying spirit (*rûaḥ šeqer*) into them, so that they would entice Ahab to disaster.

Whatever modern verdicts on false prophecy may be, it appears that two explanations of it were current in Israel. Either the prophet is not possessed, in which case the only wisdom he can summon up and the only power he can exert are his own (Jer. 14.14; 23.16,32; 27.14–16; etc.), or he was possessed by a spirit of falsehood, the purpose of which was to mislead and to ensure that the word prophesied did not come to pass (I Sam. 18.10; Jer. 4.10).

It is easy to relate this conclusion to the discussion in Chapter 5 of the nature of the biblical event. Either a divine event, of which the oracle is a part, is impending, in which case the formulae *kōh 'āmar Yhwh* and *nᵉ'um Yhwh* are appropriate, or it is not, in which case the prophets are labouring futilely to create an event for themselves. The sincerity of the prophet and the technicalities of the performance have little to do with the case. The Lord either sends the word-event or he does not. In the eyes of Old Testament writers true divine events first revealed themselves in the words of a prophet who had been called for that purpose. 'Surely the Lord God does nothing, without revealing his secret to his servants the prophets' (Amos 3.7). That was genuine prophecy. Prophecy of other kinds, whatever its source, whatever its method, whatever the conviction of its purveyors, was empty.

It may appear that this notion of prophecy goes beyond what is commonly said about the *creativity* of Yahweh's word through the prophet. On this present analysis the prophetic word is more aptly described as expressive of what is to be rather than creative. The difficulty is a real one. To call an act creative is to imply a temporal, logical, causal relationship between the act and its consequence. That is not how the Hebrew understood prophecy. Yahweh alone is creative. He creates the whole event, both the historical happening and the prophecy that is linked to it. The prophecy is a part of the event, as the man who posts the billboards is part of the circus. To speak of the prophetic word as creative is, therefore, less than exact.

In this light, one striking feature of prophecy is more easily understood. Why were oracles of doom proclaimed when there was no sign of repentance and no hope that doom would be avoided if there were? Because the prophet is not issuing a warning to make people turn from their wicked ways. He is unveiling the doom itself; his oracle is part of it. And one has the sense that the prophetic declaration would be necessary even if there were no hearers at all.[28] This is confirmed by those dramas that were carried out with no onlookers (e.g. Jer. 13.1–11). Westermann, in his study of the literary forms of prophetic oracles, points out that only after the exile did the unconditional announcement of judgment give way to an appeal for repentance.[29] Similarly, J.L. Mays draws attention to the dirges

---

[28] 'Israel too was thus aware that her language possessed possibilities other than those demanded by everyday personal conversation. She was aware of a use of language in which the primary requisite was in no sense a partner in conversation, but *just* that the words should *just* be spoken, that they should simply be brought on the scene as an objective reality endowed with mysterious power' (von Rad, *Theology II*, p. 85).

[29] Westermann, *Basic Forms*, pp. 205–9.

pronounced by prophets over living audiences.[30] The dirges are not a warning but a disclosure, a disclosure of the fate that impends and that has now become unavoidable.

To a modern critical mind prophecy is a difficult art. Different prophets will be variously successful. No prophet will be completely accurate, though some are likely to be frequently wrong. According to this approach, the distinction between true prophets and false is likely to be a matter of degree. In Israel it was not so. The distinction is between the prophet who was called and given the word by God (I Kings 18.22; 22.7) and those who deal in *šeqer*. This distinction is absolute, but, alas, not easily recognized.

[30] Mays, *Amos*, p. 103.

· II ·

TEXTS

7 · Prophetic Drama in the Deuteronomistic History

The origin of the following narratives is probably various collections of stories about individual prophets, but we encounter them as parts of the books of Samuel and Kings. Martin Noth's theory of a unified Deuteronomistic history must be accepted in broad outline, though there are many reasons for querying the details.[1] If the editing process took place during the exile, when the work of the later and greater prophets was well known, it is remarkable how little attempt was made to make these early narratives conform to the later ones. There seems real point in Childs' comment in criticism of Noth; 'The overarching theological categories which unite the four historical books did not function in such a way as to flatten or seriously to alter the earlier stages of the material's development.'[2]

If we leave Elijah's sacrifice on Mount Carmel out of account, none of the actions described here was said to have been specifically enjoined by Yahweh. These prophets seemed to operate with far greater personal freedom than was enjoyed by Jeremiah or Ezekiel. Moreover there is more than a hint in some of these narratives that use was being made of forces other than Yahweh's supreme will. The properties used in these dramas do not always appear totally neutral and insignificant. Ahijah's cloak was *new*, and that was apparently important; Elijah's mantle had a potency of its own; and both Zedekiah's horns and Elisha's arrows suggest pre-battle rituals that owe something to the common, magical traditions of the ancient Near East. The redactor may have allowed Zedekiah his folly since he was proved wrong, but in the other cases the only explanation is that the redactor was exercising restraint. The result is that the narratives in this chapter

---

[1] Noth, *The Deuteronomistic History*, 1943, ET 1981.
[2] Childs, *Introduction to the Old Testament as Scripture*, p. 235.

give a different impression from those we shall come to later, and this both complicates the task of providing a model for the understanding of prophetic drama as a whole and makes it more interesting.

The Robe-tearing at Gilgal: I Sam. 15.27f.

In this passage there is an account of Samuel's rejection of Saul which is attended and reinforced by the tearing of a garment. The source problem of I Samuel is notorious and this is a particularly difficult passage. Fohrer makes this narrative the earlier version of Saul's rejection; Caird inclines to the view that it is a later version; and again the passage may be an insertion.[3] It is impossible, therefore, to reach any conclusion about how reliable the narrative is except to say that there is nothing in the account to lead us to doubt its accuracy. In any case it is sufficient for us that it is a coherent narrative, a narrative in which Hebrew editors believed in the sense that they wished to preserve it. Most commentators would agree with the following account of the first part of the incident. Saul has failed Samuel by disobeying the command to put Amalek to the ban. The two men meet at Gilgal, though the locus of the incident in a shrine seems to have little bearing on the event. Samuel denounces Saul and declares that Yahweh has rejected him as king. Samuel then turns to go away. At this point the commentators disagree. One of the men grabbed the other's robe and it was torn. Samuel reacted to the accident by repeating the rejection in even stronger terms.

The problem arises over the 'he' and 'his' in v. 27. In English the presumption would be that the pronoun 'he' referred to the last proper noun mentioned, i.e. Samuel, but a presumption is not a rule and Hebrew is less rigid on the matter than English. There has obviously been doubt on the point for a long time because the LXX inserts 'Saul' in place of the subject 'he' and so achieves a precision which the Hebrew lacks. RSV, NEB and JB have accepted the LXX translators' interpretation. The *prima facie* case then is that Saul tore Samuel's robe. Nevertheless exegetes have frequently argued that the names should be reversed, presumably because Samuel tearing Saul's robe would make Samuel an active agent and would also provide a much

---

[3] Fohrer, *Introduction*, pp. 224f.; Caird, *I Samuel*, pp. 958, 964; H.P. Smith, *Samuel*, p. 139.

better example of a mimetic drama.[4] Tearing garments was a serious
matter, as mourning rites show. There are many references to the
tearing of a kingdom from a king in which the same Hebrew verb is
used (I Sam. 28.17; I Kings 11.11f., 31; 14.8). Royal robes were a
sign of royal dignity and defeated monarchs were humiliated by the
spoliation of their robes, either in battle or in captivity. Saul was about
to lose his kingdom, so it seems appropriate that his robe should be
the one to suffer.

On this suggestion three comments have to be made. In the first
place, the text does not imply this at all. McKane's grammatical
evidence is unconvincing, and the LXX translators were presumably
clarifying the text, as they understood it, not changing it. They could,
of course, have been wrong. Secondly, the suggestion runs counter to
any realistic understanding of the incident. Saul makes an abject
confession and begs for pardon. Samuel condemns him outright and
turns to go away. Saul grabs him. Obviously it is Samuel's robe that
gets torn. There is no sense in the supposition that Samuel turned to
go away and then deliberately turned back to tear Saul's robe. Thirdly,
the suggestion rests upon the assumption that the mimetic element
was always prominent and transparent in prophetic drama, and so the
verse must be read to ensure this. Wishing a particular understanding
onto the evidence cannot be an acceptable method and in fact
this assumption is not sound. Mauchline summarizes the contrary
argument well and his conclusion, difficult as it may be at first sight,
must be accepted.[5]

The work of Sir James Frazer has accustomed us to think of magic
in mimetic terms, but there are many reasons for not applying Frazer's
ideas to the dramas under discussion. Imitation is prominent in many
of them, but not in all; examples can be found where apparently
disconnected images are regarded as representations of the other
realities. The birth of a child is not an obvious index of the relief of a
city (Isa. 7.14–17). Giving children expressive names may be a verbal
indicator of the reality, but it is not strictly mimetic. And if we move
out of the field of drama and into the wider field of prophetic imagery,
the point is even more clear. The link between the summer fruit and
the destruction of Israel in Amos 8.2 is by means of pun rather than

---

[4] McKane, *Samuel*, pp. 102f.; Turro, *I Samuel*, pp. 170f.; Ackroyd, *Samuel*, p. 128;
the argument is older than this, however: see Goldman, *Samuel*, p. 91.

[5] Mauchline, *Samuel*, p. 125.

analogy. Amos sees *qayiṣ* (fruit) and thinks *qēṣ* (end).[6] It is surely an error to introduce the mimetic element and say that the fruit was about to go rotten. There is no overriding need, therefore, to suppose that this incident must be rendered in a way that actually mimics Saul's humiliation.

A reasonable explanation lies to hand. From the Hebrew text it is clear that Samuel is wearing a formal garment appropriate to his position (*mᵉʿîl*). In later times the priestly writers regarded this garment as part of the priestly uniform. Here it is as significant for Samuel as royal robes were for Saul.[7] When the accident happened, it was easy to see it as an outrage. Poor, disobedient Saul was led to the final misfortune of tearing his erstwhile protector's precious robe. Samuel turned the outrage back upon Saul with redoubled force. If this is the correct reading, then we have an interesting example of how dramatic actions were understood. Nobody took any initiative in the action itself, so there can be no question of a man of God injecting destructive force into the situation. The actual tearing was an accident, or so it seemed, but why did that accident take place? Because Yahweh was at work. He had already rejected Saul because of his disobedience. This accident demonstrates dramatically what was already the case in reality.

The tearing of the robe is expressive on three levels. It represents, firstly, the breach that had come to exist between Yahweh and Saul; secondly the breach between Samuel and Saul; and thirdly the breach between Saul and his kingdom. The conversation in vv. 24–26 is the verbal expression of the first two and the pronouncement in v. 28 the verbal expression of the last. Far from being simply a prophecy of something to come, the drama is, on all levels, an expression of a divine reality that has already come into being but that has not yet

---

[6] Susan Niditch's *Symbolic Vision* is relevant at this point. Niditch makes it clear that word and idea association is quite sufficient to establish the link between symbol and reality (pp. 30ff.) In this instance the word is 'tear' and the idea is the rending of something precious. There has been a tearing of the robe. There will be a tearing of the kingdom. There is no need for a full-scale mimetic drama.

[7] In a structuralist analysis of this incident Fokkelman confirms the points made here. Samuel wears a robe that is 'the symbol of his calling and dignity'. Saul, by contrast, is in distress. He 'reaches out to what he sadly lacks: unswerving faith, power, authority'. He is doubly disappointed. Samuel turns to go. The robe tears and Samuel instantly interprets this, not as an unfortunate chance, but as a sign of the irrevocability of the breach. Saul has unhappily rendered visible his own downfall (*Narrative Art II*, p. 105).

completed its course. On the third level particularly, the tearing reflects a divine activity that has four phases: first the intention to reject Saul, secondly the dramatic expression of the intention in the tearing of the robe, thirdly the verbal expression in the words of Samuel, and fourthly the fulfilment of the intention in Saul's loss of the kingdom. The tearing of the robe can be compared with the revelation of the summer fruit in Amos 8. Yahweh showed Amos the fruit and enabled him to prophesy as an intermediate stage between forming the intention to destroy Israel and the historical fulfilment of the intention. The creative power lies in the intention, not in the drama or the vision, ominous as both may be.

Historical statements can be made only with great reserve in this context. Nevertheless it is more than likely that the origin of this story is an actual incident. The narrative has a certain historical verisimilitude. The doom to which the drama witnessed continued to work itself out. From this point onwards in the narrative, attention is focussed on David.

Ahijah's Cloak: I Kings 11.29–31

Ahijah's action in tearing his cloak bears marked similarities to the story we have just discussed, but the Ahijah story is more widely regarded as an example of prophetic drama. Jeroboam is in charge of some building operations in Jerusalem, where forced labour from the north is being used; Jeroboam is already planning revolt. Ahijah, the prophet from Shiloh, wearing a new cloak, but this time a less formal garment (*salmâ*), meets him and takes him on one side so that they are alone together in open country. The LXX makes this more clear by adding, 'and he drew him out of the way'. Ahijah then removes his cloak and tears it – the same verb as in the previous story – into twelve pieces, giving ten to Jeroboam with words that suggest that ten tribes will be torn from the house of Solomon and given to him. In the Hebrew text, Ahijah appears to act on his own initiative, but there is another account of what must be the same incident in the long insertion that is found in the LXX after I Kings 12.24. Here the prophet is named as Shemaiah and he is given a command from Yahweh to perform the act. Once again doubts have been raised about who was wearing the coat, but they can be ignored.[8] The Hebrew is uncertain,

---

[8] Godbey, 'Hebrew Masal' p. 101, no doubt following Ewald, according to whom Jeroboam appeared in official dress as a servant of the regime; this was too much for Ahijah, who saw the robe as a symbol of the power of David's house that was crumbling.

but again the LXX inserts the prophet's name, Ahijah in 11.29 and
Shemaiah in 12.24o.

The drama is in two acts; first the tearing of the cloak to signify the
dividing of the kingdom and secondly the giving of ten pieces to
Jeroboam to signify his coming role. Both are interpreted by the
prophet in the accompanying formula. The undivided garment signifies the nation. The tearing and the giving signify events that Yahweh
has determined, that are already coming into being, and that will
affect the nation, and Jeroboam particularly.

There are more interesting features here. Ahijah comes from Shiloh,
a cult centre destroyed by the Philistines, which leads us to wonder
whether Ahijah was a cultic prophet. Even if he was, it hardly seems
relevant. No significance for this story can be extracted either from
Ahijah's cultic connections or from his concern for court records as
witnessed by II Chron. 9.29. More interesting is the stress laid on the
fact that the garment was new. The second of the two LXX versions
enlarges on this, 'a new cloak that had not been in water' (12.24o).
New things were supposed to have a mystic quality not possessed by
old things, hence the importance of the firstborn and the first fruits
(see too Judg. 16.7–11; I Sam. 6.7; II Kings 2.20).[9] It is clear that not
only use but washing carries this quality away, hence the comment in
the LXX.[10] If Ahijah's coat was more suited to the purpose because it
was new, it follows that prophetic drama cannot be completely
explained in terms of action without reference to peculiar objects. Nor
can it be argued that divine intention alone supplied the dynamic. The
new garment seems to have a potency of its own, a clear indication
that those who look for a single explanation for all prophetic drama,
and particularly for a 'pure' – that is to say, a non-syncretistic, non-
superstitious, sophisticated and theological – explanation will look in
vain. There must be significance too in the fact that Ahijah and
Jeroboam were alone in open country. There can hardly be any doubt
that, in the first instance, the men needed secrecy because their

[9] Amsler points out that, in those hard times, a cloak should last for years, so Ahijah's
action was deliberately shocking, as shocking as the event it prefigured (*Les Actes*,
p. 11). Certainly the action seems to represent a prodigal waste unless a new cloak was
essential to it. Nevertheless to suggest, as G.H. Jones does, that new objects were
necessary for symbolic actions is going some way beyond the evidence (*Kings*, p. 243).

[10] The importance of washing to deal with ritual uncleanness witnesses to the power
of water to disperse these mystical forces. The leprosy rite also supplies evidence (Lev.
14.5f., 50f.; Montgomery, *Kings*, p. 250).

behaviour was treasonable. The occasion may seem insignificant and the action of no practical consequence, but the prophets existed to express the divine will. Consequently this lonely encounter and its dramatic accompaniment were recognized to be momentous. Yahweh was moving into action. His intervention began in secrecy in a field, but it would soon reveal itself as a public and irreversible calamity. In I Kings 12.15 Rehoboam's stubbornness is explained as the consequence of the divine will already expressed in Ahijah's word to Jeroboam. This may be a gloss, in which case the last three words of 11.29, which refer to the secrecy of the encounter, may also be a gloss. If that is so, a Deuteronomic editor is drawing attention in a moralizing way, first to the deceptively small affair in the field, and then to its dire consequences. This is, of course, to concentrate on the interpretative rather than the historical element in the passage, but the view of the Deuteronomic editor is as interesting as that of Ahijah himself or Jeroboam.

The feature that attracts most attention in the story is the act of tearing the cloak into twelve pieces. It is difficult to know how far one should press the details. The fact that Ahijah performed the action with an article that was essentially singular may mean that propaganda on behalf of the essential unity of the Hebrew tribes is implied in the story.[11] Also the number twelve is obviously important as the ideal number of tribes.[12] But these thoughts surely belong to the literary account of the incident, when reflection had added to, ornamented and interpreted the facts. Tearing the cloak into twelve pieces must be rejected as a historical fact for two reasons. It is a difficult and impracticable thing to do. Tearing a garment once, or even twice, is admirably dramatic, but continuing laboriously until there is a heap of twelve pieces pushes the action over the edge of banality. Moreover, tearing the robe into twelve pieces has no significance in the context. Israel is not first divided into tribal groups and then distributed between two different monarchs. Israel is to be divided once into a

---

[11] Ahijah is sometimes represented as an upholder of the amphictyonic unity. See J. Gray, *Kings*, p. 295.

[12] Relating the number twelve to the actual tribes is a problem that need not concern us; modern commentators refer readers to the researches of Alt (*Essays*) and Noth (*System*). Some suggest that the number relates to the number of Solomon's administrative districts (I Kings 4.7–19), which excluded Judah. That is hardly likely and it does not help the arithmetic. See also Auld (*Kings*, p. 82) for the contention that it simply means ten times more power and responsibility for Jeroboam than for Rehoboam.

large group and a small one. It is true that the action does not have to be mimetic, but equally we should exclude extraneous and improbable actions that make the drama less mimetic than it might have been. If the drama is to be regarded as historical – and on that there is not enough evidence to reach a firm conclusion either way – then the hypothesis must be that Ahijah made a single tear and gave Jeroboam the larger portion. The editor did the rest. When the incident reached literary form, either at the hands of Ahijah himself or one of his disciples, the relevance of the schism to the religious community of Israel could be more easily expressed. This was also the point where the editor encountered the difficulty of relating the ideal tribal structure to political realities. By speaking of twelve tribes divided into ten and one (vv. 31f.,36), he lends a rough historical accuracy to the story at the expense of the arithmetic. The LXX translators, far removed from the incident, naturally turn it into ten and two.

Prophets consistently took a hand in affairs of state, particularly where religious issues were involved, so this story is not improbable. The text sets out the incident in strictly theological terms. Ahijah is not the agent but the announcer. Jeroboam must take ten pieces because Yahweh says, 'I will rend the kingdom out of the hand of Solomon, and will give ten tribes to thee' (cf. I Sam. 15.28). The event is future, the dramatic action is present; but Yahweh instigates both (cf. I Kings 12.15). There is no doubt about the historical fulfilment, for after Jeroboam's flight to Egypt, Solomon's death, Rehoboam's accession and his rash behaviour, the event foreshadowed duly came to pass.

Elijah on Carmel: I Kings 18.20–46

The encounter on Mount Carmel is in nobody's list of prophetic dramas. It might easily be passed by here, but the narrative does raise some interesting questions. The incident can be explained equally well in terms of ritual or prophetic drama, and that fact alone is of importance.

After the failure of the prophets of Baal, Elijah repairs the altar of Yahweh using twelve stones, one for each of the tribes of the sons of Jacob. Once again the amphictyonic enthusiast has shown his hand, and one suspects, with many commentators, that this detail is an addition inserted at a time when the formal structure of Israel was highly regarded. Elijah cut a trench round the altar and set out the wood and the parts of the bullock for a sacrifice. Four barrels are filled three times with water and poured over the offering. There follows no oracle but a prayer, a prayer concerned with the status of Yahweh and his prophet in Israel. Then the fire of the Lord falls, the people are convinced of the triumph of Yahweh, and very soon the drought ends with a great rain.

As it stands, the account describes a miraculous intervention by Yahweh to burn up the sacrifice, to vindicate Elijah as a true prophet and himself as the true God of Israel, and to bring rain. The pouring out of the barrels of water is connected with the altar fire, that is to say, it is interpreted by the editor as a detail, the only purpose of which was to make the burning up of the sacrifice more difficult and so heighten the effect.[13] Interpreted in this way the incident cannot be regarded as prophetic drama, but few commentators are prepared to leave the matter there. Indeed, the narrative has given rise to much discussion. Was this a momentous collision between two cults, two deities, two theologies, or simply a frontier incident between local officiants both claiming rights over the Carmel shrine? Is the chapter a unity or is it an amalgam of two separate stories, one dealing with the contest, the other dealing with the bringing of rain?[14] Was the rain-making element an example of 'sympathetic magic'? Ap-Thomas deals with all these points and argues that the chapter is a unity, that it records an event of far more than local significance, and that the essence of the contest was the bringing of rain.[15] The dance of the prophets of Baal and the self-laceration were Baalish rites to bring rain; the pouring out of the barrels of water was a Hebrew rite to the same end. Elijah's crouching posture (v. 42) was a representation of a cloud and his headlong rush before Ahab to Jezreel was an attempt to spread the rain-clouds over the parched fields of the plain.[16] The whole

---

[13] We can ignore the artless assumption that Elijah had deceitfully substituted naphtha for water. Rowley traces this notion back to Hitzig in 1869; it is only surprising that it has lasted more than a hundred years ('Elijah on Mount Carmel', *Men of God*, pp. 56f.; cf. Snaith, 'Kings', p. 157).

[14] De Vries, G.H. Jones, Alt, Fohrer, Noth and Tromp are among those who would separate the contest from the rain ritual. Eissfeldt, Ap-Thomas, Rowley and J. Gray are for taking the two together. One advantage of the former view is that it enables us to conceive of the rain ritual happening at a place where water was available.

[15] Ap-Thomas, 'Elijah on Mount Carmel', pp. 146–55.

[16] But according to De Vries, Elijah crouched 'in a profound prayer of supplication' (*I Kings*, p. 217). Similarly Tromp, 'Water and Fire on Mount Carmel', p. 486.

chapter represents the victory of Yahweh because he supplied the rain.

Not all Ap-Thomas' points are equally persuasive. But it is surely legitimate to ask whether the pouring out of the water should not be linked to the coming of rain rather than to the sacrifice. Without doubt there was a ritual related to rain in the autumn in Israel; equally without doubt there was also autumn rain.[17] It does not follow, however, that the Hebrew regarded the former as the necessary and sufficient cause of the latter. We must be satisfied with the more limited conclusion that the rain ritual and the actual rain belonged together as different aspects of the same reality. What Elijah does is prepare for, represent and celebrate rain, rather than cause it. In this sense, Elijah's action is analogous with many other prophetic acts, for none of them can be regarded as effective in an instrumental sense.

Here, then, on Mount Carmel is an example of a dramatic action which is linked with the reality signified, i.e. the rain, by actual similarity of appearance, and not, as far as the record goes, by use of an artificial formula. Elijah does not act as a free agent. He is throughout under the constraint of Yahweh (I Kings 17.1; 18.1,36f.). If this story stood alone, one might conclude that the notion of constraint from Yahweh belonged only to the final, miraculous version, but in fact this is a common feature of prophetic dramas, so much so that the first element in Fohrer's paradigm is the command from Yahweh to perform the action. So, even at this early stage, a positive Yahwist theology is present in the ritual act, which is also a prophetic act. Yahweh governs both the drama and the reality, both the rain and the ritual enactment of it. On these points the scene on Carmel is close to the other dramatic acts of the prophets. For the rest, it is a stirring but complicated story, into which we cannot probe further.

---

[17] Johnson finds indications of this ritual in his reconstruction of the autumn festival (*Sacral Kingship*, pp. 58ff., 85, 104f.). A serious study of rain-making in Israel has been made by Patai ('The "Control of Rain" in Ancient Palestine', pp. 251ff.). He accepts that I Kings 18 represents a competition in rain-making; he sees symbolism in the various details; and he regards pouring out the water as an imitative rite preserving a magical method. But the prayer interposes a divine act between the ceremony and the rain.

Elijah invests Elisha: I Kings 19.19f.

Here is another significant action involving a garment. Elijah carries it out away from the public gaze. Elisha was the entire audience. In v. 16 Elijah had received a command from Yahweh to anoint Elisha as his successor, but in the brief account given, what he actually does is to wrap his cloak around him. The encounter takes place in a field where Elisha is ploughing. No words relating to the essential point are recorded. The narrator assumes that the reader would understand the meaning of Elijah's action, and his authority for doing it, without any accompanying statement, as Elisha himself apparently did.

This simple act can be seen from two points of view. In the first place it is a conventional action. Wrapping a cloak around another person was a sign of giving protection, as can be seen in the story of Ruth (Ruth 3.9). Elijah adopts Elisha, and we can hardly avoid seeing in the action a physical means whereby the personal power of the great prophet was transferred to the other, who was younger and less dynamic.[18] If Ahijah's cloak had potency because it was new, Elijah's had potency because it was Elijah's (cf. II Kings 2.8, 13f.). In this case the cloak was the *'adderet*, the peculiar garment of a prophet, so the conventional action was used by the charismatic person in a special way, so that it had heightened meaning.

On the other hand, it would be wrong to ignore evidence of investments in a cultic context. In the two accounts of the ordination of the sons of Aaron in the Priestly tradition, robes play an important part (Ex. 28–29; Lev. 8). Ecclus. 45.6–8 refers to the ceremony and describes the robes as 'symbols of authority' (RSV, a rather free translation of σκεύη ἰσχύος). The Hebrew word for the robe is *mᵉˁîl*, and there can be no doubt that investment in it conveyed both honour and authority. Prophecy had its own garment, the *'adderet*, and though in other contexts the word is used for royal robes or rich and valuable clothing (Josh. 7.21,24; Jonah 3.6; Zech. 11.3), in this context it means the rough garment of goat's hair that Elijah wore (I Kings 19.13,19; II Kings 2.8, 13f.), and that came to be regarded as the distinctive garb of prophets (Zech. 13.4; Matt. 3.4). Assuming, as we reasonably may, that the Priestly material relates to a ritual that is at least as old as the Jerusalem cult, it follows that what Elijah carries out is a dramatic act analogous to a cultic ceremony. Nor is that surprising. Cult, convention and prophetic drama all participate in

[18] J. Gray, *Kings*, p. 413; Mauchline, 'Kings', p. 346; Snaith, 'Kings', p. 165.

the same culture. All reflect it and, to some extent, create it, so that in few instances is it possible to say which of the three is original.

The last few words of v. 20 create a difficulty; the effect of them is not to diminish Elisha's zeal but rather to strengthen it, so that he becomes a prophet, indeed, *the* prophet who will succeed to Elijah's position and influence. Yet as the text now stands, Elijah appears to tell Elisha that he can return to his parents if he wishes, and some older commentators assumed that Elijah is saying that the dramatic action meant nothing without the willing co-operation of Elisha himself.[19] This is highly improbable. The action would hardly have been carried out nor the tradition preserved if it had been meaningless. It is more likely that a word has slipped out of the text and that the end of v. 20 should read, 'Go, but remember what I have done.'

This story is a good example of the proper causal sequence in prophetic drama. Yahweh commands Elijah to anoint Elisha as his successor. The fact that Elijah did not anoint him but invested him is an awkward detail, but does not affect the main point. Yahweh commanded both the action and its fulfilment. It is idle, therefore, to say that the action was of no consequence, but equally idle to see it as an inherently effective action. Dramatic act and the reality to which it relates, in this case Elisha's commitment to the prophetic calling, stand beside each other as two aspects of one entity, both having their origin in Yahweh's will. The drama represents in a moment a state of affairs that, in another form of manifestation, spreads over the rest of Elisha's life.

Elisha's Farewell Rite: I Kings 19.21

Elisha begins his prophetic career with a dramatic gesture that marks his change of direction. He kills his pair of oxen, which symbolize his former way of life, and cooks them over a fire made out of the ploughing gear. There are two elements here, a renunciation of his former tasks and loyalties and a social event whereby old relationships were recognized and formally brought to an end. To take the second first, the verb used for killing is the normal term for sacrifice, and the events suggests a primitive peace offering. There are other examples of impromptu sacrifice in the days before cultic organization became

---

[19] Keil and Delitzsch, *Kings*, p. 261; Burney, *Kings*, p. 232.

formalized. I Sam. 6.14 is one. This was the occasion when the ark returned from the Philistines, though the sacrifice in this case was a burnt offering. Elisha was not innovating, either in the meal or in the meaning given to it, so it cannot be regarded as deliberate prophetic drama.

The example is still interesting, however, because of the former element. Slaughtering the oxen and burning the gear, on the face of it, relate entirely to Elisha's future life; but this is not the whole truth. In the first instance these actions represent a renunciation that had already taken place in the prophet's mind, and that was being put into practice at that very moment; the effects of it would, of course, continue throughout his prophetic life. The reality to which the dramatic act relates precedes, accompanies and succeeds the drama itself. This is a useful corrective to the general assumption that the drama necessarily comes first, which in turn leads to the supposition that the drama causes the fulfilment. Nothing is said about Elisha being under divine compulsion to carry out this action, though the renunciation itself is demanded by Yahweh's words to Elijah.

Zedekiah's Horns: I Kings 22.1–12; II Chron. 18.1–11

Zedekiah's action in storming around the threshing-floor of Samaria before Ahab and Jehoshaphat is interesting because it has possible cultic associations, it was carried out by a false prophet, and, despite the *bravura* performance, it was not fulfilled.[20] The year is probably 850 BCE. Ahab is in dispute with Syria. Jehoshaphat, his son-in-law, has come to Samaria to give him support. Before they march to Ramoth-Gilead, they convene an assembly of prophets and prepare to enquire of Yahweh. At the appropriate moment in the ritual, the question was put to the four hundred participating prophets and they all prophesied victory. Jehoshaphat demurs and asks if there is not another prophet of Yahweh whom they might consult. This is problematic as the four hundred were supposed to have enquired of Yahweh. Here, then is evidence of the emergence of the outsider

---

[20] We presume that the king was Ahab, but, with the exception of v. 20, the text refers to him as the king of Israel until after the account of his death in v. 37. De Vries sees two narratives entwined here and argues that in neither account was the king of Israel Ahab. The reference is to his son, Joram or Jehoram (*Kings*, pp. 265ff.; *Prophet against Prophet*, pp. 93f.).

prophet, who stands over against the group.[21] Micaiah is sent for. The story seems then to begin again and more details of the setting are given. The kings have set up their thrones in the open space by the gate. It is well known that there was a shrine of Baal in this great and still new city (I Kings 16.32), but this was, as it were, an application to Yahweh and not to Baal. Jehoshaphat was a more zealous Yahwist than Ahab. The common meaning of the word translated 'open space' is 'threshing floor', and threshing floors were often linked with solemn assemblies and sacred places in the Old Testament (Gen. 50.10; Num. 15.19f.; Judg. 6.37; II Sam. 6.6; 24.16ff; II Chron. 3.1).[22] The Hebrew is not entirely smooth but, if 'threshing floor' is correct, the site chosen was a large area, with sacral associations, but not irretrievably bound up with the Baal cult. The prophets set to work and Zedekiah emerges as more zealous than the rest. Presumably he had already taken part in the verbal prophesying. Now he took horns of iron, a well-known symbol of power (see Deut. 33.17), and apparently tried to raise his performance with them. Then, to make the matter even more clear, he produced a formula explaining what the horns meant in the circumstances. The story then reverts to Micaiah who prophesies first success and then, under pressure, disaster.

The use of horns by Zedekiah is easy to understand. The word 'horn' was common as a metaphor for strength and self-confidence, and the fact that Zedekiah's horns were made of iron simply intensifies the image. The interesting question is whether Zedekiah's prophetic action was entirely spontaneous, as at first sight it seems to be, or whether he was reproducing a familiar pre-battle performance. To take horns is to be strong and successful (Amos 6.13). To lift up the horn against someone is to act aggressively (Zech. 1.21). Cutting off the horn of a nation means disaster (Jer. 48.25). There is much more language of this kind (Deut. 33.17; Dan. 8.3; Zech. 1.18). The question is whether all these references can be explained completely

[21] That this narrative presents a fine example of prophetic conflict is not open to question, but John Gray is wrong to distinguish between Zedekiah and Micaiah in terms of a tame, time-serving professional, practising imitative magic and operating with a large entourage, versus a lone instrument of revelation. Such a distinction is too easy and begs too many questions. The inclusion of symbolic action among the characteristics of the former is a further indication of the inadequacy of the contention (*Kings*, p. 449). For the question of conflict between prophets, see Crenshaw, *Prophetic Conflict* and De Vries, *Prophet against Prophet*. The latter takes I Kings 22 as his starting-point for a literary-critical analysis of the prophets' adversarial role in society.

[22] See Porter, 'II Samuel vi', pp. 171f.

in terms of imagery or whether there lies behind them a custom in which horns were used to represent national strength. There is a partial analogy with clothing. The metaphorical language in the Old Testament about being clothed with salvation or with shame refers back to actual investments of priests and monarchs in majestic robes and others in clothes of humiliation. The language about lifting up horns may be simply metaphorical, it may refer simply to the behaviour of animals, but it may also refer to an actual ceremony in which horns played a part. There are a number of references to the horn image in the psalter. None actually requires dramatic accompaniment, but the question has often been raised whether the metaphors of the psalms were simply metaphors. We may reasonably assume that the Hebrews were as inventive in dramatic action as they were in literary expression, in which case there is a good argument for inferring a horn-lifting ceremony, perhaps even, on the basis of Ps. 75, a combat in which one horn was destroyed and another exalted. In short, it is hard to believe that Zedekiah was the first person to make use of horns in this way. It is more likely that he was making use of a familiar ritual and that, somewhere in the background, there was a pre-battle rite involving horns.[23]

Zedekiah was, of course, a false prophet. His falseness lies, not in his devotion to other gods, for he appears formally to have been a Yahwist, though doubtless a syncretizing one, nor in his lack of technique, for his action fulfils all the requirements, nor in his motives, for there is no reason to suppose that he was insincere, save that, in Ahab's court, sincerity must have been a rare virtue.[24] He was false simply because he was wrong. He was not giving expression to a victory that was in the offing. He was conducting a charade. It is easy for us, as it was easy for the editor, to see that Zedekiah's real loyalty lay with Ahab. He was anxious to provide the sign that Ahab wanted. Micaiah was a prophet of a different quality. But this does not provide justification for applying the labels 'false' and 'true' as if the two men

---

[23] See Stacey, 'A Pre-battle Rite in Ancient Israel'.

[24] In Jewish tradition the four hundred prophets consulted were reckoned to be prophets of Baal, presumably because Jezebel had slaughtered the prophets of Yahweh (I Kings 18.4, 13; 19.10, 14), but equally Elijah had purged the prophets of Baal (I Kings 18.40). Zedekiah speaks in the name of Yahweh and he bears a Yahwist name. He can hardly have been an avowed Baalist. Presumably pliant Yahwists would have survived under Jezebel, and they might have been useful when an alliance with a Yahwist king of Judah was necessary. See Slotki, *Kings*, p. 157.

represented two categories that were evidently, always and absolutely opposite to each other.[25]

Despite the failure of Zedekiah's effort, the action provides useful evidence of the way in which prophetic drama was understood. Drama and event go together. He who empowers one empowers both. In this crisis, was Yahweh compelling the dramatic action, in which case he would give the victory? Or was Zedekiah simply putting on a patriotic act? That was Ahab's, and even more Jehoshaphat's, dilemma. It was the constant dilemma of those who attended to prophecy in Old Testament times. There was no way to be sure except to wait and see (Deut. 18.22; Jer. 28.9). The editor of I Kings knew, of course, how the case had turned out, and he was happy to leave the narrative as it is. This implies that, for him, the drama had no instrumental force whatever. If Yahweh was not in the action, then Zedekiah, for all his vigour and anxiety to please, was bound to fail. It is not even true that a devout and faithful prophet always speaks and acts effectively. Faithful prophets can be wrong, and if what they say or do is not grounded in the divine intention, it will have no effect. Nobody, not even the godly prophet, could usurp Yahweh's prerogative and cause things to be.

Elisha Tears his Clothes: II Kings 2.12f.

This action is similar to the renunciation of I Kings 19.21. After Elijah is carried away and Elisha has uttered his curious lament, the young prophet tears his own, purely functional clothes in two. He picks up Elijah's mantle, which is on the ground, and returns to the Jordan. Tearing clothes, as a mourning rite, is frequent in the Old Testament and there is some discussion about what it means (Gen. 37.34; Num. 14.6; Lev. 10.6; 21.10; Josh. 7.6; I Sam. 4.12; II Sam. 1.2; 13.31). One possibility is that the torn garments are meant to be an outward expression of the sad inward disposition, just as brightly coloured garments proclaim joy. A second, less likely possibility is that the mourners were attempting to disguise, and so protect, themselves from any harm that might come to them from the departed. A third is that some kind of sympathetic burial is meant. None of these hypotheses fits here. There are no signs of grief other than the torn

---

[25] Canonically speaking, Zedekiah was a false prophet and Micaiah a true one, but, in their historical context, they were both simply prophets, Zedekiah one who enjoyed royal favour, Micaiah one who had earned grudging royal respect.

clothes, unless the exclamation, 'My father, my father' is such. One looks, therefore, for another explanation.

In II Sam. 13.18f. Tamar was wearing a brightly coloured garment which was, in the royal household, a symbol of virginity. Since Tamar had just been raped by her half-brother Amnon, she tears this garment. Doubtless grief, though not bereavement, is one factor, but another is that the garment no longer represents the true state of affairs. Rather different, but equally relevant, is the behaviour of Josiah in II Kings 22.11, 19. Josiah, aware now of the sins of Israel, tears his clothes 'before the Lord'. Again, grief is one element, but if we bear in mind that, in the Old Testament, personal identity was thought to extend into clothes, Josiah was really asking, on behalf of the nation, that the old identity should pass away and that the nation should come to a new life. 'Before the Lord' suggests a cultic procedure, and a number of psalms confirm this (30, 32, 38, etc).

In the case of Elisha, renewal is more important than grief or penitence. The old clothes belong to the old self. A new Elisha, one who might wear Elijah's mantle, was coming into being.[26] This fact required dramatic expression. In a gesture derived from both convention and the cult, Elisha expressed his own transformation. It was not so much a prophecy as a representation of the true state of affairs. Once again the chronological relationship between the action and the reality to which it relates needs to be noted. The change had already begun mentally. The dramatic action expresses it and its effects continue thereafter. It is noteworthy how anxious the redactors are to stress both Elisha's relationship to Elijah and Elisha's transformation.

Elisha's Arrows (i): II Kings 13.14–17

At the end of Elisha's life Israel was being pressed by the Syrians, and King Jehoash came to visit the sick prophet at his home. Elisha made the king take a bow and arrows; then he laid his hands on the hands of the king; then he made the king shoot an arrow through the window toward the east, towards Syria. The prophet exclaimed, 'The Lord's arrow of victory, the arrow of victory over Syria!' He continues with

---

[26] Both the idea of renunciation as suggested by J. Robinson (*Second Kings*, p. 26) and the affirmation of the sense of unworthiness, as suggested by Auld (*Kings*, p. 154), are consistent with this interpretation.

a prophecy of complete victory over the Syrians in Aphek.[27] There are two elements in this drama. In the first place, Elisha's laying his hands on the king's hands is slightly problematic. It could be understood as an indication of the transmission of power from Elisha to the king; but equally it could be understood in a purely functional way. Elisha wants to perform the act himself but lacks the strength, so the king supplies the muscle and Elisha offers what feeble help he can. Then, in the second place, shooting the arrow towards the enemy is a dramatization of a victorious battle charge. Actions of this kind are very common among tribes preparing for war.[28] The Hebrew of v. 16 is curious. Elisha's instructions contain an unusual metaphor for drawing a bow, but the effect is only to make the command more incisive.[29] Shooting the arrow is so expressive – it is reminiscent of Joshua's javelin – that no explanation is necessary, but as in the case of Zedekiah's horns, one is nonetheless given. Victory is promised and it will happen at Aphek. II King 13.25 refers to victories over Syria, but there is no mention of Aphek, which is surprising in view of the precision of the prophecy. It is possible that 'in Aphek' should be emended to 'as in Aphek', in which case it would not be a precise prophecy but a reference back to Ahab's victory over Ben-hadad in I Kings 20. It is probably coincidental, but there are two examples of pre-battle oracles in that very chapter (see vv. 13f. and 28). Bearing in mind I Kings 22, we must conclude that consulting a prophet for dramatic action before a battle was a normal thing for a king to do. It is also hard to imagine that there was anything original in Elisha's making use of a bow and arrows in this way. Fohrer includes this incident in his list although there is no specific command from Yahweh to Elisha to perform the action. These early stories commonly lack

[27] Not surprisingly, some authors regard this action as an example of instrumental magic. Bernhard Lang refers to 'Elisha's war magic which implies that the ritually shot arrow will not miss its target and ensures a future victory' (*Monotheism*, p. 89). This matter is discussed at length below in Chapter 16.

[28] For the use of arrows and other weapons in rites anticipating military victory, see Frazer, *Golden Bough*, p. 27; R.C. Thompson, *Semitic Magic*, p. 158; Fohrer, *Die Handlungen*, pp. 14, 24f.; cf. Josh. 8.18, 26; II Sam. 16.5–8.

[29] Barrick points out that the action of drawing the bow precedes the opening of the window, which is absurd. He suggests that the verb indicates stringing the bow, not drawing it, and that Elisha's hands were used simply to help; in which case the significant action is performed by the king and Elisha contributes only the potent formula (v. 17b). See 'Elisha and the Magic Bow'.

this element. The tradition seems to grant Elisha general authority and thereafter to accept what he does as an act of Yahweh.

Elisha's Arrows (ii): II Kings 13.18f.

Immediately after the first action involving arrows comes another which has similar force. Elisha tells the king to strike the ground with the arrows. He does so three times and Elisha is displeased, because three times is inadequate; it means that the king will have three victories, but no more. It is possible that this incident is nothing more than an editorial addition added to the narrative because the victorious prophecy of the preceding verse was only partly fulfilled. Jehoash recovered some cities (II Kings 13.25), but he did not smite the Syrians until he had made an end of them. Even if this hypothesis is correct, the incident remains a dramatic action, linked with a prophet and demanding explanation. But the fact that II Kings 13.17 was not completely fulfilled is hardly sufficient reason for supposing that vv. 18f. are an editorial addition. We treat them, therefore, as if they belong, with vv. 14–17, in the earliest version of the narrative.

There are two interesting questions. The first concerns what actually took place. The action, at least as RV and RSV describe it, appears to have no obvious mimetic quality. Banging arrows on the ground does not suggest defeating enemies. It is, therefore, possible that the very obscurity of the action is significant. Jehoash is being put to a test; he is not supposed to know what is happening, so that the test, which is all tied up with the drama, will be an honest one. Jehoash strikes feebly and so reveals his inadequacies. If this interpretation is accepted, then the purpose of the action was certainly not communication. But equally, the action hardly falls within our category of prophetic dramas. It was an esoteric action for a devious purpose, but not a significant act as we have defined the term. It is doubtful, however, whether this reading of the Hebrew text is correct, despite the fact that most commentators and translators appear to follow it. The verb translated 'strike' or 'smite' is a powerful one, and it is hard to link it with the apparently meaningless action of banging on the ground with a bunch of arrows. One would sympathize with Jehoash, for who would be likely to do well in such a test? It is easier to link the verb with the notion of an arrow striking a target. The same verb is used in I Kings 22.34 for the arrow that struck Ahab and pierced his armour and in I Sam. 17.49 for the stone that killed Goliath (see also II Kings

9.24). We have to distinguish, then, between the act of shooting the arrow, as in v. 17, and the consequence, the arrow striking its target. If that is the case, Elisha's second command to Jehoash is to shoot the arrows that remained into the ground. We have to assume that several were left after one had been shot eastwards. Shooting an arrow straight into the ground has all the appearance of a violent action and provides a dramatic complement to the action in v. 16. The first act is to shoot eastwards to identify the enemy, the second is to shoot repeatedly into the ground to express the violence with which he will be struck down. This interpretation provides a better understanding of the passage; it binds the two stories together as surely they need to be bound, and it provides a coherent account of a pre-battle prophetic action.

If we follow this interpretation, the whole drama is mimetic and it becomes a little more clear what the precise form of Jehoash's test was and why he failed it. Yahweh was about to show his power in Israel. Jehoash was bound to be the medium. In a drama that represented the victory it might be expected that the king would be trembling with awe and show himself almost ecstatically committed to his task. Instead he appears to act with restraint. That will not do for Elisha. and he explains that the victory that might have been devastating will be limited in scope. Tests of this kind are not unknown in the Old Testament (see Judg. 7). The test lies in the fact that the person reveals himself without realizing what is going on. It is curious that a testing of Jehoash should be all bound up with a sign of victory, but evidently what Jehoash did in the presence of Elisha was reckoned to be all of a piece with what he would do on the field of battle. There is no great problem about a significant action being performed by someone who did not realize what he was doing. Neither Jeremiah's potter nor the Rechabites were aware of what Jeremiah would see in their activities, but to the prophet himself they were of the utmost significance.

This leads to the second interesting feature of the action. It demonstrates that even the purpose of Yahweh is not always and everywhere regarded as sovereign. We have to remember that the collectors of Elisha stories do not stand high among the theologians of Israel, that they often introduce simplistic, not to say superstitious ideas. So it is perhaps not surprising that here we encounter the idea that the king's hesitancy actually interfered with Yahweh's prowess in history. We would expect Yahweh to go his own way, providing victories and requiring prophetic acts and oracles according to his own plan. Here Yahweh is frustrated by the king's lack of enthusiasm. Or, to put it another way, here we have an action that is, to some degree, effective – or should we say, ineffective? – in its own right. Later on we shall have to consider how important this fact is for the whole field of prophetic drama.

There is little evidence that the action was fulfilled in the strict sense. Three victories over Syria are mentioned in v. 25, but no details are given, so one is bound to suspect that drama and reality have been harmonized.

8 · Hosea

The book of Hosea is the first of the Twelve Prophets of the Hebrew canon, presumably because, apart from Zechariah, which is composite, it is the longest. Hosea lived in the middle of the eighth century BCE and prophesied probably in the third quarter of it, that is to say, a little after Amos and contemporary with the early part of Isaiah's work in the south. Although there was a strong prophetic tradition in the north, Hosea is the only northerner among the so-called 'writing prophets', since Amos, who prophesied in the north, was a southerner. Little is known of Hosea apart from the facts about his family life which play a dominant part in chs. 1–3, and which supply the medium for the dramatic actions that we shall discuss.

In the mid-eighth century, a time of Assyrian weakness, the northern kingdom had been enjoying a period of prosperity, but the prosperity had not gone hand in hand with religious revival; rather it magnified both social injustice and apostasy. If Amos concentrated his attack on the former, Hosea dealt faithfully with the latter. His message was undoubtedly doom-laden; whether the oracles of hope to be found in the present text also go back to Hosea himself is less certain. Hosea stands firmly by the comprehensiveness and exclusiveness of the Yahwist faith, which to him is apparently quite clearly defined, and charges his contemporaries with infidelity.

Unlike most other prophetic books, Hosea is difficult to break down into short oracles, which indicates that the work has been extensively edited. There is no agreed redactional history, but two stages, at least, can hardly be doubted. In the first place, sympathetic editors transposed the sayings of the prophet into the continuous sections we see now; then the book passed into the hands of southerners who saw its value for the Judaean situation. Some of the original text applied directly to the south, but editorial changes made it possible to claim more. Two such changes occur in passages that we shall examine (1.7; 3.5).[1]

Hosea and Gomer: Hos. 1.2f.

The marriage of Hosea provides one of the classic issues of Old Testament interpretation. In Hos. 1 and 3 there are apparently accounts of two different liaisons. They may be interpreted as two actual marriages, two relationships, one of which was not marriage, two different accounts of the same marriage, or two different incidents, one of which was marriage and the other reconciliation, in the same relationship.[2] Coupled with these problems there are textual difficulties. Sometimes the whole, sometimes parts of ch. 3 are regarded as secondary. It is fairly certain that glosses by Judaean editors are to be found in several places.[3] Nor is the problem limited to a few verses. The whole of chs. 1–3 is concerned with the relation of Israel to Yahweh, and it is discussed in terms of marriage imagery.

In view of the many problems raised by this narrative it is not surprising that some commentators in the past have relinquished the idea that we have here an incident in the life of Hosea and have interpreted the passage either as the account of a vision, or as a deliberately constructed allegory.[4] Other prophetic narratives give rise to similar reactions. Complex actions, hard to interpret, are assumed never to have happened. It is, however, one thing to have doubts about what seems impossible, quite another to reject what is merely baffling. Most modern commentators accept that there is a historical layer behind this narrative, though there is no unanimity about what it is. Whatever disagreements exist, there is widespread

[1] Other examples of southern reference are to be found in 1.1; 4.15; 5.5, 10, 12, 14; 6.4, 11; 8.14; 10.11 and 12.2. These references seem to indicate that the text of Hosea had a vigorous 'after-life'.

[2] There is an extended treatment of the question by Andersen and Freedman in *Hosea* in the Anchor Bible. See pp. 115–309. Also Rowley, 'The Marriage of Hosea', and Eybers, *Studies*. For a brief summary, see Fohrer, *Introduction*, pp. 420f. Koch takes the view that chs. 1 and 3 represent the same marriage in different words (*Prophets I*, p. 79).

[3] See especially Grace Emmerson, *Hosea: an Israelite Prophet in Judaean Perspective*, who, while recognizing the fact of southern editing, argues that great discrimination is necessary in attributing verses to this source.

[4] See Rowley, 'Marriage', *Men of God*, pp. 79ff. and of course, Maimonides (cf. Chapter 15 below).

agreement that the marriage to Gomer must be understood as prophetic drama.

The account, as it now stands, begins with an instruction from Yahweh to Hosea to marry a prostitute, or, at least, 'a wife of harlotry'; then comes an explanation that she would represent the infidelity of Israel; thirdly there is the statement that Hosea obeyed and married Gomer. The account reveals Fohrer's threefold structure, command-account-meaning, though in an unusual order, as the meaning comes before the account of the action being carried out. Even more than Jehoash in II Kings 13, Gomer is involved in the drama without knowing it. Marriage to a wife who played the harlot is a potent image, and if, as many commentators suggest, Gomer was a temple prostitute, it is even more potent. Unless we are persuaded by H.W. Wolff that sexual promiscuity has no place in ch. 1, we shall see here an example of how deeply the true prophet was committed to his vocation.

A major problem concerns the character of Gomer, named only in 1.3 and traditionally regarded, on the grounds of 1.2, as a harlot. Gomer was altogether vindicated as long ago as 1929 by L.W. Batten in a whimsical but nonetheless seriously argued article,[5] and some recent discussions also point to the conclusion that she was not a harlot when Hosea married her. Wolff argues that she was a 'wife of whoredom' only because she had submitted to a sexual ritual at a Baal shrine, the purpose of which was to ensure her fertility in marriage. It was a common social form, but to the strict Yahwist it made her a 'wife of whoredom' and the children born in the subsequent marriage, 'children of whoredom'. Hosea was allied to a tainted woman as Yahweh was allied to an Israel defiled by association with Baal worship. Wolff also points out that, if this interpretation is accepted, there is no evidence of actual adultery in ch. 1.[6]

Andersen and Freedman argue that Gomer was blameless as a bride but became disloyal some time later. The term, 'wife of whoredom', is, therefore, proleptic. This is not as illogical as it seems. According to the straightforward sense of the text, 'children of whoredom' were taken at the same time as the wife, and there can be no doubt that the children came later. Again, a marriage that begins full of promise but is injured by one partner's treachery makes a better analogy of Yahweh's relations with Israel than a marriage where the bride was

[5] 'Hosea's Message and Marriage'.
[6] Wolff, *Hosea*, pp. 14f., 60.

guilty from the first.[7] Furthermore, according to Hebrew reckoning, a woman could not commit adultery until after she was married. The real sin, therefore, came after the marriage; hence the contention that the description is proleptic. The common judgment, however, remains that Hosea married a woman already morally disreputable.

Whichever of these arguments we follow there are important consequences for this study. Before we come to them another point must be noted. On the face of it the narrative is concerned with contracting a marriage, not with living an agonized married life. The tendency, encouraged, no doubt, by the parallel in ch. 3, to suppose that it was Hosea's married state that constituted the drama, seems, therefore, misguided. But, leaving aside ch. 3, 1.2f. cannot be separated from 1.4–9. The whole story includes the birth of three children. Verse 2 itself requires Hosea to take a wife and have children. This makes it clear that the narrative has been telescoped, and that it is unwise to focus too much attention on the act of contracting the marriage, however prominent that element may at first seem to be. The traditional tendency to concentrate on the married state is thus shown to be sound. When ch. 1 is read in conjunction with chs. 2 and 3, this conclusion is confirmed.

If Wolff is right and Gomer's 'whoredom' rests in the fact that she had been initiated in a Baal temple, then the essence of the drama rests in the fact that a faithful servant of Yahweh finds himself inextricably tied to a tainted partner. There is no social uproar. Hosea does not have to explain himself; indeed explanation would be pointless, because his contemporaries would see nothing wrong in the liaison. Only the prophet understood. There is an attraction in this understatnding of the drama as Hosea's private sorrow, but it cannot really be said that Wolff's contention has been proved.

If Gomer was blameless as a bride but subsequently became unfaithful, then a number of surprising things follow. Hosea did not commit an act of unparalleled self-humiliation in his marriage, the present form of the story is misleading, and the common interpretation of the drama is incorrect. What happened was that, in the course of time, Hosea was betrayed; he came to see this betrayal as a dramatic representation of Israel's betrayal of Yahweh; he then understood his marriage as part of the divine intention to express Israel's perfidy in a living example; consequently he related the story of his marriage as if

---

[7] Andersen and Freedman, *Hosea*, pp. 115–72.

he had been commanded to ally himself with a harlot from the beginning. In fact he was not so commanded. The present text arises from this reflection on his bitter experience, not from his awareness of an actual command. This explanation is by no means impossible, but it can hardly be said to be proved.

We are left with the traditional view that Gomer was indeed already given to harlotry when Hosea married her. Contracting a marriage with a harlot is not a good image of God making a covenant with Israel, but the essence of the story is found in Israel's present relationship with Yahweh, not in the forming of the original marriage bond. The words, 'Go, take yourself a wife of harlotry', represent an instruction to Hosea to put himself in the same position in relation to Gomer as that in which Yahweh stands in relation to Israel. If Gomer was a temple prostitute, the point is sharpened. Given the three options, this remains the best choice, if only because it is the simplest hypothesis.

The next problem is whether we are to understand 1.2f. and 3.1–5 as a doublet. If so, the marriage provides a single drama stated in two different, though parallel, ways. 1.2f. is an account in the third person, and the meaning of the drama is understood in terms of the wickedness of the land; 3.1–5 is an account in the first person and the meaning is understood in terms of Yahweh's redeeming love. If ch. 1 and ch. 3 represent different incidents in the same relationship, then we have a more complicated story, particularly if ch. 2 is drawn in.[8] Gomer, if not unfaithful already, became unfaithful, fell into Baalish practices, and was eventually redeemed by her husband. A frontal attack on this problem is not possible here. Reasons are given below why it is best to treat the two passages separately but as different versions of the same, basic narrative. Nor must we forget that the marriage is not the only significant factor here. Naming the children in 1.3–9 is also part of the drama.

Several further points are worthy of attention. In the first place, Hosea is required to perform a drama expressing human infidelity rather than divine act. This appears to contradict the notion that Yahweh is responsible for both the drama and the reality dramatized. But in fact, in the holistic manner in which the Hebrews were inclined to think, sin, drama and doom are not really three separate elements. They are compounded together, so that the existence of one implies

---

[8] See Vogels, 'Hosea's Gift to Gomer (Hos. 3.2)'.

the existence of the others. In a similar way, oracles of judgment have to be spoken, whether the people listen or not, and even when it is too late for repentance. The sin and the doom require the oracle. In these circumstances it is as reasonable for the drama to express the infidelity, for which the people were responsible, as it is the consequences, for which God was responsible. We should expect a prophet to represent the latter, but, on this occasion, he represents the former. The one thing that cannot be said is that the drama causes the reality to happen. The causal relation, if we must speak in those terms, goes the other way; the infidelity causes the dramatic act. But it is better to say that the condition of disloyalty to Yahweh that abounds in Israel is focussed and expressed in the alliance of the prophet with a harlot.

Secondly, on almost any reckoning, Yahweh's word, and not any wish of Hosea, inspired this drama. If the story is factual, Hosea contracted the extraordinary alliance because it had to be. If, in fact, Gomer was unfaithful after the marriage, then the process of thought is different but no less impressive. In this case, on the face of it, Gomer's action launched the drama. But, however obvious it may seem to us, that is not how Hosea or his editors understood the matter. If the result of Gomer's action was a dramatic sign of Israel's treachery, then Yahweh was responsible for it. So, by the time ch. 1 was written down, if not before, the unequal alliance was attributed to Yahweh's command. This is an important observation, for nowhere is the prophet free to express himself in the dramas; they belong to Yahweh's will. In most cases, one can say that they belong to Yahweh's will just as much as the realities they represent. In this particular case, the reality represented, that is, the unfaithfulness, is not part of Yahweh's will; only the drama is. This example, therefore, provides a complete reversal of the common notion of prophetic drama. On the superficial level, the prophet enacts a drama; Yahweh provides the fulfilment. Here Yahweh requires the drama; the reality is Israel's doing.

Thirdly, the text contains no suggestion that Hosea should expound the matter so that his contemporaries might understand what was going on. In a case of this kind one might imagine that Hosea would be anxious to explain himself and so justify his behaviour. But, as far as the text is concerned, communication with the general public was not essential. Hosea's tragic domestic history had to be, simply because the divine relationship with Israel was tragic. When commentators represent the drama simply as an illustration of Hosea's message, they miss the real point and weaken the narrative immeasurably.

Finally, if the whole marriage and not simply the marriage contract was significant, then we have here a drama of very long duration. Most actions take only a few minutes to perform. This one took years. Equally, the reality exemplified was past, present and future. Of these the future is the least prominent. The purpose of the drama is to express what has been the case and still is now. The medium is not a pot or a garment but Hosea's life and affections. It is an awful example of how deeply the prophet participates in his message.

Hosea's Children: Hos. 1.3–9

From a literary point of view the dramatic actions expressed in the names of Hosea's three children cannot be separated from the original drama of the marriage. From a historical point of view, the series of events must be spread over several years, and many incidents and oracles must have occurred in between. As it stands, the account of the marriage and the naming of the children constitute a compact whole. The literary structure stands out even more clearly when certain obvious deletions are made. Verse 7 is most vulnerable. It represents the cause of Judah, it attempts to make a hopeful prophecy out of a drama that is essentially doom-laden, it breaks up the rhythm, and it presupposes a signal deliverance for Judah without a struggle, an idea that may well be drawn from II Kings 19.35–7. Similarly 4d, 5 and the last phrase of 6 break up the rhythm and elaborate the meaning unnecessarily. If we make these deletions from vv. 2–8, what remains is an oracle of four stanzas, each stanza being introduced by a line of narrative.

When the Lord first spoke through Hosea,

1 *Infidelity*

Introductory formula	the Lord said to Hosea,
Command	'Go, take to yourself a wife of harlotry and have children of harlotry,
Explanation	for the land commits great harlotry by forsaking the Lord'.
Account	So he went and took Gomer the daughter of Diblaim,
Narrative link	and she conceived and bore him a son.

2 *Doom of the Royal House*

Introductory formula	And the Lord said to him,
Command	'Call his name Jezreel (*yizrᵉ'ᵉel*),
Explanation	for yet a little while, and I will punish the house of Jehu for the blood of Jezreel'.
Narrative link	She conceived again and bore a daughter.

3 *Withdrawal of Compassion*

Introductory formula	And the Lord said to him,
Command	'Call her name No mercy (*lō' ruḥāmâ*),
Explanation	for I will no more have pity on the house of Israel'.
Narrative link	When she had weaned No mercy, she conceived and bore a son.

4 *Rejection of Israel*

Introductory formula	And the Lord said,
Command	'Call his name Not my people (*lō' 'ammî*),
Explanation	for you are not my people and I am not your God'.

The account of the action taking place is present only in the first stanza, though Hosea's compliance in the case of the second child, No mercy, can be inferred from the fact that a child bearing that name was weaned according to v. 8. The stanzas move nicely to a climax, beginning with infidelity, moving on to the punishment of the royal house, then to the withdrawal of compassion, and finally to the rejection of Israel as the people of God.

As with the marriage the naming drama has two levels. There is the historical level belonging to Hosea's lifetime, which includes the giving of the name but would also include the constant use of the name thereafter; and there is the literary level, belonging to a later period, when the drama was recounted in the present memorable form and the significant elements were concentrated into three brief moments involving three terse and precise commands, or four if we include the marriage itself.

Names in Israel expressed character. In the name an idea is given concrete expression, so that the character implied is more easily achieved, or, in this case, more difficult to escape. Fohrer gives some examples of names used in this way.[9] Two of these names can best be

---

[9] Fohrer, *Die Handlungen*, pp. 27f.

understood if the bearer is seen as representative of Israel, but, in the case of Jezreel, that interpretation does not help.

The most likely meaning of the name Jezreel, the one that seems to be implied in the text, is that it is a reminder of the massacre of the house of Ahab by Jehu about a century before (see II Kings 9–10). The reminder must be directed principally at Jeroboam II, the contemporary representative of the dynasty. Jezreel was the traditional battleground of ancient Israel for obvious strategic reasons, and no doubt more battles and skirmishes took place there than the Old Testament records. There Deborah and Barak overcame Sisera, Gideon defeated the Amalekites and Midianites, Saul met his end fighting the Philistines, Jehu instigated his bloody revolt by murdering two monarchs, ostensibly to avenge the blood of Naboth in the place where it was shed; there in later times Josiah was killed; and there, so the story goes, the final battle of all will be fought. In short, Jezreel meant bloodshed and death. It had the same awesome sound as the Somme and Passchendaele still have at least to the elderly in this generation. This means that the interpretation of the first of the three names is not analogous to that of the other two. No interpretation can produce an analogy, so we have to accept the fact that the three names are not all to be understood in the same way. Andersen and Freedman try to couple this ominous meaning of Jezreel with a positive one based on the actual meaning of the word, 'El sows', or 'may El sow', thus drawing attention to the goodness of God.[10] There is also the theory that Jezreel was a Baalish name and thus a proclamation of Israel's apostasy.[11] A positive sense, or indeed a Baalish sense, would have been a reasonable inference if the name had been made up artificially like the other two names and like the names that Isaiah used, but this was not the case. Jezreel was an old and familiar place name. Hosea could no more persuade his contemporaries that Jezreel stood for beneficence than First World War veterans could be persuaded to believe that Passchendaele meant spring and Easter. Moreover there is nothing positive, nor yet apostate, about the other two names; they are simply doom-laden. Jezreel must, therefore, have an ominous sense.

The next question is why Jehu's guilt should be so significant and why it must be brought home to Hosea's generation. Jeroboam II is

[10] Andersen and Freedman, *Hosea*, p. 173.
[11] See May, 'An Interpretation of the Names of Hosea's Children'.

held responsible for the sins of his predecessor. Was it because Jehu's acts set new standards in violence and that, therefore, the whole nation and especially the royal house was tainted by them? Did Hosea take the view that the house of Jehu was illegitimate since it was based on an act of usurpation? Jehu's rebellion had been inspired immediately by Elisha but ultimately by Elijah (I Kings 19.16; II Kings 9). Was Hosea accusing them of bad judgment or their protegé of going beyond his instructions? Was it that Jehu's enthusiasm for Yahweh, which commended him to his prophetic sponsors, soon waned after he came to power? II Kings 10.28–31 is sparing in praise for Jehu. He dealt with the hated Jezebel and her cult, but, for all the blood he shed, he allowed Baalish rites to thrive. It seems a clear case of history confounding hope. No doubt if Jehu had initiated a reform that had lasted, Hosea would have approved of him, despite the crude methods. But when his successors fell back into the sins of Ahab, there was every reason to scrutinize Jehu with a more critical eye. Then his bloodthirstiness, his illegitimacy, his insincerity as a supposed Yahwist, stand out clearly. Jehu appeared in one light to Elisha but in an entirely different light to a prophet living under Jeroboam II and familiar with the story of a hundred years of Jehu and his house. It was easy for Hosea to believe that Yahweh had decided to call a halt. In fact Jeroboam II's son and successor was murdered, and the house of Jehu came to an end amid much bloodshed.

The other names are easier. The second of them means, 'she finds no mercy'; the verb is not a passive participle as the RSV translation implies. There is no reason to suppose that this child was illegitimate, though the text does not say that Gomer bore the child 'to him', as it does in v. 3. According to the explanation Yahweh has suffered Israel's treacheries up to this point and treated her with mercy, but that will now cease. The child will proclaim, wherever she goes, that Yahweh has withdrawn his compassion from Israel. The third name represents the final tragedy. Israel has rejected the covenant and Yahweh has determined to accept her rejection, so Israel is 'not my people'. The explanation in Hebrew recalls the dialogue at the Burning Bush, for the verbal form translated with the negative as 'I will not be' is identical with the divine name given by God to Moses in Ex. 3.14. So we should read, 'You-not my people, and I-not *I am*, for you.'

Just as the marriage, on the historical level, was a dramatic action of many years' duration, so the naming of children was a long-lasting sign. Wherever the children went and whenever their names were spoken, the drama was re-enacted. The literary form attempts to introduce the same crisp presentation as we noticed in 1.2, and, simply on the literary level, it does so, but it takes only a moment to see through the poetic structure to the fact that the story of vv. 3–9 covers at least five years. There is no way then that this series of actions can be seen, in reality, as the affair of a moment.

A very interesting factor arises with regard to the reality that is dramatically portrayed. 'Jezreel' represents a bloody end to the house of Jehu in the future. 'No mercy' represents a condition in the present or in the immediate future. 'Not my people' represents the same. This means that within the same brief oracle of four stanzas we have all the time references possible. The marriage looked back to a state of sin that preceded it; the names of the last two children look out to the consequences that are coming into being; and the first child's name looks forward to an event yet to come. Furthermore, the marriage expressed a reality that, at first sight, appeared to be a human, not a divine, act, whereas the namings express realities that are certainly divine acts. We can only bring all this together if we adopt a holistic and not an analytical approach. The sin and the mournful consequences are to be seen together as a continuum, not as a cause and a quite separable effect. The divine judgment is inherent in the whole process and the whole composite drama expresses it. In one sense it looks back; in one sense it looks forward. In one sense it represents human infidelity, in another divine wrath. They are all part of the same continuing reality. This makes it clear that to ask how the drama is causally related to the reality dramatized is to ask the wrong question. The drama is necessary to and inseparable from the reality represented. Yahweh acts in both.

This raises the question of the inevitability of punishment. It is sometimes said that, according to the Hebrew view, the word, and even more the dramatic action, once expressed, must proceed to fulfilment.[12] What then are we to make of those positive, redemptive passages, such as 1.10f., 3.5 and 11.8–11? In particular, what are we to make of 2.21–23, which seems to be a deliberate reversal of the doom promised in 1.3–9?[13] How could it be maintained both that Israel was doomed and that God would have mercy on her? Some commentators have challenged the authenticity of these passages, but

---

[12] But see Thiselton's important article on 'The Supposed Power of Words in the Biblical Writings'.

[13] Grace Emmerson discusses this whole question in *Hosea*, ch. 1.

that simply sets the editors against the prophet and still leaves the question unanswered.[14] As far as contemporary investigation is concerned, the work of editors is as 'authentic' as the *ipsissima verba* of the prophet; the *ipsissima verba* can never be established anyway. Our concern is with Hebrew understanding and this can be traced in all who contributed to a text. As in so many other ways, the editor is as good a witness as the prophet.

The answer to the questions must be that the will of Yahweh, as the prophets and their editors understood it, was not easily charted. Apostasy-drama-doom was a comprehensible formula, but it did not lay Yahweh's mind bare. Sitting on a beach one can plot the movement of the waves and even begin to forecast their arrival, but before long unseen factors wreck the pattern. So the prophets understood the will of Yahweh. Though clear at times, they knew it to be vast as the ocean. Their visions and their oracles related to particular moments; the whole was never revealed to them. Furthermore, what Yahweh intended possessed a reality *as an intention*, and that reality could give rise to oracle and to drama. When he chose, Yahweh could disturb his own plan. Realities exist because Yahweh intends them, and so they can be expressed in prophecy. If Yahweh's intention changes, the realities cease to exist and so the prophecy simply falls away. Yahweh's intention is expressed in the reality and in the prophecy, but equally, when it so pleased him, in the diversion of the expected process. No doubt the populace was satisfied with simpler notions, but the great prophets seem to have possessed an understanding sophisticated enough to cope with this complicating factor.

Hosea and the Adulteress: Hos. 3.1–5

In 3.1–5 there is the second account of the relationship of Hosea with an immoral woman. This time it is in the first person. The fundamental structure of the two accounts is so similar that it is hard to resist the idea that originally these two passages were different versions of the same incident.

---

[14] Batten expunged all the optimistic references in 'Hosea's Message'. Toy separated chs. 1–3 from 4–14 ('Note on Hosea 1–3'). Haupt regarded chs. 1 and 2, but not 3, as a postscript ('Hosea's Erring Spouse'). This drastic way of solving difficulties is simply too easy. Modern commentators have to be ready to live with the text.

A	B
The Lord said to Hosea,	The Lord said to me,
Go, take to yourself a	Go, love a woman who is beloved of a
wife of harlotry,	paramour and is an adulteress,
for the land commits great	*even as the Lord loves the people of Israel.*
harlotry.	
So he went and took	So I bought her.
Gomer.	

The important difference is that, in the first account, the dramatic action is said to express the wickedness of Israel; in the second, it expresses Yahweh's redeeming love.[15] The basic structure has been extended in both cases, far more so in ch. 3 than in ch. 1. There is nothing antecedently improbable about this. The historical experience, which affected Hosea so deeply, could well have been applied in different ways on different occasions, and if not by Hosea, then certainly by his editors. One would also expect the explanation of the drama to be the point where the greatest extensions were made. The incident itself is not open to much embroidery, but the meaning of it could be discussed for ever. As the account of the incident is passed down through history, it is to be expected that it will be used again and again to shed light on new situations. In this way the divergences between chs. 1 and 3 can readily be explained.[16]

This, however, does not get us very far. There may be but one action on the historical level, but there are clearly two different accounts on the literary level. So ch. 3 must be studied apart from ch. 1. The author, whom we presume to be Hosea, is told to go and love an unnamed woman who is 'beloved of a paramour and an adulteress'. The first phrase is clumsy. It is possible to alter the vowels of the verb and read, 'who loves a friend', as Wolff does;[17] and it is

---

[15] Fohrer sees the two passages as two separate dramas, one expressing calamity, the other redemption (*History*, p. 247).

[16] One obvious divergence is that, in ch. 1, Hosea is commanded to have children and in ch. 3 he insists on a period of sexual abstinence. But it is widely supposed that the reference to sexual abstinence is an addendum to the basic narrative of ch. 3, and the same may be true of the reference to children in 1.2. Moreover, if two versions of the same drama existed separately, it is likely that they would come to concentrate on different aspects of the marriage relationship. Ch. 1 stresses procreation and the link with the drama of the names; ch. 3 stresses both the mercy and the discipline of Yahweh's love.

[17] Wolff, *Hosea*, p. 56.

possible, with a further alteration of vowels, to read, 'who loves evil things', as the LXX does. The sense, however, is reasonably clear. Hosea is to love an immoral woman who has already committed adultery, presumably against himself, possibly within the Baal cult; and so it is easy to read the story, on the literary level, as a sequel to ch. 1, as Amsler and many others do.[18] Love, as Wolff points out, is not to be understood emotionally or sexually, but in terms of service and loyalty.[19] The explanation, which is included in the charge, is that such paradoxical and undeserved love is similar to that which Yahweh has for Israel. Israel's wickedness is shown in turning to other gods and a desire for cakes and raisins. Consuming cakes and raisins must be a reference to the Baal cult (Jer. 7.18; 44.19) and the phrase is used here as a symbol of Baal worship in general.

The account of Hosea obeying the command is in v. 2. The woman in question is presumably for sale, or, at least, someone is in a position to accept a bid for her. The price is spelt out exactly, though it is not clear to whom Hosea paid the money. Already the performance has gone beyond the command. The prophet was told to love an unfaithful woman; in fact he redeemed an abandoned one. In v. 3 the narrative is developed still further. Hosea, the woman's saviour, now decides on a period of discipline in which she will not only not play the harlot, but not have sexual relations with any man, not even himself, her deliverer, and as many think, her husband. On his own part he guarantees a similar continence. This looks at first sight like a second act to the drama concerned, not with redemption, but with penance, and what is more, not with the present, but with the future. Some new consideration is now moulding the narrative, and in vv. 4f. we see what it is. These two verses refer to a future state of austerity for Israel when she will be deprived of all the paraphernalia of state and cult. After that she will return to seek for Yahweh her God and David her king. This last part of the chapter is very surprising. It is plainly concerned with historical considerations quite unrelated to the original command of v. 1.

How are these verses to be explained? For H.G. May the solution

---

[18] Amsler, *Les Actes*, pp. 22f.; see also Andersen and Freedman, *Hosea*, p. 293. It does not follow that ch. 1 was the first to be written. Even if it is accepted that there are two separate incidents and that ch. 1 comes chronologically first, it is best to assume that ch. 3 was first to be written. Otherwise the absence of any reference back to Gomer is hard to understand.

[19] Wolff, *Hosea*, p. 60; cf. Emmerson, *Hosea*, pp. 13f.

that beckons rules out the idea of prophetic drama altogether.[20] The
whole chapter is an allegory devised to explain the exile in terms of
the marriage laws of Deut. 24.1–4. Commentators often turn from
complex texts in despair and leap to the conclusion that allegory alone
can provide the answer, but there is no justification for such a recourse
here.[21] As far as this particular passage is concerned, it is not impossible
to overcome the difficulties and see ch. 3 as the result of a complex
literary process that began with the action of Hosea himself, the action
that involved a liaison with an immoral woman. In the present version
the long-suffering and faithful love of Yahweh is primary. Nevertheless
it was clear that catastrophe was soon to overtake the northern
kingdom. So the story is shaped to include a period of discipline, thus
holding love and catastrophe together. This editing inevitably gives
the impression that there was a second act to the drama. Hosea's
faithful editors could not leave the matter there, however. So a future
hope is introduced, a hope that, after the discipline is over, Israel
would return and put her trust in Yahweh and enjoy his goodness. So
the love is underlined. The lack of detail in v. 5 is hardly surprising
since the first editors of Hosea can have been no more certain of the
future than was Hosea himself. Eventually their positive version found
its way into the hands of southern editors who added the reference to
David in v. 5 and finally tied up the story with the exile of the southern
kingdom.

If ch. 3 and ch. 1.2f. refer to the same original incident, comment
at this point can be concerned only with the treatment that the editors
gave to the basic form. Three points are worthy of note. In the first
place, the original incident of taking or redeeming the woman, which
in the original form is made to seem like the work of a day (v. 2), is
definitely extended in v. 3. It is legitimate to ask whether this fact is
not relevant to the earlier discussion about whether the marriage
should not be seen as a life-long drama rather than as a momentary
one. Secondly, the author of v. 3 had no doubt that accepting an
extended period of misery was consistent with Hosea's understanding
of his role as a prophet; similarly, the author thought it quite fitting
to represent the history with which he was familiar in terms of the life

[20] May, 'An Interpretation of the Names of Hosea's Children', p. 286; the allegorical
view was common, not to say standard, in the pre-critical period. See also Eissfeldt,
Introduction, p. 389 and Rowley, 'Marriage', *Men of God*, p. 79.

[21] The general question of whether prophetic dramas actually happened is discussed
in Chapter 15.

story of the prophet. Thirdly, the editors did not hesitate to extend a drama that originally had to do with a contemporary state of affairs into one that involved the future as well. This apparent lack of concern regarding the time reference is a difficulty only for those who want to see the dramas as essentially effective. If the continuum of past, present and future is seen as a single intention of Yahweh, and if the drama is understood as a work of Yahweh, there is no reason why any Hebrew editor should not look outwards and forwards at the same time. In this regard the additions to the basic narrative in ch. 3 give a valuable insight into the theology of the prophetic editor.

9 · Isaiah

The book of Isaiah contains relatively few accounts of dramatic actions. If Isaiah's prophetic ministry lasted forty years or more, as seems probable, the narratives that we possess represent an unimpressive aspect of that ministry. If, as von Rad suggests, 'the preaching of Isaiah represents the theological high water mark of the whole of the Old Testament', it is both remarkable and unfortunate that so little of the prophet's message is expressed in dramatic actions.[1] There seems to be an inescapable inference that dramatic performance was not necessary to the prophetic function; at best it was an optional extra. This is damaging to any hypothesis that affirms that the purpose of the dramas was to make the message more clear or more powerful. There are only four actions to consider from the book of Isaiah, two from a single passage. All are linked to specific historical situations; the theological teaching in every case is mediated through historical comment and prediction. In this regard, Isaiah differs markedly from Hosea.

The first three examples are all linked to the year of the Syro-Ephraimite Confederacy (733 BCE). Pekah of Israel and Rezin of Syria had come to invest Jerusalem in order to persuade Ahaz to join them in a rebellion against Tiglath-Pileser, the Assyrian, who was showing himself to be a serious threat to the nations at the western end of the fertile crescent. Despite Isaiah's calm advice, Ahaz was afraid and appealed to Assyria to help. A few years later (711 BCE), there was another vain revolt against Assyria, this time led by Philistia. The dramatic action of Isa. 20 relates to this revolt, which was quickly put down.

---

[1] *Theology II*, p. 147.

Shear-jashub: Isa. 7.3

Here in this single verse we learn that Isaiah had a son called Shear-jashub (*šᵉʾār-yāšûb*). It is the time of the Syro-Ephraimite confederacy and the armies from the north are but a few hours' march from Jerusalem. Yahweh instructs Isaiah to take the boy with this elusive name and go to meet Ahaz at a specific place, there to pronounce an oracle telling the king not to be afraid. There is no account of Isaiah obeying the instruction, nor is there any explanation of why the boy had to be taken.

On the grounds of Hos. 1.3–9 and the fact that Isaiah's children are described as 'signs and wonders' in Isa. 8.18, it has been generally supposed that the name Shear-jashub has some prophetic significance. It is open to question whether the significance was originally connected with the name-giving itself, or with the enduring fact that the prophet had a son who bore that name, or with the punctual fact that Isaiah took the child, on divine instructions, to a particular meeting with Ahaz. It may be that in this one verse we have evidence, tantalizingly insufficient, of a drama in three acts, two of short duration, the other long-lasting. The actual naming is not recounted at all. A child, old enough to walk, simply appears with the name Shear-jashub. If the naming was carried out as a prophetic action at some time in the past, the account has not survived.[2] We have, therefore, to consider Shear-jashub as a permanent sign to Israel. The name means, 'a remnant will return', and it must be tied up in some way with passages such as 6.13 and 10.20–23 and with the general Isaianic remnant theology.[3]

The dramatic significance of the original circumstance can be understood in several different and, on the face of it, contradictory ways. Nevertheless, despite the apparent contradictions, it may well be that the final text embodies two or more of these interpretations.[4] An originally positive oracle may have been reinterpreted for harder times.[5] Some of the older commentators treat the verb 'return' in a moral sense and take the name to mean that a remnant will turn from the worship of false gods to the service of Yahweh, no doubt on the

[2] Clements makes the reasonable but complicating point that, if the name had been given to the child some time previously, it must, at that time, have related to some other situation. What that situation might have been is unknown (*Isaiah*, p. 83).

[3] There is little justification for repointing the Hebrew so that 'remnant' becomes 'flesh' or 'blood', as Lipiński suggests ('Isaïe VII 3').

[4] Carroll, 'Inner Tradition Shifts in Meaning in Isaiah 1–11'.

[5] As suggested by McKane in 'The Interpretation of Is. 7.14–25', for example.

grounds that a prophecy of physical return from some foreign captivity would hardly be apt in the early part of Isaiah's career.[6] 10.20f. suggests a specific occasion on which the survivors of some catastrophe will suffer a change of heart and no longer trust in foreign states but in Yahweh. On this reckoning the name is as much an expression of Yahweh's constancy as of Israel's future repentance, and a drama of long duration, such as name-bearing inevitably is, is particularly appropriate.

A second supposition is that the name should be regarded as a prophecy of doom. After some unspecified, future disaster, *only* a remnant will return home; the rest will perish ignominiously. A number of small considerations suggest that this is the proper meaning. Isaiah is primarily a prophet of judgment rather than of salvation;[7] by putting the noun before the verb, the Hebrew stresses the fact of the remnant rather than the fact of the returning; the passages that may reasonably be used for interpretation, 6.13 and 10.22f., are bleakly unpropitious in the original form;[8] it must be remembered, too, that the idea of a remnant was a matter, not primarily of theological idealism, but of harsh historical experience. Even after the most uncompromising massacres, it nearly always happened that a remnant of the vanquished people were found to have survived, though their fate was usually abysmal.[9] Amos 3.12 sets the tone; the scrap that remains is worthless. 'Return' may, therefore, mean nothing more than 'come out alive'. Against this background it is hard to construe the name very positively, and other prophetic names tend to confirm this.[10] Maher-shalal-hash-baz is a portent of disaster, though not for Israel; Hosea's names are all doom-laden. If Shear-jashub follows that precedent, it will primarily presage disaster.

Thirdly, there has been an attempt to take the name as a hopeful prophecy to the effect that Israel, through a representative remnant, would survive every disaster.[11] It is true that 7.4–9 express confidence in the future; these verses provide a positive context for the mention

---

[6] Whitehouse, *Isaiah*, p. 128; Skinner, *Isaiah*, p. 54; but see also Young, *Isaiah*, p. 271 and Jensen, *Isaiah*, p. 93.

[7] Rice, 'A Neglected Interpretation of the Immanuel Prophecy'.

[8] Blank makes this case strongly in 'The Current Misinterpretation of Isaiah's She'ar Yashub'.

[9] Von Rad, *Theology II*, pp. 21f.

[10] Immanuel, of course, is an exception.

[11] Amsler, *Les Actes*, p. 18.

of the name, but it does not follow that this one particular context expounds the meaning of the name for all other contexts. It might be argued that the name represents a theological principle, like Immanuel: in the mercy of God, always a remnant will survive. But this interpretation would be more likely to appeal to those who read of the incident retrospectively than to Isaiah's contemporaries. Scott maintains, not very convincingly, that the name was first given as a prophecy of doom, but that, after Israel had survived some disaster, it was understood in a hopeful sense.[12]

Fourthly, the fact that the presence of the child with this name was intended to be a reassuring sign to Ahaz – the oracle that was to be spoken was all about there being no cause for fear – coupled with the fact that a remnant necessarily implies a disaster, has been taken to mean that the remnant would be a Syro-Ephraimite remnant.[13] Those armies would be decimated and would return home. This is logical but improbable. One would expect the name to have direct reference to Israel rather than to her enemies, especially when one remembers that the name was not the work of a moment but an enduring witness in the life of Jerusalem.

Was the incident a warning to Ahaz that his policy would lead to a doom from which there would be few survivors? Or was it an assurance, in line with the words of the oracle, that Israel would survive? On the whole the context seems to require the latter. Isaiah was bringing confidence to a nervous king.[14] But the contradiction between the inferences we draw from the circumstances on one hand, and the probable import of the name on the other, creates a serious problem. Moreover, in this particular situation, Isaiah is not prophesying to Ahaz that a remnant will be saved, but that the whole nation will be delivered. This seems to imply two levels in Isaiah's action. On one level he is reassuring the king about the immediate situation; but on another level he is warning him about the effects of his Assyrian policy. The positive words are balanced by the presence of the child whose name suggests that Israel is always under judgment and that Yahweh will purge his people to ensure that his will is done. Unfortunately this is guesswork. There may well have been an important dramatic

---

[12] Scott, 'Isaiah', p. 244.
[13] Clements, *Isaiah 1–39*, p. 83, followed by Day, 'Shear-Jashub (Isaiah VII 3) and "The Remnant of Wrath" (Psalm LXXVI 11)'.
[14] Hammerschaimb, *Aspects of Old Testament Prophecy*, pp. 17f.

action here, but the story has not been recounted in a way that allows its full meaning to be appreciated.

It is curious that Isa. 7.3, the least clearly defined of all the prophetic acts considered so far, is the first to which the words *'ôt* (sign) and *môpēt* (wonder) are applied. The reference, in Isa. 8.18, is not to the Ahaz incident, but to the continuing existence of the children. This is a further indication that the meaning of Shear-jashub is not to be sought in the meeting with the king alone.

Immanuel: Isa. 7.10–17

This incident does not really come within our category because it does not relate to a prophetic action; it is not even a prophetic reflection on an action of someone else. It is a prophecy of an action that might be taken by someone else in the future.[15] Nevertheless a note about it is desirable for two reasons. In the first place, the passage is another of the relatively few where the word *'ôt* occurs in relation to some prophetic activity. In the second place, three significant names occur in Isa. 7 and 8; it is reasonable to assume that they interpret each other and so should be taken together.[16]

The account of the incident is well-known. While Jerusalem is still under siege Yahweh instructs Ahaz to ask for a sign. It can safely be assumed that Yahweh spoke through the voice of Isaiah and that the sign was a sign of deliverance from the besieging armies. Ahaz refuses, either because he is afraid that Isaiah is misleading him and that the demand for a sign would be blasphemous, or because he was afraid of the outcome. Isaiah is not pleased, but nevertheless continues to provide the sign. It comes in the form of a prophecy. A woman will have a child who will be named Immanuel (*'immānû-'ēl*). he will be fed on butter and honey, and before he reaches an age of discernment, the countries of the two kings at present threatening Jerusalem would be desolate.

There are a number of points at issue in this narrative and, as a full

---

[15] On one reckoning no sign was given at all, because Ahaz appealed to Assyria, thus failing to 'believe'. The purpose of the sign was to have been to confirm to Ahaz, if he had been willing to listen, that there was no need to appeal to Assyria. See Kraeling, 'The Immanuel Prophecy'.

[16] Not even this can be taken for granted. Jensen contends that, whereas 8.1–4 (Maher-shalal-hash-baz) refer to the immediate future, the Immanuel prophecy relates to a more distant deliverance and is of a quite different kind.

debate is impossible here, we shall have to content ourselves with simply indicating the preferred solution.[17] In the first place, who is the young woman who will bear the child? There is no easy answer to this.[18] Many suppose her to be the queen, but would the queen be described simply as a young woman, and how could Isaiah tell an unco-operative Ahaz what name he would give to his own child? There is much to be said for the hypothesis that the child was the prophet's own. Only in this way could the name be guaranteed, and the three names referred to in chs.7 and 8 would be analogous in that they would all be those of the prophet's children.

Secondly, is butter and honey to be regarded as the food of a prince, as many suppose, or is it the basic fare of a reduced population? 'Butter' is a doubly bad translation of *ḥem'â*. To us it means a solid substance that cannot be eaten in quantity by anyone, young or old; moreover, it is a food that only the comparatively rich can afford. 'Curds' is to be preferred on both counts. Honey, too, in a modern setting, counts as a luxury. All these indicators are wrong. In a pastoral economy, milk, meat and fruit were the three basic foods. The agriculturalist could add corn and various kinds of bread, grapes, and so wine, and herbs and spices which could either be grown on the farms or obtained by trading, but nothing could replace milk. The reference to milk in 7.15, therefore, does not suggest poverty or wealth; the primary assumption must be that it simply suggests survival. If the child was to live, it must certainly have milk; honey was used, no doubt, to make the milk more palatable after breast milk.

Commentators often seem to forget that we are dealing with a baby, and the diet of infant princes is not so very different, even today, from the diet of infant paupers. Sweetened milk follows naturally after breast milk. The point of this reference to 'curds and honey', therefore, is not to show that the baby will be either rich or poor, but to indicate a specific period in its life, the period of sweetened milk. So the passage strikes a contrast between the immediate future, the time of nursing

[17] Rice conveniently summarizes the problems and produces a complex solution of his own in 'The Interpretation of Is. 7.15–7' and 'A Neglected Interpretation of the Immanuel Prophecy'. In brief the solution is that Isaiah and his faithful followers are the sign. God is with them and, though they will not be spared judgment, they will learn to reject evil and choose good.

[18] M.E.W. Thompson has set out all the possibilities in an article, 'Isaiah's Sign of Immanuel'. See too J.T. Willis, 'The Meaning of Is. 7.14 and its Application to Mt. 1.23'.

and weaning, which corresponds to the time of the siege, and the distant future, the time of the first childish discernment, the time when the sign will be fulfilled.

Thirdly, refusing evil and choosing good suggests moral discernment to most commentators, but that requires an unacceptably long siege. Isaiah is talking in simple, practical terms about bringing up a child. The Hebrew words for good and evil are common words with a wide range of meanings and it is legitimate to render them in this context 'nice' and 'nasty'. Before the child has reached the second stage of his life, when he has developed a clear idea of what he likes and does not like, what he will eat readily and what he will refuse to eat, the besiegers will have disappeared. This cuts down the period to something much more reasonable. Even with gestation it need be no more than eighteen months or two years.

Fourthly, there is the question whether the whole should be read as a threat or a promise. Here the evidence is strongly in favour of promise.[19] The birth of a child, especially a boy, was always a happy event in Israel. To use birth as a sign of disaster results in a jangling of symbols. The naming of a child was always a significant, not to say a prophetic, event. Awful names were sometimes chosen for awful circumstances, as we have already seen, but Immanuel is a most positive name. The sign must indicate a happy future. The chief problem is the insertion of the words, 'even the king of Assyria', at the end of v. 17, but they are surely best explained as a scribal gloss linking, somewhat obscurely, the basically hopeful oracles of vv. 1–17 – and they are hopeful, despite the king's behaviour – to the gloomier prophecies of vv. 18–25. We conclude that, in a critical situation, Isaiah prophesies an event which will give rise to great rejoicing. The name of the child is a part of the sign but also the interpretation of it. The reason for the rejoicing is that God is with his people.

If we put these points together, a satisfactory explanation of the Immanuel sign is not difficult to achieve. We assume that we are dealing with a genuine historical incident, and that, when Isaiah spoke, the city was besieged and the resolution of the situation was

---

[19] Sheldon Blank, who is satisfied that vv. 17–25 are threatening and that the reference to Shear-jashub may well belong to a lost introduction to these verses, argues that vv. 1–16 represent a positive narrative, so positive indeed that it is out of place in the Isaiah corpus. But the book of Isaiah contains the work of another prophet who might well own the Immanuel prophecy. Who this prophet was and whether he was entirely factual or partly legendary is open to discussion. See Blank, 'Immanuel and Which Isaiah?'

unknown to all those present. Isaiah has a word of hope, but he has only an approximate idea of the time scale. In this he is in the same position as the apocalyptists of a later age, and he takes the same way out of the problem as they were to take. He spells out the future in terms of periods without giving a precise length to any one of them. The first period is gestation, which would naturally be understood as a hopeful image. It appears that the woman has not yet conceived, so this period is something less than a year. The second period is the birth and the naming, a period of joy and very obvious hope. There will be plenty of evidence that God is with Israel, and the naming of children will indicate this, but the final resolution of the siege will not come at this time. Hope will be deferred. How long birth, naming and feeding from the breast would last is not absolutely clear but one imagines a few months. Then comes the third period when the child is weaned. For this period he will eat infant food. No question of discrimination arises, because milky food is all the child can take. This lasts presumably a few months. Before long the fourth period arrives, when the mother tries the child on solids and the child takes some and refuses others. Before that stage happens, the siege will be lifted. In short, Isaiah is propheysing that the two kings will have departed in about two years from the time of his speaking. If this interpretation is sound, then the identity of the mother is hardly important; Isaiah may be referring to an individual or to a typical mother of the moment. The same time scale would operate in the case of any child, and if the signs of hope were strong enough, any set of parents might choose the specified name.

What does all this mean regarding the function of the sign? It has been suggested that the sign serves to authenticate the prophecy, but it is hard to understand how it could do so. Even if a specific woman was indicated and she subsequently gave birth, it would not validate the prophecy, because women are giving birth all the time. The validating would come with the departure of the besieging armies, but this event would validate Isaiah's oracles, whether there was a sign or not. A far better understanding of the sign is to see it as the expression, indeed, the introduction of the deliverance. Rejoicing begins with the birth of the child, and as the child grows, hope grows till deliverance is complete. This is an interesting pointer to how we are to understand prophetic drama.

There remains a few interesting features to note in passing. The whole drama takes place in the prophet's mind and speech. The prophecy may have been fulfilled in the terms that Isaiah indicates, but we hear no more about it. Again, as in the case of other namings, the sign has two elements, the punctual one of the naming ceremony and the permanent one of the extended presence. The implication is not simply that God would be with them in the departure of the two kings but that he would be with them all the time. Yet again, the chronological link between the sign and the reality is intricate. How the birth relates to the lifting of the siege is not absolutely clear. The giving of the name might be a prophecy of hope or even possibly a celebration of some indications of deliverance already present. What is clear is that the desolation that will come upon the enemy lands will precede a particular stage in the child's life. The growth of the child (the drama) and the process of history (the reality) will go side by side. The climactic event in the latter will precede the climactic event in the former. That is the promise. But, of course, Immanuel will be around for a long time, so we also have to think of a long-term drama corresponding to a long-term reality.

Maher-shalal-hash-baz: Isa. 8.1–4

This action is in two parts. Both are recounted in the first person. As the text stands, the two parts must be separated by the whole period of the child's gestation, since the writing is supposed to take place before the child who is to bear the name is conceived. As in the case of the naming of Hosea's children, the literary form has united in a single prophecy incidents that were in fact spaced out.

In the first part, Yahweh commands Isaiah to take a large slate and write on it, 'For Maher-shalal-hash-baz' (*mahēr-šālal-ḥāš-baz*), in the presence of two reliable witnesses. The word translated 'slate' is a curious one occurring elsewhere only in Isa. 3.23, where the meaning is even more dubious. Arguing from the meaning of the root, 'to uncover', one reaches the rather uncertain conclusion that the word has something to do with a public revelation, and that the normal word for slate was rejected because it insufficiently emphasized this point. The word used for the writing instrument is no more common and many commentators conclude that the term refers, not to the kind of pen, but to the kind of script. It was to be the common script used for everyday affairs and readable by all who could read. The force of the preposition before the name is also uncertain. RSV over-translates it as 'belonging to'; it is not at all obvious how the child's possession

of the slate could have any meaning. It is better to take it in a much
lighter sense, simply as a means of introducing the name. 'With
reference to' points in the right direction but it is much too heavy.
The message, contained in the meaning of the name, 'spoil speeds,
prey hastes', refers to a military disaster, but it is not clear at this point
who wins and who loses.[20] There are a number of other cases where
oracles that were, or could have been, spoken were also written down
(Isa. 8.16; 30.8; Jer. 36; Hab. 2.2). The point seems to be that writing
gives to words greater force, greater durability, and a more insistent
reality.[21] Why must the slate be large? Perhaps to provide a kind of
placard that could be easily read, though there is no account of a public
display and the presence of specific witnesses may even argue against
it.[22] Perhaps the large writing in the common script was simply to give
emphatic expression to the idea. The witnesses were present, not
simply to verify that the prophet had indeed made the prophecy, but
to observe that it had been given the greater reality by being written.
Even more, the witnesses represent the future populace. What is stark
and clear to them now will be equally stark and clear to the whole
nation later on. The stress in both cases is on the impossibility of
evasion.

The second part of the story contains a command from Yahweh to
give his second child the name, Maher-shalal-hash-baz. The mother
of the child is called a prophetess, which raises the question whether
she was some kind of cultic functionary.[23] The other usages of this
word refer to a charismatic, if not a cultic woman, but there is no trace
of either notion in this story. Probably, therefore, the word here
simply denotes the prophet's wife. There is an obvious escalation in
this drama. The oracle was presumably spoken by the prophet, then
certainly written and read, then finally given to a child as a name. So
it achieves further currency and greater durability, and as the child

[20] The name may not have been as strange as it seems. P. Humbert discusses a
possible Egyptian background to it ('Maher Salal Has Baz'). See also Kaiser, *Isaiah
1–12*, p. 178 and Watts, *Isaiah 1–33*, pp. 112f. Names having messages were more
common in the Old Testament than they are now (Gen. 5.29; Ex. 3.13f.; Isa. 7.14 etc.).

[21] Fohrer, *Die Handlungen*, p. 31.

[22] Renan assumed that Isaiah went round holding a placard, and he gives this action
as an example of the prophets' tendency to use 'tricks' to attract attention (*History of
the People of Israel*, Vol. II, Book IV, Ch. XVI, pp. 356f.). But Renan held a low view
of prophetic drama. See below in Chapter 17.

[23] There is no reason to infer, as Carroll seems to do, that the drama involved Isaish
in extra-marital activity (*From Chaos*, p. 313).

grows, it becomes more obtrusive. The second part of the drama has a full explanation. Damascus and Syria will be spoiled and Assyria will be the spoiler, and this will happen before the child is able to speak. This last detail is reminiscent of the Immanuel passage, especially 7.16, though in that passage there is merely the prophecy of a child's birth. Here there is an actual child already bearing a symbolic name.

In this particular instance the permanent force of the name is not easy to understand. Immanuel has permanent force as a prophetic proclamation; at least one of the meanings of Shear-jashub can be regarded as an affirmation of permanent truth; but it is hard to see Maher-shalal-hash-baz in this light. The text itself does not do so, and we are left with the uncomfortable conclusion, as far as the second part of the drama is concerned, that the prophet named a child as a dramatic act directed to one particular occasion, and that the child bore that name, somewhat irrelevantly, for the rest of its life.

The military disaster signified here duly happened. Damascus and Syria were spoiled, though eleven years elapsed between the two events. This is hardly in keeping with v. 4. We have to assume either that the future was foreshortened in the prophet's mind and the editors saw no reason to revise the text, or that the editors were responsible for v. 4 (which echoes 7. 16), so telescoping the narrative in order to make prophecy and fulfilment relate more closely. This child, together with his brother, is a sign (*'ôt*) and a wonder (*môpēt*) in Israel according to Isa. 8.18.

Isaiah's Nakedness: Isa. 20

This is one of the most celebrated prophetic dramas. It occurs in every list and is commonly discussed as a good example of the phenomenon. The terms *'ôt* and *môpēt* occur in v. 3 as a description of the action. As far as literary form is concerned, it fulfils all the requirements. It has a command, an account of the action, and an explanation, in that order, though this structure weakens as one scrutinizes it more closely.

The drama can be dated at the beginning of the rebellion against Assyria which resulted in Sargon's attack on Ashdod in 713/711 BCE.[24] A decision had been reached in Egypt, where an Ethiopian dynasty had control, that the time was ripe for revolt, but it remained uncertain

---

[24] See *ANET*, pp. 284ff.

how many of the states at the western end of the fertile crescent would follow Egypt's lead and risk a punitive mission from Assyria. While the matter was still unresolved, the command of Yahweh came to Isaiah to remove his outer garment and his sandals and go about in this destitute and humiliating condition for three years.[25]

The first question is what is meant by 'naked and barefoot'. Some have supposed that Isaiah was completely naked. Their argument is based upon the fact that the explanation in v. 4 refers to captives being led away with, according to the RSV, 'buttocks uncovered'. The Hebrew is not absolutely clear, but some shameful condition is obviously indicated. It is wrong to suppose that dramas are essentially mimetic, so that the state of the captives does not have to be portrayed to the last detail. Moreover there is something impractical about the idea of a prophet wandering around in a state of complete undress for any length of time. So we do not have to infer complete nakedness. The point is that clothing represented dignity. To be stripped was to be humiliated. Isaiah removed his outer garment and his shoes and this was enough to create the response of shocked horror that was intended.

There is a further question regarding the duration of the action. Were it not for the two words translated 'three years' in v. 3, it would be easy to understand the drama as the action of a single day, a costly but graphic warning to anyone with eyes to see of the consequences of rebellion. It is noteworthy too that the words occur, not in the command to act, nor in the account of the action, but in the explanation that follows. The evidence shows that it is in the explanation that the typical drama narrative is most vulnerable to later addition.[26] The Massoretes seem to have been aware of the problem because, against expectation, they divide v. 3 after 'naked and barefoot' so that the

[25] Sawyer (*Isaiah*, p. 180) sees a double drama here; first, the wearing of sackcloth for mourning, and secondly, the loss of even this clothing as a sign of humiliation. Sawyer is right to draw attention to the sackcloth, but we have no means of knowing for what purpose Isaiah was wearing it. There is nothing in the text to indicate that it was significant. According to Watts, the Hebrew *śaq* might be simply the basic undergarment of men, mentioned only because it had to be removed, but it is difficult to see on what this supposition is based (*Isaiah 1–33*, p. 264). Wearing sackcloth always means deliberate self-mortification in the Old Testament, even in II Kings 6.30, where it was worn secretly as an undergarment. Ridderbos thinks that the sackcloth refers to the prophetic mantle, familiar from the stories of Elijah and John the Baptist (*Isaiah*, p. 175), but in I Kings 19.19 and II Kings 2.13, the word is *'adderet* not *śaq*.

[26] See Hos. 3; Jer. 13.1–11; 16.1–7; 18.1–12; 19.1–13; etc.

'three years' are not linked with the actual walking, but with the sign and the wonder, that is to say, with the public awareness. There is, therefore, a reasonable case for the supposition that the 'three years' do not belong to the original story.[27] On the other hand, there is no manuscript evidence for dislodging the words from the text. It is just possible that Isaiah performed the drama several times over a period of years. The awkwardness of this hypothesis is that it requires us to understand 'at that time' in v. 2 as having reference to a number of occasions spread over a longer period than the actual year referred to in the previous verse, which is awkward indeed. On balance it seems better to regard the words as an editorial addition. There was a tendency for later editors to add to the stories, to make them more impressive, to make them fit the fulfilment more accurately, to make them more relevant to their own day. If the Assyrian campaign lasted three years, as appears from the inscriptions, that would supply sufficient reason for the insertion.

Some scholars, confronted with both these difficulties, have supposed that the action was not historical but imaginary. Those of a previous generation may have taken this view because they were disturbed by the idea of a prophet using immodest behaviour as the medium of his message.[28] There is, however, no need for such anxiety. In the first place, the prophets were so deeply involved in their work that again and again they were willing to surrender their own pride and dignity for its sake. Secondly, Isaiah needed to shock because the matter was indeed shocking. Thirdly, according to the view taken here, stark nakedness is not implied in the story.

The meaning of the drama is given in a first person oracle in which Yahweh is the speaker; the oracle appears to look back over the three years and provide an explanation of the action for the first time. This is very artificial. One cannot believe that Isaiah performed this action, perhaps several times, without ever saying what it meant, or, even less likely, without knowing what it meant. Surely he would have been asked to explain himself. We conclude that the explanation –

[27] Other theories are possible. G.B. Gray supposes that the three years represent the interval between the act and the explanation (*Isaiah*, pp. 347f.). Long ago Lowth produced the theory that Isaiah walked naked for three days to signify three years. In some MSS of the LXX the words 'three years' occur twice. The first occurrence could represent an original 'three days', now lost from the Hebrew text (*Isaiah*, p. 158).

[28] E.J. Young struggled with the same problem in 1969, but concluded that the action really happened (*Isaiah 2*, pp. 54f.).

including the 'three years' – belongs to the literary version and is probably an adapted summary of what Isaiah himself said at the time.

It is possible that this drama was ambiguous as far as time reference was concerned, particularly if Isaiah did repeat it over a period of years. Ashdod did, in fact, fall and its leaders suffered from the Assyrian treatment. Egypt did not, and its leaders were saved for the time being. Isaiah's drama could have had past or present reference in that it portrayed what had actually happened, or was happening, to the Philistine leaders. It could have future reference in that it portrayed what would happen to the Egyptian leaders if they continued in their folly. The attractiveness of this hypothesis rests in the fact that the drama would at least in part be linked to concrete historical fact. It is uncommon for prophets to dramatize faint and, as it turned out, unfulfilled possibilities, and perhaps even less common for editors to preserve the accounts of such dramas.[29]

The force of the drama is that Egypt and Ethiopia will be led away captive by Assyria. Isaiah is dramatizing a condition that will fall upon nations other than Israel. He cannot, therefore, represent them from within, as it were. This is an important point because there are other dramas (e.g. Jer. 32.6–15) where the prophet does represent his own group, indeed essentially so, and there may be a tendency to suppose that the significance of the drama depends upon performance by a proper representative. As the story stands at the moment, it is plainly not so. It is just possible to contend that Isaiah believed he was representing his own people, that his expectation was not fulfilled as far as Judah was concerned, and that the explanation of vv. 3–6 has been adjusted to suit the facts as they turned out. But that hypothesis calls for two comments. First, if it is granted, the editors, if not Isaiah himself, were content with a drama narrative in which the prophet represented members of a foreign community; and second, this explanation still does not accord with the facts as far as we know them. Ashdod bore the brunt of the Assyrian attack; Philistines rather than Egyptians and Ethiopians were led away captive. Distance and flagrant disloyalty to her allies protected Egypt. The rebel leader fled there from Ashdod, but he was handed over to the Assyrians, and Egypt lived on.

---

[29] Assyria defeated Egypt at Eltekeh in 701 BCE but did not invade Egypt until 671 BCE. There was a deportation of notables in 667. These facts, of course, are quite unrelated to the Assyrian campaign against Ashdod in 711, but they may not be unrelated to the way in which the story of the actions was remembered and applied.

In vv. 5f. the shame of the captives is extended to all those who were foolish enough to put their trust in Egypt. They were left militarily exposed, embarrassed and afraid. It is not clear whether the final confession of folly and shame is to be made by a Judahite or a Philistine, but it matters little. Verses 5f. may represent a later addition, because the story in vv. 1–4 is complete in itself.

10 · Micah

Micah, a countryman from Moresheth-Gath, prophesied during the same period as Hosea and Isaiah, and like them is outspoken in his denunciation of contemporary society. Micah's chief concern is with the injustices of the southern kingdom, though in the one passage that we consider, his indictment is directed towards Samaria. The redactional history of Micah is exceptionally difficult and exceptionally controversial, but there is no need for us to become involved with it.

Micah's Nakedness: Micah 1.8

This passage is far less celebrated than Isa. 20 despite the fact that its substance is similar. Micah declares that he will walk around stripped and naked, howling and wailing at the same time. The passage does not conform in any way to the familiar structure of command-account-explanation. Nor is there any clear evidence that Micah actually did what he said he would do. Nevertheless the passage can be properly treated here, because, as we shall see later on, it is unwise to make a sharp distinction between intention and performance in relation to prophetic drama. The date of the oracle must be some time shortly before the fall of Samaria. Verses 2–6, in a series of vigorous images, proclaim the doom of the northern kingdom. Her sins are incurable. They have even reached to Jerusalem so that the southern kingdom is under threat. Most commentators regard v. 7 with its precise references to idolatry and harlotry as a later addition, and it does somewhat confuse the story. Micah's doleful representation of calamity might be related to the expected destruction of Samaria (v. 6), or to the sad state of Jerusalem (v. 9), but hardly to the destruction of Samaria's idols (v. 7).

Whatever superficial similarities there may be between Micah 1.8

and Isa. 20, there are some important differences. The term 'naked' is common to both, but the other adjective is different. In Micah the construction means, 'stripped in relation to walking'. Micah's actions are those of a mourner, not a captive. This is clear from the wailing and howling as well as from the context. Self-humiliation was a common form of mourning (see above Chapter 3). Equally important is the fact that Micah belongs to the community about which he prophesies. He is speaking of the doom that awaits God's people. It does not matter whether north or south is primary in this oracle; both are God's people. Micah's expression of grief is that of a representative from within. Most important of all, Micah's action, or projected action, unlike Isaiah's has a dual time reference. In one sense Micah is looking forward to the day of doom, and mourning for it, as many will do when the day comes. If v. 8 is connected primarily with v. 6, this is the dominant sense of the drama. But, if v. 8 is connected primarily with v. 9, Micah's mourning is concerned with the present state of Judah, corrupted as she has been by the wickedness of the north. In that case, Micah is not representing in himself prophetically what many will be doing later, but responding, all alone, to a situation that cries out for penitence and grief in the present. Is the drama a prophecy of a state of affairs to come or an expression of a state of affairs already in existence? Micah and his editors seem not to have asked this question; they seem happy to allow it to be both.

11 · Jeremiah

For many decades a standard 'life of Jeremiah' has been current among scholars, which leads Otto Kaiser to say, 'Thanks to the rich tradition we are ostensibly better informed about the life of Jeremiah than about that of any other Old Testament prophet.'[1] Note the word 'ostensibly'. According to this standard life, Jeremiah began his prophetic work in the thirteenth year of Josiah's reign, that is the year 627 BCE, and he continued to prophesy until he was carried away to Egypt after the fall of Jerusalem in 586. He lived through the most critical decades in Old Testament history; he was witness to the Josianic reform and the promulgation of the Deuteronomic ideal, but also to the final follies of Jehoiakim and Zedekiah, which led to the ruin of the chosen city, the sack of the temple, the spoliation of the promised land and the captivity of the covenant people. Jeremiah bore the tragedy within his own person. He was an unwilling prophet, unable to escape from his vocation and its penalties, and deeply involved in his message. The social ostracism and physical persecution he suffered were part of his prophetic being. One reason why the nature of his ministry is so easily grasped is that it stands in sharp contrast with that of his contemporaries, those other prophets, with whom he is in such constant contention; so much so that he appears to repudiate the designation of prophet, in its common sense, altogether. 'Both prophet and priest are profane; in my house I have found their wickedness, saith the Lord' (23.11). Jeremiah was unpopular because he took the view that Judah had forfeited, at least for the time, her position of privilege, due to grievous and continuing acts of treachery; that Yahweh had appointed Babylon to be the agent of his wrath; that consequently Babylon was to enjoy a period of sovereignty; that Judah

---

[1] Kaiser, *Introduction to the Old Testament*, p. 245.

should not attempt to resist her; and that the king and the prophets who entertained and promulgated false hopes were the enemies and not the friends of the nation. It is entirely consistent with this that Jeremiah should adopt a positive attitude to the exile and write to those carried away in the first draft to accept their lot patiently and constructively.

Many would still accept this as a reasonable account of Jeremiah's life and teaching.[2] Recently, however, this standard life has been vigorously attacked by Robert Carroll in both *From Chaos to Covenant* of 1981 and his *Jeremiah* Commentary of 1986.[3] Carroll's first point is that the book of Jeremiah is, to a large extent, the product of a group of Deuteronomists who took over the original Jeremiah tradition and developed it in terms of their own ideology (Carroll's word) in the exile and thereafter. Carroll goes on to point to other complexities in the literary structure of the book and the result is that 'the historical Jeremiah' simply disappears from view.

It is, of course, true that the standard life has never been as secure as some have pretended. Throughout the whole of the twentieth century, since Duhm's commentary of 1901, an argument has continued about the literary history of the book. The disagreement between Holladay and Carroll demonstrates that it is anything but resolved today. It is relatively clear that within the book there is oracular poetry attributable to the prophet himself; some first-person prose sections; a contribution by Baruch, who wrote much of the prophecy down, although the extent of his work is disputed; a Deuteronomic contribution which may be implicit in the early material or may be an extrinsic addition by a later, alien hand; and some oracles of salvation whose provenance is also disputed. It is by no means clear how these various elements relate to each other. It is not possible or honest to try to avoid this dispute altogether. Distinctions revealed by the history of the material are important, not in order to distinguish 'the genuine' from the rest, but in order to see how editors work and how free they were to understand and apply the material in their own way. The final text is as important a witness as the actual oracles of the prophet. If it can be shown that a particular text has a significant

[2] W.L. Holladay, for example, begins his commentary by affirming that 'fairly secure settings' for Jeremiah's words and actions are attainable; he offers 'A Chronology of Jeremiah's Career' in his *Jeremiah I*, pp. 1–10.

[3] Carroll labels the approach 'Skinnerian' after John Skinner's *Prophecy and Religion* (see *From Chaos to Covenant*, pp. 5ff.).

'after-life', as, for example, Hos. 3 certainly does, that reveals something important about the way that prophetic drama was understood by those who gave it that 'after-life.'.

Jeremiah's Waistcloth: Jer. 13.1–11

This is a much discussed dramatic action. It occurs in all lists. The precise date and circumstances cannot be determined, which is one reason why commentators have found difficulty with it. As in the case of many other dramas, we must infer a complicated literary history. The drama is set out in three acts suggesting a deliberate and formal structure. The command comes from Yahweh, first to buy and wear a waistcloth, secondly to take it off and bury it in a hole in the rock (the Hebrew word means 'cliff') by the Euphrates, and thirdly to go and recover it. Each command is followed by a statement of the prophet's compliance. The third one adds the comment that the waistcloth was now good for nothing. Then comes the explanation communicated by Yahweh to the prophet, briefly in vv. 8f, at greater length in vv. 10f. Judah, called to intimacy with Yahweh, has defiled herself and will be cast away. The story is told in prose and in the first person.

The image represented by the waistcloth (*'ēzôr pištîm*) is reasonably clear. It is the most intimate of garments and it represents the position granted to Israel in the covenant. It was made of linen, unlike that of Elijah, which was made of leather (II Kings 1.8).[4] Some see in this a reference to Israel's priestly function on the grounds that linen was worn by priests, but it is more likely that linen is indicated because it was worn by the more affluent, and, of course, linen would decompose more quickly than tougher material.[5] It was to be a new waistcloth that had not been dipped in water, which is reminiscent of Ahijah's cloak. New garments had special qualities. The identification of the waistcloth with Israel is not, of course, obvious, but it is stated clearly in v. 11.

[4] It is possible that Elijah's waistcloth (*'ēzôr*) was a belt and not an undergarment. The range of meaning of the term cannot be fixed with certainty. In Jer. 13, however, an undergarment worn next to the skin fits the sense exactly.

[5] Hyatt ('Jeremiah' p. 923) and J.A. Thompson (*Jeremiah*, pp. 363f.) quote Lev. 16.4 as justification for the statement that priests wore linen, but in fact Ezek. 44.17f. is the only example of *pištîm* being used in this sense. Lev. 16.4 uses a quite different word.

For a long time commentators have been concerned about whether this drama ever took place. The old attitude, which goes back at least as far as Maimonides in the twelfth century, was that one should never attribute to prophets actions that were undignified or likely to make those who performed them into objects of ridicule. That objection is unsound. In the first place, there were no spectators to this action; in the second, suffering ridicule was sometimes the essence of prophecy. To wish onto prophets contemporary ideas, even twelfth-century ideas, of respectable behaviour is to do them a disservice.[6]

A more substantial difficulty concerns the four references in the narrative to the Euphrates. Almost every commentator points out that, as the text stands, Jeremiah is instructed to make two journeys from Judah to the Euphrates, each involving a round trip of many hundreds of miles, which would take several months. Such journeys are out of the question, but that does not mean that the drama must be reduced to a vision or an allegory or even a fabrication, nor that an unreported sojourn of Jeremiah in Babylon must be posited.

The first point to notice is that the primary meaning of the drama, that separation from Yahweh means destruction for Israel, is well expressed without any reference to a journey. The essential action is removing the waistcloth and throwing it away somewhere where it could later be found. How, then, was a journey introduced into the story? The answer given by most commentators, as in so many cases, is that a redactor introduced it. Over a century ago it was pointed out by W.F. Birch that references to the Euphrates ($p^er\bar{a}\underline{t}$) make no sense in this narrative. There are no cliffs in the southern stretch of that river where it flows through Babylon, and, when the Euphrates is mentioned in the Old Testament, the word 'river' almost always accompanies it. At the same time, there is a village three miles north east of Anathoth where there are cliffs in plenty. It is called $p\bar{a}r\hat{a}$ (see Josh. 18.23), and in the consonantal text, the difference between $p\bar{a}r\hat{a}$ and $p^er\bar{a}\underline{t}$ is very small indeed. It is extremely likely, therefore, that in the earliest version of the narrative, the Euphrates never appeared at all. A local place name did.[7] Then a later editor, conscious of the fact that Israel's turpitude had led her to exile in Babylon and struck by

[6] The matter is discussed at greater length in Chapter 15.

[7] Birch, 'Hiding-Places in Canaan I – Jeremiah's Girdle and Farah'. See also Bright, *Jeremiah*, p. 96; Paterson, 'Jeremiah', p. 547; J.A. Thompson, *Jeremiah*, pp. 364f.; Nicholson, *Jeremiah I*, p. 122; Davidson, *Jeremiah I*, p. 112; Holladay, *Jeremiah I*, p. 396, etc. The Greek version of Aquila reads εἰς Φαράν in Jer. 13. 4.

the fact that *pārâ* and *p^erāṯ* are almost the same word, had 'improved' the text to make sense, and as it now appears wrong sense, of a sign that originally had no reference to the exile.[8] Of course the sense is wrong only in terms of the original version; in terms of the editor's own day, it was the true meaning. If Birch and his followers are right, there is nothing inherently improbable about the performance of the drama in the first place, though we still need to explain why any place name occurs in the text.

This brings us to the important fact that there were no eyewitnesses. John Bright and others suppose that the sign was intended to convey a message and that, therefore, it had to be witnessed.[9] But this is to assume that the dramas had no other purpose than communication. The truth is more complex. The purpose of the drama was to give a potent, inescapable, but perhaps hidden reality another level of existence. This matter is further discussed in the final chapter. If the argument holds, the absence of spectators raises no problem. The purpose is to be sought in the reality of what it signifies, not in the perception of that reality by spectators. The drama exists for what it expresses, not, or at least not primarily, for communication.

The explanation, as it stands, speaks of a future spoliation of Judah (v. 9), her present disloyalty (v. 10), and her past privileges (v. 11), in that order. The narrative itself (vv. 1–7) simply indicates that a discarded waistcloth soon rots. There is no historical reference, not even an identification of the waistcloth with Judah. In v. 9 corruption, signified by the waistcloth, will be Judah's fate because of her pride, and this corruption will be brought about by a deliberate act of Yahweh. This is surely a thinly-veiled reference to the exile. Verses 10f. repeat this explanation and spell it out for any who have failed to grasp the point, though still without any precision about circumstances. The similarity between the latter part of v. 11 and Deut. 26.19 is unmistakable, which leads to the conclusion that a Deuteronomic editor is responsible for vv. 10f. Though the original story in vv. 1–7 does not imply any historical event, once the exile had taken place, or was even in prospect, the story would inevitably have been understood in terms of the exile. This is a factor we should have had

[8] Some commentators have argued, following a suggestion made by Rudolph, that the Euphrates is named deliberately to represent the area to the east from which came the influence that corrupted Israel. See Vawter, *The Conscience of Israel*, p. 46; Hyatt, 'Jeremiah', p. 921; J.A. Thompson, *Jeremiah*, p. 364.

[9] Bright, *Jeremiah*, p. 96.

to recognize, even if the name Euphrates had not been introduced into the text.

The recognition of a reference to the exile, however, creates a difficulty, because the introduction of the idea of historical punishment distorts the original meaning of the drama. In vv. 1–7 the waistcloth was removed while still new; it was hidden, and corruption followed as a consequence. It was not removed because it was rotten, as Israel presumably was. What Jeremiah originally demonstrates is that to be disowned by Yahweh is death for Israel. What the interpreters make of it is that Israel deserves to be disowned and will be punished in Babylon. In v. 9 Judah was already proud and stubborn before being discarded, and doom follows, not as an inevitable consequence but as a deliberate and extrinsic punishment. This is the logic of the exile, but it is not the logic of vv. 1–7. Moreover the exilic interpretation makes little sense of the third act of the drama, the finding of the waistcloth. If the pride had set in before the waistcloth was discarded, and if the corruption stood for such a patent agony as the exile, the detail of discovering the waistcloth later in a state of decomposition becomes otiose.

This calls in question not merely vv. 10f. but vv. 8f.; two points can be made against the separation of these verses from vv. 1–7. First, if vv. 8f. are detached, the story has no explicit explanation, which is strange in view of the fact that the divine commands and the account of the action are set out so clearly. Secondly, if a later editor was responsible for vv. 8f., it is surprising that he has not left clearer evidence of his work. There is nothing in v. 9 that points *directly* to the exile in Babylon. One way of dealing with this contradictory evidence is to suppose that vv. 1–9 represent the first literary version of the drama, and that this form follows some time after the original incident but precedes the final revision.

A new angle on the whole discussion appeared with an article by Charles Southwood in *Vetus Testamentum* in 1979.[10] Southwood's view was followed and elaborated by William Holladay in his massive work on Jeremiah.[11] Southwood argues that the crucial factor is the reason for hiding the waistcloth at 'Perath'. 'Perath', he thinks, must signify Babylon, but not the corrupting influence of Babylon (as Rudolph), nor the exile (as Weiser and others). It signifies the invading Babylonian

[10] 'The Spoiling of Jeremiah's Girdle (Jer. 13.1–11)'.

[11] *Jeremiah 1–25*; the second volume of this work is still awaited at the time of going to press.

army. The argument begins with the term 'hole in the rock'. The word for hole, $n^e q\hat{\imath} q$, occurs only here and in 16.16 and Isa. 7.19. In both these other contexts the people are hiding in holes in the rocks from enemies sent by Yahweh to humble them. Isa. 8.7f. and 2.6–22 are also brought into the argument, the former to show that a punishing enemy may be sent from 'the river' (i.e. Euphrates), the latter to expatiate on the moral force of the kind of disaster that drives people to hide among the rocks. Jer. 13.1–12a is thus 'a kind of midrash' (Holladay) on Isa. 2. Yahweh will humble Judah by means of the Babylonian army.

The virtues of this Southwood-Holladay argument are that it provides a possible explanation of the use of the place name, Perath, and a much better explanation of v. 9 than that of those who follow Rudolph. There are, however, strong arguments against it. In the first place, it is very elaborate. Most prophetic dramas, including those of Jeremiah, have a certain simplicity. Fohrer objects to double symbolism in the bare bones of prophetic drama. There is always, he says, a single, simple point.[12] The complexity comes always with the explanations introduced by editors who have had years to pore over the narratives and read meaning into them. Jeremiah's actions, breaking a pot, wearing a yoke, buying a field are straightforward and free from artifice. The one exception is 51.59–64, which may well not be by Jeremiah at all. It is hard to imagine that in this drama Jeremiah was consciously at work expounding two passages in Isaiah in such an oblique way. Secondly, as Southwood himself acknowledges, the hypothesis implies a basic ambiguity in the intepretation of the hiding-place. It is, at the same time, a representation of the apostasy of Judah, hiding from Yahweh for many days, and a representation of a physical hiding by the people from the Babylonian army. This ambiguity can be pressed still further. Israel deserts God and is disowned by him; corruption follows and it is represented by a dark hiding-place called Perath. Perath, however, indicates the place from which the army of judgment will come. This is not so much ambiguity as confusion. Thirdly, the force of the third command, to seek out the waistcloth and discover it to be rotten, remains unexplained.

Yet another explanation is advanced by R.P. Carroll in his commentary of 1986.[13] Carroll is not troubled by the association of prophetic

---

[12] *Die Handlungen*, pp. 87f.
[13] *Jeremiah*, p. 297.

dramas with magic and he sees a magical drama here. According to Carroll, Jeremiah marked out a symbolic Euphrates on the ground and paraded around in his waistcloth before a group of mystified spectators. He then buried the waistcloth in the 'river', waited some time, and then retrieved the garment to show the spectators that it was ruined. This is a dramatic enactment of the Babylonian exile. Carroll hesitates to say precisely what the magical force of the drama is. Perhaps Jeremiah was actually contributing to the great disaster that was to overtake Judah, but because of insufficient evidence Carroll leaves the matter open.[14] This is a highly imaginative and original hypothesis, but it cannot be allowed for at least three quite different reasons. In the first place, no spectators are mentioned in 13.1–11 and Carroll lays great stress on the spectators.[15] Secondly, a waistcloth takes time to rot. The text says that the recovery took place 'after many days'. If the whole drama took place on the same occasion – and one can hardly assume that Jeremiah assembled the same audience again several days or weeks later – the rotting must have been symbolic. This is not at all what the text says. Thirdly, as we have already argued, the reference to the exile belongs to a later period and is not to be attributed to Jeremiah himself. A fourth argument, that it is unfruitful to explain prophetic drama in terms of instrumental magic, will appear only after we have looked at the whole subject of the relation of these two phenomena. See below Chapters 16 and 17.

Let us return to the original incident and suggest another hypothesis. Let us assume that the place name Perath is not the crucial factor. The drama contains three instructions, all equally important. The third must not be overlooked. The discovery of the waistcloth is essential to the drama, for if there had been no discovery, there would have been no story at all. The waistcloth would simply have rotted and nobody would have known. Some explanations ignore the discovery (Southwood), some labour to interpret it as the return of the nation from exile – an unsatisfactory interpretation because a rotten waistcloth

---

[14] In an earlier book Carroll is less confident regarding this hypothesis. 'Reasonable but speculative' is how he describes it in *From Chaos to Covenant* (p. 131).

[15] It is important to know what kind of magic Carroll has in mind. Instrumental magic requires no audience. Indeed, some kinds of instrumental magic – especially anti-social sorcery – are essentially secret. Other forms of magical activity can be public and corporate. Carroll implies a magical act that also involves communication. There are problems of definition here, and also, of course, the hypothesis raises theological questions. See also Carroll's *When Prophecy Failed*, pp. 58–61.

can never be made good again. A simpler explanation lies to hand. It is that we are dealing with a real incident; the rediscovery is in the story, not because a certain meaning had to be expressed, but simply because it happened. Too many analyses go wrong because they put a large interpretative cart before the actual historical horse. This incident makes better sense if we see it as an actual experience of Jeremiah. In ch. 18 he saw a potter at work and related what he saw to Yahweh's dealings with Israel. Here he comes upon a rotten garment that, some time previously, he had thrown away. The experience leads to reflection, and so to the belief that this was a revelation, and so to an oracle. The burden of the revelation was that a waistcloth (Israel) belongs on the waist of a man (Yahweh). If for any reason it is removed and thrown away, it quickly becomes rotten. So powerful was the revelation to the prophet that it is easy to see how, in the course of time, he might have recounted the incident as something that was commanded. From this it is a short step to the present threefold narrative. The name Perath may have come into the story for any one of a number of reasons, perhaps, simplest of all, because that is where it actually happened. Once the name was there, extensive interpretation was bound to follow. This is purely hypothesis, but it does explain how a narrative that, at first sight looks odd, might have come about. As an explanation it would reassure even Maimonides. Thereafter, as the possibility of historical disaster became more and more obtrusive, the explanation given in vv. 8f would become more and more obvious. In the end, it could hardly be avoided, even though it distorted the original understanding.

If this is true, then this drama passed through at least four stages. First, there was the original incident with Jeremiah's reflection on it. Secondly, there was the formal account, set out carefully in three acts by Jeremiah or Baruch or one of Jeremiah's disciples. Thirdly, there was the version including the explanation in vv. 8f., which indicated a historical punishment and so changed the drama's meaning. Fourthly, there was the post-exilic version, including vv. 10f., in which further moralizing commentary was added and the word Euphrates was written in. Such a reconstruction, if granted, would demonstrate how important the dramas were to prophets and editors alike. They were more willing to give a dramatic incident an extraneous historical reference than to allow that it had none. In all probability the sense of the original incident was more theological than historical to Jeremiah, but the fact that a historical crisis intervened led the editors, and perhaps in time even Jeremiah himself, to understand the drama in terms of the coming disaster.

In conclusion, three comments can be made. In the first place, the fact that there were no spectators is of considerable importance. If the purpose of a drama is to aid communication, to perform the drama secretly and then to talk about it afterwards is the very worst way of handling it. Insisting on an audience, as Jeremiah does in 19.1–13, would make much better sense. We have evidence, therefore, to indicate that aiding communication is not the chief purpose of this drama. Secondly, if we take vv. 1–7 alone, the drama does not relate to the future but to the present. The rotten waistcloth epitomizes in a moment an eternal truth of Israel's existence. Absence from Yahweh equalled corruption. The time reference is not, therefore, forward, from a present drama to a future fulfilment, but outward, from a momentary dramatic experience to a permanent truth. Thirdly, it may well be that there is no deliberate action here at all. There does not have to be. The divine reality shows itself in all kinds of ways. Only when it is supposed that it must be the prophet who performs the creative action is it necessary to stress his positive activity. If, as is maintained here, it was supposed that the creative activity lay elsewhere and that the prophet was simply responding to it and expressing it, there is no need for us to insist that the action was performed in exactly the way that the literary version suggests.

Jeremiah Celibate: Jer. 16.1–4

It is clear from the study so far that a narrow definition of prophetic drama is not so much difficult as unprofitable. Complicated dramas can best be understood in relation to other prophetic acts and gestures and to cultic and conventional acts as well. Jeremiah's celibacy is not an obvious example of prophetic drama, and yet, in considering 16.1–9, it is impossible to ignore it.[16] The story is related in the first person. A word comes from Yahweh telling Jeremiah that he must have no wife or children, and a long explanation follows. There is no account of the drama taking place, but it is difficult to see how there could be. All three dramatic actions – or inactions – in 16.1–9 are similarly negative. In Jewish society Jeremiah's celibacy would be

---

[16] *Pace* Carroll, who contends that 'virtually all the necessary information to read the text in this way is absent from 16.1–9' (*Jeremiah*, p. 340).

almost as dramatic as Hosea's marriage, for celibacy was regarded as an unfortunate and unnatural condition. It involved the surrender of some of man's greatest blessings, the comfort and love of wife and children, the status of headship in the family, the security arising from progeny who would not only provide care in old age but also continue the name and the identity long into the future. The dramatic act, therefore, was deliberate, painful, public and permanent.

A difficulty lies with the explanation, and once again it is common to recognize the hand of the Deuteronomic editor with his knowledge of the actual fate of Judah and Jerusalem, but that does not help very much to unravel the meaning. The present text says that the offspring of contemporary marriages would die of awful diseases and lie unburied on the ground. One can understand celibacy as a prudential expedient in the circumstances, but how does it signify such a horrific fulfilment? Celibacy is not, on the face of it, an expression of general doom. If the drama looked towards an Israel full of lonely males, deprived of the love of wife and children, it would be understandable, but this is not what the explanation describes. Males and females would suffer the same fate.

There are various possible answers to the question. One is to persevere with the data and forge the best link possible between the drama and the reality. Holladay suggests that Jeremiah's lack of a wife signified the end of Yahweh's relationship with Israel, and as marriage meant children and the continuation of the line, the prophet's personal extinction signified the end of the people of God.[17] Theologically this is sound enough, but it is not a completely legitimate inference from the text. Verses 3f. do not speak so much of the end of the covenant relationship as of the violent deaths of large numbers of people.

A second answer derives from the literary structure of the whole passage, 16.1–9. If Jeremiah absented himself from the funeral rites of a kinsman, or if he rejected an invitation to a feast, his action would be public, precise and impressive; it might even cause a lasting scandal, but the refusal itself would be the work of a moment. It would also be a positive act. Remaining unmarried is not the work of a moment and it does not have the appearance of a positive act. Editing has, therefore, pressed upon Jeremiah's vocational asceticism the appearance of a significant action when in fact it was no such thing. There is nothing surprising in this. Often the drama is much sharper in the literary

---

[17] *Jeremiah 1–25*, p. 469.

form than in actual fact. The editor reckoned to see significance where the prophet saw none. As we argue below, the fact that the three actions in 16.1–9 are joined together and presented as parts of a literary whole does not mean that the original actions have to be taken as parallel. Despite the present canonical form, each may originally have had a meaning of its own. Three unusual facts about Jeremiah have been brought together in 16.1–9. Because vv. 5–7 and 8f. are easily recognizable as dramas, and because all three seem to require the same literary form, vv. 1–4 have been given the appearance of a narrative of dramatic action. This is the most likely explanation. It means that we do not know why Jeremiah was unmarried or even whether he regarded his celibacy as being a prophetic act. We only know how the editors handled the matter. So the condition of celibacy is related to the projected disaster more loosely and vaguely than is common with significant actions.

A third explanation, to a large extent consistent with the first, is that vv. 1–4 constitute a drama narrative in which the link between drama and reality is a matter of atmosphere rather than of direct representation. Celibacy is misery and deprivation, and misery and deprivation are prophesied for Israel in v. 4. If this is the true answer, we have here an example of a drama that is by no means completely mimetic, but that is not arbitrary either. There is a broad spectrum in drama narratives in this regard. At one end of the scale there is the completely mimetic action; at the other end the arbitrary drama, where one thing stands for another simply because the formula says so. This narrative is closer to the former pole.

Fourthly, it is possible that, as in Jer. 13, the explanation has been adjusted to make the significance of the action consistent with what actually happened. The drama might originally have had some other meaning, but the author of v. 4 could think of nothing but the fall of Jerusalem. So a drama that had to do with deprivation of some other kind was brought into service to relate to the awful event. It is difficult to be certain about any of this. The true explanation may involve elements of all four suggestions. The one that cannot be overlooked is the second, because the editorial contribution is so obvious in these verses.

Jeremiah forbidden to mourn: Jer. 16.5–7

Jeremiah's abstinence from mourning rites is not quite as problematic as his celibacy, but there are difficulties. Abstinence from mourning is a deliberate, public, unsocial form of behaviour, and it appears to be undertaken in response to a divine command. The literary form is exactly as in vv. 1–4, a command followed by an explanation. There is more evidence of editing, for the last part of v. 5 and the first half of v. 6 are missing from the LXX. Verse 6 is reminiscent of v. 4 and might be an addition from after the fall of Jerusalem. The reason given for the abstinence is, 'I have taken away my peace from my people.'

Once again we encounter the phenomenon of a simple narrative that has been considerably extended as far as explanation is concerned. Verse 5, even in the shortened LXX version, is a complete and coherent story by itself. Jeremiah is told to take no part in mourning rites because Yahweh has taken away *šālôm* from his people. Regardless of what was to come, the *šālôm* of Israel had already been fractured. There is, therefore, a present aspect of this drama. *Šālôm* belongs to an ordered and stable society in which everything is done according to custom. If traditional customs break down, security is gone.[18] In this case Jeremiah's action reveals a condition that, by Yahweh's word, is already in being, though not recognized by all. Yahweh has acted, security has disappeared, and Jeremiah's actions proclaim that fact. On this understanding vv. 6f are best understood as later additions by one who had seen it all happen and wanted to belabour the point.

It is possible, however, to understand 'I have taken' in v. 5 as a prophetic perfect referring to a disruption that is still to come. In that case vv. 6f describe the condition after *šālôm* is lost, when many will die without being mourned and many mourners will lack the solace of decent ritual and common sympathy. Jeremiah represents all who would wish to mourn properly but will not be able to do so. The scandalized reaction of those who observed Jeremiah's behaviour becomes part of the drama too, for their sense of outrage prefigures

---

[18] Extravagant funeral rites which involved self-laceration and shaving the head are forbidden in Deut. 14.1 and Lev. 19.28. That did not mean that they did not happen, and several references show that shaving the head, at least, was common (Isa. 22.12; Micah 1.16; Ezek. 7.18). Verse 6 implies that such practices had become so normal that their cessation would imply complete social breakdown. For the importance of proper burial and mourning rites, see de Vaux, *Ancient Israel*, p. 56 and Jacob, 'Mourning', p. 452; and see Deut. 26.14; II Sam. 1.12; 3.35; 12.16f.; Hos. 9.4; and Ezek. 24.17.

the shock that will come upon Israel when these solemn duties have to be abandoned altogether.

It is probably unnecessary to choose between the present and the future interpretations of this drama, for both are important. If the former aspect is stressed, the action in v. 5 has contemporary reference and a kind of revelatory significance. Jeremiah is dramatizing a state of affairs that already exists, but, as yet, not undeniably so. In the latter case, the drama looks to the future and, whatever its date, fulfilment in the fall of Jerusalem was not far away.

Jeremiah forbidden to feast: Jer. 16.8f.

The first point is a literary one. The three actions, or non-actions, described in 16.1–9 could only have become apparent to observers after a considerable length of time. Even if conviction on all three counts came to Jeremiah in a moment, he could express it only by extended abstinence and repeated refusals to follow the social norm. No doubt other prophetic activity took place within the period. In the literary expression, however, the three signs are drawn together and presented as a whole. This is seen in the similarity of content in all three, the similarity of literary form, and the fact that the third is dependent on the second for its introductory formula.[19] This leads to the supposition that all three, and especially the second and third, speak with a single voice. On the literary level they undoubtedly do – note the similarity between v. 4 and v. 6 – but it is legitimate to infer differences on the historical level. As they now stand, the commands in v. 5a and v. 8 are closely related; and as v. 8 is explained in terms of a future fulfilment, we are led to suppose that v. 5 must be the same. 'There will be no time for mourning, and there will be no reason for rejoicing.'[20] This, however, is true only on the literary level. An understanding of the action described in v. 5 that is quite different from the one described in v. 8 is not excluded.

It is worth noting in passing that the order of these three incidents is odd in that they proceed from the greater to the less. Anyone with minimal insight might stay away from feasts on the grounds that it was no time for rejoicing. Staying away from funerals is a much more complex and profound action. Undoubtedly it would be misunder-

[19] J.A. Thompson argues that the literary form was the work of Jeremiah himself (*Jeremiah*, p. 407).

[20] Freehof, *Jeremiah*, p. 112.

stood and cause pain. Rejecting marriage is even more serious in that it involves permanent self-negation and, almost certainly, permanent isolation.

Little more needs to be said about the third sign in the catena. The prophet must deny himself all forms of celebration. The phrase 'house of feasting' suggests social festivities in the home, especially marriage, rather than sacrificial feasting. Lonely and miserable, Jeremiah is to represent in himself the woes of the Israelites of the future. Notions of solidarity cannot be avoided here. Jeremiah often protested his own deep involvement in Israel's fate (11.14; 17.16; 18.20; 28.5f.) The pain of his ministry was, to a large extent, due to his conviction that disaster was inevitable. He sees himself as the one on whose head the future sorrows break, the one through whom the coming agony first shows itself in history.

It is difficult to avoid the conclusion that Jeremiah's behaviour in these three actions ran counter to his natural inclinations. The sense of submission to Yahweh's will is very strong. This reveals a point at which Jeremiah's dramatic actions are to be distinguished, not only from instrumental magic, but also from the activities of some of the earlier prophets, particularly Elisha.

The Potter: Jer. 18.1–12

Few commentators include this narrative in their lists of prophetic dramas. Van den Born is an exception. Fohrer refuses to do so on the grounds that the prophet does not act but simply observes, and this despite the fact that the narrative provides a perfect example of the literary form that Fohrer has defined.[21] To affirm that a drama must be an action that issues from the prophet is mistaken, for it leads to the inference that the prophet provides some creative force. In fact the evidence shows that, while in some cases drama and reality are linked in what looks like a simple, linear and causal relationship, as an overall explanation, that notion is all too simple. Sometimes it is more illuminating to conceive of the creative force flowing the other way, that is to say, to see the reality giving rise to the drama. In this instance the reality is God's sovereign power over Israel, and this reality forces itself upon Jeremiah's attention by means of a very mundane happening. There is nothing dynamic about the potter save

[21] Fohrer, *Die Handlungen*, p. 72.

in the small world of his pottery. There is nothing dynamic about Jeremiah's reflection on what he sees. The dynamic comes from the reality which communicates itself to Jeremiah by this simple means.[22]

In one sense Jeremiah's visit to the potter is not different from his experience with the waistcloth; it is simply something that happened to him by chance, as it were. The story is told in the first person. Jeremiah is instructed to go down to the potter's house where he will hear Yahweh's words. He goes and sees the potter at work. When the vessel fails to turn out as it should, the potter simply works it again into some other shape. Then an explanatory word comes to Jeremiah likening the potter to Yahweh and the clay to Israel. We need to remind ourselves of I Sam. 15.27f. and II Kings 13.18f., where persons other than the prophet carried out the critical action, and Jer. 13.1–11, where in all probability natural decay prompted the prophetic understanding.

The narrative contains an instruction from Yahweh, an account of Jeremiah doing what he is instructed to do, and a lengthy explanation. As usual it is with the explanation that the textual difficulties arise. Verses 5f. contain a simple explanation to the effect that God can deal with Israel as a potter deals with clay.[23]

Some commentators press the point of the drama too hard and ask why clay is marred in the hand of a potter. They conclude that it must be because of impurity in the clay. The failure of the potter's first attempt is thus due to the clay. If Israel is broken and re-formed, it is because of her own wickedness.[24] This interpretation shows a lively imagination, but it is illegitimate for two reasons. In the first place, there is nothing in the text to justify it. The phrase used simply indicates that the attempt went wrong and the vessel was spoiled; it was not that the clay proved impure. In the second, the inference does not fit the drama. If there are impurities in clay, the potter simply cannot start again; he must throw that clay away and take some more.

---

[22] If one takes too narrow a view of dramatic action, this point will be overlooked – as it commonly is. Not so with William Holladay's recent commentary. See especially *Jeremiah 1–25*, pp. 398f.

[23] The image of the potter also occurs in Isa. 29.16; 45.9; 64.8 and Rom. 9.19–24. In each case the force of the image is that God, the potter, is all-powerful; the clay has no say in the matter.

[24] Some commentators (Boadt, Bright, Blackwood) suggest that, if clay proves impure, the potter may choose to make a different, less delicate vessel out of it, but this is surely to read into the text of Jeremiah a notion derived from Rom. 9.21.

This line of interpretation is squeezing too much out of the drama. The sole point of vv. 1–6 is that the potter can do what he likes; the clay is simply acted upon.

When we come to vv. 7–12, we find that they contain a complicated example of the Deuteronomic pattern of history. If God plans evil against a nation and it repents, all will be well; but if he plans good and it rebels, all will be ill. Judah must be warned that God intends evil and only repentance will halt it. Such an oracle goes far beyond the implication of the drama and it bears all the marks of editorial revision. The potter has simply become the starting-point. The drama itself does not call for repentance; it does not put a choice upon Israel. It simply makes a statement about the relationship between Yahweh and Israel, a statement that differs from the thrust of vv. 7–12 in one important respect. In vv. 1–6 the stress is on Yahweh's power over Israel, and this includes the power to reshape her if she is spoiled, which, from one point of view, is good news, though not quite such good news as some suggest, for the rebirth follows only after destruction.[25] In vv. 7–12, however, the stress is on Israel's responsibility to choose the right way, which is really a contradiction of the drama in which the potter is all-powerful and the clay has no responsibility. Note too that in vv. 7–12 the image of potter and clay is forgotten save for the use of the verb *yāṣar*, shape or form, in v. 11. So we have to think of four stages in the history of this drama, the sense of compulsion experienced by the prophet, the observation in the potter's house, the theological reflection leading to the formal account in vv. 1–6, and the final stage when the Deuteronomic commentary was added.

The original drama was not primarily concerned with the future but with the eternal reality of God's relationship to Israel. The final version is concerned with the future and it introduces a very important idea. The future is not fixed and determined; no matter what the potter did with the clay, repentance can avert God's wrath. Nothing more is needed to demonstrate that, as far as the Deuteronomic editor was concerned, the drama itself was not creative and certainly not instrumentally effective. It was expressive; it revealed the true relationship between Yahweh and Israel; the consequences of that relationship

---

[25] 'Omitting the homily (i.e. vv. 7–10) makes a difference in interpretation. Without it, the parable is a blaze of hope' (Blackwood, *Jeremiah* p. 152).

would vary according to Israel's behaviour, not according to anything that the potter did.

This passage shows how necessary it is to look at a text both in terms of its literary history and its finished canonical situation. If the question is, 'How did the Hebrews understand prophetic drama?' two different answers are given here. If the text is seen in isolation, the potter's action is determinative. Yahweh can and will make of Israel what he chooses, whether Israel co-operates or not. If the text is seen in its canonical position, the potter's action is understood against a wide background of history and theology that taught a more complex lesson. Yahweh will make of Israel whatever is appropriate to her moral condition. Both answers are important for biblical theology, but, more to the point, both are important for the question of how prophetic drama was understood. Verses 1–6 appear to deal with the drama and nothing else. The editor responsible for vv. 7–12 drew his net more widely and reinterpreted the incident. The concerns of both the prophet and the editor have to be taken seriously.

Jeremiah's Earthen Flask: Jer. 19.1–13

No one doubts that Jer. 19 records a prophetic drama, though the present text is probably very different from the first version. A brief drama narrative has been greatly extended by the insertion of some rather prosaic oracular material. Jeremiah is told to buy an earthen flask and go with the elders and senior priests to the Potsherd Gate, there to smash the pot and to declaim, 'So will I break this people and this city.' On his return he may well have repeated the oracle of doom (vv. 14f.), for very soon he found himself in the stocks (20.2).

The basic story is found in vv. 1f., 10 and 11a. Verses 3–9 and 11b–13 constitute a Deuteronomic commentary on the story raising new issues and pressing different points. The concern of the commentary is the idolatry practised at Topheth. The passage joins badly onto v. 2 which needs to be followed by the action in v. 10 and only subsequently by an oracle. The intruding verses are addressed to the kings of Judah and largely repeat 7.30–34. Topheth will become a place of slaughter and Jerusalem a city of horror. Details in vv. 7 and 9 suggest not prophecies but reminiscences of the siege. There is no need to take this issue further because, unlike some other additions, the verses under discussion do not contribute anything to the understanding of prophetic drama.[26]

Even when the original drama narrative is isolated, its literary form is curious. It consists entirely of instruction. The command incorporates an explanation in the words that must be uttered as the pot was broken, but there is no explanation that stands on its own; and there is no account of the action actually taking place. That it did take place, however, need not be doubted. The consequences make that clear.

There are a number of significant details. Jeremiah had to take elders and priests with him, which suggests that communication is a primary object, but that is not the whole truth. Certainly one function of the elders was to be to be reliable witnesses, but, as in Isa. 8.1–4, the onlookers were also part of the drama. Their shocked horror when they see a flask, just purchased, broken in pieces prefigures the horror of those who will see the city fall. The reference to the valley of the son of Hinnom is difficult. When two place names – the valley and the Potsherd Gate – are mentioned for the same incident, it is right to be suspicious, and, in this case, where the two are not quite the same place and the former, the valley of the son of Hinnom, harmonizes rather too well with the secondary material, one is bound to conclude that the reference to the valley has been inserted.[27] Breaking the flask must have been one of the clearest dramatic acts that Jeremiah ever performed. As a method of execration, breaking earthenware artefacts had a long history, and no one would have been left in any doubt about Jeremiah's meaning.[28] Even in the shortest version of the story, there is a formula to identify the pot with Jerusalem. Not only was the meaning clear, but the significance of the act was not doubted either. From the opposition that followed, it is evident that the onlookers

---

[26] As is to be expected, Holladay argues that it is necessary, not simply to take vv. 1–13 together, but to treat ch. 19 with ch. 20. This is consistent with the wish of many modern commentators to treat the text in its canonical form. We can only repeat what was said in relation to 18.1–12. The finished text is important because it reveals how prophetic dramas were understood in Hebrew tradition. But equally, the original event and the original narrative reveal how the prophet himself and how his disciples understood them. Problems arise only if one or the other is neglected, or if someone tries to argue that the finished text was also the original form.

[27] The LXX also has difficulty with this name. The majority of MSS refer to an assembly place 'of the sons of their children', a very odd name and one requiring a Hebrew reading, $b^e n\hat{e}\ b^e n\hat{e}hem$, rather than $ben\ hinn\bar{o}m$.

28 Pritchard, *ANET*, pp. 328f.; Fohrer, *Die Handlungen*, pp. 13, 39f.

took the action seriously. Because the flask had been broken, the city was at risk and the population trembled. That is not to say that breaking the flask caused the fall of the city, but simply that the two go together. Yahweh caused the fall of the city; he also required the breaking of the flask so that the danger might be known. Communication is an important element here, though it is not the only element.

The precise function of the flask in the incident is uncertain. There appears to be nothing special about it. When it is broken, the pieces lie on the ground and are not heard of again. The force of the incident is to be found in the action itself, not in the flask as a material object. Sometimes, as with new cloaks and waistcloths, the quality of the object does seem to contribute something to the action, but not apparently here. It is not clear whether the purchase in v. 1 is to ensure that the pot was new or simply that a suitable, and presumably valuable, pot should be available. This indicates another variable in the field being investigated. Some dramas involve special objects, some ordinary objects, and some no objects at all.

The meaning of the drama requires no further comment, nor is there any doubt about the fact of its fulfilment. Nor can there be any doubt that Jeremiah felt himself to be under strong constraint. The message here is even bleaker than usual, for the formula ends, 'so that it can never be mended' (v. 11). This contradicts the message of the Anathoth drama of ch.32 which envisages a restoration, but this creates no real problem. These two dramas were representing different aspects of the same reality. With every calamity one may truly say, 'Things will never be the same again,' but this is not to deny the possibility of recovery. Moreover, the prophet was too passionately committed to his word to be concerned about the dangers of exaggeration. He was representing a divine intention which, in certain circumstances, would come about; and he did it with vigour. He did not, however, think that he was encompassing the end himself.

The Cup of Wrath: Jer. 25.15-29

This passage presents us with a problem. It has the appearance of a dramatic act but it cannot have taken place. Jeremiah is told to take a cup from Yahweh's hand and carry it round the nations of the Near East. The cup signifies divine fury and the nations that drink from it will stagger. Then comes a second command to deliver to the nations a particular oracle. The obvious question is: if the drama takes place purely in the imagination, why record it at all, for the full sense is carried in the oracle? The answer is that this narrative illustrates a further realm of manifestation for a divine intention. The idea of God manifesting his will in history is familiar; the idea that the historical reality is manifested in the prophetic oracle before it happens is also familiar; and the idea that the historical is recalled and preserved in cultic action is familiar. The true question is whether any limits can be set to these reverberations and extensions of the divine act. The evidence suggests that the prophets thought not. They were aware that the divine event stimulated their speech and activity so that it 'happened' in their speech and their dramas, but it also 'happened' in their minds.[29]

For the prophets it was hardly possible to distinguish between the various ways in which the divine will expressed itself. So we have oracles, dramas, visions, reflections, all centred in the divine will. It is true that all these were eventually expressed in written words – otherwise we should not know anything about them – but the prophets do not speak or act as if the written record was the critical one. They are aware of the divine reality in the mind as well as in the word. It is doubtful, therefore, whether the spoken word and the acted drama were, to Jeremiah, essentially different from the mental image. They had no significance in themselves; they all owed their existence to a divine reality of which they were the manifestations. From one point of view there is all the difference in the world between a subjective experience and a public act, but that point of view is not the prophetic one. If both were caused by a greater reality, it was of little importance whether one had its existence in the mind and the other in the market-place. This is the justification for including this passage in a series of prophetic dramas.[30]

The literary structure poses enormous difficulties. After the command, there is an explanation to the effect that the crazy staggering

[29] Here is a true story. Two inmates of Bergen-Belsen, one a professional cook, lay in their bunks allaying their hunger by exchanging recipes. The next morning the professional said to the other, 'Your recipe is wrong; I cooked it in the night and it did not work.' It proved that a vital step in the process had been overlooked. Imagination was quite sufficient to establish the point for the professional cook. In some cases the difference between imagination and objective reality is crucial; in others it is not.

[30] Cf. William Holladay in *Jeremiah 1–25*, p. 395, with reference to Jer. 13, 'It is an open question whether theologically there is a difference between an inner vision through which Yahweh reveals himself and an outer action through which he likewise reveals himself.'

of those who drink will represent the fate that will soon be theirs. Then comes the statement that Jeremiah did as he was told. Then follows a list, nine verses long, of the nations to which Jeremiah went. Then, in v. 27, Yahweh speaks again, this time in the first person without introduction, repeating the command and the explanation even more vigorously. It is unfortunate that the difficulties preclude any reconstruction of a simple and original version. Verses 15f. would almost certainly belong to it, possibly v. 17, possibly, though less likely, v. 27. The rest almost certainly would not. We can be reasonably sure that Jeremiah had a blinding vision of the leaders of certain nations staggering crazily as they drank the cup of Yahweh's wrath. In a situation where fermentation could not be measured or controlled, results could be very unpredictable; some brews could be feeble, some fiery, some perfect, and some almost poisonous. It is not difficult, therefore, to see how wine could be regarded at the same time as the cup of blessing and the cup of wrath.[31]

The reality to which the drama is directed is not a single historical occasion. There is no occasion on which all the nations experience Yahweh's wrath at the same time. Somewhat like the incident of the potter, this drama represents a telescoping of historical crises, a bringing together of a dozen disasters in order to represent the true state of affairs. Yahweh controls the nations; he brings punishment upon them; they stagger and fall. That is the permanent reality, albeit a theological one, that the drama represents.

Two further points need to be noticed, both derived from the commentary rather than the dramatic musing itself. First, the list of nations begins with Israel's traditional enemies, Egypt, Philistia, Edom, Ammon, Moab, but continues with those further afield, even including some that are very obscure.[32] The force of this is clearly that

[31] The drama itself reproduces a familiar theme. The cup of Yahweh's wrath appears in Pss. 60.3 and 75.8 (cf. Job 21.20; Hab. 2.16; Lam. 4.21; Isa. 51.17–23; Ezek. 23.32f.). Many commentators refer at this point to the trial procedure in Num. 5 which involved drinking dirty water. Here, however, we have a cup of wine. William McKane examines the themes of intoxication, poison, and trial by ordeal. All contribute something to this narrative, but McKane concludes that the dominant theme is trial by ordeal taking place at some grotesque, imagined, anti-banquet. See 'Poison, Trial by Ordeal and the Cup of Wrath'.

[32] Babylon herself is included under the code name šēšak in v. 26. The code is the simple one of reversing the alphabet. B, b, and l are the second, second and twelfth letters of the alphabet. If these same numbers are counted from the end, they become, s, s, and k. This points to a date when it was not politic to speak publicly of Babylon's doom.

Yahweh controls all nations that are, all the time. Secondly, according to vv. 18 and 29, Judah and Jerusalem are included in the list. The final text, therefore, assures us that election does not mean exemption for the people of God but that they would be first in coming under judgment.

The Yokes: Jer. 27–28

Reference has already been made to this drama and its possible relationship with I Kings 22. The textual difficulties are again severe, though it is relatively easy to distinguish what form the drama took. As in most cases, secondary elaboration comes with the explanation. Jer. 27.1 is a curious introduction. It is a third-person addition to a first-person narrative, plainly incorrect, and missing from the LXX.[33] The Hebrew word for 'yoke' is a plural, due, no doubt, to the fact that a yoke consisted of three bars joined together; the reference in v. 2, therefore, is to one yoke, not several (as AV and RV). Following the LXX we should delete the suffix from the verb 'send', leaving the verb without an object.[34] This clarifies the action, which consists in the prophet wearing a yoke, not in his sending yokes round to neighbouring monarchs. To them he simply sends a message. The message, a rather rambling affair contained in vv. 4–11, gives an explanation of the wearing of the yoke. Everything down to v. 11 is stated in the form of an instruction from Yahweh. In v. 12 the format changes and Jeremiah gives a first-person account of two further addresses that he made with reference to the yoke, one to the king (vv. 12–15) and one to priests and people (vv. 16–22). There is no account of him actually making the yoke, but he must have done so because of Hananiah's action in the next chapter.

The year is 594/3 BCE. Neighbouring kings have sent envoys to the court of Zedekiah, the puppet king set up by the Babylonians, to discuss the possibility of rebellion against the common overlord. Patriotic spirit is abroad. The prophets were already hard at work, if we can trust vv. 9 and 14–6. A similar circumstance pertained in I Kings 22 when Jehoshaphat had come to Samaria to discuss a campaign against Syria, and when the prophet Zedekiah had made

[33] Most Hebrew MSS read 'Jehoiakim' in 27.1, although the narrative relates to the reign of Zedekiah.

[34] The RSV 'send word' is an overtranslation of the Hebrew, which, with the suffix, reads, 'send them'.

his horns.[35] In Jer. 27 there is no reference to a cultic performance, although vv. 16–22 are addressed to priests and others concerned with temple affairs. Presumably Jeremiah was to appear before the envoys wearing his apparatus and telling them that they must all suffer Babylon's yoke, because Yahweh had decreed it. The yoke is a symbol of submission and no long oracle was necessary to make the point. On the primary level, therefore, the sign represents the submission that Yahweh had decreed and that was already being expressed increasingly in harsh political reality. Submission to Babylon did not necessarily mean the sack of Jerusalem.

It is difficult now to determine where the explanation belonging to the original drama is to be found, though the sense of it is probably preserved in vv. 6f., now part of the address to the envoys. It is, as one would expect, very general. The full text of the addresses to the envoys, to Zedekiah, and to the priests provides more explicit information. At this point the LXX is more economical, so we may suspect some elaboration. The points made in the first two speeches are: (i) it is Yahweh's will that Nebuchadnezzar is to be master for the time being; (ii) the hopeful prophets, who urge resistance to Babylon, are all in total error; this point is made with great emphasis in all three speeches, indeed, it might be said that this idea dominates all three speeches; (iii) those who reconcile themselves to Yahweh's will may hope to live in reasonable comfort under Babylon's yoke, and in their own land, according to the first speech; and (iv) those who believe the hopeful prophets and resist will suffer sword, famine and pestilence as a divine punishment. The third speech repeats the first three points, but misses out the sword, famine and pestilence in favour of a prophecy that all the remaining holy treasure will be taken to Babylon. The Hebrew text concludes with an assurance that it will one day be brought back, but the LXX has no such assurance.

Beside this we must consider what actually happened: (i) Babylon gained the ascendancy until the arrival of Cyrus; (ii) Hananiah and his supporters, who affirmed that Babylon would be defeated, were proved totally wrong; (iii) Jehoiachin, who had submitted to Babylon,

---

[35] It is interesting, and perhaps not coincidental, that the two artefacts would look much the same. Two uprights, bound together with a cross-piece at one end, would suffice for both. Zedekiah wore them pointing upwards for horns; Jeremiah wore them pointing downwards for a yoke. If, as I have suggested in 'A Pre-battle Rite', horns figured in warlike, patriotic ceremonies, Jeremiah's dramatic symbolism would be all the more telling – and offensive.

eventually lived in relative comfort, though not for a long time and not in his own land (II Kings 25.27–30).[36]; (iv) Zedekiah, who refused to submit, brought siege, famine and total ruin on Jerusalem, and a gruesome fate on himself (II Kings 24.20; 25.1–7).[37] The bronze pillars and holy vessels were carried off to Babylon (II Kings 24.13ff.) from whence, according to Ezra 1.5–11 and 7.19, they were eventually brought back. The correspondence between the speeches and the facts is almost complete. The one point where the speeches seem to fail is in the promise that those who submit will survive in their own land. This point, of course, was never tested; Zedekiah did not submit and Jerusalem was sacked.

This makes plain the problem that Jeremiah's editors faced. The prophet had manifested a divine intention that was punitive but not utterly devastating. The future, however, had not unfolded entirely according to this plan, because the general folly, promoted by lying prophets, had frustrated it. Something had to be done, therefore, to link Jeremiah's dramatic action, ignored as it was, with the subsequent course of events. Those who edited the speeches adopt two devices to achieve this end. In the first place they treat the drama, not as an unveiling of the future, but as an indication of what Yahweh *willed* Israel to do, and as a representation of how faithful, wise and compliant Israelites should behave. So it becomes ground for exhortation rather than an indication of what will happen. Secondly, an alternative fate is devised to show that Yahweh will not be frustrated. Submission is Yahweh's will, but if submission is resisted, then sword and famine and pestilence are the alternative. In this way the drama is preserved as a significant action, closely related to the subsequent course of history, but not as an unveiling of the future in the simple sense. How much of this divergent interpretation was contributed by Jeremiah himself and how much by editors of a later day it is impossible to tell.

[36] Pritchard's *ANET* provides a few scraps of evidence in the form of tablets listing supplies provided for Jehoiachin and his household in Babylon (pp. 308; see also D. Winton Thomas, *Documents from Old Testament Times*, pp. 84–6).

[37] Looking back at the period from a distance, it may appear that Israel did submit tamely to Nebuchadnezzar. Amsler maintains that Israel's quiescence is proof that Jeremiah's spectacular intervention was effective (*Les Actes*, p. 66). But those who lived through the decade 597–586 BCE would doubtless tell a different story. See, for example, the situation described in the Lachish ostraca (*ANET*, pp. 321f.) and also Jer. 34. 6f. and 38. 1–6.

We have to assume that the present text has been thoroughly worked over.[38]

The difference between the original implication of the drama and the interpretation found in the speeches must not be exaggerated. Wearing a yoke can represent being conquered. The difference is that Jeremiah believed the submission should be voluntary, and in fact it was enforced. Nevertheless two points of interest arise from the way in which the incident is handled. In the first place, there can be no question of instrumental efficacy in relation to this drama, either in the original incident or in the later interpretation. The fact that the interpreters are able to treat the drama as prescriptive, that is, as a recommendation that was not accepted, shows that no such notion was present to their minds any more than to Jeremiah's. Secondly, the interpreters regarded themselves as having considerable freedom in how they went about their task. There was no closely defined system whereby they were supposed to work. They inferred meaning as best they could, and later generations accepted their word. In short, when the drama, which was undoubtedly an unveiling of what God *intended* for Israel, proved to be only partially fulfilled in fact, a more complex understanding was devised; it involved rendering the drama as an exhortation to make one future possible rather than as a revelation of a future that was bound to be. This has an important bearing on the understanding of the dramas. Normally we have the series, God's will/prophetic drama/historical reality. Here we have the shorter series, God's will/prophetic drama and no historical reality. To the interpreter, however, this shortened series was just as much an event as the normal longer one. The crucial factor in the whole concept is not what actually happened but what Yahweh wills to be.

Chapter 28 is an account in the third person, after v. 1, of how Hananiah attempted to counter Jeremiah's action.[39] It begins with a date, still not entirely clear, but comprehensible. It is the fourth year of Zedekiah's reign – the LXX (35.1) has it right – and the year that Psammetichus II came to the Egyptian throne. Jeremiah and Hananiah confront each other in the temple in the presence of the priests and the people. It may have been a formal ceremony. Hananiah begins with an oracle deliberately phrased to counter the effect of the yoke

[38] Carroll regards the whole cycle of chs. 27–29 as a literary creation rather than history. He further argues that 28 is a variant of 27.16–22.

[39] 28. 1 actually begins the narrative in the first person, but, in accordance with vv. 5ff., 'to me' is probably an error or an abbreviation of 'to Jeremiah'.

that Jeremiah was wearing. Within two years the yoke of Babylon would be broken and the wealth of the temple restored. Verse 4 speaks of the restoration of Jeconiah (Jehoiachin), the son of Jehoiakim, as the rightful king of Judah, but presumably such a statement would have been treasonable, and unlikely to be found on the lips of a compliant prophet. Jeremiah replies that he would agree if he could, but honest prophecy is often full of foreboding. The yoke represents Yahweh's will.

What is emerging is a kind of prophetic contest. Both prophets are claiming to represent a divine reality, the reality that is to be.[40] They disagreed, so one of them was wrong. But which one? Doubtless in critical situations prophets often disagreed; but before the nation could act, there had to be unanimity – not so much because unity is strength, but because the nation needed the assurance that they were pursuing the divine intention; they needed to know that God was on their side. This explains the performance in I Kings 22 which may well be repeated here. The prophets come together and set to work to see which way the word runs. Before long one party outdoes the others in enthusiasm and a unified fervour takes over. The dissidents either surrender or disappear. What is and what is to be stands revealed. Bearing in mind that many prophets were royal time-servers, the dissidents were not likely to have been numerous or persistent. This explanation fits I Kings 22, where Jehoshaphat showed himself afraid that the emerging fervour was bogus and premature. It fits Jer. 28 equally well. Jeremiah begins the process with his yoke sign. Hananiah, baldly described as a false prophet in the LXX, counters with an

[40] The matter is, of course, treated quite differently by sociologists who look for reasons for prophetic conflict which satisfy the modern observer. Our concern is not with modern explanations, however sound, but with ancient explanations, whether true or false. Robert Wilson has worked out a contrast between Jeremiah and Hananiah using sociological methods (*Sociological Approaches*, pp. 77–80). Jeremiah was from the priestly family at Anathoth (Jer. 1.1; cf. I Kings 2.26f.); he was the upholder of the Deuteronomistic theological traditions; he was a prophet 'like unto me' (Moses), who speaks God's words directly (Deut. 18.9–22; cf. Jer. 1.4–10); but he was an outsider to the Jerusalem establishment. Hananiah was versed in the royal theology of Zion; he had a place at court; he was part of the religious establishment. But, according to Jeremiah's accusation, he did not stand in God's council, he concocted his oracles out of visions and dreams of his own making (Jer. 23.15–32). However, B.O. Long, using a similar approach, comes to a quite different conclusion in 'Social Dimensions'. See also H. Mottu, 'Jeremiah vs. Hananiah' and R.P. Carroll, *When Prophecy Failed*, pp. 184–98. The whole subject has been well treated by James Crenshaw in *Prophetic Conflict*.

oracle affirming, in the name of Yahweh, that Babylon is finished. Jeremiah replies by casting doubt on Hananiah's integrity. Hananiah then takes the yoke and breaks it. It is important that he does not ignore the yoke or mock it. He accepts it as a sign of Babylonian dominance and uses it to produce a counter-sign. Babylon's power would be broken. He adds an explanatory oracle, and Jeremiah, momentarily nonplussed, goes his way.[41] It is worth pointing out that Hananiah is not exhorting the nation to break Babylon's yoke, but announcing that it will be broken.

Hananiah's action is described in the same way as normal prophetic dramas. There is an account of the action and a brief oracle explaining its force. There is, of course, no instruction from Yahweh, for, by the time the passage was edited, the whole truth was known; but the form is still recognizable. Hananiah's dramatic action in breaking the yoke, like Zedekiah's in wearing horns, was not fulfilled, but it is still a good example of the genre. The narrative shows clearly how dramatic actions relating to the future are to be understood. The prophet is not causing things to happen; he is striving to express what is to be. His action may have been demanded by Yahweh, in which case it is an essential part of the total reality of the event; or the prophet may be false, in which case he is expressing nothing at all. Everyone would have been in broad agreement that this was the case, though Hananiah and no doubt many of the populace would have expressed it more crudely than would Jeremiah. The question was which prophet was in touch with Yahweh and the true event, and which was not. This was always the problem with prophecy: at the material time, there was no empirical difference between the true and the false. It was so much easier for the editors. They knew not only of the competing dramatic actions but of the actual reality, and they could edit accordingly.

Jeremiah came back some days later to speak of a counter-counter-drama, a yoke that no one can break. Whether he made such a yoke,

[41] Many commentators remark on the pause between the first round, which Jeremiah is supposed to have lost, and the second round, when he returns with an even harsher oracle. Overholt explains this in terms of his hypothesis that the audience has a significant part to play in the prophetic process. Jeremiah went off to consider before God the feed-back from the first round ('Jeremiah and the Prophetic Process'). A less elaborate hypothesis is that prophecy is far removed from the art of repartee. It is commonly stated that the prophet's word was not his own but was given by God. Whatever view one has of the prophetic process, spur-of-the-moment inspiration is unlikely to accord with it.

or whether he was simply speaking graphically of the heavier yoke that Hananiah's folly would bring upon the nation, we do not know, but the chapter concludes with another attack by Jeremiah on his rival and a prophecy of his impending death.

Anathoth: Jer. 32.1–15

The purchase of the field at Anathoth might be explained as a practical statement of faith without reference to the notion of prophetic drama; but once the significance of the actions of prophets, particularly in moments of crisis, is recognized, the simple explanation appears inadequate. The action was both a statement of faith and a deliberate drama, and that is how it appears in the record. The oracles of hope are treated with suspicion by some scholars, chs.30–33 coming under particularly close scrutiny. As Childs points out, however, the double commission to destroy and to build up is expressed in the call narrative (1.9), and expressions of hope appear, in a subdued form, throughout the prophecy.[42] The sentiments of chs.30–33 are not, therefore, alien to Jeremiah; they are simply made more explicit in these chapters. There is no reason to reject the Anathoth incident as a later fabrication. The narrative is contained within a third-person passage, though the drama itself is recounted by Jeremiah, as it were, in direct speech.

The year is 588 BCE. Jerusalem is besieged and Jeremiah is in prison in the court of the guard.[43] He has been accused, not simply of lowering morale, but of giving prophetic voice to the unthinkable notion that Jerusalem would fall to the Babylonians, a much more serious matter. In prison he receives word from Yahweh that his cousin Hanamel will come to ask him to fulfil his family duty and buy a field from the home town which, according to custom, should be kept in the family. The nice point regarding the transaction was that the field was actually in the hands of the Babylonians when Jeremiah was asked to buy it. Hanamel arrives and Jeremiah interprets his request as a command from Yahweh. He buys the field for what appears to be the full price, in the presence of witnesses, with all the formalities, and he hands the deeds to Baruch for safe keeping. He explains that, siege notwithstanding, according to the word of Yahweh, houses and fields and vineyards would be bought and sold again in Israel.

[42] *Introduction*, p. 351.

[43] Ch. 37 gives what appears to be another account of the same incident, though Anathoth is not mentioned by name and there are considerable differences.

The relation of vv. 1–5 to 6–15 is awkward. Verse 1 gives the date; vv. 2–5 give an elaborate account in the third person of why Jeremiah was shut up in prison. The real narrative begins in v. 6 and it is recounted in the first person. This seems to suggest that we have to consider at least three different phases for this incident: first, an actual event which there is no reason to doubt; second, an autobiographical account of it by Jeremiah himself (vv. 6–15); and third, a later edited version (vv. 1–15), in which it is necessary to set the scene. In this case, however, there is no reason to suppose that the significance of the action changes with editing; on the contrary, the message remains the same.

The command from Yahweh to buy the field is presented in a complicated way. First, it is revealed to Jeremiah that Hanamel will come and urge Jeremiah to play the part of *gō'ēl*; secondly, there is an account of Hanamel's arrival and request; thirdly, there is the recognition by Jeremiah of where his duty lay. This is an interesting commentary on the sense of compulsion that dominates prophecy. One may reasonably suppose that what began as an urgent request from Hanamel ended as a clear word from Yahweh. The account of the action is given in great detail and it is evident that a full, legal transaction is described here. There are one or two difficulties, but they do not affect the understanding of the incident as prophetic drama.[44] The explanation, contained in Jeremiah's final sentence to Baruch, is brief but comprehensive. The text is, therefore, a good example of the threefold structure regarded by Fohrer as indicative of a true symbolic action narrative.

Unlike contrived and artificial actions – wearing a yoke or breaking a pot – buying a field is a commonplace, normal action. The circumstances, however, were peculiar and so the commonplace action was given extra significance. In a society that is breaking up, people shirk their long-term duties and concentrate on survival. This is why the formalities of the sale are so important. A slipshod transaction would imply that the deal was largely meaningless. But according to the word that Jeremiah had received, the ultimate restoration of normal business was Yahweh's will for Israel. By carrying out his family duties Jeremiah was asserting that Hebrew society was not about to lose its identity

---

[44] The chief difficulties are in v. 11. The words translated 'terms and conditions' are grammatically difficult and best left out as in the LXX. The idea of a sealed copy and an open copy makes good sense, but commentators are not agreed on the precise form. See Hyatt, 'Jeremiah', pp. 1044f. and contrast Paterson, 'Jeremiah', p. 556.

and that family and property together would endure until legal rights were again recognized and exercised in Israel.

This action is not a miniature of a larger event as breaking the pot was. Rather it is one action to represent a series. Just as the first word represents the book to the Hebrew, so this purchase represents a hundred other purchases that would take place when the crisis was over. This seems the major point. There is, however, another aspect of the incident of perhaps even greater importance. It is explicitly set out in vv. 36–44 which appear to be a later comment on the purchase. Boadt makes the point that the laws of property were determined by the Hebrew belief that the land was God's gift to Israel as part of the covenant. Ownership of the land had, therefore, to be protected and controlled. If a piece of land came on the market, then, according to Lev. 25.23–34, it was the duty of the next of kin to buy it, to keep it safely within the covenant community.[45] By upholding the law and valuing the land and treating ownership of it with great care, Jeremiah is affirming the continuing significance of the land to Yahweh against all appearances, and affirming, too, that the covenant between Yahweh and Israel, in which the land played so vital a part, was still in being. If the Babylonian invasion had led to the panic selling of land – and silly optimism can quickly turn into panic – then Jeremiah's action would be all the more significant. This drama, therefore, is partly an anticipation of many similar acts in the future and partly a declaration of a continuing relationship between Yahweh and his people. The prevailing circumstances do not reveal the whole truth. The prophetic action does.

Jeremiah and the Rechabites: Jer.35

Jeremiah's dealings with the Rechabites do not constitute the most obvious example of a prophetic drama, but on closer inspection there is here an action that signifies something beyond itself, and the literary structure is suggestive. The date of the incident is uncertain, but from the evidence available (Jer. 35.1, 11; II Kings 24.2), it can be deduced that the year was probably 598 BCE. The Rechabites were in the city because of the state of war in the country and this is the point of departure for interpreting the whole passage. As was clear in the previous section, faithful observance of the normalities of life was a

---

[45] Boadt, *Jeremiah 26–52*, pp. 61f.

way of expressing confidence in the future. Failure to observe these normalities was both an index and a cause of breakdown. The presence of the Rechabites in the city was not normal (v. 11), and it was, therefore, to Jeremiah and his contemporaries, a pointer towards a general collapse. The purpose of this action by Jeremiah was not simply to reverse that impression but to cause the Rechabites to display a fidelity that would be creative in the sense that it would give rise to a whole series of faithful acts that would continue for ever.

According to the biblical evidence, the Rechabites were a community that looked back to Jonadab, son of Rechab, as their founder. This man shared with Jehu in the slaughter of Baalish worshippers in II Kings 10. Thereafter, it has been generally supposed, his descendants continued their protest against Baalism – which they identified with the Canaanite agrarian way of life – by living in tents as nomads, rejecting agriculture as a means of subsistence, and drinking no wine. This account has, however, been contested by F.S. Frick in 'The Rechabites Reconsidered'.[46] Frick regards this supposed devotion to the desert way of life, this 'backward social evolution', as a scholarly mirage. According to him, Jonadab's name means that he was a chariot-maker, who did business with Jehu. His Rechabite descendants may well have been members of a craft guild who, for professional reasons, followed a unique way of life. Their teetotalism was not an indication of nomadic sympathies but a practical requirement to ensure that the secrets of their trade were protected. The Rechabite way of life was not a religious, still less an anti-Baalish, affirmation. Frick may well be right. The point of the story is not the theology of the Rechabites but their constancy.

Jeremiah was commanded by Yahweh to go to the Rechabites and take them into one of the small chambers of the temple and there offer them wine. He did and they refused. Perhaps the most curious thing about the incident is its location. The room is defined with some care as the chamber of the sons of Hanan, the son of Igdaliah, which was by the chamber of the princes, which was above the chamber of Maaseiah, the son of Shallum, the keeper of the door (v. 4). Two things seem evident. The formal refusal was not a public act. Presumably it could have been arranged in public, but Jeremiah had something else in mind. Though it was not public, it was not secret either, because

[46] *JBL* 90 1971, pp. 279–87. Frick is supported by N.K. Gottwald, *The Tribes of Yahweh*, pp. 321, 577–80.

the subsequent speeches proclaim it. Secondly, though it was private, great care is taken to affirm the fact of the refusal and to locate it precisely in the most holy of contexts. We can therefore conclude that the drama was not intended as a visual aid, nor even as a public example, but as a secure fact, a firm and incontestable reality; and like the purchase of the field at Anathoth, the first in a series of acts that will make up the greater reality of Israel's enduring loyalty to Yahweh. There is no need to deny a prescriptive element – that this is how Israel ought to act – but the prescriptive is not necessarily primary.

This interpretation is confirmed by the literary structure. The story vacillates between first and third person; it begins with an instruction to Jeremiah to offer the Rechabites wine. This and their refusal takes up six verses. The rest of the chapter is made up of speeches. The first is an extended explanation of the position of the Rechabites, which seems to be directed more to informing the reader who the Rechabites were than to justifying their refusal. Then comes the Deuteronomic sermon in vv. 12–17, which dominates the chapter, extolling the virtues of the Rechabites and promising judgment for Jerusalem. Thirdly, in vv. 18f, Jeremiah addresses the Rechabites and assures them that, because of their constancy, their family will never disappear.

It is noteworthy that narratives of prophetic drama often attract lengthy and varied interpretations, and this is undoubtedly what we have here. On a signal occasion the Rechabites refused wine. That was a text on which many could preach. Stripped to its essentials the passage relates a story that has much in common with the Anathoth narrative. In both cases the temptation was to repudiate traditional duties that seemed no longer meaningful, and in both cases the principals demonstrate constancy and confidence. That constancy is understood in two quite different ways in the speeches. In vv. 12–17 it is an example to move the feckless Hebrews to shame, albeit too late to save them. In vv. 18f., it is an act of virtue that secures a reward, the reward of survival come what may. Neither of these interpretations pays any attention to the Rechabites' action as a significant drama, and it could be argued that, if the text fails to do so, it is wrong for us to try. Nevertheless vv. 1–6 have so much the flavour of a dramatic narrative that it is reasonable to speculate about the original happening and the original version. If the purchase of the field at Anathoth is accepted as a guide, we have here another example of the stable conduct that witnesses to and helps to secure the stability of Israel as the people of God. If there was an original explanation along these lines, it has been surrendered to allow for the speeches of vv. 6–11, 12–17, and 18f.

Jeremiah's Scroll: Jer. 36

This is a complex chapter. It contains three dramatic narratives, or perhaps one narrative in three phrases. It is reminiscent of the account of the yokes in chs.27–28 in that there is a dramatic act, a counteract, and a reaffirmation of the original act. The complexity may well belong to history. It is not, this time, a case of a simple story being complicated by editorial revision and addition. Rather the account has been written to make the original action itself stand out more clearly as a significant prophetic drama.[47]

In the first phase, vv. 1–8, Jeremiah is told to take a scroll and write on it all the oracles that he has declaimed against Judah.[48] The purpose is to make the nation repent. Jeremiah obeys the instruction, using Baruch as his amanuensis. Verse 5 carries the story a stage further, for Jeremiah instructs Baruch to read the scroll in the temple on a fast day, as he himself was under some kind of restraint.[49] If cultic prophets had a part to play in the ceremonies that marked the crisis points in

[47] R.P. Carroll takes the view that this account was fabricated by Deuteronomistic scribes in order to legitimize their role in the development of the Jeremiah tradition (*From Chaos to Covenant*, pp. 15f.). Lawrence Boadt, among others, draws attention to the similarity between this chapter and II Kings 22–23. In both cases there is a narrative of a king, a prophet and a book, but the structure works out in directly opposite ways. II Kings 22 concludes with Huldah's prophecy that Josiah would be gathered to his grave in peace. Jer. 36 concludes with Jeremiah's prophecy that Jehoiakim's body would be cast out, to the heat by day and to the frost by night. According to Boadt, Jeremiah's editors have organized the account in Jer. 36 to highlight the difference between the two monarchs' responses to the divine word (*Jeremiah 26–52*, p. 83).

[48] The Hebrew speaks of all the oracles against Israel, Judah and all the nations. This must be an exaggeration and probably a gloss. Jeremiah had been prophesying for twenty years, but, if the account here is taken seriously, the resultant scroll could be read through fairly quickly – three times in one day, quite apart from the attendant discussions. This suggests that only a selection of the oracles was included; the rest of the story suggests that they were largely oracles against Judah.

[49] The fast day of v. 6, which may or may not have been the same occasion as that referred to in v. 9, was probably a special occasion and not anything to do with the regular cultus. Fasts were proclaimed in times of war, drought and other calamities (Judg. 20.26; I Sam. 14.24; I Kings 21.9; I Macc. 3.47; see Ehrlich, *Kultsymbolik*, pp. 82ff.).

the life of the nation, it is reasonable to expect that Jeremiah would want to be heard at a time of national mortification; the incident occurs around the time of the battle of Carchemish, when Babylon first appears as a threat to Judah. From v. 3 it appears that, if the nation repented, there was still a possibility that the prophesied doom could be averted. Baruch did as he was instructed both in writing and reading. Verse 8, therefore, appears to conclude a drama narrative that is complete in itself.

It might, of course, be argued that what was happening was purely functional. Jeremiah was prevented from speaking in the temple, so Baruch spoke for him. The Babylonian threat might have made Jeremiah anxious to secure his oracles for posterity. In any case it was normal for oracles to be written down (cf. Isa. 8.16f; 30.8; Hab. 2.2f.). The editorial process, however, makes it clear that the writing down was understood as more than merely functional. There are three points to note. First, the story begins with a divine command followed by an account of the prophet carrying it out, which is at least reminiscent of the form recognized by Fohrer as the classic form for symbolic actions. Secondly, it must be supposed that the actual content of the written oracles would not have come as much of a surprise; nevertheless reactions to the writing are carefully chronicled in the rest of the chapter; these reactions are hard to explain if the act of writing was not thought to have had a special significance in itself. Thirdly, all our present prophetic oracles must have been soon committed to writing for practical purposes, but this incident is preserved and reported in a special way. It must be concluded that the editor of Jer. 36 saw this incident as a peculiarly significant action and not simply a functional one.

In v. 9 it is a year later. At another fast Baruch read the oracles again, first in the temple, and then, under duress, to some of the princes. The dating is awkward. If vv. 9ff. are an expansion of v. 8 and both refer to the same occasion, there is a considerable delay between Jeremiah's instructions and Baruch's compliance with them. The LXX makes it worse by speaking of a four-year gap between v. 1 and v. 9 (see LXX 43.9). The most probable explanation is that there is a mistake in the numbers. The whole chapter is meant to be read as a single episode. That, however, sets a question mark against v. 8. If the chapter records a single incident having three acts, what is the point of a verse that rounds off the first act and makes it complete in itself? Bright assumes that the last half of the verse is a gloss.[50] Or perhaps the verse belongs to a different redaction when the first part of the chapter existed on its own.

In the present version Baruch reads the scroll to the people at large in a room in the temple. The news is reported to the princes of Judah who were gathered near by. They summon Baruch, have the scroll read again, are overcome with fear, and report the matter to the king. The king is not so easily swayed. As the scroll is read to him, he snips off the part that is done with and burns it, until it is all gone. The spirits of the princes are then remarkably restored. In the third phase Jeremiah is told to write the scroll again and add to it a prophecy of doom for Jehoiakim and his house.[51] This, with Baruch's help, he does.

In the story of the yokes in Jer. 27–28 we encountered the phenomenon of the action and the counteraction. In fact other Old Testament incidents are illuminated by the notion that one dramatic action can be the means of counteracting another. In this case there are three actions to consider, the original writing and reading, the cutting and burning by the king, and the second writing. The first writing was a significant action, or so the king thought, and so thought Elnathan, Delaiah and Gemariah (v. 25), and so thought the editor of the chapter. By putting his oracles in writing Jeremiah was making them, not merely more permanent, but more vigorous.[52] Jehoiakim acts deliberately to bring the oracles to nothing, and the effect of his action at the very least is to change the attitude of the princes. When the words were first read, they were afraid; but as soon as the scroll was consigned to the flames, the fear left them. Jehoiakim had evidently acted boldly and, so they seemed to think, effectively to forestall the doom that was written.[53] The third phase follows naturally as does the third phase in 28.12–16. Jeremiah counters the counteraction with another action of his own. This time the words are written but not read; the record is sufficient.

This chapter raises three issues that are often raised in the discussion of prophetic drama. In vv. 3 and 7 it is stated that the written

[50] Bright, *Jeremiah*, p. 180.

[51] For a theory regarding the contents of the two scrolls, see William Holladay, 'The Identification of the Two Scrolls of Jeremiah'.

[52] Kessler, 'The Significance of Jer. 36'.

[53] See Tucker, 'The Role of the Prophets', p. 169; Blank, *Jeremiah: Man and Prophet*, p. 29.

prophecies need not be fulfilled, need not, that is, if Israel repents in time. It is clear then that no account of prophetic drama will suffice if it represents the action as inevitably effective. At the very most this drama is conditionally effective, but a better way of putting it is that several possible futures exist in Yahweh's hand. They all have the reality of Yahweh's power and purpose. Which of them extends into earthly reality has yet to be decided. In the meantime the oracle or the drama represents a reality that is quite real enough for Israel's comfort.

The second phase, however, gives quite the opposite impression. Jehoiakim acts as if the destruction of the scroll was sufficient to guarantee a desirable future.[54] Notions of instrumental effectiveness are certainly lurking here. There is no reason to suppose, however, that either in historical fact or in the written record, Jeremiah and Jehoiakim shared the same beliefs about dramatic action. Jehoiakim and his supporters seem convinced that the king's vigorous action would be both psychologically and instrumentally effective; Jeremiah would be outfaced and his prophecies reversed. Jeremiah takes a different view. It may be that Jeremiah was convinced that, on this occasion, the quasi-magical action would not work, because he had Yahweh on his side; but it is more likely that Jeremiah's understanding of dramatic action was totally at odds with that of Jehoiakim. It was not a case of spell and counter-spell, but of submission to God on one hand and an empty performance on the other. There is nothing surprising in that. It was not the first time, nor would it be the last, when a monarch and a prophet differed, not simply on practical ethics, but on theology and metaphysics.

Thirdly, when the scroll was written again, it contained a prophecy that was not fulfilled. According to II Kings 24.6 Jehoiakim slept with his fathers and was succeeded by his son. The fate foretold in Jer. 36.30 did not overtake him, and it was not due to repentance on his part. We need then to find an explanation of prophetic activity that embraces both the successes and the failures of prophecy. Jeremiah believed his oracles to be God-given expressions of God-given historical realities; oracle and historical reality were different aspects of the same divine intention. Inscribing the oracles was simply a way of extending the intention still further. Jehoiakim, buoyed up by wishful thinking and a less profound theology, believed that, by attacking the scroll,

---

[54] Ideas of this kind are frequently, if vaguely, called magical. See Fohrer, 'Prophetie und Magie', pp. 44f.

he could frustrate the intention expressed in it. Jeremiah returned to the charge. The divine intention is firm; it must be expressed; so a further oracle and a further scroll are necessary. This time Jeremiah made an error in detail and surprisingly his editors let it stand. Plainly the prophetic process was not infallible. However sensitive and profound the prophet may be, however deeply convinced he, his disciples and his editors were of the genuineness of his revelations, nobody could suppose that they would be entirely free from error.

Tah'panhes: Jer. 43.8–13

It is generally recognized that this is an example of prophetic drama. There is a clear instruction to Jeremiah to perform the action and to explain what he is doing, though there is no account of him actually doing it. Jeremiah is in Egypt against his will. He is at the frontier town of Tah'panhes and Yahweh instructs him to bury some large stones in the courtyard outside the royal residence.[55] The men of Judah are to see him do it and they are to be given an explanation. It is that there is no escape from Yahweh's justice. Nebuchadnezzar would pursue them to Egypt. The stones signify the foundations of his throne which would be set up at that very place. Tah'panhes was the first town that an invader would conquer and the royal residence there would provide a splendid opportunity for triumphal display. When Nebuchadnezzar ascended the throne, the pestilence, captivity and slaughter that these Hebrews had attempted to escape would be let loose in Egypt. He would burn the temples and break down the obelisks of Heliopolis.[56]

From one point of view Jeremiah's action was mimetic. In burying the stones he was imitating the workmen who would make the pedestal for the throne when the conqueror arrived. But perhaps the action is more easily understood as inceptive rather than mimetic. Jeremiah is

[55] There is an insoluble textual problem about where the stones are to go. The meaning of the two words in the MT is a mystery. The LXX reads something quite different and the Vulgate, with three Greek versions, reads something different again. These last give the meaning 'in secret' which, if it can be accepted, gives a very convincing picture. Jeremiah is to steal out with some of his fellow refugees and perform a dramatic action which would have been impossible in the full light of day because of its treasonable import.

[56] The reference to Heliopolis, Beth-shemesh in Hebrew, occurs only in v. 13, which otherwise only repeats the sense of v. 12. It is probably an addition, perhaps an aetiological one.

laying the first stone, others will continue to work and Nebuchadnezzar's ascent of the throne will complete the event. The drama and the
reality are part of the same whole. The one difficulty here is finding
assurance that the reality actually took place. Josephus refers to a
Babylonian victory in Egypt, but most commentators take the view
that his account of Nebuchadnezzar's doings in Egypt in 582 BCE is
based, not upon extra-biblical evidence, but upon this prophecy of
Jeremiah.[57] Otherwise we have only a damaged Babylonian text
relating to an invasion of Egypt in 568 BCE, some nineteen years after
Jeremiah's action.[58] Even this is treated with reserve by commentators,
though a punitive mission, as distinct from a colonizing campaign, is
more than likely. There is no real problem as far as prophetic drama
is concerned. Evidence has been building up in this section to show
that there was no belief that fulfilment was inevitable. The fact that
an editor might have recorded a dramatic act without any conviction
that it was followed by fulfilment provides an interesting datum that
must be worked into any final account of prophetic drama.

The Book about Babylon: Jer. 51.59–64

The last drama from the book of Jeremiah is against Babylon. On
closer inspection it appears to be two actions rather than one. First,
Jeremiah writes out the doom of Babylon in a book and commissions
Seraiah to take it with him to Babylon when he goes there in 594 BCE
with Zedekiah the king, and to read it, presumably aloud, on arrival.
This is reminiscent of the dictation to Baruch in Jer. 36 and, from a
comparison of 32.12 and 51.59, it seems easy to deduce that Baruch
and Seraiah were brothers or even, conceivably, two names for the
same person. Events that are coming into being move one stage nearer
to reality when the account of them is written down. Secondly, when
he has finished reading, Seraiah is to tie a stone to the book and sink
it in the Euphrates, at the same time affirming that Babylon will sink
and never rise again. In the first act, the words represent events, and
the words are to be sunk in the Euphrates, in the place where the
events are to take place, and in such a way that the words cannot be
recovered or revoked; in the second act, the book represents Babylon
itself. As prophetic dramas both acts are easily intelligible, but they
are not without difficulties.

---

[57] *Antiquities*, 10.9.7.
[58] See Pritchard, *ANET*, p. 308.

In the first place, there is a considerable body of opinion that 50.1–51.58 cannot be attributed to Jeremiah. These oracles deal with the downfall of Babylon and are much later than the last date when Jeremiah could have been in Jerusalem. The question arises as to how vv. 59–64 are related to this secondary material.[59] There are indications that these verses have simply been grafted onto it. Verse 60b looks like a deliberate attempt to relate the passage to the preceding material and v. 62 echoes 50.3 and 51.26. If these elements are removed, the story is improved. One possibility is, therefore, that a genuine oracle about Babylon by Jeremiah has been gathered up with secondary material on Babylon and has then suffered editing to make it appear to be in place; but this does not solve all the problems. The narrative of vv. 59–64 exhibits a different attitude to Babylon from that which appears in the bulk of the book, even though it is the same attitude as that in the rest of chs.50–51. Can the author of 51.63 be the author of 27.6, 29.7 or 43.10?[60] This leads to the conclusion that the narrative is not to be attributed to Jeremiah.

A second difficulty arises from the historical implications of 51.59. On the basis of 27.2ff. it has been assumed that a rebellion against Babylon was planned, and that Zedekiah had subsequently to travel to Babylon to extricate himself by diplomacy from the dangerous situation into which his folly had plunged him. That there was a conspiracy need not be doubted, but, apart from 51.59, there is no record of any diplomatic journey. Even here it is not entirely clear who is supposed to have gone to Babylon. The Hebrew says Zedekiah and Seraiah, but the LXX implies Seraiah alone. This is not a very serious problem because it was the presence of Seraiah in Babylon that alone matters.

Thirdly, this drama is very different from the others in Jeremiah in terms of theology. The story opens with a command, not from Yahweh but from the prophet himself. There is then an account of Jeremiah writing the book of evils and then further instructions to Seraiah. The

[59] Hyatt ('Jeremiah', pp. 1123, 1136) argues that the whole of 50–51 is secondary, but others, while allowing that there is secondary material in these two chapters, regard some verses, usually including vv. 59–64, as from Jeremiah (Streane, *Jeremiah*, p. 310; Binns, *Jeremiah*, p. 375; Bright, *Jeremiah*, p. 212). See also R.M. Paterson, 'Reinterpretation in the Book of Jeremiah'.

[60] Van den Born comes up with the colourful theory that the narrative might be a forgery, an underground political pamphlet, distributed by false and anti-Babylonian prophets in Babylon, to offset the effects of Jeremiah's tranquillizing letter in 29.4–23 (*Profetie Metterdaad*, p. 28).

second act has more instruction from Jeremiah to Seraiah and a brief explanation. If this were simply a variation of what is admittedly a very loose literary format, it would not be important, but the problem is not literary; it is theological. The element of submission to Yahweh is absent altogether. The deity is mentioned only in v. 62, a verse that was probably added later. Instead we have what amounts to a curse formula in v. 64.[61] It would be helpful if we knew precisely what Seraiah's position was and whether he performed the same functions as Baruch, but *šār m^enû ḥâ* (RSV quartermaster) in v. 59 is most elusive. Godbey asserts that the term is associated with sorcery and that Seraiah was the real actor in the story, not Jeremiah.[62] There is some doubt, therefore, whether this incident can be regarded as a prophetic drama carried out by Jeremiah or not. The weight of evidence seems to be against it.

Even if the story is secondary, it remains interesting. Perhaps, indeed, it is more interesting because it gives a slant on prophetic drama other than that supplied by dedicated Yahwistic theologians. In the search for an adequate model, the distinction between the sophisticated understanding and the demotic one is crucial. This narrative may be a valuable pointer towards the latter.

Little more needs to be said about the first act, as writing dramas have been considered already. Babylon's doom is made to appear more certain when the words are given the permanence and objectivity of the written form. If all other things were equal, there would be no objection to an action of this kind being attributed to Jeremiah. He had done the same kind of thing before. In the second act, however, the book changes its nature and the process of the drama is different. The book now stands, not for the doom of Babylon, but for Babylon itself and the drama becomes mimetic, at least in a metaphorical way. Babylon will not actually sink in water as the book does, but she will be overwhelmed and lost. What then is the relation of the two acts to

---

[61] Bernhard Lang links this incident with 'Elisha's war magic' in II Kings 13.14–19 and makes this comment, 'Here the law of "mystical participation" (Lucien Lévy-Bruhl) reigns. "Pre-imitation" of the future, the magical act (the sinking of Jeremiah's scroll in the Euphrates) paves the way for the historical event (the decline of the Babylonian power). In a mystical way the historical event participates in the magical game and is set in motion by the latter' (*Monotheism*, p. 89). This matter is discussed in Chapter 16. Carroll also takes the view that this drama is a good example of magical activity. The purpose was to damn Babylon (*Jeremiah*, pp. 295f.).

[62] 'The Hebrew Masal'; the Hebrew is not easily understood as it stands, and LXX, Syriac and Vulgate all provide different solutions.

each other? Though they can be seen separately, they are linked by the appearance of the book in both. The first act is clearly the basic form. Someone with no love for Babylon produced a narrative that superficially resembles another narrative from the life of the great prophet. It is easy to see why the message of catastrophe should be taken to Babylon – for the same reason that Baruch's book had to be read in the temple – to lodge it securely in the place where it was to be fulfilled and to inaugurate the event with which it was concerned. Even the submerging of the book at this point would not be inappropriate. The indicator of the doom of Babylon would then be sunk in her famous river, like a time bomb ticking away beneath a city. Then it happened that someone appeared who could not leave the text alone. The imagery was too suggestive. So what begins as a lodging becomes a drowning; and the addition of the curse formula of v. 64 makes the submerging into a second act of the drama, or, to be more accurate, a second instruction to perform a second act.

This requires us to consider again the question whether the story is historically possible. If Jeremiah had been the author, and if Seraiah was about to depart for Babylon, it is possible to imagine Jeremiah performing the first act and perhaps even giving instructions for the second. But that possibility has been ruled out. If someone other than Jeremiah was the author, and if he was constructing a supposed incident in Jeremiah's life, it is hard to see how either act could have taken place. It must also be remembered that there is nothing to suggest that the second act ever did happen. There is simply an instruction, nothing more. The most probable hypothesis, therefore, is that an anti-Babylonian enthusiast produced the first act under the influence of the incident recorded in Jer. 36. Subsequently he, or someone of the same persuasion, gilded the lily by adding vv. 63f. with the second act and the curse formula. Finally the story was incorporated into the collection of anti-Babylonian oracles. It is interesting to speculate what understanding the person who added the curse formula had of prophetic drama and how it differed from that of Jeremiah himself.

12 · Ezekiel

The book of Ezekiel has always proved daunting to students, partly because of the obscurity of the language and the strangeness of the images, and partly because of the problems of literary history that have been evident since Hölscher published his critical analysis in 1924. Only about one-seventh of the book survived Hölscher's pruning, and so for more than sixty years studies of Ezekiel have been carried on under the influence of the hypothesis that 85 per cent of the book was not 'genuine'. Not all the difficulties have yet been overcome, but the appearance of Zimmerli's great two-volume commentary in 1969 (ET 1978 and 1983) does mean that a new and more positive era in Ezekiel studies has now begun. From our point of view Ezekiel is a most important text, difficult without a doubt, but also very rewarding.

On the basis of the biblical material a broad outline of Ezekiel's life story can be constructed; this provides us with a working hypothesis for the study of the book. It is not reasonable to expect anything more. Ezekiel, the man, was a priest living in Jerusalem until the Babylonian army arrived in 597. Jerusalem was besieged but then surrendered, so that the city was not sacked. All the notables, including king Jehoiachin and Ezekiel himself, were carried off captive. The poor were left behind with Zedekiah as their king (II Kings 24.8–17). Ezekiel settled at Tel-abib by the river Chebar, and there, in 593 BCE, he received a call, characteristically abstruse, to become a prophet. Much of his work was done and many of his dramatic actions were performed in the next few years, before Zedekiah foolishly rebelled and Jerusalem was thoroughly destroyed (II Kings 25).

There has been some discussion in the past about whether Ezekiel was permanently settled in Babylon or whether he returned to prophesy in Jerusalem for a period, especially in the light of chs.8–11, which seem to require Jerusalem as a locus. It is quite true that these chapters are about Jerusalem and the text says that Ezekiel was actually transported there (8.3; 11.1), but there is no reason for supposing that physical presence is implied. There is ample evidence that Ezekiel was a highly imaginative person and that he could be totally absorbed in his imaginative world; he also knew the city well from his youth. The whole episode could well have taken place in his mind, and, indeed, almost certainly did so. A large contingent of people who were deeply concerned about Jerusalem's fate, and also morally responsible for her grievous condition, was present with Ezekiel in Babylon. These were the people he needed to address; some of his oracles were in the form of judgments upon them and some of his dramatic acts had the precise purpose of making the conditions in Jerusalem evident to those who were so far away. This is an unusual prophetic task, but not one that is hard to comprehend. This minor complexity is aggravated by the prophet's language. Without a doubt he was a most unusual person. His flights of fancy, his visions, his allegories, his images are so inventive and so detailed – the word 'bizarre' crops up frequently in the commentaries – that no modern scholar can feel confident that he has grasped all the nuances.[1] Most of the dramatic actions we consider here exist only in the form of instructions that Ezekiel received in his mind. The accounts of him actually performing the dramas are usually lacking.

What we know of Ezekiel the man confirms what we infer from his book. He was liable to attacks of trembling, dumbness and paralysis (3.15,26; 4.4; 12.17; 21.6) which, though they cannot be diagnosed clinically, can scarcely be called normal. We have, therefore, to envisage a person of rare mental intensity who is so taken up with his woeful message that appropriate symptoms appear in his own body. Or, to put it another way, Ezekiel saw in his own physical state indications of his message. Between these two ways of putting the case, there is a great gulf in terms of causality, but this is a point where the modern observer sees more than the participant. To Ezekiel affliction and reality, suffering and message, were all the same.

Not all the message was condemnatory. The last fifteen chapters of the book contain oracles of hope, including the vision of the valley of dry bones and concluding with the account of the new temple and

---

[1] It is hardly surprising that many scholars trace the apocalyptic style of writing back to Ezekiel.

priesthood. Some scholars still view these chapters with suspicion. It is unnecessary for us to debate the point, because only one prophetic drama is found within these chapters, and, in the case of Ezekiel more than any other prophetic book, the question of 'genuineness' is really a diversion. It is impossible to determine what oracles were actually spoken by Ezekiel, and it would not help us very much if we knew.

Like Hosea and unlike Isaiah, Ezekiel consists of extended sections rather than short oracles. The passages are usually written in the first person, yet it is hard to think of the prophet declaiming them in their present form. One must assume that the actual oracles have been extended in a conscious literary way. The subject matter confirms this impression. The reapplication of the message seems to have begun almost at once and to have continued for a generation or two without losing the sense of the cohesion of the whole. The 'genuine' Ezekiel can hardly be found now, though this in no way invalidates the integrity of the book of Ezekiel. A continuous process of redaction makes the determination of particular stages in the process impossible except in an approximate way. The adaptation of 4.9–17 (the baking of strange bread) took place almost at once, and the representation of the people being taken into captivity (12.1–16) was probably revised to concentrate on the fate of Zedekiah soon after the unhappy king died. Joining the sticks in 37.15–19 must have been developed during the better days of the exile, for it is hard to think of any editor writing the words of vv. 20–28 after the realities of the return were known. On the other hand, the action with the hair in 5.1–4 seems to have been worked over several times, the final form not emerging until the exile was over. The action with the sword in ch.21 is a similar case. The fact that editors made such positive use of the text, giving it an 'after-life' of greater significance than the original form – or so we must suppose – is an important factor in assessing how those theological interpreters understood the material with which we are dealing.

Ezekiel, both man and book, present the most daunting problems in the whole field of prophetic studies. It is fortunate that we come to him towards the end of the survey, for by now the key points have been marked out. It is reasonably clear what material is definitive, what is marginal, and what is to be excluded. If it had been necessary to begin with Ezekiel, this would not have been clear at all.

Ezekiel's Scroll: Ezek.2.8–3.3

The first narrative comes in the marginal category. In many ways it is reminiscent of passages in Jeremiah. Jer. 1.9 recounts a call to prophesy in similarly graphic style; Jer. 36 deals with prophetic oracles in written form; and Jer. 25.15–29 presents a similar example of a drama narrative which fits well into the category, save that it could never have happened.

The story begins with a command to the prophet to open his mouth and eat what is put before him. The prophet sees before him a scroll with writing on both back and front. The writing proves to be oracles of woe. The command to eat is repeated, actually repeated twice, and there is a further command to prophesy to the house of Israel. Then the command to eat is repeated yet again, this time in basic language, 'Let your belly eat, let your stomach be filled.' The prophet obeys and finds the scroll sweet to the taste. The literary structure is complicated because the command is given four times in different terms and the account of the action comes in two stages. There is no explicit explanation of the action, but the words, 'Go, speak to the house of Israel,' are an implicit one and nothing more is needed.

The scroll clearly represents God's word given to the prophet. Yahweh put his words into Jeremiah's mouth (Jer. 1.9) and subsequently Jeremiah had them written down (Jer. 36). Ezekiel telescopes these two ideas and has the words, already written, presented to the prophet's mouth. There is an obvious kinship of ideas here and Zimmerli leans to the view that Ezekiel, as a priest in the temple, was around when the incident recounted in Jer. 36 took place.[2] The writing on both sides suggests a long and detailed series of oracles, for normally only one writing surface was used. Some critics have been concerned that the implication of these verses is that what they regard as the brilliant spontaneity of the prophetic oracle is now a thing of the past; the word has become static like the law. But this contention fails to take account of two important facts about how prophecy was understood. In the first place, though the prophet might appear to speak spontaneously, his word, if it was a true word, was always reckoned to have been given to him ready-made by Yahweh. The spontaneity, if there was any, concerned the appearance, not the content. Secondly, the writing down

---

[2] Zimmerli, *Ezekiel I*, p. 137.

of words simply represents another stage in their actualization (see above on Jer. 36). The great event which begins with divine intent and ends in historical fulfilment may move through an intermediate stage of prophetic speech, or even two stages of speech and writing. If this happens, we are not to conclude that prophetic oracles in general have become fixed, only that, according to contemporary understanding, these particular oracles are moving ineluctably nearer to actualization.

Ezekiel eats the scroll, showing that he takes the word totally into himself, and showing, too, his absolute obedience to the command of Yahweh.[3] The basic language is important, for it stresses that prophet and word are to be identified; the word becomes part of him and he becomes part of the word and the event that the word prefigures. The sweet taste of the scroll relates, not to the content of the oracles, which were laden with doom, but to the recognition that to accept Yahweh's command is, of itself, a blessing, regardless of what is involved in it. This is all reasonably clear, but eating a scroll must be regarded as an impossibility, even for Ezekiel. It is, therefore, necessary to recall what was said with regard to Jer. 25.15–29. This event was a real part of Ezekiel's experience. It could not have been more real to him had there been a scroll that other people saw him eat. In practical terms, the experience was determinative for Ezekiel's life. In this example the reality indicated by the dramatic action was Ezekiel's prophetic vocation and practice. The drama took place only in his mind. It remained, however, an important element of the reality, that is, Ezekiel's prophetic work. To apply, at this point, a distinction between subjective and objective happenings is simply not appropriate; so it is possible to argue that this narrative has a place within the category of prophetic dramas.

Another interesting feature of the story is that the prophet is not simply the visionary but also the audience. The drama is addressed to himself. This has a bearing on the discussion whether a primary purpose of prophetic drama was to make obscure meaning clear. No such possibility exists here. Ezekiel is the only person concerned. Yet the account he gives of the matter includes, not simply the charge to prophesy, but the eating of a scroll. The action, albeit in a vision, seems to be necessary, even though the meaning is clear

[3] Greenberg, *Ezekiel 1–20*, p. 73.

without it. There is a need for expressive action over and beyond communication.

Ezekiel's Dumbness: Ezek. 3.22–27; 24.25–27; 33.21f.

Strictly speaking 3.22–7 contains two elements. Ezekiel is first commanded to shut himself up in his house, where, it appears, some further restrictions will be placed upon him. It is possible that presence in the house stands for something significant in its own right,[4] but more likely that this restriction is simply another aspect of the dumbness. We must return to this point when considering 4.8. For the moment, because 24.25–27 and 33.21f. make no mention of confinement, we shall restrict ourselves to a discussion of Ezekiel's dumbness.

The matter is referred to three times. In 3.22–27 there is an account of a visionary experience when the Spirit tells Ezekiel that he will be restricted, unable to go out, and struck dumb. This account is not dated, but from its position in the narrative we infer that it belongs to the beginning of Ezekiel's ministry.[5] In 24.25–27, dated in the ninth year, presumably of his captivity, Ezekiel's dumbness is taken for granted, and the word from Yahweh is that his voice will be restored when a fugitive arrives with the news that Jerusalem has fallen. This happening will be a sign (môpēt) to the people. 33.21f. describe the fulfilment of this word. The date of the fugitive's arrival is given – the twelfth year of our exile. The prophet's voice was restored at that very time. Superficially, therefore, the passages are consistent, but no commentator is satisfied.

The first consideration is that 3.22–27, which are in the form of a prophecy, do not relate the dumbness to the fall of Jerusalem at all. The onset of dumbness is a separate and self-contained incident and no term is placed upon it. Ezekiel is told that he will be dumb and unable to reprove the people. The thought of Ezekiel being unable to speak for a long period, however, was obviously problematic because of the profusion of his oracles. Verse 27, therefore, appears to tidy this up. It does not set a term on the dumbness, as the other two

---

[4] Eichrodt thought that he was confined due to the hostility of the exiles (*Ezekiel*, p. 160).

[5] Greenberg makes it seven days after the eating of the scroll, no doubt on the basis of 3.15f. On Greenberg's reckoning the total period of restraint is seven and a half years ('On Ezekiel's Dumbness').

passages do, but it says that God will open Ezekiel's mouth *on particular occasions*.[6] It is notable, however, that the language of 4.8 (where Ezekiel is to lie on his side) is similar to that of 3.25. Both speak of a physical restraint and both use the same image of being bound. 4.8 is directly related to the fall of Jerusalem; so it is easy, though not necessarily correct, to suppose that the context of 3.25 is the same as that of 4.8. In this way a link between 3.22–27 and the fall of Jerusalem has been inferred by the editor though the passage does not actually mention it. This in turn means that 3.22–27 should be placed later in the prophecy, nearer to the calamity, and a shorter period of dumbness is implied.

The second passage, 24.25–27, is not, in fact, consistent with 3.27. It is also in the form of a prophecy; it states that Ezekiel's mouth will be opened, presumably permanently, when a fugitive arrives with the news that Jerusalem has fallen. The text actually states that Ezekiel would hear the news on the same day as the city fell, but that would be a practical impossibility. The emphatic 'on that day' must surely refer to the temporal link between the arrival of the news and the departure of the affliction. The removal of 'on that day' from v. 26, on the assumption of dittography, or better still the removal of the whole verse as a gloss, would overcome this difficulty, but the disparity with 3.27 would remain. In 3.27 God opens the prophet's mouth only when it was necessary for him to prophesy. In 24.25–27 his mouth remains closed until the fugitive arrives, after which he is no longer dumb.

The third passage, which is in the form of autobiography, gives a precise date, the twelfth year of the exile.[7] A fugitive arrives with the news of the fall of Jerusalem. It appears that Ezekiel's voice returned at this point, perhaps on the previous night, though the text is not at all clear. This implies that 24.25–27 and 33.21f. relate to each other as prophecy and fulfilment, the more so as the intervening chapters

---

[6] This is disputed. Greenberg argues that a single, unbroken period of restriction is intended ('On Ezekiel's Dumbness'). Robert Wilson follows Greenberg in rejecting the idea of sporadic dumbness, asking why 3.22–27 is placed where it now is. He answers this question by saying that 3.22–27 is essentially a modification of Ezekiel's call and is consequently placed next to the call narrative. Unlike other prophets, who were able to plead with Yahweh for the people and to proclaim oracles of salvation, Ezekiel was limited to oracles of doom until Jerusalem fell and he was released ('An interpretation of Ezekiel's Dumbness'; see too Sherlock, 'Ezekiel's Dumbness').

[7] Eichrodt argues cogently that the *eleventh* year is correct (*Ezekiel*, pp. 457f.). There is much discussion of the matter.

25–32 are a collection of oracles against foreign nations which were inserted between 24.27 and 33.1 at a late stage of the editorial process.

The evidence, then, as we have it in these three passages, suggests that (i) at the beginning of his ministry, Ezekiel was confined to his house and struck dumb, (ii) he was nonetheless charged to prophesy, (iii) he was assured that his tongue would be loosed and that he would be able to prophesy when a fugitive arrived from Jerusalem, and (iv) after some years of exile the fugitive did arrive and Ezekiel was able to speak. This evidence has usually been resolved in one of two ways. Either the period of dumbness is reckoned to be long, but the dumbness to be only sporadic, so that Ezekiel could continue to prophesy, or the length of the period is contracted to a relatively brief time just before the fall of Jerusalem, which means that 3.24–27 is placed too early and the figures in 24.1 and 33.21 need adjustment.[8]

A proper treatment of this issue would require a full-scale enquiry into the chronology of Ezekiel's prophecy and a discussion of the vexed question of whether he functioned in Babylon, as the present text implies, or Jerusalem, as some critics have contended. The latter cannot be completely avoided and it is discussed below. The former is impossible here, and it would, in any case, do little to help the enquiry. At this point, therefore, we shall restrict ourselves to the basic question concerning how the dumbness itself was understood.

From the uneven material the only relevant facts about which we can be sure are that Ezekiel was liable to suffer periods of speechlessness, that one particular attack was related to the fall of Jerusalem, and that he, or his editors, or more probably both, saw his speechlessness as a significant element in his prophetic ministry. It seems certain that Ezekiel suffered from a malady that repeatedly affected both movement and speech.[9] This hypothesis was first put forward more than a century ago and the evidence is still strongly in its favour.[10] Ezekiel's painful experience is comparable to Hosea's marriage and Jeremiah's celibacy in that the conditions of life that the

[8] Greenberg's solution is that Ezekiel was housebound and unable to speak as a normal prophet would over the whole period. He was, however, able to pronounce God's word of doom. He stayed miserably at home contemplating the fall of Jerusalem and pouring out doom-laden prophecies when people came to his house. Greenberg draws attention to a remarkable parallel in Josephus, *War* 6.5.3.

[9] Apart from the three passages under consideration here, 3.14f., 12.17–20, 21.6f. and 24.16f. imply curious physical reactions.

[10] See Rowley, 'The Book of Ezekiel in Modern Study', *Men of God*, pp. 207f.

three prophets had to suffer were in each case interpreted positively as a specific sign for the nation.[11] Ezekiel was totally taken up with his mission. He had ingested the divine word. Whatever happened to him thereafter must be related to his identity as a prophet. So when he had an illness that prevented him from prophesying, it became a sign for him, perhaps a series of signs.

Once the affliction is interpreted in this way, it becomes clear how the tradition recounts the evidence in order to bring out its significant quality. The first two passages do not describe a condition that already pertained but announce one that is imminent. So, in the record, the dumbness does not fall on Ezekiel unawares; it is prophesied; it is part of God's determined will. The link with the fall of Jerusalem provides a complication. There is no difficulty for us in accepting that the news would deeply affect a person of Ezekiel's temperament. Clinically it is quite possible that the shock would bring back his voice. The problem lies in the way that the editors have handled the incident. The affliction is a recurrent condition in 3.27, and a prolonged but finite condition in 24.27. Speech is to be restored when the fugitive arrives in 24.27, and it is restored on the preceding night in 33.22. This is a puzzle and it suggests different editors handling the known facts differently. Fortunately the understanding of the material as prophetic drama does not have to wait upon the resolution of this difficulty.

In this drama, as Ezekiel works it out, the prophet personates Yahweh. In the calamity that had overcome the nation, divine guidance ceases. The word that might be spoken is not spoken; Ezekiel will be unable to reprove Israel because her guilt is too great. The divine word is a privilege and Israel has to be without it in order to learn how great a privilege it is. The word is restored when the city falls, perhaps because the punishment has now taken place and it is time for the healing work to begin.[12] There is nothing surprising in the fact that silence is called a sign (*môpēt*) in 24.27. Signs do not have to be active performances. Amos could conceive of a famine of the words of Yahweh (Amos 8.11f.) and what better sign for such a state than speechlessness in the prophet? Restoration of the word was equally a

[11] In other respects the afflictions were quite different. One was caused by another person's infidelity, one was self-inflicted, and one was a natural misfortune. In no case, however, is the text interested in these causes; consequently the differences do not affect the way in which the afflictions were understood.

[12] See TeStroete, 'Ezekiel 24.15–27: The Meaning of a Symbolic Act'.

sign of hope. In this instance drama and reality are hardly to be separated. Because Yahweh is silent, the prophet is silent and vice versa. The emptiness is both sign and fulfilment, drama and reality. This is the best example we have yet seen of the idea that the drama participates in the reality, and that the prophet's action, or inaction, is the immediate and perceptible aspect of a divine reality that, although terribly real, is not so easily perceived.

The Siege in Miniature: Ezek. 4.1–3, 7

Ezekiel 4 contains a series of dramatic actions, some related to the fall of Jerusalem, some to the exile itself. They have been heavily edited and it is not easy now to disentangle them or to determine their original form.[13] Their sense is even more elusive. The first one appears simply as an instruction from Yahweh. There is no account of Ezekiel carrying out the instruction, and the only explanation is woven into the charge. Ezekiel is told to take a brick of soft clay and make a model, or perhaps a ground plan, of a besieged city.[14] All the details of a siege, the wall, the mound, the camps, the battering rams, are to be added. Verse 3 complicates the picture. The prophet is to take an iron plate and set it up between himself and the model. He must set his face toward the city and press the siege against it. This is a sign ('ôṯ) for the house of Israel.[15]

It was customary at one time to say that this drama never took place, but archaeological discoveries reveal that there is nothing very improbable about it. Sieges are depicted in Babylonian reliefs, and city plans inscribed on clay have survived.[16] Dramas often have a mimetic quality, but this is the only case where there is an attempt to

---

[13] For a discussion of the literary structure of the whole passage 4.1–5.4, see Zimmerli, *Ezekiel I*, pp. 101ff. He concludes that there are three basic actions, 4.1f., 4.9–11 minus the last half of 9, and 5.1–3 with certain deletions. They represent the beginning of the siege, its severity and its end. C. Uehlinger has recently produced an important study of this whole passage in *Jerusalem: Texte-Bilder-Steine*, a Festschrift for Hildi and Othmar Keel. It is ' "Zeichne eine Stadt . . . und belagere sie!" Bild und Wort in einer Zeichenhandlung Ezechiels gegen Jerusalem (Ez. 4f.)', pp. 111–200.

[14] The nature of the model is discussed at some length by Uehlinger.

[15] On the face of it, this is a good example of what Bernhard Lang calls prophetic 'street theatre' (*Monotheism and the Prophetic Minority*, p. 81), but there are difficulties with that explanation even in this example, and far greater difficulties elsewhere. See below Chapter 17.

[16] Pritchard, *ANEP*, pp. 129–32.

create a realistic copy of the reality that is being expressed. The undertaking was complicated and must have taken some time to carry out. There is no mention of an audience, but there is the comment at the end of v. 3 that this is a sign for the house of Israel. If, as seems likely, it is essential to the meaning of the word *'ôṯ* that the deed be visible, then it must have been public. On the other hand, if it had been public, some explanation would have been needed, and no explanation is given. So, either the explanation went unrecorded and is now lost, or the comment at the end of v. 3, including the word *'ôṯ*, does not belong to the original incident, but is an editorial comment.

Eichrodt considers that the identity of the city portrayed in the drama was not revealed, but this is most unlikely.[17] It is true that the words 'even Jerusalem' in v. 1 are probably a gloss, and maybe 4.7, which seems to tie up the whole passage with Jerusalem, is the product of later editing. Nevertheless, there is still the common-sense question whether, at that time and place, a besieged city would suggest any place other than Jerusalem, whether named or not. It is possible that the original action was not public, that it was a drama for the prophet himself, like Jeremiah's experience with the waistcloth, but it is not credible that it was done in public, as Eichrodt suggests, without anyone knowing to which city it referred.

There is widespread agreement among commentators that, in this action, Ezekiel personates Yahweh, but, even without the precise instructions in v. 3b, he personates the besiegers as well. Yahweh has raised up a human agency to lay siege to his own city and Ezekiel, in dramatizing the event, represents both parties. Setting the face towards or against the city is a strong phrase. On the basis of other usages in Ezekiel, where a weaker verb is used (13.17; 15.7; 20.46, etc.), it must be understood in a hostile sense. The eye emitted personal force, the glowering countenance conveyed destructive energy. The world of ideas connected with sorcery is not far away, but Ezekiel is not putting a spell on the city; he is representing the anger of Yahweh, and anger, being personal, is not regarded as a condition or an attitude, but as a precisely directed activity.

This brings us to the difficulty in v. 3. What purpose does the iron plate serve? If it represents the fortifications of the city, it is redundant, for the model of v. 1 must include walls. A second suggestion is that it shows the severity of the siege, the 'inexorable grasp' of Yahweh,

---

[17] Eichrodt, *Ezekiel*, p. 83.

in which case it is a remarkably inexpressive detail in a very carefully worked out drama.[18] Thirdly, the plate might represent an impenetrable barrier which rules out the possibility of any intervention, even divine intervention, from outside. The point of the iron is then clear. Iron is stronger than the material used for the rest of the drama. Jerusalem is not afflicted merely by an enemy at the gates, which has happened before, but is now cut off by divine judgment so that nothing will interfere with her doom.[19] This option may seem the most likely, but there is still a contradiction of images. The plate is a barrier to divine intervention but not to Ezekiel's bellicose grimaces. Fourthly, the plate may represent a barrier between the prophet and the city, interrupting temporarily the prophet's sense of identity with the unhappy inhabitants.[20] Bearing in mind these difficulties, it seems best to suppose that v. 3 is an editorial attempt, and a confusing and unnecessary one, to strengthen the imagery of vv.1f.

What is most interesting about this drama is its purpose, and the definition of that will depend upon solving the question of where Ezekiel was at the material time. There has been considerable controversy on the point since critical scholarship began; it is an issue that bears, not only on this passage, but on most of the drama narratives in Ezekiel. The majority view now is that Ezekiel's own account of his ministry is substantially correct (1.1; 3.15, etc.), that is to say, he was taken into exile in 597 BCE and prophesied from Babylon. The alternative view, that his base was Jerusalem, is hard to accept for the following reasons. In the first place, almost every scholar who doubts that Ezekiel worked largely in Babylon produces a hypothesis of his own, and to a large extent these hypotheses conflict with each other. Secondly, the Jerusalem hypothesis is not simply a new interpretation of the data. It is a hypothesis based on other hypotheses. A new account of the literary history of the book of Ezekiel must first be worked out and find favour before it is even possible to address the question of the prophet's location. This leads to such complexity that it would be wiser to declare for agnosticism than actually to put faith in any such theory. Thirdly, the argument rests largely on the fact that much of Ezekiel's prophecy is concerned with judgment on Jerusalem, but it is an error to suppose that this must be addressed to

[18] Davidson and Streane, *Ezekiel*, p. 32; Zimmerli, *Ezekiel I*, pp. 162f.; Zimmerli regards v. 3 as a later addition, but possibly by Ezekiel himself.

[19] So Greenberg, *Ezekiel 1–20*, p. 104.

[20] So Uehlinger, ' "Zeichne eine Stadt" '.

the inhabitants of that city. If the people of Israel were to have any future, the lessons to be learnt from the last days of Jerusalem were of crucial importance, not so much to the inhabitants, who were doomed, but to the exiles, who represented the future. Fourthly, Ezekiel has much to say about the fall of Jerusalem, and his dramatic actions emphasize the pain and horror of the event. That would hardly be necessary if he was prophesying to the people who were about to experience it. It would, however, be vitally important in Babylon, where the people would not know and where, perhaps, some would not care.

It is wise, therefore, to assume that this dramatic action and those that follow took place while Ezekiel was among the exiles at Tel-abib (cf.3.15). Jerusalem was many hundreds of miles away by the shortest route, but concern for the fate of the city would be uppermost in the minds of the faithful and should be uppermost in the minds of all. Ezekiel makes his model to bring the siege home to them. The overwhelming fact of Yahweh's wrath against the city and its consequential downfall has to express itself, not only where the loss takes place, but where it is most significant and where it is most felt. Hence this drama. If this is the true explanation of the act, then we have here, not a prediction of a future event, but an extension of a present one. The divine reality manifests itself in Judah as a siege and in Babylon as a drama. This explanation holds, even if the drama were performed in private. The main thrust is not towards the communication of a message but towards the extension of a divine act.

Ezekiel Lies on his Side: Ezek. 4.4–6

That a dramatic action is recorded in 4.4–6, in which Ezekiel is told to lie on his side for a long period, is clear, but there, alas, clarity ends. The prophet is instructed to lie on his left side for 390 days to bear the punishment of Israel, the left side representing the north, and one day representing one year of punishment. Then he must lie on his right side for 40 days to bear the punishment of Judah. The LXX changes 390 to 190 both here and in v. 9, where the figure occurs again, but this does little to help. There is no account of Ezekiel carrying out the charge and there is no explanation other than that which is implicit in the charge itself.

The problems are in four areas. There are textual difficulties; the meaning is dubious; the numbers resist logical explanation; and the whole thing seems impossible.

The textual difficulties are not confined to this one narrative, but this is a convenient point to treat them. The evidence considered already suggests that in the passage beginning in 3.22 we have accounts of actions, not in themselves simple, that have become more obscure because of later additions. Already we have had difficulty with 4.3 and concluded that it is probably an editorial addition. The same conclusion must be reached over 4.7f. These verses are concerned with extending and cross-referencing what is said elsewhere. In v. 7 the editor returns to the subject of the siege. A detail from v. 3, 'set your face toward the siege', is repeated, and an instruction is given to Ezekiel to bare his arm and prophesy against the city. Neither of these actions is easy to reconcile with the enforced immobility. Nevertheless, by means of the reference to the siege in v. 7a, vv. 1–7 are locked together, the kernel of the passage being two short prophetic actions, the siege drama, which we have already discussed, and the lying down, the discussion of which is still to come. But v. 8, while still relating to the siege, also goes back to 3.25, making an even larger bracket with three prophetic actions in it. Verse 8 also speaks bafflingly about 'the days of your siege'. There is nothing in the siege narrative itself that requires activity over a length of days; the number of days comes from the following narratives. Verse 8 also states that, despite the barely conceivable discomfort of lying so long on one side, the malady will prevent the prophet from turning over.[21] By these various allusions, dumbness, siege and lying down are inextricably tied together. Then, to complete the picture, v. 9, with its reference to 390 days, which belongs to the next narrative, connects with v. 5, so interlocking four drama narratives. One can only suppose that this is literary artifice and that the basic stories must be considered first without the additions, though the fact that they were later bound together so intricately shows that those who gave us the final text were anxious that we should not treat the incidents separately, but allow each to interpret the others. One thing seems to be clear, that the editor who wrote 4.8 interpreted Ezekiel's immobility in 3.25 as a malady imposed by God. This is fatal to Eichrodt's theory that Ezekiel's confinement was due to hostility from exiles. It also indicates that, in the editor's

---

[21] Verse 6, of course, instructs the prophet to turn over, but once only, between the two periods.

understanding at least, there was nothing significant about the prophet's house. The significance attached to the prophet's physical condition.

We now return to the story in 4.4–6. It has two elements, 390 days for Israel and 40 days for Judah. The first question is whether the reference to Judah is original. Verse 9b, one of the insertions that bind the whole passage together, refers only to the 390 days for Israel. The LXX has the two elements, but leaves out the word for 'a second time' in v. 6. The most important consideration, however, is whether Ezekiel, whose prophecies at this point are so deeply concerned with Jerusalem and the Judahite exiles, would have any reason for performing a dramatic action relating to the northern kingdom, which had ceased to exist for more than 120 years. If the action is essentially a drama about Judah, then the references to the house of Israel in vv. 4f. must be understood as relating to Judah, and paradoxically, v. 6, with its reference to Judah, must disappear. The word 'left' in v. 4 would probably have to go, too. The use of 'the house of Israel' is consistent with Ezekiel's usage. His prophetic call was to prophesy to the house of Israel (3.1). The editor of the passage may well have agreed with Ezekiel about this, for he had just used the same phrase for Judah in v. 3. But, if that is so, who could possibly have added v. 6? Whoever did so took 'the house of Israel' to mean the northern kingdom. So either vv. 3 and 5 are consistent, in which case v. 6 is contradictory, or vv. 5 and 6 are consistent, in which case vv. 3 and 5 are at odds and v. 5 is at odds with Ezekiel's general usage. Only a speculative theory of editorial redaction can solve this problem and any such would be very hypothetical. This is one of those cases where one has to work on, recognizing that the problem cannot be solved. It is also one of those cases where holistic treatment of a complete passage (3.22–5.4) seems attractive until it is actually undertaken; then old problems present themselves in a new guise.

What is reasonably certain is that here an action is recounted in which Ezekiel represents the Jewish community in exile. The community is under constraint as a punishment and their sad condition is focussed in a special constraint placed on the prophet himself. The drama is thus expressive, not causative, and this well suits the early years of the exile. It is not a matter of communicating facts to people who did not know them, but of recognizing a reality that is coming into being and responding to its compulsion in a dramatic way. The suggestion that the days of constraint represent 390 years of Israel's sinning misses the point of the symbolism which relates to punishment and not to rebellion. The years of sinning have been converted into so many days of vicarious punishment (cf. Num. 14.34). One can legitimately say with von Rad, that the prophetic office invades the prophet's private life and leads him to suffer vicariously.[22] This interpretation stands even if the constraint was not artificial and deliberate but the result of an illness. Prophecy itself was compulsive. Prophets, particularly the great prophets, were not free men. The constraint of Yahweh's word and the constraint of illness, so different to a modern reader, would be much the same thing to them. The logic goes like this. There is a striking event – illness; there is a significant interpretation – punishment. Therefore the event is a sign, and if a sign, a deliberate act of God to express his intent.

Can we conceive of the action having taken place? There is no account of it actually happening, and if the numbers are taken seriously, surely it must be regarded as impossible. But the numbers probably obscure the point and it is no great loss to reject them as unreliable. Commentators have wrestled with them for years without success. It makes little difference whether the numbers are regarded as original or a later addition.[23] What is likely is that Ezekiel suffered an illness in which he was forced to lie still or was unable to move, and he afterward interpreted his affliction as a divine word. This is consistent with the account of his occasional dumbness in 3.22–27. If the action is understood in this basic sense, then it was certainly very expressive. The constraint evident in Ezekiel's body epitomized a long-lasting constraint on the whole kingdom.

Strange Bread: Ezek. 4.9–17

Ezekiel is instructed to make bread of poor quality by gathering different kinds of grain. He is to eat it once a day in small measure. Similarly he is to allow himself only a small ration of water. The bread,

[22] Von Rad, *Theology II*, p. 275; see also McConville, 'The Place of Ritual in Old Testament Religion'.

[23] The numbers problem is complicated by the uncertainty regarding the meaning of 'the house of Israel' in v. 4. If the story is taken as it stands, and if 'house of Israel' means Israel over against Judah, then neither 390 nor 190 gives a correct answer, for the northern kingdom never saw the end of her punishment. If, however, v. 5 refers to Judah, the number must have been altered when v. 6 was added, but what the original number was and why it was altered to 390 remain mysteries. For a discussion of the problem of numbers, see Greenberg, *Ezekiel 1–20*, pp. 105f.

he is now told, must be baked on human dung and in public. He protests that he has never defiled himself by eating impure food before and is then allowed to use cow dung. There is no account of the action actually being performed.

Verse 9b must be extracted. It refers again to the 390 days; it disrupts the sense, and it must be regarded as an editorial reference back to vv. 4–8. The problem then is that the passage has two quite different themes, and two different explanations are offered for the drama. The first theme is famine. Verses 16f. imply that Ezekiel will be representing the besieged in Jerusalem on crude, hard rations. The second theme is uncleanness. Verse 13 implies that Ezekiel will be representing Israel in exile, eating unclean bread 'among the nations'. The confusion is made worse by the facts that v. 9a, which contains the primary command, can apparently be taken either way, and that v. 12, which contains the reference to human dung, might be part of the original drama, implying that fuel was also short, or it might be part of the secondary version, raising the question of uncleanness.

A reasonable solution is not impossible. We begin with v. 9a. It is commonly said that the reference to a mixture of several kinds of grain is ambiguous. It could mean that there was not enough good grain, which would imply siege conditions and point to Jerusalem. Or it could mean that the mixture of seeds implied uncleanness and so points to the exile. In fact there is no evidence that a mixture of this kind was unclean.[24] The texts usually cited, Deut. 22.9f and Lev. 19.19, refer to sowing in a field, not baking in a cake. The notion that the mixture of grains is unclean is read back into the preliminary account from the explanation, and, as we shall see, from a secondary explanation at that. The description in v. 9a definitely suggests conditions of shortage and it may reasonably be assumed that the drama began its course as a representation of the conditions of life in besieged Jerusalem. The people had only half a pound of coarse bread and perhaps a pint of water a day. In this case, vv. 16f. provide the appropriate explanation. The drama has much in common with 4.1–3 and 12.17–20. Ezekiel is exhibiting the siege of Jerusalem before the eyes of the exiles, so that those far removed from the scene may none the less enter into its pathos.

The complication arises with the reference to human dung in v. 12

[24] A fact pointed out by Zimmerli, *Ezekiel I*, p. 169; see too Carmichael, 'Forbidden Mixtures'.

Deut. 23.12–14 makes clear the Hebrew attitude to this matter of elementary hygiene and we are left wondering whether the use of human excreta is a part of the original drama, thus making the conditions in Jerusalem appear all the more shocking, or whether the detail has been deliberately added to divert the story from the theme of privation to the theme of impurity. The position of the verse settles the question in favour of the latter interpretation. If the detail had been part of the original version, the correct place for it would have been between vv. 9a and 9b and certainly before v. 10. Its appearance after v. 11, that is, after the reference to drink, shows that it is no part of the original but that it belongs to the secondary version, calling for a different explanation. Here, then, we suggest, is a drama, or rather a command to perform a drama, in which Ezekiel acts out in Babylon the painful experiences of Jews still living in Jerusalem. As such the drama is expressive but in no sense causative. Then, at a later stage, someone wished to relate the action, not to Jews still in Jerusalem, but to the exiles themselves. Their problem was not shortage but an unclean environment. Verse 12 was added to change the emphasis. The food supply was not so much exiguous as impure. Where was Israel obliged to suffer by eating impure food? Of course, in an unclean land, that is, in exile (cf. Amos 7.17). The ceremonial implications of Ezekiel's supposed action in v. 12 were severe and the editor could not allow the prophet to receive the command without protest. So, after the new explanation set out in v. 13, Ezekiel is allowed to make an objection and cow dung, a common and legitimate fuel, is allowed instead.

As far as prophetic drama is concerned, both these versions point in the same direction, but they do not operate in exactly the same way. If the story concerns the representation of the famine in Jerusalem, then the drama is a means whereby a reality is extended in space. The time reference is unclear, even unimportant. What matters is that, by means of the drama, the reality is established in Babylon. This makes it an interesting and important example of how the relationship between drama and reality was understood. It is noteworthy that, if v. 12 is attached to the secondary explanation, there is no reference to an audience for the drama at all. This may be simply fortuitous, but the notion of a private action cannot be ruled out.[25] The editor who

---

[25] This suggestion is, of course, at odds with the views of those who still see dramas primarily as visual aids. Lang, for example, who regards Ezekiel as a 'creative

added the secondary explanation in vv. 12–15 had a rather different idea. He saw the drama as epitomizing Israel's real plight in the exile that was just beginning. The tragedy is expressed in the action of the prophet who was required by Yahweh to break the laws of purity. What Ezekiel was commanded to do on one occasion, the whole people would have to do over a period of years. This makes two powerful points. In the first place, exile, appalling as it was, was Yahweh's decree. The people was to be defiled by his will. Secondly, if some of the people were inclined to take exile too lightly, and for some it turned out to be less disastrous than might have been expected, the drama demonstrates its true nature. The editor uses the narrative to bring into sharp focus a reality that was being enacted at that very time and place, but which was not being properly appreciated for the tragedy it was. This second interpretation may well have originated soon after the first. It would be immediately topical. It is even possible that the new interpretation was not the work of an editor, recounting Ezekiel's words and deeds some time in the middle of the sixth century, but of Ezekiel himself, though it is hard to believe that he actually performed the drama a second time in a different form. In either case, drama and reality are related in a most instructive way.

Shaving the Hair: Ezek. 5.1–4

The last of this group of drama narratives is also concerned with the fall of Jerusalem. Ezekiel is instructed to take a sword or dagger and, using it as a razor, shave his head and beard. He was to collect the hair, weigh it, and divide it into three parts. One part was to be burnt, one part was to be cut up with the sword, and the third part was to be scattered to the winds. In all probability that was the end of the original action. Verse 2 concludes with three problematic Hebrew words. They constitute a first-person statement, presumably by Yahweh, underlining the disaster. Taken as they stand, these words imply that Yahweh himself will become involved in the drama. The statement seems to have found its way into this verse from v. 12, where it is part

---

performer', considers this action as another example of 'street theatre', 'an open-air demonstration of how to prepare simple wartime meals that would, however, not necessarily meet all the standards of ritual purity and gourmet taste' ('Street Theater, Raising the Dead and the Zoroastrian Connection in Ezekiel's Prophecy', p. 298). Lang's writing is lively but not persuasive.

of an extended explanation and where it makes better sense. Verse 12 may in turn be an echo of the doom threatened in Lev. 26.33.

As so often in Ezekiel, the drama consists of a command only, with no account of the prophet complying. Subsequently extra details were added in vv. 3f., and a long explanation taking up all the rest of the chapter appended. Verses 1f. may well pre-date the fall of Jerusalem. They are harsh and hopeless; but a later editor, conscious of the vocation of the covenant people, and perhaps cheered by the situation in Babylon, insisted that Ezekiel, who was at this point personating Yahweh, should preserve a small remnant in the border of his robe. Yet another editor, with a bitter experience of the exile, saw that even the remnant was vulnerable, and he wrote this factor into the narrative.

Despite the bizarre impression created by the present text, the symbolism is not at all difficult. Hair was regarded both as a pride and a glory and as the actual locus of physical strength (Judg. 16.19).[26] Cut hair was not simply the stuff that was swept up off the barber's floor but a symbol of the personality and, therefore, an appropriate material to be used in the representation of the inhabitants of Jerusalem. Moreover shaving the head and beard was a sign of humiliation and sorrow (II Sam. 10.4f.; Isa. 15.2; Jer. 16.6; 41.5; 48.37), so the detail is doubly significant. One complication in the account is that shaving the head is forbidden to a priest in Lev. 21.5 and Ezek. 44.20. That, however, does not argue against the drama being enacted; rather it underlines the affliction that comes to the prophet through expressing the divine will. A further complication is that the prophet is required to personate both the righteous judge and the guilty victim at the same time. In Isa. 7.20 Yahweh's action against Israel is expressed under the image of a comprehensive shaving, and no doubt that oracle lies behind this passage.

The instruction to Ezekiel is to take a sword and use it as a razor, a curious and perhaps significant detail. As the drama represents the final carnage for the people of Jerusalem, a sword is a more suitable tool than a domestic razor. This, at any rate, holds for the written account. It is more difficult to see how, in practice, the prophet could shave himself with a sword, but perhaps we think of shaving in too modern a sense. A sword would do simply to hack off his hair and his beard. The result does not have to be a smooth skin. Ezekiel takes the sword to perform the act of humiliation, but he performs it on himself.

---

[26] Fohrer, *Die Handlungen*, pp. 14, 53f.

He thus represents Israel, who is about to suffer judgment. This is not the end of the complication, for the hair, once cut off, becomes a property for a further act of the drama. The hair itself now becomes the people of Israel. The thought process is not easy but it is comprehensible. The balances seem over-elaborate; they must be supposed to signify the extreme care with which Yahweh works out his will in history. Nothing, it might be thought, is more random than the slaughter that ensues when a city falls, but it was not random to Ezekiel. Everything happened according to the exact judgment of Yahweh.

The import of the basic action in vv. 1f. would, therefore, have been reasonably clear. The sword meant military force. Burning hair 'in the midst of the city' – does this mean the model of 4.1–3? – is expressive enough. A third of the people would suffer as the city was sacked; a third would die in the ensuing battle; and a third would be deported and scattered. Complex this may be, but only a relatively simple formula would have been necessary to make it all clear to Ezekiel's contemporaries at the beginning of the exile, if indeed this was his purpose. The additions are another matter. Both vv. 3 and 4 suggest ornamentation at the literary stage and the long explanation in vv. 5–17 is too long and too wide-ranging to belong to the original occasion. These verses contain a comprehensive prophecy of doom relating back to all the dramas in this group but including in v. 12 a specific reference to 5.1f.

Those whose chief concern is whether the incidents under scrutiny actually happened tend to point to this narrative as an example of a drama that is completely incredible, but this judgment is unsound. It is a complex act of a complex person, and it is made more complex in transmission, but an actual performance is still discernible, quite credible, and by no means incomprehensible. The difficulty is that the drama proved to be inaccurate or not sufficiently subtle and vv. 3f. were added at the literary stage to make the whole more in line with events. The time reference in this narrative is, therefore, interesting. In vv. 1f. there is every reason to suppose that Ezekiel is continuing the purpose revealed in the previous drama of bringing home to the exiles the awful fate of Jerusalem and its people. There may be a predictive element here, but the drama would be equally effective if Jerusalem had already fallen. Verses 3f., however, deal with the fate of the third part that was scattered. They too had varied fortunes; the sword followed them; some were protected – presumably that is how we are to understand, 'bind them in the skirts of your robe'; and some were destroyed in the fire. No doubt this addition was made, as a *vaticinium ex eventu*, to give as accurate an account as possible of what actually happened. But in inserting this addition into the narrative, the editor made it into a thoroughly predictive one. Plainly he had no qualms about this. He was governed by the principle that drama and reality belong together as part of the same whole. As he had, from his position in history, superior knowledge of the reality, he thought it right that he should adjust the drama accordingly.

Clapping and Stamping: Ezek. 6.11–14

Once again, in a pattern that has become familiar in Ezekiel, we find an instruction to perform some dramatic gestures followed by a lengthy explanation, all part of the instruction, and no account of the gestures actually being carried out. They are clapping the hands, stamping the foot, and making an exclamation. These are conventional actions, no doubt clear to Ezekiel's audience, but not so clear to us. The explanatory formula is not directly related to the actions in that it explains why some actions are to be carried out, but not why these particular actions are appropriate. As so often, the explanatory formula has been extended so that the balance of the passage is lost. A brief command – six words in Hebrew – becomes the text of a disproportionately detailed sermon.

Clapping the hands occurs in the Old Testament as a gesture of excitement with a number of different associations. Four different verbs are used. Some instances suggest rejoicing, particularly cultic rejoicing (II Kings 11.12; Isa. 55.12; Pss. 47.1; 98.8). Others suggest gratification at an enemy's downfall (Lam. 2.15; Nahum 3.19; Ezek. 25.6; Job 27.23; 34.37). Others suggest anger (Num. 24.10; Ezek. 21.14,17; 22.13).[27] Stamping the foot is less common. It occurs only here and in Ezek. 25.6, where it refers to the malevolent glee of the Ammonites over Israel. The exclamation, 'Ah' ('Alas' in RSV), is no more helpful. In the only other occurrence, Ezek. 21.15, it implies enthusiastic excitement over slaughter.

A certain pattern emerges from this material. Anger fulfilling itself in destruction and leading, therefore, to wild satisfaction is implied.

---

[27] There is a late usage in Prov. 17.18 and 22.26, where clapping the hands signifies giving a promise. It can hardly be relevant here.

There is no need to emend *'āḥ* to *he'āḥ*, which usually expresses satisfaction,[28] despite the fact that *he'āḥ* occurs in Ezek. 25.3, 26.2 and 36.2; *'āḥ* is simply a blank to be filled in by the context. The probability is that Ezekiel is being asked to personate, not the foreign conqueror, but Yahweh himself, who brings home justice to his people. The similarity between 6.12d and 5.13, 7.8, 20.8, 20.21, and 22.22 makes this fairly certain, even though unbecoming passions are thereby attributed to the deity. The actions involved are conventional, but their performance on this occasion was given a specific and elevated meaning.

Going into Exile: Ezek. 12.1–16

From many points of view this is the clearest example of prophetic drama in Ezekiel. The action can be dated around the year 592 BCE. Ezekiel is told to gather together the meagre belongings that one going into exile could take with him. He is to be sure that his fellow Jews see what he is doing; indeed, the point is laboured: 'in their sight' occurs six times in four verses. Then, at night but still in the presence of onlookers, he must dig his way through a wall, presumably, if this detail is original, the wall of the hut in which he lived in Tel-abib. He must lift his baggage onto his shoulder and, covering his face, carry it away. This detailed command is followed in v. 7 by the statement in the first person that it was actually carried out. Then comes an explanation which is even more detailed than the instruction. It relates the action to Zedekiah, the puppet king of Israel, who would suffer the fate that Ezekiel had dramatized. The end would be that Israel would at last know the power of Yahweh. Here then, for the only time in Ezekiel, we have Fohrer's ideal structure of *Befehl*, *Bericht* and *Deutung* in a single narrative. Furthermore, in vv. 6 and 12, Ezekiel's action is described as a *môpēt* to the onlookers.

A simple drama relating to the departure of the inhabitants of Jerusalem into captivity lies behind these verses, but the passage has been added to, perhaps more than once, by editors who were familiar with the historical facts, particularly those relating to Zedekiah. So, in the present version, Ezekiel is to be seen personating the king rather than the ordinary Jerusalemite. The clearest indication of the revision of the story is to be seen in vv. 10 and 11. In v. 11 it is asserted that

---

[28] As Zimmerli (*Ezekiel I*, p. 180) and others suggest.

the sign relates, as one would expect, to all those who would go into exile. Verse 10, an obvious intrusion, relates the sign specifically to the king. II Kings 25.1–6 reveals the source of some of the other details that have been added. The digging through the wall of v. 5 derives from II Kings 25.4; the details are not clear, but Zedekiah evidently escaped by a gap in the wall rather than by the gates. The covering of the face (vv. 6 and 12) is a puzzling detail. It can hardly refer to the fact that Zedekiah was subsequently blinded. Perhaps the LXX has it right. In v. 12 the LXX has a passive; the face was covered, not to stop the king seeing, but so that he might not be seen. This at least makes better sense. Verse 13 must surely be a reference to Zedekiah's wretched fate recorded in II Kings 25.7. Verse 16 looks like another addendum. It is reminiscent of 5.3 and suggests a period, late in the exile, when faith and confidence were beginning to revive. The original drama is, therefore, probably to be found in vv. 1–4, 7–9, and 11, but even these verses have been worked over.

In that Jerusalem had not yet fallen, there is a predictive element in this dramatic action, but it still remains primarily expressive rather than predictive. Ezekiel is certainly not causing the fall of a city hundreds of miles away. He is transporting the Jerusalem crisis to Babylon and enabling his hearers to participate in the coming event. The doom is already created in the mind of Yahweh and it is slowly coming into actuality before the eyes of men. Several times it is reiterated that the drama must be done in public and v. 2 gives the explanation. The reality of God's righteous action in history has not been grasped by Israel. The people remain stubborn and rebellious. Consequently the appalling facts have to be thrust before their eyes. They must be witnesses to the deportation. On the face of it this looks like an argument for the old-fashioned view that the dramas were merely visual aids to make the prophetic message clear, but this contention falls far short of the truth. The drama does not derive from a prophet who is having difficulty with communication. It derives from Yahweh who is angered by the fact that the people, who understand the prophetic word well enough, are not impressed by it. They remain a rebellious house. So the word must be made more insistent, more aggressive, more inescapable. The reality of divine judgment must be forced on their attention. With the drama the reality approaches one step nearer. It becomes less and less easy to live in blind ignorance. By this drama Ezekiel extends the plight of Jerusalem to Babylon, so that the rebellious will not be able to escape it. It is not necessarily in order that they may repent, for repentance is not mentioned until the addition in v. 16, but simply that the divine action might be fully realized and the truth manifested. For this reason, if for no other, we should reject Eichrodt's curious view that the drama was ambiguous until verbal explanation was given. Even though the action was carried out in silence, the demeanour of the prophet must have been unmistakable. Even in mime good news is easily distinguished from bad; how much more the best from the worst.

Eating and Drinking in Fear: Ezek. 12.17–20

Yahweh commands the prophet to eat bread and drink water while giving expression to a state of terror. At the same time he is to proclaim that the inhabitants of Jerusalem will eat and drink in a similar condition because of the violence that is coming upon them. There is no account of the action being carried out and all the explanation is contained in the oracle which is a part of the dramatic action itself.

It is not entirely clear whom Ezekiel is addressing. Three prepositions occur in the first half of v. 19. If each is taken in its simplest sense, then Ezekiel is commanded to address the inhabitants of Jerusalem.[29] But the oracle then proceeds with a description of the people of Jerusalem in the third person. Zimmerli points out that the book of Ezekiel is given to blurring the distinction between ʾ*el* and *ʿal*, so it is probably best to take it that Ezekiel is to speak, not to, but *about* the people of Jerusalem, who would be absent.[30] This agrees with the general contention that Ezekiel's prophetic ministry took place in Babylon and the specific point that this series of dramas all represent the fall of Jerusalem in one way or another to people who could not experience it. Ezekiel is speaking to the exiles, described with some irony as 'the people of the land', about a state of affairs in Jerusalem. If the previous drama was about deportation, this one relates to the conditions after it. It expresses not so much a shortage of sustenance (as in 4.16), but the emotions of those who had to suffer it.

The interesting question is whether Ezekiel trembles and quakes

---

[29] It is hardly surprising that this passage figures in the argument about where Ezekiel was when he prophesied. Eichrodt recognizes the problem and puts forward the proposition that Ezekiel was addressing the former landowners of Judah in their captivity (*Ezekiel*, p. 154f.).

[30] Zimmerli, *Ezekiel I*, p. 85f.

deliberately in response to the divine command or whether the trembling came first as a sympton of an illness and Ezekiel inferred a word of God from it, as may well be the case with his dumbness. It is the kind of issue where we have to be satisfied with probability rather than certainty. Three arguments tell in favour of this drama being an inference from a natural condition rather than a contrived action. First, it is hard to see how the prophet could represent terror by the way in which he ate and drank. This action was to be performed in public and, according to v. 20, communication was its chief purpose. If that was really the aim, this action is a poor way of achieving it. Secondly, it is clear that Ezekiel was prone to psychological disturbances which are impossible now to diagnose, but which are consistent with bouts of shaking and trembling. One who was at times dumb and at times prostrate could hardly have been free from such indications of physical weakness. Thirdly, both Hosea and Jeremiah interpreted apparently natural experiences as divine words. Ezekiel almost certainly did the same with his dumbness and his immobility. It must, therefore, be presumed that something similar happened here. While he was suffering this particular affliction, he came to understand it as a dramatic representation of how the inhabitants of Jerusalem would suffer after the siege.

*   *   *

The whole of ch. 21 would contribute considerably to our understanding of the subject if we had a clear account of the prophet's actions or even a complete text and some idea of the literary history. None of these is available, and this is doubtless the reason why van den Born, Fohrer and others pass over much of the material. A thorough textual study would require more space than we can allow and would still not provide a version that would inspire complete confidence; nevertheless the material is too valuable to ignore completely.

It is reasonably clear that in ch. 21 a number of passages of different provenance are tied together by the word 'sword'. The word first appears in v. 3. Three times the text speaks of a sword that Yahweh will draw from its sheath to cut off both the righteous and the wicked in Israel. The reality is clear – destruction by an invader's sword from south to north. But there is no dramatic action at this stage, only an oracle. The text continues with the action of sighing which we will consider in a moment. We return to the sword in v. 9 and again in the words of an oracle. Even though the sword is sharpened and polished, it still has not appeared in a visible dramatic action. On the contrary, we stay, for the time being, with the sighs of grief, 'cry and wail' and 'smite upon your thigh'. In vv. 14–17 the prophet is told to make cutting movements with the sword, and so the spoken oracle passes over into the acted drama. Verses 18–27 continue the sword theme with a reference to the king of Babylon at the parting of the ways (see below). Verses 28–32 return to the sword waving of vv. 14–17.

From this tangled skein we extract three possible dramatic acts, the sighs of grief, the sword waving, and the king at the parting of the ways.

Sighs of Grief: Ezek. 21.6f., 12 [21.11f., 17 in Hebrew]

This is a drama narrative in miniature. After prophecy against Israel which includes a promise that the sword of Yahweh would work havoc through the land, there follows the present instruction-with-explanation which is typical of drama narratives in Ezekiel. The prophet is told to sigh deeply and show outward signs of grief. When questioned he is to explain that he is doing what everyone will do when the ill news comes from Jerusalem. Later in the chapter he is told to cry and wail and smite upon his thigh. The last is an action we have not encountered before. From Jer. 31.19 we can deduce that it is some kind of self-chastisement to express intensity of emotion. There is no account of the actions being carried out.

Only a few brief comments are necessary. In the first place, Ezekiel is personating the whole people in exile. As a prophet to whom God's intention is known, he already stands in the presence of the awful reality. As yet the people do not, but they soon will. He is representing them in their future state, but this is not foresight; nor is it instrumental action to bring about disaster. It is, as far as Ezekiel and his editors are concerned, exposure to an actual event, which already exists in the will of Yahweh, which has come to exist in the experience of the prophet, and which will soon become an actuality in the experience of everyone. Like Jeremiah's action in buying the field of Anathoth, Ezekiel's action is the first of a series. He sighs now, but many will sigh hereafter. Also like Jeremiah, Ezekiel is not indulging in mere mimicry; there was a real field and there is real grief. Others may misunderstand; the contemporary situation may give an air of unreality both to the ownership of the field and the expression of grief, but things are not what they seem. What Yahweh wills exists. Jeremiah and Ezekiel are not looking ahead; they are simply in touch with the true nature of things; they are already sharing in what is coming to be.

Secondly this story confirms that dramatic actions do not have a function essentially different from oracles. An audience is necessary here. The sighing must be 'before their eyes'. In Amos 5.1ff. there is a dirge oracle against the northern kingdom which has the same force as Ezekiel's sighing.[31] Nevertheless it would be wrong to argue from this that the sole, or even the primary purpose of the prophetic action is communication. A different interpretation fits all the evidence better. Both word and action are aspects of the full reality. What is to be will express itself in verbal form as well as historical form. In many cases the verbal form will serve the purpose of communication, but it need not be so. The prophetic word and the prophetic action are linked essentially to the activity of Yahweh who gives them, and not *essentially* to the eyes and ears of the people who receive them. Words and actions are, therefore, alike in that they are responses to divine prompting. Actions may appear more dynamic than words, and there may be special circumstances that make actions appropriate, but fundamentally they operate in the same way.[32]

Thirdly it is worth pointing out that the time reference may be less important than the space reference in this story. The prophet is unveiling an experience that belongs to a distant land. The people will sigh when they hear the news – for them the word will travel overland – but the prophet is already taken up into the Jerusalem event. The drama expresses a tragedy that is present to him.

Fourthly, there is the question whether Ezekiel's action owes anything to the ritual lament. Ritual mourning had an important function in the ancient Near East, and the fact that weeping for Tammuz was an abomination (Ezek. 8.14) does not mean that all ritual mourning was apostasy. On the contrary, sighing, in its purely natural form, would probably go unnoticed. It seems necessary, especially in view of v. 12, to posit a formalized and dramatic expression of grief and cultic procedure might be expected to supply the form. There is no reason to doubt, therefore, that these actions were derived from well-known cultic procedures. As actions they are not unique,

---

[31] Dirge oracles of this kind are common in the prophetic books. See Westermann, *Basic Forms*, pp. 202f.

[32] Amsler devotes the first chapter of *Les Actes* to this point.

but, on this particular occasion, they are raised to a unique level of meaning.

The Sword: Ezek. 21.8–17, 28–32 [21.13–22, 33–3 in Hebrew]

When the sword is introduced in v. 3, it appears as an image, something that is simply spoken about, but in vv. 14 and 16 the instructions include details about what to do with a real sword. The prophet is to bring it down three times and to cut to the right and the left with it.[33] Clapping the hands also appears here, an action too imprecise to be clearly understood and difficult to associate with sword waving. The important factor is the way that the text proceeds from oracles about a sword to actions with a sword. On this three comments can be made. First, the process from oracle to action implies some escalation in the intensity of the prophetic action. Secondly, the confusion between oracle and action appears not to have concerned the editors of this chapter. Oracle and action stand so close together in the minds of the editors that it is not necessary to be clear, at any given moment, which one is being spoken about. Thirdly, this factor makes it impossible to satisfy the modern desire to know what actually happened. This is of no great moment to us, because we are concerned with the way these things were thought about, but it troubled those commentators of a previous generation who were anxious to know the 'real facts of the case'. Fortunately there are other 'real facts of the case' besides what actually happened.

Mock warfare has already been discussed in relation to Joshua's use of the javelin at Ai (Josh. 8.18), Elisha's arrow against the Syrians (II Kings 13.17), and Zedekiah's horns (I Kings 22.11). A similar action with a sword occasions no surprise. The question is whether the action was in any sense formalized, whether it was derivative from 'weapon magic', or whether it was a relatively spontaneous action. Eichrodt, following van den Born, shows some interest in weapon magic, but is concerned to show that Ezekiel's Yahwist faith was not compromised.[34] No one can say much more than that. The use of weapons in dramatic actions of all kinds is widespread and well-known, but the precise details of one such action in ancient Israel are inevitably lost to us.

In vv. 28–32 the sword image is taken up again in order to

---

[33] Some doubt arises about the doubling and trebling in the action in v. 14b, but nothing more precise can be said in view of the corrupt state of the text.

[34] Eichrodt, *Ezekiel*, pp. 293f.

bring the chapter to an acceptable conclusion. In the middle section (vv. 18–27), Jerusalem was chosen for judgment and Ammon appeared to be spared. Ammon, however, has no right to survive, so here the sword is drawn for Ammon. But Babylon, herself, the victorious nation, is only an instrument in the hand of God. Her time too would come; her sword would be returned to its sheath; and she would suffer judgment.[35]

Whatever origins may be sought for these verses in the prophetic ministry of Ezekiel, it seems extremely probable that the present account owes a great deal to the editorial stage of the prophecy. The account, as far as v. 27, leaves Jerusalem on the point of destruction, Ammon exempt and Babylon triumphant. This cannot be the end of the story. The sword action must be rehearsed twice more; first it must be drawn for Ammon, and then it must be sheathed as a sign that Babylon's destructive power is limited. It is, of course, possible that Ezekiel used a sword on a number of occasions and for different purposes, but it is more likely that a relatively simple action for one occasion has been extended and made comprehensive by later reflection. In the end sword actions are directed against all the three nations involved. As far as the meaning of prophetic drama is concerned, this last section adds nothing to what we have discovered already. The sword is used, at least in imagination, to signify swift and devastating judgment. It is sheathed to signify the helplessness of even the greatest nations before Yahweh.

It is interesting to note that Cooke, writing in 1936, found difficulty in attributing to Yahweh the violent attitudes expressed here.[36] Rather than tolerate such an idea he overturned the whole theological basis of Old Testament prophecy and made the prophet the author of the oracle. Yahweh was brought into the action, so Cooke maintained, only by later scribes. Such a hypothesis is quite intolerable. In this chapter, as everywhere else, the prophet is reckoned to be under constraint. The drama is not his because the reality is not his, and

---

[35] It cannot be denied that this understanding, though supported by some (Stalker, Zimmerli), is strongly contested by others (Davidson, Cooke, Taylor). Some vacillate or opt for middle ways (Eichrodt, Wevers). The text is difficult and nobody can feel too certain. An alternative is that the sword represents Ammon's attack on stricken Jerusalem and the sheathing of the sword the moment when Yahweh brings Ammon to judgment. Whichever interpretation is accepted the understanding of the significant action remains much the same.

[36] Cooke, *Ezekiel*, p. 229.

even if the key figure is the editor, it makes no difference. The process is supposed to rest on a divine movement in history, what the prophet says and does is part of that movement. To give the initiative to the prophet is to misrepresent the Hebrew understanding of the prophetic phenomenon completely.

Nebuchadnezzar at the Parting of the Ways: Ezek. 21.18–22 [21.23–27 in Hebrew]

This story is easily related to the historical background. About the year 589 BCE, Judah and Ammon had been plotting to throw off the Babylonian yoke (Jer. 27.1–7), and Nebuchadnezzar inevitably marched westwards. Ezekiel then received instruction from Yahweh to make some kind of map or plan of Nebuchadnezzar's route from Babylon and to set up a sign-post at the place where the road to Rabbath-Ammon and the road to Jerusalem divide. Just where the fork was to be is of no consequence. It might have been Riblah on the Orontes, where Nebuchadnezzar was encamped (II Kings 25.6,21), or Damascus, or somewhere further south. The point is that Nebuchadnezzar had to make a decision about which rebel he would subdue first. Surprisingly the instruction to Ezekiel stops at this point. The prophet is not charged to do anything with the map nor to personate Nebuchadnezzar in his decision. This is odd; the story appears truncated, for the explanation which begins in v. 21 goes much further than the dramatic action itself. The explanation speaks in some detail of Nebuchadnezzar standing at the fork in the road and using three kinds of divination to determine his choice. Jerusalem is indicated as the first place to be attacked.[37]

Verse 22 probably marks the end of the original narrative. What is added in the next few verses is theological comment rather than further explanation of the drama. Verse 23 is a justification of the whole invasion. Nebuchadnezzar is being used, as Assyria was used in Isaiah's day (Isa. 10.5), to execute Yahweh's will on the guilty. The word *mazkîr* is used in v. 23; it is a technical term for the public prosecutor, the one who brings guilt to remembrance. Mention of this root (*z-k-r*) leads on to an oracle against Judah (v. 24) in which Judah is held to be her own prosecutor because her wickedness is

---

[37] Jerusalem had, of course, already been subdued by Nebuchadnezzar in 597 BCE. Some captives, including Ezekiel, had been taken away, but the city lived on.

unconcealed. Then follows an oracle against Zedekiah. By this time we have got completely out of touch with the dramatic action, which was concerned, not with the guilt of Jerusalem, but simply with the fact of Nebuchadnezzar's choice. The theological explanation is, therefore, of little help in solving the puzzle of the form and purpose of the dramatic action.

Nonetheless it is possible to return to the original story and see something of what Ezekiel was doing. He is prophesying in Babylon to those who knew that Nebuchadnezzar was campaigning in the west but who could not believe that the doom would fall on Jerusalem. Hananiah might be dead, but his brand of political optimism lived on. Right to the last the hopeful would believe that Nebuchadnezzar's destination was somewhere else. Ezekiel performed an action which, in the first place, brought home to the exiles the awful fact that Nebuchadnezzar was in a position to choose. Even now he was standing at the cross roads deliberating. Would it be Jerusalem or Rabbath-Ammon? This in itself would be drama enough, and if we rest with the command, that is the end of the story. But the explanation in vv. 21f. carries the incident on to the divination and the choice of Jerusalem. Unfortunately there is no account of the action to arbitrate between the command and the explanation. We must conclude either that the instruction is truncated or that the explanation goes beyond the performance. Either conclusion would be tolerable. The real theological accretions do not begin until v. 23.

It is unfortunately not clear how the drama relates to the reality dramatized in terms of time. No doubt optimism prevailed in Jerusalem, but we have concluded on other grounds that Ezekiel was not ministering there. Among the exiles the drama could also be a forecast, but it could equally be an action to make the crucial events in Jerusalem's tragedy present to those in a distant country. In Babylon the chief function of the action would be to overcome space rather than time. When news travels slowly, it is impossible for those at a distance to live in the same moment as those at the centre of things. The question, 'What has happened since the messenger left?' tends to limit the value of 'news'. The unveiling of the distant event is, therefore, of all the greater significance, and this is the most likely explanation here. At the same time it should be pointed out that there is no mention of any audience in vv. 18–22. Making a distant event present without anybody realizing it may seem a pointless exercise, but the fact must be properly considered. It may be that the editors took an audience for granted. But, whether they did or not, it was clearly not important to them to mention the audience. What they do mention is that it was part of Ezekiel's prophetic ministry to give expression to a distant and painful but divine reality. If that was the important point to them, it is important to us.

Inscribing the Date: Ezek. 24.1f.

This is a brief narrative but one of considerable interest. Inscriptions of one kind or another figure several times in the prophetic books (Isa. 8.1, 16; 30.8; Jer. 36; Hab. 2.2), and the general force seems to be that the word gains greater fixity and authority when it is written down. In this case, however, Ezekiel is not told to write down an oracle but a date, that is, a precise day at the turn of the year 589–8 BCE, the ninth of Zedekiah's reign. There are two difficulties. First, v. 2 provides what looks like an example of dittography, 'the name of this day, this very day'.[38] Secondly, the date is not expressed in Ezekiel's usual style.[39] Editorial harmonization with II Kings 25.1 and, therefore, indirectly with Jer. 39.1 and 52.4 is a distinct possibility. But neither of these difficulties alters the fact that Ezekiel was commanded to make an inscription of a certain date and that date was to be the day on which the siege of Jerusalem began.

Ezekiel in Babylon writes down the date on which Jerusalem's siege was beginning. We do not need to raise the questions of whether he was right or how he knew.[40] The important fact is that a far-off event, in which the exiles were unwilling to believe, and which consequently was to them nothing more than an unpleasant dream, is confirmed and made concrete by the prophetic action. The date represents the event as the name the man. The awful reality of the Jerusalem situation is thus established in Babylon.

There are three ways in which this simple incident might be understood. First, it is sometimes suggested that the action was an attempt to record a prophecy so that, when the news came through, Ezekiel could claim to have been right all along. This sounds very

[38] The LXX preserves the dittography but does not translate the word šēm ('name').

[39] There are a number of dates in Ezekiel and the way they are set out follows a fairly consistent pattern. This one differs from the others in that it does not come first in the sentence and the word ḥōdeš occurs twice.

[40] Concern with these questions so fascinates commentators that few of them give any thought to the meaning of the action.

practical but is least likely to represent the mind of the prophet. Secondly, it could be an attempt to bring the exiles in touch with the reality as it took place, perhaps even to force it on their attention. The day of doom cannot so easily be denied when it is represented, microcosmically, before your eyes. This is the most obvious way of interpreting the incident – to see it in terms of communication, but there is no mention of an audience until v. 3 which begins a new section. So there is a third possibility. Ezekiel's purpose may have been simply to bow to reality, to attest the fact, not in order to pass on information, but simply because it was a fact, a divine fact, to which his prophetic ministry was subservient.

The Rusty Cauldron: Ezek. 24.3–14

This passage is another tangled skein. The difficulties are such that all conclusions will be hypothetical and such conclusions can contribute little to a comprehensive account of prophetic drama. In the first place, it is not clear that this is a prophetic *action* at all. The command in v. 3 may simply mean, 'devise an allegory', though practical demonstration would be equally acceptable, and v. 10 does imply action rather than speech.[41] More difficult is the fact that this story, unlike most other drama narratives, does not reveal a simple message, boldly stated. Rather, in the way of allegories, it offers a complex message in which all the details count. In the *māšāl*, as we have it here, there are four elements. First, a cauldron full of meat prepared for cooking is set on the fire; this is stated in a kind of work-song, in which the various tasks are enumerated in verse. Secondly, the cauldron is discovered to be rusty; this is stated in a doom-oracle. Thirdly, the contents are taken out; the instruction here is very complex. Fourthly, the cauldron is set empty upon the fire and heated till its rust is gone. The immediate reaction is to suppose that a simple action has been allegorized, but if so, it is difficult to deduce what the simple action was.

The meaning of the complex version seems to be that the pot is Jerusalem and the flesh its inhabitants. This has already been stated in 11.1–11, especially v. 3, though whether the cauldron represents an image of security or constraint is not certain. Setting the cauldron on the fire means that the city comes under siege. Rust means that the

---

[41] See the discussion of *māšāl* in Chapter 2.

cauldron is unfit for use. The word ḥel'â occurs only in this passage, but it must refer to some kind of discoloration or impurity.[42] Taking out the contents must refer to the inhabitants who were carried away into exile, and the subsequent burning depicts the fate of the guilty city.

There are textual problems that cannot be avoided. Verse 9a is an exact repetition of 6a and most of the material in between deals with one particular ceremonial sin (cf. Deut. 12.16, 24; Lev. 17.13). Verses 7f. could well be an editorial intrusion. Further, both 6b and 10 deal with the removal of things from the pot, v. 6b stressing the lack of discrimination in the way in which the pieces are removed and v. 10 referring to the residue when the broth is poured out. One or other should be deleted. This would leave us with an allegory in verse form (vv. 3–5) about the preparation of a meal and completely neutral in sense, perhaps even part of a familiar song. This is followed by a prose oracle against Jerusalem (v. 6a and some part of vv. 9–14), as a city fit only for destruction, and making use of the cauldron image. The two halves of the passage do not fit very neatly together even after deletions.

We are left with a dramatic action that might just have taken place. Ezekiel either deliberately took a cauldron that was corroded, or alternatively, while preparing a meal, found a pot to be corroded. He then burnt it, perhaps with some bones inside, until the corrosion was gone and the stench of disaster had been spread around. This gives expression to the state of affairs in Jerusalem. Unfortunately there is too much guesswork here for us to be able to put forward any interpretation with much confidence. The one thing that appears certain is that the prophet is trying to make the guilt and doom of Jerusalem a present reality in Babylon.

Ezekiel Refrains from Mourning: Ezek. 24.15–24

This is one of the best known dramatic actions in Ezekiel and, like most of the others, it relates to the period of the siege of Jerusalem. The phrase, 'the delight of your eyes', in v. 16 must be a reference to Ezekiel's wife. Yahweh tells the prophet that she is to die suddenly. Though he will be heart-broken, he is not to make any public demonstration of mourning. He is not to go barefoot or bareheaded,

---

[42] Kelso draws on some metallurgical expertise to expound this aspect of the narrative. See 'Ezekiel's Parable of the Corroded Copper Cauldron'.

nor to observe the normal conventions. As the text stands, the command from Yahweh ends at v. 17; v. 18 gives an account of the instruction being carried out, and then follows, in response to a request from the people, an explanatory oracle. This is not usual in Ezekiel. We are normally left to infer from the command that something happened, but there is no reason for changing the text. When Ezekiel obeys the command and the people question his behaviour, he replies with an oracle to the effect that they will lose the temple and many of their relatives in Jerusalem, and yet, in that awful loss, they will have no opportunity for the decencies of mourning.

The oracle is plainly composite. The format of vv. 21–24 is a speech by Yahweh to the prophet, but in v. 22 Ezekiel is speaking in the first person about his own strange behaviour. Verses 22f. seem to be largely derivative from vv. 16f. and they could well be a later insertion. The sense would be better without them, and the oracle would then move smoothly to its climax in the statement that Ezekiel would be a *môpēt* to Israel. This word, which also occurs in 12.6 (the miniature siege) and 24.27 (release from dumbness) is an indication that the action of the prophet was taken to have deep and special significance.

It is clear that Ezekiel's wife represents Jerusalem, the beloved city, and the temple. Her death represent the city's destruction with all the attendant loss of life. But the crux of the drama is the absence of the mourning conventions which, when properly carried out, had the double effect of honouring the dead and assuaging the grief.[43] Whom is the prophet personating? The obvious answer is that he is personating the people of Jerusalem who will not be able to carry out the rites of grief because of the chaos, but wilful abstention from mourning rites is not a very expressive representation of the deprivation forced upon those who have to endure the destruction of their city. It is more likely that Ezekiel is personating the people in exile, whose children and friends in Jerusalem will be butchered and not mourned because the exiles will not know of the disaster. This makes the action – that is, the inaction – very apt. Ezekiel walks around in normal garb, though his wife lies dead, just as the exiles will proceed with the normal business of life while Jerusalem is sacked and its people stricken. This is consistent with v. 24b which states that Ezekiel's action will be repeated in due time by all his hearers.

---

[43] For a full summary of various views on the reason Israel is not to mourn the loss of Zion, see TeStroete, 'Ezekiel 24.15–27: The Meaning of a Symbolic Act'.

There are one or two other points to notice. First, the bereavement may well be another incident in the life of Ezekiel, akin to 4.4–6 and 12.17–20, which is perceived as significant only after it has happened. There is a difference, however, in that in those other cases the affliction (the paralysis, the trembling) came upon the prophet himself, and the affliction alone was interpreted as significant. Here someone else is mortally involved; the significant element lies in both the death and the prophet's reaction to it. The point is, however, that the drama begins with a calamity that is interpreted as significant, not with a contrived action. Secondly, Ezekiel is so conscious of being, by his prophetic vocation, a representative of Israel that he responds to his own personal tragedy in a representative way. He sees the shock of his bereavement as the first of a series of shocks that will overcome God's people as the divine will unfolds. Thirdly, this is not an action that could be performed with detachment. Like Hosea in his marriage, Ezekiel is plunged into it. There is no question of prophetic technique; it is simply a matter of commitment. This action cannot possibly be regarded as a formal procedure which must be performed according to a correct pattern. A large gulf exists, therefore, between actions of this deeply personal kind and both ritual procedures on one hand and acts of instrumental magic on the other.

Joining the Sticks: Ezek. 37.15–28

The prophet is commanded to take two sticks and inscribe them with the names of Judah and Joseph. He is then to join the two sticks in his hand so that they appear one. When asked what this means, he is to explain that Yahweh will similarly join the two groups together and restore king, law, land, covenant and sanctuary. There is no account of the action being carried out. An explanation is contained in the reply that the prophet is instructed to give to enquirers.

As commonly with Ezekiel, the impression that a simple story has been expanded is irresistible. The narrative could well finish after v. 19 because, by this point, a clear, brief, but adequate explanation of the action has been given. Judah and Ephraim will be joined again. Verses 20ff. provide an expanded version of the same explanation. Verse 20 gives a short summary of the action, and v. 21 then begins with the same formula as v. 19, so that the notion that vv. 20–28 are a longer alternative to v. 19 is hard to resist. Verses 21–28 work through the whole programme of restoration, even introducing eschatological elements. The directness and simplicity of the action contrasts sharply with the prolixity of the explanation. It is best, therefore, to assume that the drama dealt only with the reunion of the tribes, and that, when hopes of restoration were in the air, Ezekiel's editors overreached themselves and used the action as a pretext for their larger-than-life expectations.

As a simple drama, the story has one or two interesting features. In the first place, the reality expressed never happened. This is one of a relatively small number of prophecies and actions that had no fulfilment. No doubt its preservation is a witness to the hope that it would be fulfilled one day and, in that sense, it takes its place as part of Israel's eschatology. There can be no doubt that it must be included in the category under investigation, even though no account of the relationship between drama and reality can be posited. Secondly, there is a sense in which the inclusion of this narrative guarantees the integrity of Ezekiel's editors. If the only evidence we had was of them operating by hindsight, we could not be certain how they viewed their material. But here we have a narrative where the reality indicated remains hidden. They do not hesitate to preserve it and thus prove that, for them, the appearance of the reality was only a matter of time. Thirdly, v. 19 implies that an action similar to that performed by Ezekiel will be repeated by Yahweh in order to bring into being the reality. This is significant. It provides an example of the extended identity of the event. Ezekiel's act, Yahweh's act, the historical fulfilment are all representations of what is essentially the same reality. This is a crucial matter for the understanding of prophetic drama.

13 · Zechariah

If 'bizarre' is the commentators' word for Ezekiel, 'obscure' (Jerome's epithet) is the word for Zechariah. There is wide agreement that a division must be made between chs. 1–8 and 9–14, and that the two sections can be treated almost as different books. It is also widely accepted that the prophet Zechariah, who figures with Haggai in Ezra's account of the return, is responsible for the basic visions of chs. 1–8. But regarding the date and nature of the second part, and the redactional history of both parts, there is little unanimity.

Two prophetic dramas are to be found in the biblical Zechariah. Inevitably they are treated by scholars in different ways. Not only are there the usual doubts about what actually happened, but there are also difficulties about what the best text is, and still more, what it actually means. In the circumstances, expectations in this chapter must be modest; it is possible to discover ways in which the narratives confirm discoveries made elsewhere, but little can be built on these texts alone.

The Coronation: Zech. 6.9–15

Despite the problems of the text, there is general agreement that this coronation represents a prophetic drama. As it stands, the narrative consists of a long instruction from Yahweh, which includes an explanation, but no account of the action taking place. Zechariah is told to approach three or four returned exiles, presumably to be witnesses, but also because they possessed the gold, and in their presence to make a crown – though the word is a plural – and set it on the head of Joshua, the high priest. Then Zechariah is instructed to make reference to a man whose name is ṣemaḥ, 'branch', who will rebuild the temple, bear royal honour, and sit upon a throne with a priest at his side. Afterwards the crown is to be left in the temple as a reminder (*zikkārôn*). Verse 15 provides a threefold conclusion: a prophecy that other returning exiles would help in rebuilding the temple, an affirmation that the probity of the prophet would thus be demonstrated, and a caution that the fulfilment would depend on the people's obedience.

The chief problems here are whether there were two crowns or one, where, if at all, Zerubbabel figures in the story, and whether vv. 12f. are part of a coherent narrative or an insertion.

Let us begin with the problem of the crown or crowns. In v. 11 the word occurs in the plural (*ʿᵃṭārôt*) and again in v. 14 it has a plural form. But in v. 14 the verb it governs, 'shall be', is a singular;[1] some Greek MSS, but not the LXX, read the singular *ʿᵃṭeret* and translate στέφανος in v. 11, and the LXX does the same in v. 14. Lipiński has argued that *ʿᵃṭārôt* is only an apparent plural, that it is, in fact, an archaic form of the feminine singular.[2] There is also the possibility that the plural, if it is right, means a single crown with several tiers. Another possibility is that a plural is correct in v. 11, where the crowns are made, and a singular in v. 14, where, perhaps, only one of the two is kept as a memorial.

To turn now to vv. 12f., many commentators are satisfied that they refer to Zerubbabel, the grandson of Jehoiachin. His name means 'sprout of Babylon', which agrees neatly with 'whose name is the Branch' in v. 12 (cf. Hag. 2.23), and almost everything in vv. 12f. requires a king rather than a priest as the central figure. This raises the question: what is an oracle concerning the dignity of a king doing in a passage concerned with the crowning of a priest?

One explanation is that vv. 12f. represent a separate instruction which has nothing to do with the crowning and which has been inserted awkwardly into a passage concerned with Joshua, the priest. In this case the symbolic action is found only in vv. 9–11 and 14f. Another explanation is that the whole oracle concerns Zerubbabel and that his name originally stood in v. 11 in place of Joshua's. This would make sense of some but not all of the clauses in vv. 12f., and it is just possible to argue that the names were changed, either when Zerubbabel

---

[1] The MT certainly has a plural in both cases, but the plural is expressed fully with a *wāw* in v. 11 and only vocally in v. 14. This makes it a little more easy to argue that it should be read as a singular in v. 14. See C.L. and E.M. Meyers, *Haggai, Zechariah 1–8*, p. 363.

[2] 'Recherches sur le livre de Zacharie', pp. 34f.

dropped out of favour with the Persian court or when priestly interest became predominant in Israel. In view of the fact that Zerubbabel remained a hero of Jewish tradition, neither of these occasions seems probable.

Both these explanations assume that there was a single crown. It has been argued, however, that there was a double coronation of both a royal and a priestly figure who would co-operate freely together (v. 13d). In the Ezra account of the return and the prophecy of Haggai, Zerubbabel and Joshua the priest work in consort, and in the vision of the golden lampstand in Zech. 4.1–4, the two olive trees stand for the two anointed ones (lit. 'sons of oil') who 'stand by the Lord of the whole earth'.[3] This explanation is suggestive of the two messiahs of Qumran, but it requires us to explain why reference to Zerubbabel is now missing from v. 11. A fourth hypothesis is that Joshua was to be crowned in place of Zerubbabel, the priest taking the place of the monarch, giving us a symbol within a symbol.[4] The reason for the substitution was either that Zerubbabel had not yet arrived in Jerusalem or that crowning a royal figure would have appeared to be an act of rebellion.

These solutions are all imaginative and they all depend on reading details into the text rather than out of it. Recent commentators have been more inclined to wrestle with the text as it is and to solve problems of meaning without depending on a hypothetical literary history. Petersen recognizes vv. 12f. to be a separate oracle, but sees its insertion into the surrounding 'envelope' as the work of 'an accomplished literary architect'.[5] The resulting text sets out the relative positions of Joshua and Zerubbabel in the community of Israel. Petersen accepts that two crowns were made. The fact that Joshua was to wear one helps to establish the subtle balance between him and the figure of vv. 12f. who was to build the temple and bear the glory, and whom Petersen, with many others, takes to be Zerubbabel. Both crowns are to be placed in the temple as a memorial to those who had provided the gold and silver from which the crowns were made. Petersen certainly addresses himself to the text as it stands, but two questions remain. Can nothing be inferred from these verses about the function of the second crown other than that it was to stand

[3] For Petersen this is a clear indication of a diarchic polity for Israel which reappears in Zech. 6.9–15 (*Haggai and Zechariah 1–8*, p. 118).

[4] Ackroyd, *Exile and Restoration*, pp. 196ff.

[5] *Haggai and Zechariah 1–8*, p. 273.

with Joshua's crown as a memorial? And were the crowns to act as a memorial simply to the generosity of the four men named?

Carol and Eric Meyers contend that the narrative can be well understood with only the slightest emendation of the MT. They argue that Zechariah is instructed to make two crowns, one of silver and one of gold, and to place the silver one on the head of Joshua, the high priest. The gold crown is not to be worn for the moment but to be placed in the temple. The oracle of vv. 12f. is addressed by Zechariah to Joshua. It refers, not to Zerubbabel, but to a Davidic ruler of the future who would wear the golden crown and share his authority with the priest. It is not certain that the crowning actually took place, but the impact of the narrative is clear. The dramatic actions described in it are to be seen as symbolic representations of the future governance of Israel. The witnesses are important because they are part of the drama; they represent the various elements of the fragmented community that will be drawn into one when the new day dawns.

If only one crown was made, it is possible to read this passage as an extended prophetic action involving the making of a crown, placing it on the appropriate head, and then storing it in the temple as a permanent reminder. The drama then bears some resemblance to the naming of children, which is done in a moment, though the name remains for years as a reminder. If, however, the Meyers are right, there are two elements here, one the act of crowning, the other scarcely an action at all; the crown that is not placed on a head remains as a material symbol in itself. This latter element raises intriguing questions, and we can only regret that we do not have a clearer picture of what the text actually says.

The one factor that stands out clearly is the anticipatory nature of the coronation. Joshua was a priest already, and, in any case, crowning was not the means of installing a priest, nor yet a high priest. The rite, therefore, could have nothing to do with normal procedure. We have to assume that it indicates some added glory that he was presently lacking, presumably because of the conditions under which the community of Israel existed at the time. So the crowning looks forward to a day when Joshua would exercise the fullness of priestly authority in a renewed community, patently established as the people of God. If vv. 12f. are taken as an essential part of the story, the passage looks forward to a time when priest and king would together exercise their proper authorities in that community. Whether the realization of this community is to be understood in historical or eschatological terms is not clear, but this does not affect the force of the actions. The crowning begins a new day for Israel; the completion of the reality signified, the dominion and the glory, lies in the future.

This brings us to the second element, the keeping of a crown permanently in the temple as a reminder. The Meyers point out that the term *zikkārôn* often occurs together with *'ôt*.[6] This is true, but when the two terms occur together, it is usually in relation to something that lies in the past. Israel is to remember the past and take it as a sign for the future. The stones from the Jordan were set up as a sign of the safe passage of the ark and so that they would become a memorial for ever (Josh. 4.6f.; cf. Ex. 12.13f.; 13.9; Num. 16.38–40). In Zech. 6.14 the precise function of the memorial is not stated, but the context makes it clear that the crown will serve as a promise of a future messianic kingdom, a reminder of the true state of affairs when appearances give contrary evidence, and an exhortation to the community to live as the people that they truly were and one day would be manifestly shown to be.[7]

The act of crowning is the first appearance of the reality; the presence of the crown in the temple is a constant reaffirmation of the true state of affairs, and so, perhaps, a permanent factor in the struggles of the community. This is as far as we can go with this tangled story. That the happy situation envisaged did not come about in historical terms does not detract from the meaning of the drama or the purpose of the prophet when he carried it out.

The Shepherd: Zech. 11.4–17

There are many reasons for passing over this passage. It is obscure; it is a complex allegory that needs to be explained line by line; it is a literary creation rather than an account of an action; and it belongs only marginally to the prophetic tradition. Nonetheless there are elements here that are so obviously linked with prophetic drama that

[6] *Haggai and Zechariah 1–8*, p. 363.

[7] Petersen suggests that the fact that the crown was kept as a memorial object 'should dissuade us from construing Zechariah's action here as a mere symbolic action' (*Haggai and Zechariah 1–8*, p. 279). The word 'mere' is unfortunate. Symbolic actions sometimes embrace objects and there is no reason at all why the permanent presence of the object should not be understood as an essential part of the dramatic action. D.R. Jones is nearer the point: 'The crown was the significant symbol, continuing the life of Zechariah's symbolic act' (*Haggai, Zechariah and Malachi*, pp. 93).

some comment is required. The uncertainty of interpretation gives unlimited scope for imagination and originality, but this is a temptation to resist; we must limit ourselves to those features which are germane to the study and not too contentious.

The passage refers to a whole series of actions, some of which Yahweh instructs the prophet to carry out and some of which he does of his own accord. He becomes a shepherd, takes two staves, calls them Grace (nōʾam) and Union (ḥōbᵉlîm), resigns his position, breaks the first staff, demands wages, casts them into the treasury, breaks the second staff, and takes up the implements of a shepherd again. Of these actions only the first and the last and the casting of the money into the treasury are the result of divine instruction, but there is an account of all of them being performed save the last, which remains simply a divine instruction. Explanations are entangled in the material throughout.

Four points need to be noted. First, the passage is based upon a positive understanding of prophetic action. Whether these actions were carried out or not, the author was aware that similar actions were performed by prophets, and were performed necessarily and to good purpose. Secondly, the passage may well contain a comment on Ezek. 37.15–28, the joining of the two sticks. That passage contained a prophecy that Judah and Israel would be reunited. Here in v. 14, the second staff is broken to destroy the bond between Judah and Israel, presumably for ever. Thirdly, the action of breaking the staves, whether it actually took place or not, was conceived of as essentially bound up with the signified reality. The language could not be more powerful, 'I broke it, annulling the covenant;' 'I broke my second staff Union, annulling the brotherhood between Judah and Israel.' This at least indicates how one post-exilic writer conceived of prophetic action. Fourthly, acting the part of the shepherd is both predictive and expressive. The purpose of the action is to make stark and clear something that is imminent but unrecognized.

There can be no discussion of whether these actions took place. The passage raises too many problems to make such an enquiry possible; but it reveals something of how prophetic action was understood.

· III ·

INTERPRETATION

14 · Summary and Analysis

It is now possible to survey, analyse and classify the prophetic dramas. The first question to be asked concerns the *circumstances* in which the dramas take place. One answer is that they emerge only in the most critical circumstances, when words have proved inadequate; that is to say, they provide some kind of escalation. One wonders how many times Jeremiah had prophesied the fall of Jerusalem before he broke the flask in the presence of the elders of the city (Jer. 19), and it is certain that his wearing of the yoke took place in the latter part of his ministry, after Nebuchadnezzar's first attack and when the situation, to any rational eye, was desperate. None·the less this is not the complete answer. The evidence rather suggests that gestures and actions were an important concomitant of all deliberate expressions in Israel, and it is probable that more significant actions took place than are recorded.[1] To search for particular circumstances in which dramatic actions took place is, therefore, probably misguided. A more important question is why some actions have been recorded while others have been allowed to disappear. The answer probably rests on three factors: first that some actions are peculiarly memorable and demand a record, second, that some oracles are inextricably entwined with actions so that one cannot exist without the other, and third, that most oracles can be transmitted adequately, without loss of meaning, in the oracular form alone.

Secondly, if we ask what is the *typical* prophetic action, the answer is that there is none, because the actions are baffling in their diversity. In many cases the prophetic action is deliberately contrived. Tearing

---

[1] There is an interesting discussion of the importance of signs in ordinary communication in Lévy-Bruhl, *How Natives Think*, pp. 161ff.

a garment, making and wearing horns, walking naked, breaking a flask, making a model siege, these are not natural gestures but carefully thought out actions. In one or two cases, however, the action is not contrived but is a conventional act which already has some symbolic meaning. The prophet performs it in such a way that its common meaning is elevated and made more specific. When Elijah wrapped his cloak around Elisha, he was carrying out a simple protection ceremony, though much more than simple protection is implied (I Kings 19.19–21). Naming children in an expressive way was the custom. Both Hosea and Isaiah followed the custom and took it further (Hos. 1.4–9; Isa. 7.3; 8.1–4). Jeremiah's obedience to custom in buying the field at Anathoth was given more than customary meaning (Jer. 32.6–15).

Actions, whether deliberately contrived or conventional, represent the norm, but there are cases where it is not action by the prophet but inaction which provides the drama. Jeremiah does not marry, he does not mourn, he does not feast. Ezekiel does not speak, he does not mourn for his wife. In one or two cases, the drama takes place in the mental activity of the prophet. In Jer. 18, Jeremiah is constrained to go and watch a potter at work. When the pot turns out badly, the potter simply reduces the clay to a lump and begins again. Jeremiah was impressed and interpreted it as a dramatic representation of what Yahweh would do with Israel. The significance comes to light in Jeremiah's mind; it was not that the potter was doing anything unusual. Something similar may be true of the discarded waist-cloth in Jer. 13, and it is hard to interpret the cup of wrath in Jer. 25 in any way other than mental activity. Nor can Ezekiel be supposed to have swallowed a real scroll in Ezek. 3.2. This is a dramatic action carried out in a dream or vision.

There are cases where the critical action is performed by someone other than the prophet. In the arrow-shooting in II Kings 13, Joash actually shot the arrow, though it might be argued that Elisha, by laying his hands on the king's hands, made him his surrogate.[2] In the next verse, although Elisha was in charge, it was the king's performance with the arrows that was held to be significant. Similarly in Jer. 35, Jeremiah set up the incident, but the significant act, the refusal of the wine, was the act of the Rechabites. Again, in the next chapter,

---

[2] See Barrick, 'Elisha and the Magic Bow'.

Jeremiah received the command from Yahweh, but the work of writing and reading was done by Baruch.[3]

Most interesting are those cases where natural conditions or happenings provide the substance of the drama. The tearing of the robe in I Sam. 15.27f. was an accident; nevertheless it was interpreted by Samuel as a sign. Something similar is true of Ezekiel's physical afflictions. Jeremiah might have carried out an elaborate performance with his waist-cloth and Ezekiel with a cauldron, but both stories are better explained if the incidents were normal happenings. Despite all the difficulties attaching to Hos. 1 and 3, it is still most likely that the pain that Hosea experienced caused him to understand his marital relationship in terms of Yahweh's relations with Israel. In these cases the crucial activity of the prophet lies in the 'seeing' and in the interpretation, rather than in the conditions themselves.

The action of a drama usually requires only a brief period of time, but some take place over a much longer period. Names, which express a prophetic message and which are given to children, become a more or less permanent sign, as did the crown of Zechariah, which became a *zikkārôn*. Hosea's marriage extended over a long period. So, too, did Jeremiah's celibacy and his regular absence from funerals and festivities. Ezekiel, too, was involved in extended actions; even if we ignore the three hundred and ninety days of Ezek. 4.5, the paralysis was not momentary and the dumbness was recurrent and extended.

A further variant is found in the parts played by the prophet in prophetic action. Often his representative capacity is prominent. Isaiah personates and represents refugees in Isa. 20; Jeremiah personates Edom, Ammon, and Moab (Jer. 27), and Israelites of the future (Jer. 32.6–15). Often the prophet personates Yahweh. Ahijah tears the cloak as Yahweh tears the kingdom (I Kings 11.29–31); Ezekiel divides up his hair as Yahweh divides up the people (Ezek. 5.1–17).

It is commonly supposed that the drama was, or ought to be, a miniature of the reality, and nearly always there is some element in the action that tolerably represents the reality in appearance or at least in mood. Rarely, however, is the action so explicit that no explanation is necessary. Explanations occur regularly in the written record, though they vary considerably in detail. No explanation is necessary

[3] Interesting questions are raised about the position of the various children given symbolic names; presumably they are unwitting participants. But what of Hosea's partner, who is instructed by Hosea to act in a significant way in 3.3–5a? On this latter point, see Schmidt, 'Prophetic Delegation: a Form-Critical Enquiry'.

when Elijah wraps his mantle around Elisha (I Kings 19.19–21). Horns, too, represent strength, so Zedekiah's action needed no commentary, though one is given (I Kings 22.11). Jeremiah's buying the field at Anathoth was a vote of confidence in the future for all to see (Jer. 32.6–15), and there was no room for doubt as to the reason that Hananiah broke Jeremiah's yoke (Jer. 28.10). In a large number of cases, however, the meaning of the actions is not clear by itself. Perhaps it was obvious that Isaiah was imitating the plight of the refugee, but it was still necessary to say that the nations concerned were Egypt and Ethiopia (Isa. 20.3). Would Jeremiah's contemporaries have grasped the point of his celibacy, and would they have understood the message of the discarded waistcloth, if they had known about it? Surely not. Few of Ezekiel's actions, if they were performed as described, could have made sense to the onlookers. There is, therefore, considerable variation in the clarity of the actions, a difficulty that the written records strive to overcome. Altogether the variety displayed in the narratives is so great that one can hardly speak of a typical prophetic action.

Sometimes *material objects* are used in dramatic actions: Samuel's robe, Ahijah's cloak, Elijah's mantle, Zedekiah's horns, Elisha's arrows, Isaiah's slate, Jeremiah's waistcloth, his yoke, Ezekiel's brick, his hair, Zechariah's crown, and so on. The link between the object and what it stands for can be obvious, in which case no formula is necessary, though one usually occurs. In other cases the link is artificial, in which case a formula is necessary, at least if communication is the chief end. In fact, however, a linking formula does not always occur, not even in those cases where the object in no way resembles the reality it stands for. Apparently it is only necessary for the prophet to entertain the idea that one thing represents another and the link is formed. In the story of Jeremiah's waistcloth (Jer. 13), the waistcloth is taken by Jeremiah to signify Israel; there is no formula. On the other hand, with Ezekiel's divided hair, there is a definite formula, 'This is Jerusalem' (Ezek. 5.5).

There is only one example of an attempt to construct a small-scale model of the reality. This is in Ezek. 4.1–3, where Ezekiel makes a model of Jerusalem and then constructs siege works all around it to signify Jerusalem's fate. There are several examples where the object is suggestive rather than imitative. Jeremiah's yoke, while not an actual representation of Babylon, points to the condition of servitude. Zedekiah's horns, while not actual weapons, portray the strength and confidence of the warrior. In most cases, however, objects signify realities simply because the prophet brings the two things together by artificial contrivance. There is no reason why Ahijah's cloak should represent the kingdom or Jeremiah's flask the city other than that one is easy to tear and the other to break and so the prophets chose them for that particular purpose.

It is clear, then, that physical objects are not an essential feature of prophetic drama. Some involve weapons, but there is no hint of weapon magic. Prophets manage just as well without any objects at all. Moreover, it is worth noting that the objects used are not in any way changed by the usage. There is no suggestion that the relationship established in the action is permanent, nor that the object acquires significance in itself, nor that the object contributes any substantial potency of its own, as, for example, blood may do to sacrifice.[4] The action is everything. The object participates temporarily in the identity of the reality signified, but that is all. One possible exception is Zedekiah's crown. Quite apart from the dramatic action when the crown is set on the head by the prophet, the crown itself signifies majesty and dominion for the person to whom it belongs. A crown kept in the temple signifies majesty and dominion for some person yet to emerge. In this case, more than any other, the material object exists as a symbol in its own right.

Next there is the question of onlookers. In the majority of cases, the actions are carried out in public, and sometimes it is specifically stated in the command of Yahweh that it should be done 'in the sight of men'. Ezekiel is told to make all the preparations for going into exile in public (12.3); the purpose is that the onlookers might understand their sin and its impending punishment. The crude rations

---

[4] It may seem that Elijah's mantle is an exception. According to II Kings 2.13f. it appears that the mantle possessed extraordinary powers, even after Elijah had discarded it. A number of points must be borne in mind: (i) this is an early story which, like other stories in the Elisha cycle, lacks the theological sophistication that is found, for example, in the work of Jeremiah; (ii) the dynamic really belongs to Elijah rather than to the mantle; Elijah's personal identity extends into objects closely associated with him, so it is wrong to think of the mantle as possessing an impersonal and instrumental force; (iii) we hear no more about the mantle, so it is reasonable to assume that, once the association with Elijah faded into the background, the mantle lost whatever power it was reckoned to have; (iv) the incident of II Kings 2.13f. does not follow the pattern of prophetic dramas in that, though there is a dramatic effect, the action does not relate to a corresponding reality on a larger scale; and (v) the same mantle is used in the story of I Kings 19.19, where there is no suggestion that it possessed extraordinary powers.

of Ezek. 4.9–17 must be prepared in public. Ezekiel must sigh and display grief for all men to see (Ezek. 21.6); and he must hold the two sticks he has joined together as a sign 'before their eyes' while he proclaims the hopeful oracle of 37.15–28. Jeremiah, too, must carry out his curious action outside Pharaoh's palace at Tah'panhes before the eyes of the men of Judah who were with him in Egypt (Jer. 43.9), and his flask had to be broken in the presence of elders deliberately gathered for that purpose (Jer. 19.1–13). Other actions are, by their very nature, public: marrying or remaining celibate, abstaining from mourning rites, fasting, wearing a yoke or a refugee's clothing continuously, giving expressive names to children. It is hard to believe that public awareness of these actions was not important, but that does not mean that they were done in order to convey a message.

In a few cases the prophet is concerned with one other person only. The other person may be present simply because the action requires a second party, as, for example in the purchase of the field at Anathoth, where Hanamel participates in the action to enable it to happen but is no part of the reality. More important are the cases where a second party is incorporated in the action because he is involved in the fulfilment. This applies to Elijah's wrapping his mantle around Elisha (I Kings 19.19–21); to the two arrow signs that Elisha carries out with Joash (II Kings 13.14–19); to Ahijah's action before Jeroboam (I Kings 11.29–31), and to several other incidents.

There are actions where the audience appears to be irrelevant. In some cases this may be accidental, due to the brevity of the account, but this is not the complete explanation. The presence of a long proclamation with the hair sign of Ezek. 5 leads one to suppose that weighing and dividing the hair was not done privately, though no audience is mentioned. The siege drama has no audience, but it concludes with the phrase, 'This is a sign ($'\hat{o}t$) for the house of Israel.' This does not necessarily mean that the public observed it. Ezekiel saw and took part in the action and Ezekiel represented Israel.[5] Two dramas remain where the action itself seems all-important and no communication is made to anyone. Both come from Jeremiah. The waist-cloth, which is taken off and buried, and which subsequently rots, is never exhibited to Israel (Jer. 13.1–11). As it stands, this is a

[5] It could be argued that communication in the fullest sense is not involved in $'\hat{o}t$. $'\hat{O}t$ means a mark, a proof, a pledge, a guarantee, but the sense is perfectly fulfilled if the proof or pledge exists and is acknowledged by Yahweh and a representative Israelite. It does not have to be widely published to be an effective guarantee.

drama that Jeremiah works through, that he understands himself, but that he never communicates to Israel, save in the sense that his whole prophecy is an exposition of the reality expressed. The second example is the book that Jeremiah wrote, or is said to have written, concerning the doom of Babylon (Jer. 51.59–64). Seraiah, the quarter-master, is merely a necessary participant. He is not an audience. He is to read the book and to throw it into the Euphrates with an appropriate formula. There is no mention of anyone being told. It is reasonable to infer that the action was considered to be important in itself and not as a means of raising morale among the exiles.

Always dramatic action is related to some other, greater reality. The action may be expressive of a straightforward historical event or a universal truth or a judgment that Yahweh has made, but reality there must be, for the drama is bound up with what it represents so closely that it is reasonable to say that one is a part of the other. A problem arises, therefore, with those actions that are carefully recorded but appear never to have reached fulfilment. Zedekiah's horns did not inaugurate victory for Ahab. Hananiah did not herald the end of the Babylonian threat. In these cases the editors make it clear that the agents were false prophets. They were not representing divine reality; they were simply play-acting, though few people knew it at the time.

However, Jeremiah's action in Egypt, which anticipated Nebuchadnezzar's conquest, may well come in the same category (Jer. 43.8–13). The only text that might indicate fulfilment is so brief and difficult to decipher that nothing can be based upon it. Then there is the joining of the two sticks in Ezek. 37.15–28, which looks forward to the reunification of Israel and Judah under a Davidic prince. Ezekiel anticipated a full restoration with a new cult and a new temple as soon as Babylonian power collapsed. The editors of a later day, who worked over the prophecy, knew that this had not taken place, but they did not conclude that the sign had been performed in vain. They simply pushed the fulfilment into the future. Eschatology developed as the situation worsened and expectation was not diminished but heightened. The Testament of Benjamin still speaks of a gathering of the twelve tribes in the temple of God in the late second century BCE (9.2). This evidence shows that the Hebrew prophets and their editors took the view that the true pophetic action was essentially the unveiling of an unseen or unrecognized reality. What was, or was to be, appeared first, or perhaps most strikingly, in the word and act of the prophet. The editors were, of course, in the happy position of being able to say which prophets were true and which were false; their only difficulty was in dealing with the occasional action of an evidently true prophet, which appeared not to have been fulfilled.

Finally, there is considerable variation in the chronological relationship between the drama and the reality. The simplest and commonest example is when a prophet performs a momentary action which relates to a relatively finite event in the future. Ahijah tears a cloak to indicate that the kingdom will be divided. More than half the narratives fit into this pattern, but the remainder display considerable variety. We have already noted that some dramas are not momentary. It is equally true that some of the realities indicated are not finite events. Hosea's marriage represents an infidelity on the part of Israel extending through many generations, and the names of his second and third children indicate a state of dereliction that might be permanent. The potter, whom Jeremiah observes, affirms an eternal truth, and his ascetic way of life a lengthy travail for his people. But the point that is least appreciated is that dramas do not necessarily point forward to fulfilment. Some have the purpose of making the present more real; this particularly applies to the dramas Ezekiel performs in Babylon with reference to Jerusalem. And some point backwards rather than forwards; Saul has already been rejected when the cloak is torn; Israel has already been unfaithful when Hosea marries Gomer; the bloody deeds of Jezreel are long past when the child is named; Elisha has already renounced his former life when he destroys his plough and tears his clothes. All these actions stand in relation to other realities, but the relationship is more elusive than that of simple prediction.

This summary of the drama narratives leaves an impression of enormous diversity. There are few constant features. The only recognizable unity is one of mental conception. The dramas all exhibit the same understanding of the relation between the prophetic office and the activity of Yahweh; and this view, demonstrated so clearly in these incidents and their interpretation, is consistent with all the rest of the prophetic literature. The rationale of prophetic drama, if there is such a thing, can, therefore, only be understood from within Hebrew thought and culture and, indeed, theology.

15 · The Question of Objectivity

An important question, often discussed in the past, is whether the dramas recorded in the Old Testament actually took place. The extreme improbability of one or two dramas has already suggested that there is a serious issue to be discussed. Did they all happen? Did none of them happen? Did some happen and others not? If the last is true, what is the difference in force between dramas that actually happened and dramas that were merely thought about or recounted? We encounter the problem on three levels: first, as regards all Old Testament incidents, secondly, with specific reference to incidents centred on prophets, and thirdly, in relation to particular dramas.

The general problems of establishing the historicity of Old Testament incidents are well known and need not delay us long. Since the critical age began, scholars have been concerned with this question, and at times there has been a tendency to assume that everything hinged upon the answer. Indeed, for some, the question became the dominant issue in Old Testament scholarship.[1] Historical questions of the what-actually happened? kind are difficult to resolve, even with regard to fairly recent events, and where Old Testament events are concerned, the difficulties are enormous. The evidence is tenuous, usually lacking corroboration; it is often complex and ambiguous; the events concerned are frequently so improbable that exceptionally good evidence is required to substantiate them. The relevant texts have passed through many hands (and ears and mouths); they have been read, edited, copied, in many situations. New historical contexts meant new readings and new editorial adaptations. The transmission

---

[1] It is fair to say that theological presuppositions had much to do with attitudes on this point, so the various answers, 'It did', 'It must have', 'We do not know', 'It does not matter', may reveal more about the theological position of the writer than the strength of the evidence.

was vulnerable to all the normal accidents that befall ancient records; even so, normal accidents are not the chief problem. The records were preserved and transmitted for a purpose, and that purpose determined the way in which the material was handled. So often was the story retold and relived that it is easy to see how we can have lost touch with the original event. This is a general comment about all Old Testament records; it certainly applies to incidents in the lives of the prophets.

A special problem arises, however, with narratives relating to prophets because of the esteem in which prophets were held in after years. They were not treated as if they were for ever locked into their own contexts. On the contrary, it was expected that their words and deeds would speak directly to later generations. So the oracles and narratives were edited to make their contemporary relevance clear; the task of the redactor was as much to interpret as to preserve.

In its historical journey from the prophet himself to its final place in the Old Testament canon a prophetic text had to pass through a number of crises. If we take Hosea as an example, what he said and did was first weighed by his diciples who had the advantage of outliving him. They could see every individual word and act in the context of his whole life and its consequences, and even these first disciples had reasons of their own for preserving what they did. The whole text would be read again in a new light after the fall of Samaria. Then, without doubt, the text was carried to the south, where it was read in the light of its relevance to Judah's problems. Then it was carried into exile and brought back. At every point it was open to reinterpretation and adaptation, and it is hard to suppose that none of these crises affected the basic historical record in any way. The evidence from Hos. 3, for example, argues powerfully for exactly the opposite conclusion. Redaction criticism, for all its difficulties, has added excitement to Old Testament studies in recent years, but it has not helped in answering the old question: did it actually happen?

These, however, were not the issues that troubled the scholars of a generation and more ago. They were concerned about the appropriateness of some of the dramas, performed, as they were said to be, by men called by God. Patrick Fairbairn, writing in the mid-nineteenth century, took it for granted that few serious people would regard the dramatic acts as 'occurrences of actual life'. Had they actually happened, onlookers would have regarded them as 'puerile and ludicrous'. Some of the actions were physically impossible, others morally so.[2] A.B. Davidson shows the same embarrassment. In the large work on prophecy, compiled from his writings by J.A. Paterson after Davidson's death in 1902, he tends to avoid the subject and, when brought face to face with it in the commentary on *Ezekiel*, he tries to show that, though a few happened indisputably, the majority simply passed through the prophet's mind.[3] Davidson is actually following the great mediaeval Jewish scholar, Maimonides, who lists a number of the more problematic dramas (Hosea's marriage, Isaiah's nakedness, Jeremiah's waist-cloth, and all those in Ezek. 4 and 5) and states that they were revealed to the prophets as allegories in visions. 'God forbid to assume that God would make His prophets appear an object of ridicule and sport in the eyes of the ignorant, and order them to perform foolish acts.'[4] Regnier (1923) stresses the literary aspect of the study and doubts whether the question of objectivity is really important. It is notable, however, that, for him, Hos. 1 and 3 provide, not history, but an idealistic story, a parable.[5]

While it is possible to make some kind of case in Davidson's favour, it is rather more easy to suggest the unstated reasons why he and his contemporaries took the position they did. These reasons are not very persuasive today. First, the narratives imply that God required some very queer behaviour from his prophets: walking about naked, lying rigid on one side for days, playing at sieges, baking bread with human excreta. 'Odd', 'crude', 'childish', 'bizarre', these words crop up again and again in the comments.[6] To suppose that great men of God behaved in this way and that God required it was against the spirit of the times. The prophets were regarded as pioneers of progress, the architects of a lofty, ethical monotheism, who, more than any others, freed Israel from 'primitive' ways of thought and practice and prepared the way for the New Testament. Symbolic behaviour, ecstasy and trance did not fit well into this picture, so there was a tendency to play them down.[7] Secondly, the indifference shown by Regnier to the question of whether the actions happened or not reveals a failure to

---

[2] Fairbairn, *Ezekiel and the Book of his Prophecy: an Exposition*.

[3] Davidson, *Old Testament Prophecy*; Davidson and Streane, *Ezekiel*, pp. xxviiif., 30f. Many others took a similar view.

[4] *The Guide of the Perplexed*, Part II, Chapter 46.

[5] Regnier, 'Le réalisme dans les Symboles des Prophètes'.

[6] See Rowley, 'The Nature of Prophecy'.

[7] As recently as 1963, Whitley wrote that the prophetic dramas were survivals from the style of the old *nᵉbî'îm* and were of little help in understanding the canonical prophets (*The Prophetic Achievement*, pp. 14f.).

grasp the significant fact that words and actions were necessary realities *in themselves*. For Regnier, and for many others who discussed the matter after his day, it was the import of the drama that was significant. The search was for the meaning, the thesis behind the particular action. How the meaning was expressed was less important. If the prophet was able to make his point without dramatic action, then what need was there for the action actually to be carried out? Did it matter if it was or not? All the work that has been done on Hebraic thought in the last half a century shows how wrong this approach was. J.L. Mays, in discussing the historical aspect of Hosea's marriage, points out, 'The very character of prophetic symbolism requires that the divine word be actualized in a representative event.'[8] Recent commentators tend to agree. Yahweh wills, not simply the reality, but the drama also. Thirdly, the link between prophetic drama and magic caused difficulty. It was as clear in the early years of the century as it is now that there was such a link, but it was much harder to acknowledge in those days because anthropologists and theologians had little common ground. Magic, so it was said, depended upon specific actions that, if performed correctly, acted *ex opere operato* to the exclusion of all moral factors. If prophetic drama had something in common with magic, then theologians were confronted with an awkward problem. They took the view that moral factors dominated the work of the prophets, that, in God's world, no charm could ever work automatically, that ritual was ineffective without repentance. Since, in appearance, prophetic drama was so close to magical action, the point at which the differentiation could be made had to be on the necessity of the actual performance. Correct performance was essential to magic, but, with prophetic drama, moral factors were so dominant that it mattered little whether the action took place or not.[9] That, at least, is how the matter appeared to many in the early part of this century.

More recently the case for the non-historical nature of prophetic drama has been argued by Groenman in a monograph that deals simply with this point.[10] Groenman argues that his predecessor, van den Born, accepted the historicity of the dramas simply because there

[8] Mays, *Hosea*, p. 23.

[9] It must be remembered that scholars of the period were under pressure from both critical anthropologists and from members of the *Religionsgeschichtliche* school. The Old Testament scholar often tended to be something of an apologist as well.

[10] Groenman, *Het Karakter*.

seemed to be no adequate reason for doubting it.[11] It is Groenman's wish to provide objective criteria for settling the issue. He refers to the obvious arguments: that some of the actions described are impossible, that some of them are crude, that some were supposedly carried out without witnesses; then he passes on to something more cogent and more interesting. The real force of the drama narratives, he says, lies not in the actions themselves, which may be ambiguous and confusing, but in the explanations that follow. If the explanation is the crux, then the actual performance is irrelevant. The explanation will be as effective if it refers to something that happened in the mind as it would be if it related to an actual happening. Why, then, do the accounts suggest historicity when, in all probability, the events never took place? Groenman feels himself equal to the question. The Hebrew practice is to express theology in the form of narrative. This is what gives rise to the category of myth in Old Testament studies. In prophecy the prophet is entirely taken over by the spirit of Yahweh, so that the words and acts of the prophet are to be regarded as the words and acts of Yahweh. What more natural then that they should take the mythic form of quasi-historical narrative? A true understanding of the Hebrew mind, therefore, leads, according to Groenman, to the conclusion that the dramas are related in the form of historical narrative, as are the myths, but, like the myths, they are actually unhistorical.[12]

Groenman's argument is unsatisfactory for at least two reasons. First of all, he assumes without question that the purpose of dramas is some kind of communication. This alone explains his attempt to shift the emphasis from the act to the explanation. He seems not to consider the significance and the necessity of the act itself, apart from any commentary. Secondly, Groenman is led into a false position by his readiness to isolate prophetic drama from other significant action. He speaks of Yahweh's spirit entering the prophet, as if this gives rise to a qualitative difference between prophetic activity and all other significant activity. So he can go on to provide a mythic explanation in this one peculiar case. But can this distinction possibly be maintained? Spirit possession is not confined to the prophets in the Old Testament;

[11] Van den Born, *Profetie Metterdaad*, pp. 16ff.

[12] Robert Wilson, writing about Ezekiel, seems to be in broad agreement with Groenman. Ezekiel's symbolic acts 'are likely to be the product of literary activity, for they are too complex to have been comprehensible, and some of them are physically impossible' (*Prophecy and Society*, p. 283).

nor is significant activity. Once prophetic dramas are set in their right context with all other significant actions, this point is lost.[13] Moreover, despite the extensive use of myth by Old Testament writers, Yahweh's activity is not regarded as essentially unhistorical. Theology is expressed in historical as well as mythical language. Granted the word 'historical' means different things in different cultures, it remains that the Old Testament does contain plenty of theological writing that, at the same time, strives to keep in contact with what actually happened.

These arguments are outlined because the question raised is a real one. In terms of historical probability the prophetic dramas vary enormously. The three actions associated with Jeremiah's asceticism, for example, are historically probable, since the alternative would make the passage meaningless. Other narratives may have incidental difficulties. Did Jeremiah bury his waistcloth by the Euphrates (Jer. 13.6), or Isaiah go naked for three years (Isa. 20.3), or Ezekiel lie on his side for so many days (Ezek. 4.4–6), or go through all that rigmarole with his hair (Ezek. 5.1–4)? Nevertheless fundamentally these narratives are not beyond credibility. Then there are one or two narratives which, almost by definition, could not have taken place. Jeremiah could not have taken a cup from the Lord's hand and made the nations drink from it (Jer. 25.17) and Ezekiel could not have eaten a written scroll (Ezek. 3.1). These actions could have taken place only in the imagination of the prophet; the only objectivity they could have had is in the form of words.[14]

These last examples raise a fundamental question. If Yahweh wills the drama as well as the reality, how can the action that is only conceived and described stand with the action that is actually carried out? Is not the objective reality of the action supremely important? Some scholars have tried to protest that descriptive language alone is sufficiently objective to sustain the theological point. Engnell, in his discussion of figurative language in the Old Testament, argues that prophetic language has the same intrinsic relation to the other reality

[13] A further misfortune for Groenman's argument is that the stories that are most open to historical doubt, that is, the Elisha cycle, are the least patient of the explanation that the prophet is entirely taken over by the spirit of Yahweh.

[14] What is, or is not, reckoned to be impossible is, to some extent a subjective matter, and, in this regard, a separate discussion has to take place regarding each narrative. See the appropriate chapters in the section that deals with texts. See also van den Born, *De Symbolische Handelingen* and *Profetie Metterdaad*. What is under discussion here is the question whether there is any presumption that dramas probably happened or probably did not.

it describes as, according to our contention, dramatic actions have.[15] Fohrer contends that, in later times, prophets could describe imaginary actions, and the description would have the same potency as the actions would have had, if they had been carried out.[16] Where, then, is the necessity for action, and, when difficulties arise in action stories, why is it not immediately assumed that the actions are simply imaginary?

For the answer to these queries it is necessary to consider the relation of thought, vision, and inner perception to words and oracles, and words and oracles to dramatic actions. In general it appears that oracles and actions serve the same purpose, and that there are no special circumstances which require dramatic action rather than oracles. There is, however, one piece of evidence that points in the opposite direction. Prophets sometimes set down oracles in writing when writing was not needed either for communication or for making a record. The reason, so it appears, was that giving the oracle objective expression on a slate or a scroll also gave it greater force and durability.[17] Isaiah commanded persons unknown to write his gloomy message on a tablet (Isa. 8.16). The verse suggests a prophetic testament. Isaiah was about to retire and wished his words to be given more permanent expression. Similarly in 30.8 he asks that the accusation he is making be written in a book that it may stand for ever. Jeremiah dictated to Baruch what must be presumed to have been a summary of his oracles, because Jeremiah himself was not free to speak. Jehoiakim cut the scroll up and burnt it (Jer. 36). Jeremiah's response was to write another roll. This is similar to the yoke story. Assertion and denial seem to escalate into action and counter-action. The book on Babylon's doom (Jer. 51.59–64) may have been a practical necessity if Seraiah's memory could not be trusted, but that the book was more than a record is shown by the fact that, after the reading, it had to be sunk in the Euphrates. Habakkuk is commanded to write his vision in a book so that its force would not be lost as time passed (Hab. 2.2f.).[18]

---

[15] Engnell, 'Figurative Language', p. 246f.; cf. Knight, *Hebrew Prophetic Consciousness*, p. 54.

[16] Fohrer, *Die Handlungen*, pp. 72f.; see too van den Born, *Profetie Metterdaad*, p. 31.

[17] Cf. the jealousy rite in Num. 5, especially v. 23. The curse is written down and then somehow washed into the water which is drunk. See Fohrer, 'Prophetie und Magie', p. 261.

[18] These verses have a claim to be included in a list of prophetic actions; they were excluded because the reference is so brief.

These references imply that, when an oracle passes from the spoken to the written word, it gains in force and validity. In Isa. 8.3f. the writing is followed by a further sign. The message of doom was not only written on a slate but given as a name to a child who would bear it for years. Is this further escalation?

It would be overstating the case to say that the objective drama was qualitatively different from the spoken oracle or even from the vision, but it seems necessary to recognize a difference in vitality between them. Thought, word and deed represent a progression whereby, in everyday affairs, a notion conceived in a person's mind comes into being and takes effect. It is legitimate, therefore, to see in the series, thought-speech-writing-action, a progression in the realization of the reality to which all four are directed.[19] It can all be seen in Jeremiah. The central event, the reality towards which the whole prophecy is orientated, is the spoliation of Jerusalem. This can be seen in his thoughts, his spoken words, his manner of life, his script, the shattering of his pot, and then, finally, in the disaster itself.

The conclusion is that, as the awareness of the central event becomes more and more intense in the prophet's mind, so he is moved to express himself more and more clearly. One would, therefore, expect him to translate his words into action fairly often, indeed, whenever the pressure of the coming event forced him to do so. For this reason it cannot be said that the question of objectivity is of no importance. It *is* important, though it cannot always be resolved with complete confidence. There are many reasons why it may be necessary to hesitate before accepting the objectivity of any particular action, though the fact that, by modern standards, it might be called vulgar is not one of them. Van den Born reaches the conclusion that, whenever a prophet is said to perform a dramatic action, and whenever there is no insuperable difficulty, he did, in fact, do so.[20] While allowing for the parables, the allegories, the signs that could not have happened (e.g. Zech. 11.4–17; 13.7–9; Jer. 25.15ff.), he draws attention to the presence of witnesses who were actually involved. This, he maintains, with reasonable justification, removes the action from the realm of

---

[19] With this conclusion a number of scholars who have written on the subject appear to be in broad agreement: Lods, *The Prophets and the Rise of Judaism*, pp. 54, 215; H.W. Robinson, 'Hebrew Sacrifice', p. 132; Fohrer, *Introduction*, p. 349; von Rad, *Theology II*, p. 96; Ringgren, *Israelite Religion*, pp. 214, 257; Lindblom, *Prophecy*, p. 172; Jensen, *Isaiah*, p. 172.

[20] Van den Born, *Profetie Metterdaad*, pp. 18ff.

imagination. Furthermore, the fact that many drama stories are recounted in the third person, van den Born regards, less justifiably, as evidence that the incident was objective and did not exist simply in the prophet's mind.

All this argumentation is interesting, but it has a rather old-fashioned look. It tends to assume that, if a narrative states that something happened, and if the happening is not impossible or inappropriate, it did indeed happen. The matter seems much more complicated today. We have already seen that the basic facts of the life of Jeremiah have been assessed in totally different ways.[21] It is now a commonplace that large questions have to be asked about the literary history of the prophetic books before questions of the what-actually-happened? kind can even be raised. The one conclusion that can be drawn with reasonable certainty is that those who gave us the Old Testament believed that the prophets performed dramatic acts and that the fact of performance was of great importance to them, so much so that highly improbable actions were represented as having been performed. Whether those who gave us the Old Testament were right in these beliefs is another matter, but the fact that they believed them helps us to grasp how prophetic drama was understood by them.

[21] See above, Chapter 11.

16 · Prophetic Drama and Magic

Many authors suggest that there is a link between prophetic drama and magic, but few pause to define the link with clarity or authority. The problems of the undertaking are daunting. There is the difficulty of producing a standard account of prophetic drama on one hand, and the immense complexity of the field of study that goes under the name of 'magic' on the other. Old Testament scholars, in general, have not given the subject as much thought as it deserves; and at times there has been a dispiriting tendency to fall into clichés. The issue really resolves itself into two questions. First, what exactly do we mean by magic? And second, how far is a comparison between prophetic drama and magical acts illuminating?

More than forty years ago, H.W. Robinson, leaning heavily on the work of J.G. Frazer, produced a rather trite formula in his article, 'Hebrew Sacrifice and Prophetic Symbolism'. 'Magic constrains the unseen; religion means surrender to it.'[1] The prophets were devoted to Yahweh; their own will was nothing; therefore their symbolic actions can be sharply distinguished from magic. Robinson allowed that there was a historical connexion of form between symbolic magic and prophetic action, but the latter was carried out 'not to constrain Him, but as constrained by Him'.[2] Many other scholars have followed in Robinson's wake. Harold Knight can be taken as an example. 'The prophet acts in obedience and self-surrender to the declared will of Yahwé. . . . The magician, on the contrary, acts in independence of, and is indifferent to, the will of God. His mimetic acts are the private manipulation of reality for the satisfaction of personal desire. The acted drama of the prophet is the pledge of his loving self-identification

---

[1] H.W. Robinson, 'Hebrew Sacrifice', p. 132; cf. Mauss, *Magic*, pp. 12f.
[2] 'Hebrew Sacrifice', p. 137; *Inspiration*, p. 227; *Two Hebrew Prophets*, p. 85.

with his God: the act of the magician is a defiant coercion of God.'[3]
Lindblom, while allowing that the common people may have had
other, less creditable, ideas, carefully stresses both the points in
question. Magical actions were directed to personal ends and were
inherently effective. Prophetic actions derived both aim and power
from Yahweh's will.[4] This hypothesis has the advantages of clarity
and simplicity, but abbreviative formulae often mislead through their
brevity, and this is a case in point.

In the first place, magic is a very comprehensive term. There is
good magic and bad magic, private and public magic, witchcraft,
sorcery, divination and many other manifestations of this elusive
practice. The word conveys different meanings in different contexts.
Field-work in the last half century has demonstrated how erroneous
generalizations can be. Robinson's slogan might have been more
acceptable if it had referred to the particular kind of magic evidenced
in Palestine in the first half of the first millenium before the Common
Era, but there is no hint of such a limitation.[5]

Secondly, magic is a complex phenomenon. To say simply, 'magic
constrains', is not to do it justice. Robinson's formula rests on out-
moded anthropology. Robertson Smith certainly argued in the last
century that magical ceremonies were antisocial, that they applied
force to demoniacal powers, that, 'in all well-ordered states they were
regarded as illicit'.[6] Frazer, too, was quite willing to speak of constraint
and coercion of the unseen. But much has happened since Robertson
Smith and Frazer. More and more interest has been shown in the
thesis that magic is essentially a response to experience rather than a
direct attempt to control it, and the positive, social function of magic
has been brought to light.[7] The 'primitive man' who believed that
certain words, 'had an objective efficacy that nothing could defeat' is,

<hr>

[3] Knight, *The Hebrew Prophetic Consciousness*, pp. 50, 85.

[4] *Prophecy*, p. 172.

[5] Long ago Mowinckel made the suggestion that magic should be considered, not
primarily in terms of the varied rites and performances, but as a particular world-view
which gives rise to various practical expressions. Unfortunately this does not advance
the argument very much, for, though the idea that the metaphysics of magic are constant
is attractive, it rests on speculation rather than evidence.

[6] W. Robertson Smith, *The Religion of the Semites*, pp. 263f. The reference is to the
second edition. The Burnett lectures were given by Robertson Smith in 1888–9.

[7] Despite the progress that has been made in the study of magic, Fohrer still works
with a definition that implies mechanical causation. See 'Prophetie und Magie',
pp. 244f.; *Die Handlungen*, p. 10.

to a large extent, a figment of nineteenth-century imagination.[8] It needs only a little reflection to realize that magic cannot have existed down through the centuries purely on the basis of belief in its instrumental efficacy. Undoubtedly it worked sometimes; undoubtedly it sometimes failed; equally undoubtedly so-called primitive man was aware of these facts. This notion that magic must always be understood in terms of its inherent effectiveness rests partly on discredited anthropology, partly on the desire to establish clear and simple definitions, and partly on the wish to enunciate an acceptable distinction between prophetic activity, which was in general approved by contemporary students of the Old Testament, and other kinds of dramatic and imitative activity, which received widespread disapproval.

Thirdly, religion is an even more complex phenomenon than magic, and one wonders why the slogan, 'religion means surrender' has been tolerated so long. The pleas of the Psalter, the practice of sacrifice, the celebration of the festivals show the Hebrew worshipper to be much concerned with his own well-being. To call such an attitude 'submissive' is to strain the meaning of the word. The distinction between surrendering to the deity and attempting to constrain him is often blurred, and if, as is commonly stated, the rites of the temple had a certain thrust towards realization, then activities that are normally regarded as mainline Old Testament religion are not so far removed from acts that are supposed to be inherently effective.[9] Moreover, within the religious field, prophetic acts themselves vary considerably. They are not all related to magic in the same way, however it is defined. The confrontation of Elijah with the priests of Baal may be represented as an act of submission, but the rain ritual cannot be overlooked. Is it magic or religion? Similarly, some of the acts of Elisha are as self-centred as anything that can be found in the lore of Israel's neighbours, and that is partly the reason that they have been excluded from this

[8] Nonetheless the words are taken from a book published in 1947; see Knight, *The Hebrew Prophetic Consciousness*, p. 36.

[9] Mowinckel makes an interesting point when replying to an accusation by H.H. Rowley. Rowley had stated that Mowinckel's views of cultic action reduced the cult to magic (*Re-Discovery*, pp. 126f., 174). Mowinckel replies, 'That something really "happens" in the cult does not make it into "magic"; I doubt the legitimacy of using this notion in the world of religion. If the drama of the Israelite new year festival . . . be "magic" then the Orthodox, Roman, Anglican and in fact even the Lutheran cult must be "magic" as well' (*The Psalms in Israel's Worship I*, p. 182). Rowley modified his tone, though not perhaps his basic view, in *Worship in Ancient Israel*, pp. 192–9.

survey. Are they magic or religion? Perhaps the formula is meant to apply only to the actions of Hosea, Jeremiah, and prophets of that weight, in which case it needs to be pointed out that appreciation of the theological convictions of those prophets does not necessitate a general castigation of magic.

Fourthly, H.W. Robinson's formula implies too simple a view of causation and time and, therefore, does not satisfactorily explain a large number of prophetic actions. The supposition is that, in magic, the action and the fulfilment stand in a direct, linear relationship, the first being the sufficient cause of the second. In the first place, as we shall see, magic is not generally understood in this way now; and in the second, such a view could never apply to all the prophetic actions. Even when it is granted that Yahweh, rather than the prophet, is the true agent, the implication of Robinson's argument remains that the drama must precede and play a part in causing the reality. In many instances, as we have seen, this is not the case. The notion of a dramatic action that affects the future and the future only is too restrictive both for magic and prophetic drama. A more complicated and more subtle formula is called for.

Part of the problem is that scholars of a previous generation tended to approach the subject of magic with a great sense of superiority. Sir James Frazer, for long the doyen of British anthropologists, shows little sympathy for the magician and his arts. 'The acuter minds perceive how easy it is to dupe their weaker brother and to play on his superstition for their own advantage. Not that the sorcerer is always a knave and impostor; he is often sincerely convinced that he really possesses those wonderful powers which the credulity of his fellows ascribes to him. But the more sagacious he is, the more likely he is to see through the fallacies which impose on duller wits. Thus the ablest members of the profession must tend to be more or less conscious deceivers . . . For it must always be remembered that every single profession and claim put forward by the magician as such is false; not one of them can be maintained without deception, conscious or unconscious.'[10] This kind of statement explains why, in 1965, it was necessary for Evans-Pritchard to make the plea that magic should be treated as a serious subject.[11]

Writers from ecclesiastical camps revealed the same attitude. Magic

[10] Frazer, *Golden Bough*, p. 46. Mary Douglas refers to Frazer's 'complacency and undisguised contempt for primitive society' (*Purity*, p. 24).

[11] *Theories*, p. 4.

was either rejected outright, or, in accordance with contemporary ideas of progress, put down as the 'cramping chrysalis' out of which the lofty theology of Second Isaiah grew.[12] This explains why books on Old Testament religion and Old Testament theology tended to dispose of magic quickly and why authors who mention the subject in relation to prophetic drama usually eliminate it from discussion after a paragraph or so. It is hard to avoid the conclusion that there is an *a priori* judgment here: magic is primitive, it has nothing to contribute to Old Testament religion, and, therefore, it provides no means of understanding religion. Fortunately, in recent times there has been a welcome change of direction in Old Testament studies. The relevance of anthropological and sociological theories is much more widely appreciated today.[13]

It is now necessary to look more closely at the subject of magic by considering the work of a number of anthropologists who have made a significant contribution to the study in the last century. Frazer has already been mentioned. For him, magic was, 'a spurious system of natural law', not based on reflection or abstract reasoning but simply inferred, incorrectly, from practice.[14] Magic rests upon two principles which are 'two different misapplications of the association of ideas'.[15] The first is that, when two things have been in contact, they each retain an element of the other's identity, so that to act on one is, in effect, to act on the other; and the second, that like produces like, that effects resemble causes, so that the magician has only to perform an action of a particular kind for it to produce an effect of a similar kind. Frazer was able to illustrate both principles with hundreds of examples; indeed, the profusion of examples reveals the lack of balance in Frazer's work. He compiled material assiduously, but rarely paused to give any thought to the rationale of magic or to the magician's

---

[12] Guillaume, *Prophecy and Divination*, p. 176.

[13] Four cheering signs are: Rogerson's *Anthropology and the Old Testament*, 1979; vol. 21 of *Semeia*, edited by Robert C. Culley and Thomas W. Overholt and called *Anthropological Perspectives on Old Testament Prophecy*, 1982; Bernhard Lang's 'Old Testament and Anthropology: A Preliminary Bibliography' (*Biblische Notizen*, 1983); and the work of a number of other scholars with an interest in sociology. A useful summary of this area is John S. Kselman's article, 'The Social World of the Israelite Prophets: a Review Article'.

[14] Frazer, *Golden Bough*, p. 11; Frazer seems to contradict himself at this point. If magic is entirely spurious, as he affirms, how did it ever come to be inferred from practice?

[15] Frazer, *Golden Bough*, p. 10.

world-view, or to what he himself called 'theoretical magic'.[16] He does, however, make one important assertion, that magic depends upon a conception of nature in which effect follows cause according to immutable laws. The magical action must be instrumentally and impersonally effective. There is no room for chance or for the intervention of higher powers, least of all for an omnipotent and wilful deity.[17] This led Frazer to make his unfortunate distinction between magic and religion.[18] He argued that, when man failed with magic, that is with the coercion of the powers that be, as fail he must, he tried again with acts of propitiation and supplication, that is with religion. So religion is a later stage of development than magic.[19] Science is, of course, the third and highest stage.

Frazer's view has been very influential. It is surprising how often magic is put down as simply an attempt to coerce whatever deities may be, and so characterized as primitive and naive. Equally unsatisfactory is the notion that religion is a logical development from magic, based upon the supposition that the gods cannot be coerced but only entreated. The nineteenth century was too fond of such developmental systems. As far as prophetic drama is concerned, it is clear that many prophetic actions seem to function in an imitative way, but it would be leaping a long way ahead of the evidence to follow Frazer and suppose that they were attempts to operate the principle that like will produce like.

Emile Durkheim criticizes Frazer's account of sympathetic magic on the grounds that the two principles are anything but parallel. In contactual magic there is simply an attack on the whole through one of its parts. If it is believed that the identity of a person extends to all the physical objects that have been in touch with him, then it is reasonable to suppose that action against any one of those objects is an action against the person. If the identity extends to images, then action against an image is action against the person. This may be called imitative in the sense that it is hoped that the action against the object or the image will be reproduced elsewhere in greater measure, but it

---

[16] See Hahn, *The Old Testament in Modern Research*, pp. 56f.

[17] Frazer, *Golden Bough*, p. 49. Frazer is hardly consistent here, since he often refers to demons and other spiritual beings that act positively.

[18] Unfortunate, at least, because magic and religion are often found intermingled in a single rite.

[19] *Golden Bough*, pp. 48ff.; cf. Norbeck, *Religion in Primitive Society*, p. 34; van der Leeuw, *Religion in Essence and Manifestation*, p. 547.

is not imitative magic in the pure sense. The term properly belongs to a magical action in which no part or image of an intended target is conceivable. The action is pure drama representing a conclusion that has not yet appeared. The actors imitate the sound of wind or falling water in the hope that wind and rain will thereby come to be. This means that the imitative action is expected to create something entirely new.[20] This kind of action Durkheim puts in a religious setting. He thus reaches the conclusion that Frazer's order is wrong. Religion provides the basis for magic rather than magic for religion.

Religion, for Durkheim, is a function of the group. It is not simply that members of the group share beliefs, but that the beliefs are an important constituent of the group. They help to create its unity. 'The idea of society is the soul of religion.'[21] Religious rites, of course, have no instrumental efficacy. They are so obviously ineffective that the question must be asked why tribes persist with them. Durkheim's answer is that the performance of social rituals has an adventitious influence over the worshippers who take part in them. The performance re-forges their moral nature and this, in turn, leads to the conclusion that the rituals have succeeded. 'Thus it comes about that men attribute creative virtues to their gestures, which in themselves are vain. The moral efficacy of the rite, which is real, leads to the belief in its physical efficacy, which is imaginary.'[22] This belief is confirmed by the fact that many of the ends to which religious rites are directed do happen anyway in the natural process. Durkheim considers that illustrations of this process are to be found in the attitudes of modern, sophisticated, religious believers. They may have rational doubts about the efficacy of individual rituals, but they continue to participate in the cult. To give up the whole religious undertaking would simply launch them into moral confusion. Religion is not, fundamentally, a way of achieving an end, but a means of undergirding moral security.

Durkheim is certain that Frazer's principle of like producing like could never have been devised by the magicians upon the basis of empirical evidence. It must have its origins, therefore, in religious practice which, of course, is effective only obliquely. The magicians took over the notion and exploited it successfully for limited and practical ends. Their crude industry could never have come into being

[20] Durkheim, *Elementary Forms*, pp. 356f.

[21] Ibid., pp. 43f., 419.

[22] Ibid., p. 359.

on its own. It was born of, and is a particular and generally destructive application of, religious practice.

In one important respect, R.R. Marett also turns Frazer's system on its head.[23] Magic, according to Marett, does not begin with reflection about like producing like or any other such generalization. It begins with customs which develop in association with recurrent situations in social life. Hunting and fighting are two examples. Many of these situations give rise to powerful emotions which must somehow be discharged. That raises no problem for the actual hunters and fighters; they can pour all their excitement into the practical activity, but what about other members of the community? They are caught up in the excitement but have no function to perform. Imitative behaviour provides the outlet. So dances and mimes appear as an adjunct to the functional activity. They mimic the primary activity, but they have no practical function. In the course of time, however, the non-functional behaviour calls for explanation and there is a natural reluctance, or perhaps an inability, to draw a sharp distinction between the functional and the ancillary. So it is taken for granted that the ritual action possesses some kind of power which helps the primary activity along. If this is the case, then Frazer puts the cart before the horse. Imitative rituals are not based upon a belief that like produces like. On the contrary, the fact that imitative rituals happen gives rise, by a process of rationalization, to a notion of sympathetic involvement and then, eventually, sympathetic causation.

The difference between Frazer and Marett in the interpretation of evidence is of great interest because it suggests that a similar difference may exist in the interpretation of prophetic actions. For Frazer the drama precedes and produces the situation, but for Marett the situation produces the drama. Does that parallel suggest that the prophetic action should not be seen as preceding and predicting and producing the event but as deriving from it? Or perhaps the sharp distinction between the two is unsound; perhaps it depends too much upon our wish to establish an order of causation. Perhaps in the mind of the Hebrew, as in the mind of those who go in for war dances and hunting dances, the ritual and the reality cohere. They are seen to share in a composite identity so that the question of priority and causation is not relevant.

After the First World War, the study of magic was much influenced

---

[23] Marett, 'Magic', p. 247.

by the writings of the French anthropologist, Lucien Lévy-Bruhl. Lévy-Bruhl had attempted to analyse the thinking processes of so-called 'primitive man' and he produced two books with the revealing titles, *Primitive Mentality* and *How Natives Think*.[24] His thesis was that the primitive was entirely mystical in outlook, devoid of reasoning power, and he coined the phrase 'pre-logical mentality' to describe this lowly condition. The pre-logical mentality was not given to analysis. It grasped reality in terms of undifferentiated wholes and was, therefore, 'essentially synthetic'. It did not ask the right questions concerning causation, so natural causes tended to be ignored and curious phenomena were explained in terms of unseen, spiritual powers. A further shortcoming of the pre-logical mentality was that it did not bind itself down, as our thought is supposed to do, to avoiding contradiction. All this is very paternalistic and Lévy-Bruhl has been duly criticized, but it represents only the worst side of his achievements. In his day he was distinguished and influential.[25]

One of Lévy-Bruhl's harshest critics was Bronislaw Malinowski, who worked in England between the wars. From his own research he disproved Lévy-Bruhl's contentions that primitive man was 'mystical' in outlook, devoid of reasoning power, and 'pre-logical'. Malinowski shows that the Melanesians he studied have a wide and accurate knowledge of agriculture based on experiment but, side by side with it, a clearly defined magical practice. In some areas it is recognized that hard work provides the answer, in others hard work is of no avail. So, to deal with pests, bad weather, and ill-fortune, Melanesians turn to magic.[26] The existence of scientific method does not by any means prove that faith in magic has disappeared. On the contrary, belief in magic co-exists with all kinds of sophisticated systems of thought.

Following Marett, Malinowski argues that magic arises from the natural reactions induced in moments of intense stress. It is common, at such times, to go through the motions associated with the desire, to shake the fist at the enemy that has escaped, to embrace the lover that is gone. These are, 'extended expressions of emotion in act and word'.[27] They are effective in that they give vent to feelings, a fact

---

[24] The original titles were *La Mentalité Primitive* (1922) and *Les Fonctions Mentales dans les Sociétés Inférieures* (1910).

[25] See *Primitive Mentality*, p. 36; *The 'Soul' of the Primitive*, pp. 112f.; *How Natives Think*, pp. 73f., 78f., 108, 229.

[26] Malinowski, 'Magic, Science and Religion', pp. 29ff.

[27] Ibid., p. 74.

which leads on to the more dubious assumption that they are effective in other ways. This phenomenon is 'not only one of the sources but the very fountainhead of magical belief'.[28] In the course of time magic develops into a system governed by complex techniques, esoteric formulae and the like, which must be studied by the magician with the utmost care, but it is never thought to be dramatically effective. Rather it is a 'sober, prosaic, even clumsy art, enacted for purely practical reasons'. Malinowski thus dispels some of the melodramatic overtones that magic had acquired.[29] One conclusion at this point is that it is necessary to take care over the use of the word 'effective' in relation to ritual acts, because they can be effective in the Malinowski sense without being effective in the Frazer sense at all.

It is clear that, by the nineteen twenties, anthropologists had given up the contention that 'magic constrains', at least as a comprehensive statement. The final word on that phase of the argument came in a book published in Paris in 1950 by the French scholar, Marcel Mauss.[30] Mauss sees magic as an indeterminate phenomenon lying somewhere between technology, in which you achieve precise aims by precise methods, and religion, where aims are not precise and so the question of achievement does not arise. Magic is an intensely compact social phenomenon born out of social need. Magic exists simply because people need it. The magician is no fool. He is aware that magic is rarely practically effective; he is aware that he himself conjures up effects to make it seem more effective than it is. But both he and his clients continue to believe in it. It is a strange, circular logic. 'He is serious about it because he is taken seriously, and he is taken seriously because people have need of him.'[31] If the magician falls ill, he himself seeks the help of another medicine man. Knowledge of his own failings does not weaken his acceptance of the social conviction that the general procedure is sound. Magic is thus self-propagating. Even the failure of a magical rite can become an argument for the magician, for the failure may be thought to be due to counter-magic, and then the magician is more than ever necessary to defeat the enemy. To sum up, magic is, 'a system of *a priori* inductions, operating under the pressure of the needs of groups of individuals'.[32]

[28] Ibid., p. 75.
[29] Ibid., p. 65.
[30] The English translation appeared in 1972 with the title, *A General Theory of Magic*.
[31] Mauss, *Magic*, p. 96.
[32] Ibid., p. 126.

This is very important, for it shows that the crucial factor is the world of thought and practice spun out by society to answer its needs. Mechanical efficacy may be hoped for, but it is rarely achieved.

The whole discussion takes a new turn with the work of more recent writers such as Godfrey Lienhardt and Mary Douglas. Lienhardt, unlike so many anthropologists of a previous generation, eschewed theorizing and concentrated on detailed study of a specific field. The results are most illuminating.[33] Lienhardt gives a number of examples of symbolic actions among the Dinka, and demonstrates quite clearly that, though the actions were regarded as important, and indeed, necessary, the idea of instrumental efficacy was largely absent. The rite to cure malaria and the rite to bring rain take place when the malaria season is declining and when the rain is due. In these regular ceremonies, 'their human symbolic action moves with the rhythm of the natural world around them, re-creating that rhythm in moral terms and not merely attempting to *coerce* it to conformity with human desires'.[34] As far as malaria is concerned, those who perform the ritual are also eager to go to the clinic for treatment. In no way does the ritual render practical steps unnecessary, but equally, in no way do the practical steps render the ritual unnecessary. When a lion troubles the village, the 'masters of the fishing-spear' will take a stone and tie it in a kind of grass. So the lion, represented by the stone, is constrained and restricted. But immediately thereafter a hunt will be organized to deal with the lion in a more practical way. 'This "mystical" action is not a substitute for practical or technical action, but a complement to it and a preparation for it'.[35] It would not be true to say that ritual action was thought to exert no control whatever over the objective situation, but exerting control is not its primary justification. Primarily the ritual affects the participants; it affects their attitudes, their emotions, their whole disposition towards the objective situation, so that it is experienced in a new way; and the consequences of the change of attitude may be very far-reaching. If Frazer thought that magic was an attempt to affect objective circumstances, Lienhardt contends, more subtly, that it affects not so much the circumstances themselves, as the way in which those circumstances are experienced.

Mary Douglas begins her *Purity and Danger* with a critique of Robertson Smith, Durkheim and Frazer. The first two win her

---

[33] Lienhardt, *Divinity and Experience*, 1961.

[34] Ibid., p. 280.

[35] Ibid., p. 283.

approval for the emphasis they lay on the social aspect of primitive religion, but they are found wanting in that they suppose magic to lie outside the social processes. A true estimate of ritual behaviour, according to Professor Douglas, embraces both the religious and the magical. Frazer is criticized more sharply.[36] He failed to grasp the importance of sociological factors and so came to understand magic as an individual belief in non-ethical rites that work *ex opere operato*. This led to his theory of progress – magic giving way to religion and both giving way to science – in which magic and religion are distinguished absolutely. Malinowski is also criticized for accepting from Frazer the notion that magic can be easily distinguished from religion. Magic, for Malinowski, was 'a kind of poor man's whisky, used for gaining conviviality and courage against daunting odds'.[37]

Mary Douglas then turns to comment on the work of Lienhardt, and concludes first, that the notion of instrumental efficacy has been wrongly applied to magic, mostly by Europeans whose understanding was imperfect, and secondly, that magic cannot be easily distinguished from religion.[38] The study of primitive ritual has been beggared by simple-minded observers who have taken the ritual at its 'Aladdin-and-the-lamp face value'. Ceremonies are performed, as we have seen, not to bring rain or to cure malaria, but at the time when the rain is due to fall and the malaria to abate. If the officiant ends the ceremony by urging the congregation to attend the clinic to keep healthy, then it cannot be that the magic was thought to be instrumentally effective.[39] It must mean that the magic has some other, social function related to the cycle of the year. Both Lienhardt and Douglas assert that ritual – the distinction between magic and religion disappears at this point – is a symbolic activity that moves parallel to experience. It evokes common experience, represents it, deepens it, refashions it where it has gone awry, and, within certain limits, controls it.[40] If the rituals 'do not change actual historical or physical events – as the Dinka in some cases believe them to do – they do change and regulate the Dinkas' experience of those events'.[41] Mary Douglas continues with an illuminating analogy between ritual and currency. Mauss had

---

[36] *Purity*, pp. 22ff.
[37] Ibid., p. 74.
[38] Ibid., pp. 66ff.
[39] Ibid., p. 73.
[40] Ibid., p. 67.
[41] Lienhardt, *Divinity and Experience*, p. 291.

remarked that magic was a false currency. Not so, says Mary Douglas, ritual – she prefers the more comprehensive term – is a regular coinage, socially useful, even necessary, with a clearly defined function, but, if public confidence is lost, valueless and futile.

This point ought to have been obvious to us all along. Leaving aside the rituals of the churches, secular occasions in Britain are simply loaded with ritual. What, for example, is the point of Trooping the Colour? It does not win any battles. It is not a secret weapon against the enemies of the state. It is a means of expressing loyalty, patriotism, continuity with the past, confidence in the future. In other words, it evokes, extends and deepens social solidarity and social experience. It does not change the world situation, it changes our attitude to it. The spectators go home with a sense of security rather than with security itself. Something similar is true of all grand celebrations. There is plenty of spontaneous behaviour at the Cup Final, but there is much ritual behaviour too. Before the match there is the wearing of colours, the chanting of slogans, the bellicose gestures performed in concert. After the match there is the public display, the lap of honour, the tour on the open topped bus. The central phenomenon is a game of football, but the surrounding ritual attracts an extraordinary amount of attention. The Sunday papers lead, not with a photograph from the game itself, but of the winning captain holding the trophy aloft – the ritual, not the reality!

With this notion of the function of ritual we are in a new world. The relevance to the study of prophetic drama can hardly be overrated. Nevertheless, we must be careful not to overstate the case. It is arguable that Lienhardt overplays the expressive element in ritual and underestimates the element of instrumental efficacy.[42] Neither magic nor religion exists in any society in pure and uncorrupted form. Wishful thinking is found everywhere, and crude, shallow, and foolishly optimistic expressions of the pervasive social doctrine and social practice follow from it. Without casting any doubt upon the researches of modern anthropologists, we have to recognize that in Israel, as everywhere else, there would have been many who saw ritual action, quite wrongly, as a mysterious but relatively cheap means of getting their own way. Moreoever, we have to recognize that sorcerers of one kind or another exist in most societies. They work secretly, outside the social programme but parasitic upon it, and they depend

---

[42] Douglas, *Natural Symbols*, p. 17.

absolutely on their clients' belief in the instrumental efficacy of their rites. The analysis of ritual in terms of social function does not, therefore, cover the whole field. There remains a category of symbolic actions that have to be called magical in an instrumental sense.[43] Recent research has diminished the size of this category and drawn attention to other, more interesting and more significant, symbolic actions, but the category has not disappeared altogether.

This fact leads to problems of definition. On one hand we recognize the perceptiveness of anthropologists who have seen that some rites, which appear to operate with instrumental efficacy, in fact do not do so. This leads to a definition of magic that does not imply wilful and effective constraint on the powers that be. On the other hand we have to find a name for the rites that still do appear wilful and instrumentally effective. If we continue to use the word 'magic' in both senses, we shall have to employ adjectives to define the meaning more closely.

It is now clear just what H.W. Robinson was doing in defining his slogan, 'Magic constrains the unseen; religion means surrender to it.' He was comparing the crudest and most unsophisticated form of magic with the most refined and selfless expression of religion. The formula is not, therefore, simply too brief to be helpful; it is so heavily loaded that it is misleading.

Before passing on it is worth pointing out that magic, even in its crudest form, is not necessarily either silly or reprehensible. It may be seen as an understandable, though not always successful, attempt on the part of embattled people to shape the environment a little more to their liking. Frazer may be right to see some link between magic and science in that the same motives prompt the rain-rituals of the ancient Near East and the building of the Aswan dam. The magician who claimed to bring down rain – and despite all we now say about rain-rituals, there is little doubt that some did so claim – may have been ineffective, but nobody knew this for certain. It may have seemed that he was trying to achieve a rational end by the only means available. It is often assumed that to put any trust in such figures is folly, because the claim cannot pass any empirical test; but is this so? There are at

---

[43] Fohrer really makes the same point ('Prophetie und Magie', p. 244). He describes an early magico-religious complex from which both magic and religion emerge by a process of polarization. The polarization is never complete, but a distinction is clear in prophetic times. Fohrer then goes on to define the magical element in terms of mechanical causality. Magicians continued to exist in Israel right down to New Testament times and beyond.

least four reasons why devotees of instrumental magic may have been confirmed in their beliefs.[44] First, there is the problematic nature of causality itself. It always does rain on the Carmel range in the autumn. As the long, hot summer wears away, the magicians turn to their arts. How is it to be established that *post hoc* is not *propter hoc*? Secondly, there is the fact of coincidence. The taxi-driver who leaves his St Christopher medallion at home and then drives into a lamp-post will find it hard to exclude the idea that there is some causal nexus here. Coincidences happen, and of course, one positive example will outweigh dozens of negative ones. Thirdly, there is the psychological factor. The *placebo* works in medicine because a person who expects to be cured may well be cured due to the release of tension. The curse will work if the cursed person really fears it. Fourthly, one must not overlook the shrewdness of the magician himself and the foresight that is bound up with his art. Long practice will reveal to him the situations in which his magic is likely to succeed and he will be wise enough to practice on those occasions and avoid the others. By this means his success rate will be improved and his credibility enhanced. Magic, then, even private magic, implies neither villainy nor folly on the part of its devotees, though it may be clear to us that, in many circumstances, it is not successful in the way that it claims to be.

We must now consider whether any useful comparison can be made between prophetic drama and magic of any kind. There is one great difficulty. Whereas we have some knowledge of the Old Testament understanding of prophetic drama from the texts studied in Chapters 7–13, we have very little knowledge of how magic was apprehended and used in ancient Israel. There are texts from Israel's neighbours and a few slanting references in the Old Testament that the editors have allowed us to see, but there is nothing approaching an adequate corpus of material. In these days of field studies the information we have must be counted as very scanty. We proceed, therefore, with great hesitation, for we are comparing a phenomenon about which we are reasonably well informed with another which is defined only in terms of very general inferences.

Most Old Testament scholars consider that, whatever may be the subsequent differences, prophetic dramas derive, historically speaking, from a world of thought and practice that may as well be

---

[44] For a full treatment of this issue, see Skorupski, *Symbol and Theory*.

called magical as religious.[45] The ground for this view is the familiar practice of the earliest prophets, not simply the despised $n^e\underline{b}\hat{\imath}\,'\hat{\imath}m$, but the heroic figures of the early period as well. The most remarkable feats are attributed to them, feats which suggest that they possessed powers far beyond the understanding of ordinary men. Whether these feats are to be regarded as within the field of magic or of religion is simply a matter of definition. The element of caprice that exists in some cases suggests that the actions ought to be disowned as instrumental magic, but the fame of the agents ensures that they are accepted as part of the authentic Hebrew tradition. This makes it clear that we have exactly the same spectrum in Old Testament religion as we have discovered in the field of magic. The actions include Moses' tricks with his rod and the plagues that he brought on Egypt (Ex. 4.1–5, 7–10; 14.16; 17.1–7, etc.), Balaam's technical skill in blessing and cursing (Num. 22–24), Samuel's secret knowledge (I Sam. 9.1–10.16), the actions of the man of God in I Kings 13 who broke the altar and paralysed Jeroboam's hand with a word, the remarkable prescience of the blind Ahijah (I Kings 14.1–20), and much of what is recorded of Elijah and Elisha. The Zarephath story (I Kings 17.8–24) implies two miracles. Elijah's foreknowledge of Ahaziah's death and his swift despatch of Ahaziah's squadrons by means of fire from heaven, continue the theme (II Kings 1.1–18), as do the final scene at the Jordan and the chariot ride to heaven (II Kings 2).

The Elisha cycle provides further and even stronger evidence of a world of thought in which instrumental magic and religion are confused. 'Frankly a Shamanistic wonder-worker', is one scholar's comment on Elisha.[46] Elisha purified springs, cursed children, produced water in the desert, frightened off the Moabites, multiplied oil and bread, raised a dead child, made poisoned food edible, cured a leper, caused leprosy, made iron float, used clairvoyance against the Syrians – all this in II Kings 2–6 – and, on his death-bed, set in train their defeat (II Kings 13.14–19). Even from the grave he managed one miracle (II Kings 13.20f.). Some of these stories are a serious

---

[45] Lods, *Israel from its Beginnings*, p. 446; Johnson, *The One and the Many*, p. 21; H.W. Robinson, 'Hebrew Sacrifice', p. 137; Johnson, *Cultic Prophet*, pp. 38f.; Fohrer, 'Prophetie und Magie', pp. 247, 250; *Die Handlungen*, pp. 10–14; *History*, p. 234; Engnell, 'Prophets and Prophetism', p. 150; Fohrer, *Introduction*, p. 349. Despite the sharp distinction he draws in later times, this is also Knight's view (*Hebrew Prophetic Consciousness*, p. 35).

[46] Knight, *Hebrew Prophetic Consciousness*, p. 47.

embarrassment for those who contend that, whereas the magician was wilful and malicious, the prophet was submissive to Yahweh's will. A more reasonable conclusion is that the prophet inherited the prestige, the power, even the methods of the magician, with the single reservation that the prophet belonged to the Hebrew tradition and used the name of Yahweh.

It must not be supposed that these actions were all of a kind or that they can all be explained in the same way. Nevertheless it is fair to say that no clear distinction between instrumental magic and what normally goes by the name of religion in the period under discussion can be charted in these traditions, particularly if we are looking for a distinction that implies disapproval for one and approval for the other. Indeed, if we were to encounter such stories outside the canon of Holy Scripture, we should give them very low marks. Later on it becomes easier to distinguish between prophetic drama and instrumental magic, but both have their origin in the same complex of thought and action. And it has to be remembered that, where theological conceptions are concerned, prophetic actions do not constitute a homogeneous category. There are important similarities between the stories of Zedekiah with his horns, Elisha with his arrows, and Jeremiah with his yoke, but the theological conceptions implicit in them are very different.

There is also a link in outward appearance between the public magical action and prophetic drama. This link is seen throughout the whole period. It is as obvious in Jeremiah as it is in the historical books.[47] Externally the prophetic drama involves a notable charismatic figure, distinguished by prestige, social role, dress, habit, and 'life-style'. Officiants of most magical cults have a similar status and similar personal attributes.[48] There are differences, of course, but the differences do not nullify the link.[49] Further, the rites performed by these mysterious figures are not easily distinguished. Scholars looking for parallels have found numerous examples to work on.[50] Some

[47] Jer. 19.1–13 and 51.59–64 are, in appearance, as much like magical stories as anything in the Old Testament. See van den Born, *De Handelingen*, p. 27.

[48] Malinowski, 'Magic, Science and Religion', p. 76.

[49] Little of Mauss's description of the magician (*Magic*, pp. 25–44) applies to the prophet.

[50] Fohrer, *Die Handlungen; History of Israelite Religion*, pp. 232f.; Gaster, *Myth, Legend and Custom*; Keller, *Das Wort OTH*, pp. 49f., 55f.; Overholt deals with a modern parallel and finds that, in terms of *activity*, as distinct from content, there is plenty of correspondence ('Prophecy: the Problem', p. 63).

prophetic acts, like Jeremiah's breaking of the pot, have obvious parallels near at hand.[51] Others lack obvious parallels, but it is still clear that they bear no distinguishing mark to demonstrate that these are the actions of Yahwist prophets and not of non-Yahwist magicians or even sorcerers. When a man tears a coat into pieces, or shoots an arrow, or ties two sticks together, it is not evident that he is doing it in the service of Yahweh. Prophetic acts and magical acts are both done with ceremony, both have a certain dramatic effect, both have reference to some other state of affairs to which the action is directed, both provide many examples of mimetic actions, and both may be accompanied by a verbal formula. In appearance, therefore, the link is real enough.

There is a link, to speak in very general terms, between the various mental conceptions on which the two kinds of action are based. Fundamental to both worlds of thought is the notion that there is a bond of identity between the ritual and the reality, between the war dance and the battle, between the pouring of water and the falling of rain, between the breaking of the pot and the sack of the city, between raising the cup and winning the game. Which of the two comes first in the process of time is not important, at this point. Nor does it matter that, in some cases, human agents are active only in the ritual, whereas in others they are active in both. The important feature to note is the bond between the dramatic action and the reality. This thought world is not specifically religious nor specifically magical, but it forms a link between the most exalted prophetic act on one hand and the most arrant sorcery on the other.

Another element in what one might call the metaphysics of ritual actions is the positive significance attached to the action itself in both prophetic dramas and magical performances. But both kinds of action are effective. The problem relating to the use of the word 'effective' has been discussed above. Efficacy is normally construed in terms of instrumental efficacy, which, of course, begs the question, but ritual action is effective, not necessarily in the sense of achieving a determined end, but in the sense of expressing what needs to be expressed, adding to, deepening, and modifying experience, releasing emotion, and enabling those present to appreciate and respond to a new situation. Both prophetic dramas and magic reflect this background, though in

[51] Pritchard, *ANET*, pp. 328f.

different ways; both kinds of action are necessary, they are not ornaments, they are essential.

It would be foolish to pursue this kind of discussion without recognizing that in Israel, as in all other societies, there were different levels of perception in these metaphysical matters. We encounter the spectrum again. Jehoshaphat seems to have been well able to distinguish between Zedekiah and Micaiah ben Imlah in terms of effectiveness (I Kings 22). The former's dramatic action carried little weight with Jehoshaphat, but what did Ahab think and what about the onlookers? It is impossible to imagine that there was a unanimously agreed account of the effectiveness of prophetic action in ancient Israel. Even supposing there was, the effectiveness would depend upon the genuineness of the prophet, and there could never be unanimous agreement on that. Two examples of counteractivity confirm this point. Hananiah broke Jeremiah's yoke and Jehoiakim cut his scroll in pieces (Jer. 27–28; 36). These counteractions suggest the belief that prophetic dramas were effective rituals that could be nullified if a more powerful and determined practitioner set to work against them. We can hardly resist the conclusion that Jeremiah understood his actions in one sense, and many of the onlookers understood them in another. Indeed, there appear to be three quite different metaphysical concepts here. There is the way Jeremiah understood his work in the service of God; there is the way Jeremiah understood his opponents' actions, that is, as bogus and deceitful fabrications; and there is the way those opponents understood their own performances, and possibly his too, that is, as dynamic and effective actions. The case for a link between prophetic dramas and magic in terms of effectiveness does not, therefore, rest upon our ability to define effectiveness in each case and to show a similarity, but simply on the fact that, in their different constituencies and in ways appropriate to those constituencies, both kinds of action were regarded as effective.

We have now to consider the fact that the Old Testament identifies certain practices without defining them very closely and regularly deplores them.[52] These practices can hardly be called anything but

---

[52] The practices and the practitioners include the following: The *'ōḇ* who was primarily concerned with necromancy (Deut. 18.9–11; Isa. 8.19; 19.3; etc.); *qesem*, the art of discovering secret knowledge, especially with regard to the future, though the word is used fairly generally (II Kings 17.17; Jer. 27.9; 29.8; etc.) and is linked with false prophecy in Ezek. 13.6, which shows that one man's diviner is another man's

magical, so another sense is added to that overworked term. The number of different functions involved is surprising. Among the practitioners condemned are the *ḥōlēm ḥᵃlôm* (dreamer of dreams) and the *nᵉbî'îm* (Deut. 13.1–3 [2–4 in Hebrew]; Jer. 23.26f; 27.9; 29.8 etc.). Classical prophets are never described by the former term and, in Jeremiah at least, the latter is regularly used of a group of disreputable prophets. Nevertheless it is surprising to see dreamers and prophets lined up with sorcerers, enchanters and soothsayers for denunciation, but so it is. It appears from all the references that, to the common people at the material time, prophets belonged to a group of specialists who dealt in strange arts, a group which also included some who practised instrumental magic. The existence of these specialists represents a point of contact; the denunciation of them establishes the contrast. Furthermore, Hebrew tradition – and this term includes people who were disciples and contemporaries of the men concerned – chose certain figures from this mass, preserved their oracles, revered their memory, and canonized them as the only true prophets. This continues the point of contrast, for it never happened to Israelite magicians. In the surviving tradition they are consistently condemned. By what criteria was the category of true prophet established? The fact that their oracles proved to be accurate is of some importance, as the Old Testament itself says (Deut. 18.22; Jer. 28.9), but there must have been successful wizards and shrewd forecasters of the future in Israel, and they never received the same honour. The answer must lie in theology, in the theology of the prophets themselves and the theology of the later arbiters of the canon. This is a point to which we must return. Once the category of 'true prophet' was

---

prophet; *yiddᵉ'ōnî* is one who is in touch with the unseen world (I Sam. 28.3; Deut. 18.11); *'-n-n*, a root that means to practise some kind of fortune-telling, which can hardly have been forbidden in Israel, though certain methods were presumably banned (Lev. 19.26; Deut. 18.10; II Kings 21.6; Isa. 2.6; Micah 5.12 [11 in Hebrew]; Jer. 27.9; the root *n-ḥ-š* similarly suggests divination by the use of omens (Lev. 19.26; Deut. 18.10; II Kings 17.17; 21.6); *kešep*, sorcery or witchcraft (Micah 5.12 again and Ex. 22.18 [17 in Hebrew]); and the root *ḥ-b-r*, which means, among other things, weaving spells or charms (Deut. 18.11; Ps. 58.5 [6 in Hebrew]). It is not always clear how these various practices were carried out nor what effect they were thought to have. The subject is not well documented. See Oesterley and Robinson, *Hebrew Religion*, pp. 71ff.; R.C. Thompson, *Semitic Magic*; Witton Davies, *Magic, Demonology and Witchcraft among the Hebrews*; Guillaume, *Prophecy and Divination*, particularly pp. 233ff.; Wright, *The Old Testament against its Environment*, pp. 77ff.; Kapelrud, 'Shamanistic Features in the Old Testament'.

established, it is easy to see how it was extended backwards to include heroes and charismatic figures like Samuel and Elisha, to whom some of the defining features of true prophecy did not apply. This explains how Elisha, whose activities seem at times so much like magical stunts, was accepted by Hebrew tradition when magic itself was condemned.[53]

Before coming to the main issues, several smaller points regarding the distinction between prophecy and magic need to be made. They are primarily concerned, not with magic in general, but with sorcery. First, it is noteworthy how simple and straightforward prophetic actions are. To speak generally, prophetic dramas are not complex, technical, esoteric actions, such as would normally be associated with sorcery; they are not difficult; they do not hint at the miraculous; they do not suggest mystical power and activity. Some of Ezekiel's actions may be exceptions to some of these rules, but the general principle stands.

Secondly, though prophetic drama was an act carried out by an individual, in few cases did the reality to which it was related involve only one individual. The concern of prophecy is normally with communities, not, as is so often the case with sorcery, with individuals.[54] In one or two cases individuals figure prominently in the reality – Saul in I Sam. 15.27f., Jeroboam in I Kings 11.29–31, Ahab in I Kings 22.11, Joash in II Kings 13.14–19 – but it is significant that all these men were, or were about to become, kings. The drama involves the nation through its representative. Particularly is this true of the classical prophets. All their dramas had social reference. Usually they concerned Israel, sometimes other nations, but never do they have reference to the weal or woe of single individuals.[55] The classical prophets saw themselves as representative individuals and acted in this capacity. Prophetic acts may, therefore, be akin to the public performances of ritual magic, but

[53] R.B.Y. Scott oversteps the mark in his anxiety to free the great prophets from any charge of wonder-working (*Relevance*, pp. 55f., 98f.). He drives a wedge between the classical prophets and the early prophets. 'A difference of degree has become a difference in kind.' That makes the place of Elijah and Elisha in the prophetic tradition very insecure. Granted the differences, the evidence hardly calls for so drastic a conclusion.

[54] Once again we have to give thought to definitions. Magic is a general term that includes both social and individual action. Sorcery refers to individual action only. Distinguishing between prophetic dramas and sorcery does not, therefore, necessarily imply a distinction between dramas and magic.

[55] The actions of Elisha are, of course, excepted.

they are distinguished absolutely from acts of sorcery which attempted to gratify the private and malevolent wishes of ordinary individuals.

Thirdly and somewhat paradoxically, prophetic dramas differ, not simply from sorcery, but from all types of magic in that the dramas were usually worked out by the prophet to be used on one particular occasion. Magical acts are not simply invented by the magician; they belong to a traditional programme. The magician is knowledgeable in magical lore; he is not a creative artist, but he knows what to do in any set of circumstances. The prophet, on the other hand, gives the appearance of thinking for himself and devising one-off dramas. This means that the magician's performance, and even that of the sorcerer, is more in line with cultic action than with that of the prophet, which may seem surprising, but it is true.

Fourthly, although some dramas are carried out with no audience, secrecy is not essential to them. In most cases there is an audience, and in some cases the audience is essential. Prophetic dramas are not, therefore, a secret art. Without suggesting that the dramas can properly be explained as visual aids, we can say that the phenomenon existed out in the open and that communication was a common, if not essential, element in them. This is confirmed by the explanations that accompanied many of the prophetic actions and that became a feature of the drama stories. This overtness is in marked contrast to the work of enchanters whose business depended on the preservation of their secrets. Fohrer is at pains to point this out.[56]

Fifthly, coming closer to the heart of the matter, the qualifications of the prophet differ significantly from those normally required of both the magician and the sorcerer. The chief qualification for prophecy in the Old Testament was a sense of divine call, of being, from time to time, possessed by the word of God. Nothing else appears to be of much importance, not even abnormal psychological experiences, for, though such conditions occur frequently in the prophetic books, they vary enormously, and some prophets show no sign of them. As for the technical qualifications for prophecy, there were none. There was no trade to be learned, no skill to be acquired. The only prophet in the record who carries out what looks like a

[56] 'Die Gattung', pp. 94ff., 107f.; *Die Handlungen*, pp. 17ff.; 'Prophetie und Magie', p. 245.

technical action at the request of a client is Zedekiah in I Kings 22, and he was not a prophet who won the approval of later generations. Zedekiah has something in common with the magician, and many of his contemporaries, no doubt, took him seriously; but Hosea, Isaiah, Jeremiah and Ezekiel functioned at no one's request and were often at odds with the society they believed they were serving. In some cases the prophets acted to their own detriment: Hosea endured all that misery over the years in the belief that he was doing it under divine compulsion; Jeremiah, too, hated his message and would gladly have resigned, if he could. No known form of magic would require the magician to carry out actions which would indicate the destruction of his own city, the captivity of his own people, and his own exile.

This last point begins to go to the root of the matter. The prophet has no plan of his own and no universally recognized programme. He waits to be acted upon. A survey of all the different kinds of prophetic drama reveals that there is no system that the prophet controls, but simply a large number of occasions on which the prophet feels himself compelled to act or think or respond in a way that he believes is determined by Yahweh and not by himself. Some dramas are contrived performances in which the prophet acts as he believes himself to have been commanded, but others are interpretations of the actions of others or of events in the prophet's own life. This indicates that the essence of prophetic drama is not a positive and effective performance by the prophet, but the recognition by the prophet of a bond between an immediate condition – whether contrived by him or not – and a more distant reality. The one who is responsible for both the immediate condition and the distant reality, and who determines the bond between them, is Yahweh. Performing the action is the less important factor in the prophet's function; recognizing and interpreting the bond is crucial; this in turn rests on hearing and obeying the divine command.

We have now moved a long way from the simple comparison of magical and prophetic phenomena; we have come to the fundamental factor of world-view. How does the universe operate? What works and what does not work? Because there is no empirical answer to these questions, there are many speculative answers. Israel's answer was a theological one; it worked itself out in the days of the monarchy and resulted in the establishment of a clear distinction between prophetic actions and acts of instrumental magic, despite the similarity of form.[57] This process took place in Israel dramatically, even at times violently, as Yahwism came to its full vigour. The evidence does not suggest that theological beliefs were homogeneous throughout Israel, but a concept of Yahwism did develop in some quarters that made any notion of constraint on the deity impossible. The canonical prophets from Amos and Hosea onwards contributed to this concept and ultimately it had the greatest possible influence on the compilers of the Old Testament. In other quarters, no doubt, less sophisticated theology continued to flourish. Many of the kings, and perhaps many of the people most of the time, clung to this shallower view, but, in the fulness of time, it was condemned. This, at least, is how Ezekiel interpreted the tragedy of the exile. The difference between the dramas of the classical prophets and acts of instrumental magic is, therefore, a theological one. The history, the ritual form, even, to some extent, the modes of thought, are the same, but different concepts of deity inform them. It is not what the prophets actually do, but what they think about what they do that is important.[58]

The Yahwistic theology to which we refer implies belief in the historical activity of a sovereign deity whose actions are beyond man's power to understand, to constrain or to predict. Yahweh's power is illimitable and he chooses to exercise it on behalf of Israel, not to please Israel, but to bring Israel to please himself. Yahweh scorns other deities, humiliates them when it pleases him, and shows them to be no more effective than lumps of wood. His own people are required to blot other deities out of their minds and offer appropriate service to him alone. Appropriate service is total service. So speaks the Holy One of Israel.

The precise dates of the growth of this sophisticated Yahwism are

[57] Perhaps this is most clearly seen in the way in which conflict between prophets is handled by the ancient editors of the prophetic books. There is no doubt that individual magicians and sorcerers clashed, and it was presumably assumed that victory went to the one who could exert most power. There is much evidence of prophetic conflict in the Old Testament; it is not, however, recounted in terms of competing powers, but in terms of truth and falsehood. One prophet possessed the word of Yahweh, the other did not. See Crenshaw, *Prophetic Conflict*, de Vries, *Prophet against Prophet*.

[58] Claus Westermann provides an interesting parallel in his discussion of the relation of prophetic judgment oracles to curses. Curse formulae are unsatisfactory to the prophet who thinks of history as the arena of God's activity. So the notion of the curse was rethought to take account of the sovereign will of Yahweh, and the judgment oracle is the result. No doubt curses, thought to be effective, continued on the lips of non-Yahwists and half-Yahwists unchecked (*Basic Forms*, pp. 194ff.).

a matter of debate. Particularly it is difficult to say when and where it achieved the definition outlined in the previous paragraph. Some scholars attribute the theology almost entirely to Moses.[59] Others look to the author of the Yahwist saga,[60] or to Elijah,[61] or to the classical prophets.[62] The soundest conclusion is surely that this positive theology achieved clarity of definition only after long debate, that it was partly the product of and partly an influence on the classical prophets, that it made possible a distinction between the dramatic actions of the great prophets, and not only contemporary magic, but also the dramatic actions of others in Israel, who had come before them, and who had not understood Yahwism in this thoroughgoing way. These early figures were Yahwists, but their Yahwism had not been defined so precisely as to proscribe the quasi-magical act.

The relevance of this developed Yahwism to the dramas of the prophets is inescapable. It affirms that the autonomy of man is severely limited; his glory is a derived glory; his greatness rests in the fact that he bears the divine image; his dominion over the world is ambassadorial in that he exercises it on behalf of Yahweh whose dominion is absolute. This is seen nowhere more clearly than in the course of history, which Yahweh directs for his own purposes and which man can do little to control. One inference from the story in I Kings 22 of Ahab and Jehoshaphat seeking prophetic help before a battle is that Jehoshaphat, at least, feared that prophetic activity did not control history and that Yahweh did. The classical prophets do not give the impression that they determine history themselves. They are mere instruments. Whatever is spoken or done, Yahweh is the power behind it. The initiative, not simply for the historical event, but for the prophetic act

---

[59] Albright, *From the Stone Age to Christianity*, pp. 257ff.; Kaufmann, *The Religion of Israel from its Beginnings to the Babylonian Exile*, pp. 223ff.

[60] James, *Personalities of the Old Testament*, pp. 196ff.; Ellis, *The Yahwist: The Bible's First Theologian*.

[61] Pedersen, 'The Rôle Played by Inspired Persons', pp. 140f. Pedersen does not suggest that Elijah was the originator of Yahwism but that he grasped the true nature of the faith and inaugurated a movement towards Yahwist distinctiveness and Hebrew nationalism.

[62] There can hardly be a simple answer to this question. Fohrer addresses it in 'Remarks on Modern Interpretation of the Prophets', and argues that the prophets were not simply interpreters of tradition (contra Bright), but innovators. Not absolute innovators because they began with the vigorous faith of the Mosaic age, but innovators in the sense that they expanded the Mosaic faith to meet wholly new situations. See also von Rad, *Theology I*, pp. 66f.

itself, comes from Yahweh and not from the prophet himself. This is a difficult matter to expound because it carries us deep into the realm of motive. Who can know just what went on in the prophet's mind? Did prophets never try to take a hand in the revelation, to steer the oracle in the direction they themselves approved? In theory, the answers to these questions may be no, but in practice the questions are unanswerable. Nevertheless, it is possible to trace in the great prophetic acts a certain moral and theological consistency. Israel has sinned, Israel will be punished, a remnant will be saved to inherit the promises. Most of the prophetic acts fit into this scheme, which argues that the prophet believed himself to be acting in submission to a greater plan rather than in the service of his own wishes. Moreover, the way in which the dramas were understood in later times shows that they were not regarded as acts of prophetic initiative. It is taken for granted that the prophet believed himself to be overwhelmed by Yahweh, and he was certainly believed by others, both at the time and in later generations, to be so overwhelmed. The abstruse actions of Ezekiel make it evident that the ideas were mediated through the prophet's personality and bear the prophet's own personal stamp. This may constitute a problem for theologians – and an opportunity for rationalists – but it does not affect the fundamental point of the way in which dramas were understood. To the onlookers and the editors, the act was no less Yahweh's because it was also Ezekiel's.

All this indicates that each action and each prophet has to be considered in its own right. The actions of Elisha will not profit much from the arguments that have just been put forward, which explains why he has been largely left out of the enquiry, but as far as the other prophets are concerned, it should be possible, on the criteria set out here, to draw distinctions between them and various kinds of magician. In one or two areas the enquiry reveals, not distinctions, but positive points of comparison, which lead to a better understanding of prophecy.

17 · The Function of Prophetic Drama

When a prophetic drama takes place, an action, a person or persons, and possibly an object belonging to the everyday world are deliberately brought into relationship with some unseen event or reality, usually something on a much larger scale than the drama itself.[1] The dramas point away from themselves towards the unseen element in the conjunction. The purpose of this final chapter is to determine as precisely as possible the relationship between these two elements as it was understood by all those who, in their several ways, gave us the Old Testament.

It has to be recognized that a single and simple account that covers the relationship of all the dramas to all the realities is not possible. There is too much variation between the dramas themselves; there is variation between the original sense of the drama and the sense expressed in the later record; and there is very considerable variation in the way in which different people understood the dramas at the material time. That is to say nothing about how differently they have been understood since biblical times. If we keep within the Old Testament itself, at least five different kinds of people have to be considered: there is the prophet himself acting under a sense of divine compulsion; there is the uncomprehending, syncretizing Hebrew onlooker; there are the prophet's disciples who made the first record and who must have carried out some selection and rejection; there are the theologically sophisticated editors of the prophetic text; and there are the believing communities that produced the canon and inevitably interpreted the individual prophet's work in terms of the whole. Even

---

[1] Dillistone speaks of 'metaphorical conjunction between present situations and future events' (*Christianity and Symbolism*, p. 275). In this book the terms drama and reality have been used. The problem of the logic involved in these terms has been discussed in Chapter 2.

this analysis is a patent over-simplification – one cannot even talk about 'the prophet' or 'the editors' as if there was a common mind among them – and yet it embraces some who see the dramas as something near to sorcery and others who regard them as a word of God, not only to the prophet's generation, but to their own. We need to tread warily.

It needs to be noted, too, that modern interest is not divided equally between the five groups. Because most people who read the Old Testament today read it for theological reasons, or hear it read in a liturgical context, interest is concentrated on the first and fifth groups. We are interested in what the prophet thought he was doing, and we are interested in what the Bible, the revered, holy, canonical text, represents as the meaning of prophetic activity. The views of disciples and editors are of interest only to biblical scholars, and the views of the unsophisticated onlookers are of interest only to scholars whose approach to the biblical text includes an anthropological element. This explains the proportions displayed in this chapter. No doubt the second group was much larger than the third or fourth, but it was less significant for later thinking. There is also the question of evidence. The attitudes of the second group find their way into Scripture by chance, whereas the whole text gives evidence of the beliefs of the others.

The most obvious variation is that between what seems to be the view of the earliest prophets and that of Jeremiah and Ezekiel. They are separated by more than three centuries, centuries which included periods of intense theological activity. It would be possible to write down the arrow dramas in II Kings 13 as acts of imitative magic designed to influence the deity, and then to suggest a quite different explanation for the actions of the great prophets.[2] In that case the difficulty becomes one of continuity. A rough and ready way of solving that problem is to say that the acts of the great prophets preserve the form of imitative magic but not the content. The prophets act to arrest attention, to impress an audience, to reveal an idea, rather than to implant anything in the mind of the deity. It remains awkwardly true, however, that the editors of the Deuteronomistic history still saw fit to preserve the earlier stories, including those surrounding Elisha, so presumably it must have been possible for Jews of the post-exilic age to see virtue in both kinds of activity. Von Rad explains the

---

[2] See, for example, J. Gray, *Kings*, pp. 599f.; cf. Sawyer, *Isaiah*, p. 180.

development by saying that the earlier actions were directed to the future in a creative way, whereas the actions of the great prophets were more concerned with proclamation in the present. They not only prefigure the future but prepare the people to meet it.[3] In the case of Jeremiah's yoke, says von Rad, the concept underwent an even more radical change, for the drama concerns a possible future, not necessarily the actual one. The issue is thus forcibly pressed upon the onlookers, but, as far as creative action is concerned, the hope must have been that it would not operate at all.

The conclusion from this must be that a single explanation for all dramas will not do. We must take account of growth and theological change, and at the same time try to preserve some sense of continuity. It is not enough to say that the outward form of the action did not change. In view of the diverse nature of the actions at all periods, that statement is almost meaningless. What one hopes for is an explanation that gives a coherent account of both the diversity and the development of the understanding of dramatic action, and yet also pays due regard to the theology of the most profound prophets.

Broadly speaking, the explanations that have been given in the past fall into three groups. The first two are manifestly inadequate, the last more subtly so.

Some scholars of a previous generation concentrated their attention on the psychological condition of the prophet and thought little of what he himself thought he was doing and how his actions were understood by his contemporaries. These scholars did not scrutinize the dramatic acts for positive meaning but wrote them off as the products – sometimes interesting, often embarrassing – of an over-charged psyche. One has to recognize the pressures of the period. Earlier in this century Christianity, indeed all religious belief and behaviour, suffered an onslaught of reductionism from Freudian psychologists. Anything that appeared odd or irrational by contemporary standards was seized on and held to be evidence, not of divine influence, but of some deep-seated, psychological malady. In the field of prophecy, Hölscher's work of 1914 had used ecstasy as a sufficient explanation for much of what had previously been regarded as divine inspiration. Some Old Testament commentators all but surrendered to the pressure. O.R. Sellers of McCormick Theological Seminary, writing in 1924, diagnosed in Hosea introspection, an inferiority

---

[3] Von Rad, *Theology II*, pp. 97f.

complex, a martyr complex, sadism, exhibitionism, jealousy and a desire for revenge. He had married Gomer out of physical attraction but was then anxious to clothe his motives in religion. Sellers was equally disgusted with Isaiah for exposing himself in the streets of Jerusalem, 'a clear-cut case of exhibitionism, a tendency which may be observed at any bathing-beach'.[4] Ezekiel was an even easier target. He was often suspected of instability and his behaviour was said to be due to a disturbed mind. W.F. Lofthouse, by no means a rash critic, also took the psychologists seriously. He concluded that Ezekiel, acting under deep, religious excitement, tended to behave impulsively and then to attribute the impulse to God. Jeremiah, too, performed some of his dramas as a way of finding relief from pent-up emotions. Lofthouse seems to surrender a lot of ground, but he also contends that the deeper level of consciousness in which these strange impulses originated was the point of true religious inspiration.[5]

At this point we are in danger of plunging into confusion. Three different contentions must be distinguished. It might be argued that the prophets were merely acting under psychological duress, and mistakenly supposing that their actions had some religious significance. It might be argued that the prophets' religious experience was the dominant factor, that they believed themselves to be obeying the word of Yahweh, and that the modern psychological reduction, though interesting, is best regarded as an irrelevance. And it might be argued that the prophets were indeed obeying the inscrutable word of God and that any 'explanation' that takes no account of this is of no consequence whatever. The first is sceptical, the third theological, and both must be disregarded here because they depend upon highly determinative presuppositions. We must endeavour to seek the middle way and minimize our presuppositions. That means recognizing the importance of the theological convictions of prophets, onlookers, editors, and interpreting the actions in the light of these, while at the same time taking care not to invoke our own theological convictions. Difficult as that is, and, to be realistic, ultimately impossible, nevertheless that method is the only one to be adopted if we are to understand the Old Testament in its own terms. The theological – or the sceptical – enterprise has to follow after this work is done.

It follows that the psychological explanation of prophetic drama is

---

[4] Sellers, 'Hosea's Motives'.
[5] Lofthouse, 'Thus hath Jahveh Said'.

almost useless. Indeed it is not an explanation at all. It tells us what the modern psychologist thinks the prophets were doing. It does not tell us what the prophets themselves thought they were doing, which is what we really want to know. It implies that the dramas were by-products of prophecy, adding nothing and often subtracting from the dignity of the message. For our purposes the method is all wrong, because it is the product of distant observation. Disturbed or not, Ezekiel and all the other prophets were acting in a way that their contemporaries took seriously. What concerns us is how the behaviour was understood by those contemporaries, not how Ezekiel would have fared on a modern psychiatrist's couch.

The second attempt to explain prophetic drama is found in the contention that they were illustrations, visual aids, whose purpose was to make a difficult message more clear and more memorable. What is seen is more easily grasped than what is received verbally.[6] The prophets now appear, not as sufferers from a psychological malady, but as exponents of a psychological technique. This explanation of prophetic drama was expounded by Buzy in 1923 and it has found supporters here and there ever since.[7] Engnell suggests that the dramas were 'consciously sensational'.[8] So strong is the sense that any dramatic performance must have the purpose of making things clear that John Bright insists that Jeremiah's action with the waistcloth must have had an audience and Robert Wilson is convinced that, because Ezekiel's acts were too complex to be comprehensible, they could not have happened at all. The possibility that a drama might have a purpose other than communication is not even considered.[9] As recently as 1983 we find Bernhard Lang expounding the methods of prophetic communication and including, 'the performance of street

---

[6] It is interesting to note that some scholars who could not bear to think that the dramas were actually performed were none the less willing to recognize their value as visual aids. As regards Ezekiel, for example, Fairbairn approved of the dramatic acts as long as they were understood to be 'visions', perceived and thought about but not actually carried out (*Ezekiel*, pp. 48f.). Similarly I.G. Matthews was happy if the narratives were 'the literary product of a Babylonian editor'. The historical Ezekiel could then be described as, 'a normal, healthy-minded, vigorous prophet' (*Ezekiel*, pp. xxiif.).

[7] Buzy, *Les Symboles*, p. 156; see also Farbridge, *Studies in Biblical and Semitic Symbolism*, p. 10; Kuhl, *Prophets*, p. 35; May, 'Ezekiel', p. 86; J. Gray, *Kings*, p. 599.

[8] Engnell, 'Prophets and Prophetism in the Old Testament', p. 151.

[9] Bright, *Jeremiah*, p. 96; Wilson, *Prophecy and Society*, p. 283; see too E.R. Fraser, 'Symbolic Acts', p. 49.

theatre in which the prophet illustrates his word by game, mime and props'. Several dramas are mentioned as means of 'obtaining a hearing and giving weight to the word of their god'. In this regard the prophets were 'showmen'![10] Burke Long takes the same view, 'It is clear from the prophetic traditions that the acts were primarily used to dramatize and underscore what the prophets were saying.'[11] To be fair to Lang, he does not think of 'street theatre' purely in terms of a visual aid. For him the prophet is a political activist, not simply bringing news, but calling for decision and action; his aim is not simply to communicate, but to shock, to stir, to move. Involving onlookers in a piece of drama is a powerful way of furthering this aim.

All this is well said. This explanation, unlike the previous one, has the virtue of setting out what the prophet himself thought he was doing. It does not take the haughty line that we know what he was up to and he did not know himself. But the suspicion remains that this explanation wishes onto the prophets some very modern notions about the process of communication and persuasion; perhaps more to the point, this explanation is not sufficient to account for all the facts.

There are these objections. In the first place, the explanation fails to take account of those dramas that were not performed before an audience, or, equally important, that were not recorded as having taken place before an audience. This matter has already been discussed in Chapter 14. Elisha did not tear his clothes nor Ezekiel eat his scroll in public (II Kings 2.12; Ezek. 2.8–3.3). Was this because those actions related to themselves alone? Hosea may have married Gomer in public, but the significance of the action as prophetic drama was evident only to himself. Jeremiah had no audience for his performance with the waistcloth (Jer. 13) and Ezekiel had none for his performance with his hair (Ezek. 5.1–4). The book on the doom of Babylon was not used as a visual aid (Jer. 51), and in several other stories an audience is either not mentioned or treated as an irrelevance.

Secondly, many dramatic acts are, in fact, less clear than the oracles

---

[10] Lang, *Monotheism*, pp. 81f., 88f.; Uehlinger takes a similar view in his discussion of Ezek. 4–5. Lang quotes with some approval the words of Renan, who describes the prophet as 'un journaliste en plein air', who gathers a crowd with publicity-seeking tricks. Buffoonery was apparently put to the service of piety (*History of the People of Israel II*, Book IV, Ch. 16, pp. 356f.). Renan does not have to be taken too seriously. Nevertheless his low view of prophetic drama has proved convincing to many, even today.

[11] Long, *I Kings*, p. 129.

they are supposed to illustrate. Ezekiel's actions may arrest attention, but few of them can be said to communicate meaning more easily than words. Often oracles are necessary to make clear what the dramas mean. There may be some sense in which the performance of a drama represents an escalation in expression, but it is by no means always an escalation in clarity. Neither must we forget the actions where a visual aid is totally unnecessary. In every case where an audience of one person is involved the message would be simple and clear without any embellishment. How easy to tell Jeroboam that Yahweh will prosper his rebellion; how laborious and unnecessary to tear up a new cloak into all those pieces! Amsler's point must not be forgotten: why waste a valuable cloak?[12]

Thirdly, several dramas appear to involve contests. Leaving aside the competition on Mount Carmel, there are the clashes between Zedekiah and Micaiah ben Imlah (I Kings 22), Jeremiah and Hananiah (Jer. 27–2) and Jeremiah and Jehoiakim (Jer. 36). The purpose of the contest is to establish which prophet is speaking the truth. In no case is there any doubt about the content of the message, the doubt concerns its reliability. So it is not enough for Hananiah to deny Jeremiah's contention or to make him go away; the yoke had to be broken. Similarly Jehoiakim's dramatic gesture was unnecessary for the purpose of communication, and Jeremiah's response – to have the scroll re-written – was even more unnecessary for that purpose. It is evident that the dramatic acts were taken much more seriously than they would have been if their purpose had been simply to clarify the message.

Fourthly, in at least one case, the onlooker who was most concerned, never really understood what was going on. Elisha does not communicate very well with Joash in II Kings 13, and the poor king is reprimanded in the end. In that example it almost appears that Joash was not meant to know the meaning of the drama until it was too late.

Fifthly, we have to remember those dramas that were not artificially contrived. The tearing of Samuel's robe, the work of the potter, the various afflictions of Ezekiel were neutral happenings before they were invested with prophetic significance. In no way can they be regarded as visual aids to elucidate a pre-determined message.

---

[12] It is only fair to point out that Amsler's own answer to this question is quite different from the one implied here. He says that the new cloak was torn, in true prophetic style, to shock the audience into taking notice. In other words, he sees the dramas as essentially aids to communication (*Les Actes*, pp. 11, 61ff.).

Sixthly, the notion of language that lies behind this approach is at odds with what we find in the Bible. If words are simply a practical code for communicating intelligence from one person to another, then it is conceivable that the code might break down and a second interpretative medium be required. A modern observer might understand language and dramatic action in that way.[13] But that, of course, is not how the Hebrew understood words. As we have argued above, words were not simply a code for communication, they were centres of power. If they fell short, they needed to be fortified, not clarified.

If a prophet resorts to dramatic action, it is much more likely to be because the word was not powerful enough rather than not clear enough. This is confirmed by the treatment of the drama narratives by later editors. Their additions frequently complicate the meaning of the action and never clarify it. The reason is that the action is not thought of primarily as a means of bringing home a message, but as a divine creation in its own right. The prophet was moved by God to perform this action; therefore the action will continue to have significance. If the original reality to which it bore witness is no longer relevant, then the action will move on to relate to something else. It does not exist to make a single message clear but to represent a divine initiative in the world, and as that initiative moves through history, so the drama comes to signify new meaning.

From time to time variations of this explanation appear. It is sometimes affirmed that the dramas were not intended to make the message more clear but more authentic. They were supposed to reveal the prophet as a peculiarly gifted person and thus to validate his message. No doubt a prophet engaged in drama was more impressive than a prophet declaiming oracles, and this factor may contribute something to the way the dramas were understood, but this explanation cannot have satisfied the more sophisticated onlookers and it clearly did not satisfy the prophetic editors. Two of the most impressive dramas in the Old Testament were the work of false prophets. Zedekiah made horns and Hananiah broke Jeremiah's yoke; they were in error, and the editors knew they were in error, but they still recount the actions in all their impressiveness. Impressiveness is evidently not the point. Impressiveness plays no part in the well-known test of prophecy in Deut. 18.22. Thomas Overholt considers this question

---

[13] Many modern observers *think* they understand language in this rational way, but do they? Many of us are haunted by the idea that words have power even when reason assures us they have not.

in an article in 1982.[14] He contends that acts of power are intended to give authenticity to the prophet, but he distinguishes between dramas as we have defined them and actions that appear to abrogate 'the laws of nature'. The latter – largely associated with Elijah and Elisha – provide the ground for Overholt's argument. On the basis of texts like I Kings 17.24, II Kings 2.15, 4.37 and 8.4–6, it is easy for him to make his case, but they represent a different kind of narrative from those we are studying. These narratives raise quite different questions and would need to be treated in a different book.

Samuel Amsler takes a somewhat similar line.[15] He approaches the subject by way of the modern study of communication theory. That means, in the first place, recognizing that a relationship already existed between the prophet and his audience, and that the relationship could easily become blocked. If the prophet's chief intention was to move, shock, disturb his audience, then some new means of producing an effect had to be devised, a non-verbal means which would draw the audience into the action and so make effective communication possible. While this hypothesis might well have a bearing on some of the drama narratives, it does not, for reasons already given, provide an explanation for them all; and, as far as the literary stage of the process is concerned, it has little to offer.

Some scholars in recent times have taken a different direction and produced a third explanation of prophetic drama. It has now become commonplace to suppose that, in the biblical world, words and actions were regarded as 'dynamic'. Making things clear may be a subsidiary purpose of dramatic actions, but the main significance is independent of the effect on the audience; it is to achieve a positive end. Consequently, the public dramas, often thought to be typical – Jeremiah's breaking of the flask, for example – may actually mislead, because they divert attention from the main point. This approach represents a complete reversal of the argument that the dramas were visual aids. Dramatic actions do not exist primarily to convey intelligence but to exert power. Many scholars are now inclined to refer to the creative power of the prophetic word and the prophetic action.[16]

[14] Overholt, 'Seeing is Believing: the Social Setting of Prophetic Acts of Power'.

[15] 'Les Actes et la Communication par les Actes'.

[16] Bernhard Lang is one of relatively few scholars to protest at this suggestion. See his introduction to the collection of essays he himself edits, *Anthropological Approaches to the Old Testament*, pp. 7f. His resolution of the problem is scarcely an advance, however. See above n. 10. Perhaps the best antidote to the whole thesis is supplied by Thiselton in 'The Supposed Power of Words in the Biblical Writings'.

The dangers here are obvious. Is it seriously being implied that prophets thought that, by their own words and actions, they could cause great events to happen? Is prophetic drama, then, the Old Testament version of instrumental magic? Not really, for few argue that the words and actions are dynamic *in themselves*. The one who comes closest to this position is R.P. Carroll. He sees a clear link between prophetic drama and magic, and he does not confine himself to those actions that patently 'abrogate the laws of nature', as Overholt does. Fohrer and many others see links in history and in outward appearance, but Carroll goes much further. Carroll holds that prophetic dramas 'belong to an epistemological framework where divination and incantation represent power transmitted through words and gestures . . . These are not just actions which illustrate words with gestures but are part of the creation of the thing itself – they make things happen. The performed action, accompanied by the ritualized words and gestures, is causal.'[17] These words might just about be tolerated if Carroll were to allow that the true agent was not the prophet but Yahweh. However, he rejects such sophisticated theology. It 'fails to allow for the extent to which belief in magic dominated the ancient world.'[18] The Jeremiah tradition, he maintains, is full of magical elements.[19] They should be recognized and not dissolved away by anachronistic explanations. The weakness of this position is tied up in the two phrases 'belief in magic' and 'the ancient world'. Enough has been said about the former to make it clear that such generalizations add little light to the question, but the second phrase is equally unhelpful. There certainly was belief in magic of various kinds in the ancient world and there are abundant texts to prove it, but one cannot infer any such belief where there are no texts to prove it, least of all where what texts do exist point the other way. The evidence of the prophetic dramas shows that similarities can be traced between some dramatic actions and some kinds of magic, but very few imply the kind of similarity to which Carroll refers.[20] As a

---

[17] Carroll, *Jeremiah*, p. 295.

[18] ibid., pp. 296.

[19] 'Ritual magic is characteristic of the presentation of Jeremiah in certain strands of the tradition (e.g. 13.1–11; 19.1–2, 10–11; 25.15–17; 51.59–64). He creates and presides over the annihilation of the enemy (e.g. Judah, Jerusalem, Egypt, Babylon) by his performance of certain acts accompanied by incantations, curses and magical utterances' (ibid., p. 727).

[20] Jer. 51.59–64 might be an exception and a case can be argued regarding some of those recorded in Samuel and Kings.

general explanation of the function of prophetic drama, therefore, Carroll's thesis is unacceptable.

Carroll, however, must be respected for his boldness. Many other commentators show a tendency to have it both ways at this point. On the one hand, in order to stress the vitality of the prophetic act, they speak of dramatic actions being effective and ensuring fulfilment; on the other, when considering the larger theological issue, they draw back from the brink, modify their language, and make Yahweh the true agent. It is necessary to be quite clear about this. Is the prophet effective because his actions are dynamic, or because Yahweh prompts him? And if Yahweh prompts him, is it necessary also to make use of the notion of the dynamic quality of prophetic action? This point must be cleared up before it can be said that prophetic drama has been explained.

Perhaps, then, those people who speak about word and drama as dynamic are being imprecise. It is not difficult to believe that some of the early dramatic actions were popularly understood as being instrumentally effective, but that explanation will not do for them all; and it will not do for any once they are seen within the context of the whole prophetic corpus. Prophets had neither the power nor the intention to act in this way. Nevertheless it can fairly be said that a version of this theory of dynamic drama is the one that holds the field at the moment. In a sentence, the common thesis is that prophetic drama preserves the outward form of instrumental magic but the inner substance of Yahwist theology. Zimmerli's great commentary on *Ezekiel* provides an excellent example. In one column he states the thesis with great vigour, 'By this action, which is more than mere symbolism, the prophet prefigures as an event what he proclaims through his word. More precisely this event is brought into effect by the prophet and is commanded to happen. By accomplishing this action the prophet guarantees the coming event.'[21] If it were left at that, we should have to conclude that, according to Zimmerli, the prophet's actions were instrumentally effective. But in the next column he writes that, 'the sign-action is not to be regarded as an "actualizing" of the prophet's message which he has ingeniously devised, but that it is wholly given through God's sending and empowering him. Furthermore the sign-action is throughout only a living manifestation of the word of Yahweh.'

[21] *Ezekiel 1*, p. 156, col. 1.

Prophetic dramas preserve the outward appearance of acts of instrumental magic, that is to say, they are performed by a specially gifted person, they frequently mimic the end sought after, they are attended by an air of mystery and by the belief that, once carried out, they will proceed irrevocably to their fulfilment.[22] At the same time the theology is Yahwist, that is to say, the prophet takes no initiative and has no power of his own. He performs his dramas in obedience to Yahweh and it is Yahweh's power that ensures their fulfilment. Prophetic dramas are, therefore, explained as an amalgam of Yahwist theology and magical form.[23] They are effective acts, but they fall within the concept of Yahweh's control of history. Fohrer argues in this way.[24] He reckons that the world of magic provides the historical context out of which the prophetic dramas arose and he allows that a magical element persists in some Old Testament narratives. His list of symbolic actions, however, excludes the magical and he denies that any act of the classical prophets can legitimately be called magical. Nevertheless he spends a lot of time providing parallels between the prophetic actions and those from various other cultures around the world that can be called magical; these parallels are, of course, in appearance only; the Hebrew prophet acts by Yahweh's command and the power of the action depends on Yahweh alone.

Most of the writers who recognize prophetic drama to be more than a visual aid argue in this way. Yahweh's sovereignty does not make dramatic actions unncessary, nor rob them of their effectiveness. On the contrary, he wills to speak and act in this way. The dramas are both necessary and effective. They depend for their proper functioning upon a proper relationship between Yahweh and the prophet, hence the emphasis laid on the prophet's call and on the command to perform the actions; but they remain, in appearance, much like magical acts, though exceptions have to be made in the case of actions that were burdensome to the performer. These exceptions are in fact illuminating because they reveal that the supreme actor was not the prophet but Yahweh. They also reveal that we have not quite reached the end of our journey.

This explanation gives an apparently satisfactory account of most of the data. It tends to represent the dramas as predictions that proceed

[22] J. Gray, *Kings*, pp. 413, 449, 592, 599.

[23] See Sawyer, *Prophecy*, pp. 10f. and Overholt, 'Prophecy: The Problem', p. 63.

[24] Fohrer, 'Prophetie und Magie', pp. 25ff.; *Die Handlungen*, pp. 10ff.; *History*, pp. 234, 241, 243, 286.

to fulfilment, which is appropriate for many of the narratives, but not all. It sheds a little light on the problematic fact that prophets often pronounce judgment without any call to repentance, even sometimes when the time for repentance is past. The word and the drama are the beginning of the doom; through them Yahweh moves on to the historical consummation on which he has decided. This explanation is also consistent with the idea – prevalent, so it seems, in the Old Testament – that the course of history might be diverted if the prophet was silenced and his drama annulled.[25] It may seem dangerous to try to interfere with God's will, but presumably the prophets' antagonists had a different idea of what God's will was. That, however, is not quite the point. The point is that everyone agreed that it was not enough to disbelieve or denounce the drama. The drama had inherent power – even those who did not believe in the direction of its thrust recognized that it had power – so it had to be destroyed.

This explanation also has the virtue of ambiguity, ambiguity which is not, perhaps, intended but which none the less helps us to interpret some of the different views that were held in Israel. Dramatic action is always impressive, the more so if the performer displays the mystique of other-worldly powers. Those with a profound trust in Yahweh would see through the performance to the power of Yahweh evidenced in it. Those with a feeble grasp of the theology would simply be impressed by the mystique. Jeremiah's confrontation with Jehoiakim shows two people, both concerned with the same actions and realities, both aware of the significance of dramatic action and of divine will; but they differed in where they laid the stress. For Jeremiah, Yahweh's will was dominant and his own action was simply the expression of it. For Jehoiakim, the right action was all-important and Yahweh's will could be expected to conform to it. Broadly speaking, they both took the view that the prophetic drama was an amalgam of mysterious, impressive performance and a divine act to complement it.

This explanation is, therefore, valuable, but it is by no means perfect. In the first place, it is never quite clear whether the analysis belongs to a modern, theological approach to the data, or whether it is supposed that the prophets themselves thought in these terms. If, as one suspects, the former is the case, then the explanation does not answer the question we are raising. If the latter is the case, then it

---

[25] See, for example, I Kings 22; Jer. 20.1f.; 28.10f.; 32.2–5; 36.23; 37.15, 21.

seems that we are wishing onto the prophets a degree of analytical and theological sophistication that belongs to our world rather than theirs. This is not to deny theological depth to the prophets, but to suggest that their theological awareness needs to be set out in terms appropriate to their situation.

In the second place, it is not profitable to talk about prophetic drama having the outward appearance of magic. This question has been discussed at length in the previous chapter and there is little need to say more now. Magic, in the primary sense, is now understood as part of the social programme. A magical action takes place when the community, following community tradition, goes to work with the deity. Solitary actions by individuals, which, because they are solitary, may well be anti-communal, represent a debased form of magic and may even deserve the name of sorcery. The sorcerer is intent on fulfilling his own will and that of his client; he proceeds by traditional methods, for no sorcerer simply makes up a charm out of his own head. The prophet does not express his own will; in many cases the prophet's own wishes are not referred to, and when they are referred to, they are frequently set on one side. Equally, the prophet is not bound by tradition. He acts, believing himself to be under divine constraint, in all kinds of novel and imaginative ways. It may be that we do not know much about Israel's arcane tradition, but whatever it contained, we may be sure that marrying a prostitute, appearing in public naked or yoked, and burying a waistcloth were not included in it. To suggest, therefore, that prophetic dramas have the outward appearance of magic is, at best, to be imprecise.

The reference to magic, however, is not essential to the position under discussion, which is really concerned with the dynamic nature of Yahweh's word through the prophet. Zimmerli makes out this case without mentioning magic at all. Nevertheless there are other serious weaknesses in this explanation of the function of prophetic drama. In the third place then, it tends to assume a simple, linear view of time and causation in which drama always precedes fulfilment. It may be remembered from Chapters 4 and 16 that cultic activity and some expressions of magic warn against this presumption, and as a matter of fact, there are many prophetic dramas that cannot be explained exhaustively, or even explained at all, if they are regarded as actions to introduce or bring about future events.

Some of the dramas are best understood, not as introductions of future events, but as dramatic expressions of present ones. Hosea's unhappy alliance with Gomer is not a prediction of future infidelity; it is a powerful expression of how Yahweh relates to Israel. A universal fact is brought into dramatic focus in the marriage. Similarly the potter in Jer. 18 is expressing God's power over the nation. Only in a very reduced sense is that expression predictive. Again, Micah's announcement that he will go about naked is a response to a bleak situation. In one sense it initiates a future condition of mourning, but in another it is an actual mourning for Israel's present state. The action is weakened if it is reckoned to have only future reference. Again, the very complex drama of Jeremiah's waistcloth is, in the first instance, a theological reflection rather than a prediction. It is an eternal truth of Israel's existence that to be separated from Yahweh means corruption and ruin. Many of the dramatic actions of Ezekiel relate to events that are happening at a distance in space, not in time. Ezekiel in Babylon is living out the tragedy of Jerusalem, and some of his dramas express the agony of that city. The siege story of Ezek. 4 makes little sense as a prediction, but it makes great sense if it is reckoned to express in Babylon the precise conditions in Judah. Similarly, Ezekiel, lying on his side (4.4–6) expresses a state of affairs that already is; he does not cause it. The eating of strange bread (4.9–17) is an attempt to reproduce the conditions of the siege and the two dramatic actions of Ezek. 12 (replicating the scene when the captives are carried off and eating and drinking in fear), are an attempt to involve the exiles in the predicament of their compatriots in Zion. Some dramas look back as much as they look forward. In the robe-tearing scene at Gilgal (I Sam. 15.27f), Saul has already been rejected when the incident happens. Elisha burning his plough and boiling his oxen (I Kings 19.21) is saying goodbye to the old life and, in tearing his clothes (II Kings 2.12f.), he is denying the old identity before he takes on the new. The naming of Hosea's children (Hos. 1.4–9) involves the representation of past sins with their consequences much more than any prophecy about the future. An explanation that does not take account of these variations in the chronological relation of drama to reality is bound to be inadequate.

Fourthly, if God's dynamic activity through the prophet is understood through the model of instrumental magic, it must follow that a reality, once brought into being by prophetic drama, is bound to continue to its conclusion, for though magicians may fail, God presumably may not. This is very dangerous ground.[26] Every Israelite knew that fulfilment of any dramatic act could be frustrated – for all Zedekiah's efforts, Ahab lost – and in at least one case, Ezek. 37.15–28, the prophet was simply wrong. But more important, some dramas take place in circumstances where repentance is still possible and fulfilment not inevitable. Although the potter reworked the clay in Jer. 18, v. 8 shows that it is not certain that Israel will be 'reworked'. It depends upon whether Israel turns from its evil way.[27] Similarly, in Jer. 27 a choice is available to the people, though it is a dusty one: either submit to the yoke of Babylon or suffer from sword, famine and pestilence. The drama indicates the better way, though the choice is still open.[28]

From all this it is clear that a new hypothesis is necessary; one that is concerned with more than prediction and fulfilment; that is not so strong on the dynamic force of the dramas themselves, but allows for the fact that they frequently exist to express reality rather than to cause it; one that is more in touch with the notion of time revealed in the cult and less tied to the simple, linear notion of time and causation; one that allows for the possibility of variation in the reality, even when a predictive action has been carried out; and above all, one that is rooted in the Hebrew world and is not informed by twentieth-century attitudes.

In the work of A. Lods there is the suggestion of an interesting alternative. In his essay of 1927 it is only a hint, but it is raised again in just a few lines in his work on the prophets of 1937.[29] Lods asks whether prophetic dramas create the future or whether they are not best understood as unveiling realities that exist but are as yet unseen

[26] The Old Testament is so far from this mechanistic view of the universe that it allows that God can change his mind: Gen. 6.5–7; 18.16–33; Ex. 32.11–14; I Sam. 2.30f.; 15.11; Amos 7.1–6, etc.

[27] Jeremiah 'is convinced that he is proclaiming not an immutable decree of Yahweh but rather a plan that allows God to "repent" if the people repent' (Gunkel, 'The Prophets as Writers and Poets', p. 62; the whole section, pp. 61–3, is interesting and provides many other references).

[28] This human involvement in the course of history, whereby Israel co-operates or fails to co-operate, raises large theological questions about how God was understood to act. Israel was free to repent, but presumably Babylon was not free to call off the siege once it had been decreed from above. How much freedom had Assyria in Isa. 10.5f.? Much discussion of so-called 'divine events' in the Old Testament is beggared by this problem. It is too large a subject to be pursued here.

[29] 'Le Rôle des Idées Magiques dans la Mentalité Israélite', p. 59; *The Prophets and the Rise of Judaism*, p. 54.

or unappreciated. 'One wonders whether the prophet's act was supposed to influence the future or whether the future was reflected in the action of "the man of the spirit".' Lods goes no further and the hint has generally been ignored. Von Rad speaks of the fall of Jerusalem 'casting its shadow before it', but he does not expand on the subject.[30] The evidence, however, suggests that these two scholars are looking in the right direction for a solution.

In modern discussion of the cult, it seems that the ritual drama played out at the festivals on Mount Zion is suspended between two great events in the story of God's dealings with his people. On one hand there is the ancient event – the creation, the escape from Egypt – which is being recalled; on the other hand there is a great victory of the future, which is being anticipated. Contemporary victories also come into the reckoning and hoped for victories in imminent battles. The celebration is not, therefore, just a memorial, nor just an anticipation, but a telescoping of history, a drawing together of all events, past, present and future in the cultic day. It is as though the divine action shows itself in the world in a number of different modes, by our categories mythological (the creation), historical (the battle just won), ritual (the cultic drama), and the eschatological (God's final triumph). All are drawn together and expressed in the same celebration. To ask which of these causes the others is to ask the wrong question, for all are manifestations of the divine will. Equally, to suppose that they are all separate entities is to miss the point, for they are all different expressions of the same divine triumph.[31]

Cultic celebration demands a modification of the straightforward linear view of past, present and future, and the notion of causation that goes with it. The past is not drifting ever further away and the future is not blankly inaccessible. They exist in the divine will and they are brought together on the great occasion. This biblical understanding has remained with the Jewish people ever since. The Passover is a different kind of memorial from the annual service at the Cenotaph. Each year the marchers in Whitehall get older, and one has the sense that gradually we are losing touch with the past. Nobody can recall Ladysmith now, few the Somme, and before very long, few will recall El Alamein. Not so with the Passover.

[30] Von Rad, *Theology II*, p. 232.
[31] See above Chapter 5.

The escape from Egypt, escape from the holocaust, the founding of the State of Israel, and many other events, ancient and modern, together with eschatological visions of a glorious future, coalesce in the one celebration. Two different conceptions of time inform these two examples. The Old Testament with its theocentric view of history sees events, not as a series of sequential happenings spread out along a line, but as different aspects of the great divine activity in history in which all times and all places are drawn together.

When we discuss the bearing of this on prophecy, a similar number of guises of the divine event appear. An event has an existence in the will of Yahweh, in the mind of the prophet, in his oracle, in his drama, in the arena of history, and in the historical record.[32] Which of these manifestations comes first in the chronological sense is unimportant. Because the will of Yahweh is hidden, the first appearance of an event may well be in the word or drama of the prophet, in which case we may be misled into speaking of the word or action of the prophet being dynamic and *causing* a certain outcome. But that is unfortunate, for in fact, the whole complex has one cause, the divine intention. This explanation holds good for those dramas that are not predictive. In the case of Hosea's marriage, the critical factor – Yahweh's constant love for his unfaithful people – in the current state of affairs is hidden. The drama expresses that critical factor. It may not communicate widely, but that is not the point. The reality is focussed and manifested in the dramatic action even if it is unappreciated. If one asks, 'What is the point, if it is unappreciated?' the answer is that what is must proceed into expression because of the very weight of its being. It is expressed because it is true, and truth demands expression, whether it is apprehended or not. Even if it is not apprehended by people, it is apprehended by God. Jeremiah's action with the waistcloth expresses what needed to be expressed. More obviously, Ezekiel's dramatic acts relating to the fall of Jerusalem extend to Babylon a reality that had its locus hundreds of miles away.

This hypothesis is strengthened by considerations from two different directions. In the first place, the discussion of terminology in Chapter 2 revealed something interesting about the meaning of the words *'ôt* and *māšāl*. In Isa. 7 Isaiah prophesies the break-up of the

---

[32] Susan Niditch makes a somewhat similar point in *Symbolic Vision*, (pp. 33f.), but she unhelpfully ties it up with sympathetic magic.

Syro-Ephraimite confederacy. He then offers Ahaz a sign of the fulfilment of his prophecy. The sign is the birth of a child, and as the child grows, the deliverance takes shape. The purpose of the sign is to bind together the prophecy and the deliverance, so that the word, the growing child and the departure of the two kings are seen as a single divine reality. Something not too dissimilar is true of the typical *māšāl*. The *māšāl* represents a concretization of a universal truth. That sounds very abstract, but if the universal truth is Yahweh's hatred of infidelity and Israel is being punished for infidelity, then Israel has become a *māšāl*, a particular expression of a divine attitude. What exists in extension also exists at a particular point through the *māšāl*. One element does not cause the other. They are both aspects of the same reality.

The second confirmation derives from what was said in the previous chapter about the modern understanding of magic. In many cases the magical performance is not seen as a mechanism to bring about a particular effect. Rather the performance and the reality to which it relates are seen as different aspects of the same entity. There is rain, but there is also need for rain and gratitude for rain. There is war, but there is also fear of war and experience of war. The rain and the war themselves cannot be brought under control, but the experience of them can. So the hopes, joys, fears are worked out in the magical ceremonies so that the realities, when they happen, can be enjoyed or endured positively, successfully and to the full. Rain and rain rites, war and war rites belong together. But to decode these things in terms of our own notions of time and causation is to impose the wrong pattern upon them. It is considerations like these that help to unlock the Hebrew mind.

If we are to keep in touch with biblical understanding, we need to think of events in the Bible as complex entities existing on different levels or in different modes. The fall of Jerusalem is a divine act, a prophetic oracle, a flask broken before the elders, an actual horror, a series of dramatic actions in Babylon, and a bitter record. The deliverance at the Red Sea is an actual happening, an oral record, a written text, a constantly renewed celebration, plus all those later deliverances in which the prototype is recapitulated and renewed, and finally the great Messianic deliverance of the future when all the promises will be fulfilled. That is some event, but if we are to understand the idea properly, we must look at the whole rather than the parts.[33] The various elements are not to be logically disconnected. They are best understood as one integer with many different modes of expression. This way of thinking may seem strange, but it requires little effort to apply it to our own situation. What is marriage? It is a piece of paper, a gold ring, a ritual drama, a series of spoken words, an emotional attitude, a social status, a sexual act, a prolonged cohabitation, a new family unit. In one sense, none of these *is* marriage, but they are all aspects or expressions of one complex entity. It is in this sense that we have to understand drama and reality in the Old Testament.

The simplest and easiest application of this principle to prophecy is, of course, in the divine will-oracle-drama-fulfilment sequence. We simply need to recognize that it is not the word or the drama, but the divine will, that is dynamic. Diagrammatically,

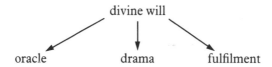

is more correct than divine will → oracle → drama → fulfilment.

When the circus comes to town, the first indication is the man who posts the bills and then the caravan from which the tickets are sold. The clowns and the animals are still a long way off. The first lorry brings the four posts of the big top; then comes the tent itself; then at last comes the procession, and the circus is here. The performance takes place; and then it all moves away, leaving behind a few men to clean the site. The bill-posters come first, but they do not *cause* the show. They and the performers are part of the same enterprise, and they are all under the control of the circus-master. He is not bound by the bill-posters – they are bound by him – but his circus needs them. The circus is a complex reality with many modes of existence, all interrelated, all necessary and all dependent upon the one who is in charge.

This illustration fails, however, in that it deals only with the simplest

---

[33] To take an example from outside the Old Testament, the most complex biblical entity of all is probably the resurrection, which exists in history (the resurrection of Jesus, however understood) in story (the kerygma), in ritual sign (baptism), in personal experience (repentance and faith), in practical ethics (so Paul continually hopes) and in eschatology (the consummation).

and commonest case of prophetic drama; it links one element and the next in a linear and sequential, though not causal, way. A comprehensive account of the relationship of prophetic drama to reality is not so easily illustrated. Perhaps the word 'drama' was a wise choice because of the complexity and elusiveness of the relation of all drama to reality. The drama stands over against reality; it holds up a mirror to it, it represents, it informs, it interprets; it heightens reality by highlighting it and revealing its inner nature; the drama affects the way that reality is experienced. And so we could go on. Prophetic drama hovers around the reality and gives it further 'presence'. It is another form of manifestation of the reality itself.

It is wise to point out that the hypothesis we are putting forward is not necessarily theological; it has to do with Hebrew thought-forms rather than with Hebrew faith, though the latter is included in the former. Jehoiakim would have shared these ideas with Jeremiah. There is, however, a difference in the way the two men operated the concept, and this difference *is* theological. The common element is that word, act, fulfilment, record, etc. are all parts of the same reality. Diagrammatically, we have a kind of wheel.

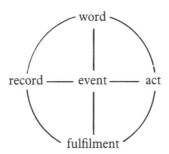

The theological question is where Yahweh fits into the diagram, where the dynamic force comes from, what turns the wheel. According to the 'low' theology prevalent in Jehoiakim's court – and prevalent, without doubt, through much of Israel and most of the ancient Near East – the divine activity is but one more element in the event, and so is located on the circumference. The dynamic can be exerted through the word and the act; human agents can bear upon the divine and so bring about the fulfilment. According to the 'high' Yahwist theology, no human being can exert control over the Holy One of Israel. The whole event belongs to him. If he wills it, all the elements happen; if he does not, none of them do, or, if words are spoken and actions performed, they are powerless. There can be no dynamic from the circumference; if the wheel turns, it turns from the hub.

Some such conception alone allows us to take account of all the factors that have come to the surface in this study. It makes it possible to explain the shift in theology and the difference in understanding between the Jeremiahs and the Jehoiakims. The great prophets were possessed of an idea of the sovereignty of Yahweh that was not fully worked out in the earliest traditions nor comprehended by the mass of the people. To return to the circus illustration, the early stories imply too much power in the hands of the bill-poster, and Jehoiakim and his courtiers never got beyond this understanding. The great prophets recognized the power of the circus-master and realized that they themselves had no power of initiative at all. We can thus explain the sense of compulsion felt by the prophet. Yahweh called into being both the reality and the drama. We can also explain the relatively few cases where allowance must be made for possible repentance. Yahweh is not bound by the historical process as human beings are. The future is what he wills it to be, and his will constitutes reality, as nothing else does. That reality may break into human consciousness by prophetic act or word, and there is nothing spurious about these acts and words. If Yahweh's will changes, however, the future is different, and different acts and oracles are called for. In both cases the prophetic activity is authentic because it represents a reality that has its being in God. That only one future can actually happen does not invalidate either prophetic exercise. In a similar way dramas and oracles that are delivered when the time for repentance is past are explained. The work of the prophet is primarily related to Yahweh and his historical activity, not to his audience and their response. If Yahweh decrees that a reality is to be, then oracle and drama go with it, regardless of whether anyone is listening or watching. We have also to explain prophetic contests. On this reckoning there is an absolute difference between a true prophet and a false one, a difference that is not in any way diminished by the fact that, in any given instance, nobody can be sure which is which. The true prophet signifies a world-shattering reality. The false one signifies what is in his own imagination. The contest is an attempt, sometimes a vain attempt, to put the issue to the test. Even then, as I Kings 22 makes clear, nobody can be sure. Only time reveals the truth.

Drama and reality stand over against each other, mutually dependent and interpreting each other. The drama presents, focusses, interprets and mediates the reality. It also modifies the reality, because, in so far as the attitude of the people is a significant element in the total event, response to the drama contributes something to the reality. Such a view of prophetic drama helps to unlock the world of the prophets and the thought of the Old Testament. It may also take us further. So much of the New Testament is written in Old Testament style, and Old Testament thought patterns persist in the New Testament. Beyond that, much Christian doctrine is conceived in terms of biblical ideas. It may be, then, that an enquiry of this kind has a bearing both on our understanding of the New Testament and on the starting-point of Christian doctrine. Perhaps the most interesting of the possibilities in this regard is in relation to the theology of the sacraments.

Bibliography

Books are referred to in the notes by means of the author's name and either a full title or an easily recognized abbreviation.

Ackroyd, P.R., 'Hosea' and 'Zechariah', *PC*, London and Edinburgh 1963
— *Exile and Restoration, a Study of Hebrew Thought of the Sixth Century BC*, OTL, London 1968
— *Israel under Babylon and Persia*, ONC vol. 4, London 1970
— *The First Book of Samuel*, CBC, Cambridge 1971
Addinall, Peter, 'The Soul in Pedersen's Israel', *ExpTim* 92, 1981, pp. 299–303
Albright, W.F., *Archaeology and the Religion of Israel*, 2nd edition, Baltimore 1946
— *From the Stone Age to Christianity; Monotheism and the Historical Process*, 2nd edition with new introduction, New York 1957
— *Yahweh and the Gods of Canaan; a Historical Analysis of Two Contrasting Faiths*, London 1968
Allen, Leslie C., 'Ezekiel 24.3–14: A Rhetorical Perspective', *CBQ* 49, 1987, pp. 404–14
Alt, Albrecht, *Essays on Old Testament History and Religion*, ET Oxford 1966
Amsler, S., *Les Actes des Prophètes*, Essais Bibliques 9, Geneva 1985
— 'Les Prophètes et la Communication par les Actes', *Werden und Wirken des Alten Testament*, ed. R. Albertz et al., Göttingen and Neukirken-Vluyn 1980, pp. 194–201
Andersen, F.I. and Freedman, D.N., *Hosea*, AB, New York 1980
Anderson, A.A., *Psalms*, 2 vols., London 1972
Anderson, B.W. and Harrelson, W. (eds), *Israel's Prophetic Heritage*, London 1962

Anderson, G.W., 'Hebrew Religion', *The Old Testament and Modern Study*, ed. H.H. Rowley, London 1951, pp. 283–310

— 'The Psalms', *PC*, London and Edinburgh 1963

— *The History and Religion of Israel*, ONC vol. 1, London 1966

— (ed.), *Tradition and Interpretation: Essays by Members of The Society for Old Testament Study*, Oxford 1979

Ap-Thomas, D.R., 'Elijah on Mount Carmel', *PEQ*, 92, 1960, pp. 146–55

Auerbach, Erich, *Mimesis: The Representation of Reality in Western Literature*, Berne 1946, ET Princeton, N.J. 1953

Auld, A. Graeme, 'Prophets through the Looking Glass: Between Writings and Moses', *JSOT* 27, 1983, pp. 3–23

— 'Prophets and Prophecy in Jeremiah and Kings', *ZAW* 96, 1984, pp. 66–82

— *I and II Kings*, DSB, Edinburgh 1986

Auzou, G., *La Danse devant l'Arche*, Paris 1968

Balentine, S.E., 'The Prophet as Intercessor: a Reassessment', *JBL* 103, 1984, pp. 161–73

Barr, J., *The Semantics of Biblical Language*, Oxford 1961

— *Old and New in Interpretation: a Study of the Two Testaments*, London 1966

Barrick, W. Boyd, 'Elisha and the Magic Bow: A Note on II Kings XIII 15–17', *VT* 35, 1985, pp. 355–63

Barton, John, *Oracles of God: Perceptions of Ancient Prophecy After the Exile*, London 1986

Batten, L.W., 'Hosea's Message and Marriage', *JBL* 48, 1929, pp. 257–73

Bentzen, A., *King and Messiah*, Zürich 1948, ET London 1955

Bevan, E., *Symbolism and Belief*, London 1938

Binns, L.E., *Jeremiah*, Westminster Commentaries, London 1919

Birch, W.F., 'Hiding-Places in Canaan I – Jeremiah's Girdle and Farah', *PEFQS*, 1880, pp. 235f.

Blackwood, Andrew W., jnr., *Commentary on Jeremiah*, Waco, Texas 1977

Blank, S.H., 'The Current Misinterpretation of Isaiah's She'ar Yashub', *JBL* 67, 1948, pp. 211–5

— 'Immanuel and Which Isaiah?' *JNES* 13, 1954, pp. 83f

— *Jeremiah: Man and Prophet*, Cincinnati 1961

— 'The Prophet as Paradigm', *Essays in Old Testament Ethics*, ed. J.L. Crenshaw and J.T. Willis, New York 1974, pp. 111–30

Blenkinsopp, Joseph, *A History of Prophecy in Israel From the Settlement in the Land to the Hellenistic Period*, London 1984

Boadt, Lawrence, CSP, *Jeremiah 1–25*, Wilmington, Delaware 1982

— *Jeremiah 26–52*, Wilmington, Delaware 1982

Boman, T., *Hebrew Thought compared with Greek*, Göttingen 1954, ET London 1960

Born, A. van den, *De Symbolische Handelingen der Oud-Testamentische Profeten*, Utrecht-Nijmegen 1935

— *Profetie Metterdaad*, Roermond-Maaseik 1947

Bouyer, L., *Rite and Man*, ET London 1963

Bowker, J.W., 'Prophetic Action and Sacramental Form', *Studia Evangelica*, vol.III part II, ed. F.L. Cross, TU 88, Berlin 1964, pp. 129–37

Brandon, S.G.F., *Creation Legends of the Ancient Near East*, London 1963

Bright, J., 'Isaiah', *PC*, London and Edinburgh 1963

— *Jeremiah*, AB, New York 1965

— *A History of Israel*, OTL Revised Edition, London 1972

— *Covenant and Promise*, London 1977

Brockington, L.H., 'The Lord Shewed Me: the Correlation of Natural and Spiritual in Prophetic Experience', *Studies in History and Religion*, ed. E.A. Payne, London 1942

Brown, S.L., *The Book of Hosea*, WC, London 1932

Brownlee, W.H., *Ezekiel 1–19*, WBC, Waco, Texas 1986

Brueggemann, W., 'From Hurt to Joy, from Death to Life', *Int 28*, 1974, pp. 3–19

Buber, M., *The Prophetic Faith*, New York 1949

Burney, C.F., *Notes on the Hebrew Text of the Books of Kings*, Oxford 1903

Burton, E.D., *Spirit, Soul and Flesh*, Chicago 1918

Buss, M.J., 'The Social Psychology of Prophecy', *Prophecy: Essays Presented to Georg Fohrer*, ed. J.A. Emerton, Berlin and New York 1980, pp. 1–11

Buttenweiser, M., *The Psalms Chronologically Treated with a New Translation*, Chicago 1938

Buzy, D., *Les Symboles de l'Ancien Testament*, Paris 1923

Caird, G.B., 'I Samuel', *IB* vol. 2, New York and Nashville 1953

Campbell, A.F., *The Ark Narrative*, SBL Dissertation Series 16, Missoula, Montana 1975

Carley, K.W., *The Book of the Prophet Ezekiel*, CBC, Cambridge 1974

Carmichael, Calum M., 'Forbidden Mixtures', *VT* 32, 1982, pp. 394–415

Carroll, R.P., 'Inner Tradition Shifts in Meaning in Isaiah 1–11' *ExpTim* 89, 1978, pp. 301–4

— *When Prophecy Failed: Reactions and Responses to Failure in Old Testament Prophetic Traditions*, London 1979

— *From Chaos to Covenant: Uses of Prophecy in the Book of Jeremiah*, London 1981

— 'Poets not Prophets', *JSOT* 27, 1983, pp. 25–31

— *Jeremiah*, OTL, London 1986

Cawley, F. and Millard, A.R., 'Jeremiah', *NBCR*, London 1970

Chamberlayne, J.H., *Man in Society*, London 1966

Charles, R.H., *Daniel*, Oxford 1929

Cheyne, T.K., *The Prophecies of Isaiah I and II*, London 1886

— *The Book of Psalms*, London 1888

Childs, B.S., *Myth and Reality in the Old Testament*, SBT 27, London 1960

— *Memory and Tradition in Israel*, SBT 37, London 1962

— *Introduction to the Old Testament as Scripture*, London 1979

Clements, R.E., *God and Temple*, Oxford 1965

— *Prophecy and Covenant*, SBT 43, London 1965

— *Prophecy and Tradition*, Oxford 1975

— *Isaiah 1–39*, NCB, London 1981

Coggins, Richard, Phillips, Anthony and Knibb, Michael, (eds) *Israel's Prophetic Tradition*, Cambridge 1982

Cooke, G.A., *The Book of Ezekiel*, ICC, Edinburgh 1936

Cope, G., *Symbolism in the Bible and the Church*, London 1959

Cox, D., 'Psychology and Symbolism', *Myth and Symbol*, ed. F.W. Dillistone, London 1966

Crenshaw, J.L., *Prophetic Conflict: its Effect upon Israelite Religion*, BZAW 124, Berlin 1971

Crenshaw J.L. and Willis, J.T. (eds), *Essays in Old Testament Ethics*, New York 1974

Culley, R.C., 'Anthropology and Old Testament Studies: An Introductory Comment', *Anthropological Perspectives on Old Testament Prophecy: Semeia 21*, ed. R.C. Culley and T.W. Overholt, SBL, Chico, California 1982, pp. 1–5

Curtis, E.L., and Madsen, A.L., *The Books of Chronicles*, ICC, Edinburgh 1910

Dahood, M., *Psalms*, 3 vols (1–50, 51–100, 101–150), AB, New York 1966, 1968, 1970

Danby, Herbert, *The Mishnah*, Oxford 1933

Davidson, A.B., *Old Testament Prophecy*, ed. J.A. Paterson, Edinburgh 1903

Davidson, A.B., and Streane, A.W., *Ezekiel*, CBSC Revised Edition, Cambridge 1916

Davidson, Robert, *Jeremiah, Volume 1*, DSB, Edinburgh 1983

— *Jeremiah, Volume II and Lamentations*, DSB, Edinburgh 1985

Davies, G. Henton, 'The Ark in the Psalms', *Promise and Fulfilment*, ed. F.F. Bruce, Edinburgh 1963, pp. 51–61

Davies, T. Witton, *Magic, Demonology and Witchcraft among the Hebrews and their Neighbours*, London 1898

Day, John, 'Shear-Jashub (Isaiah VII 3) and "The Remnant of Wrath" (Psalm LXXVI 11)', *VT* 31, 1981, pp. 76–8

Delitzsch, Franz, *The Prophecies of Isaiah I*, Edinburgh 1890

Dillistone, F.W., *Christianity and Symbolism*, London 1955

— 'The Functions of Symbols in Religious Experience' and 'Conclusion', *Metaphor and Symbol*, ed. L.C. Knights and B. Cottle, London 1960, also in *Myth and Symbol*, ed. F.W. Dillistone, London 1966, pp. 1–14

Douglas, M., *Purity and Danger*, London 1966, Pelican edition 1970

— *Natural Symbols*, London 1970

Driver, S.R., *Deuteronomy*, ICC, Edinburgh 1895

— *The Book of the Prophet Jeremiah*, London 1906

— *The Book of Exodus*, CBSC, Cambridge 1929

Durkheim, Emile, *The Elementary Forms of Religious Life*, London 1915

Eaton, J.H., *Obadiah, Nahum, Habakkuk, Zephaniah*, TBC, London 1961

— *Vision in Worship: The Relation of Prophecy and Liturgy in the Old Testament*, London 1981

Ehrlich, E.L., *Die Kultsymbolik im Alten Testament und im nachbiblischen Judentum*, Stuttgart 1959

Eichrodt, W., *Theology of the Old Testament*, vol. I, Stuttgart 1959, ET OTL, 1961; vol. II, Stuttgart 1964, ET OTL, London 1967

— *Ezekiel*, ATD, Göttingen 1965–6, ET OTL, London 1970

Eissfeldt, O., 'The Prophetic Literature' *The Old Testament and Modern Study* ed. H.H. Rowley, London 1951, pp. 115–61

Eissfeldt, *The Old Testament: an Introduction*, Tübingen 1934, ET from third edition, Oxford 1965

Ellis, Peter F., *The Yahwist: The Bible's First Theologian*, Notre Dame, Indiana 1968

Ellison, H.L., 'I and II Kings', *NBC*, ed. F. Davidson, London 1953

— 'The Prophecy of Jeremiah: Jeremiah's Symbolism', *EvQ* 40, 1968, pp. 34–40

— *The Prophets of Israel from Ahijah to Hosea*, Exeter 1967

Emmerson, Grace I., *Hosea: an Israelite Prophet in Judean Perspective*, Sheffield 1984

Engnell, I., *Studies in Divine Kingship in the Ancient Near East*, Uppsala 1943

— 'Prophets and Prophetism in the Old Testament', 'The Book of Psalms', and 'The Figurative Language of the Old Testament', *Critical Essays on the Old Testament*, Stockholm 1962, ET London 1970

Evans-Pritchard, E.E., *Witchcraft, Oracles and Magic among the Azande*, Oxford 1937

— *Theories of Primitive Religion*, Oxford 1965

Everson, A. Joseph, 'The Days of Yahweh', *JBL* 93, 1974, pp. 329–37

Ewald, H., *The History of Israel*, Göttingen 1864–8, ET 8 vols, London 1867–86

Eybers, I.H., (ed), *Studies on the Books of Hosea and Amos*, Potchefstroom 1966

Fairbairn, P., *Ezekiel and the Book of his Prophecy*, 3rd edition, Edinburgh 1863

Farbridge, M.H., *Studies in Biblical and Semitic Symbolism*, London 1923

Fohrer, G., 'Die Gattung der Berichte über symbolische Handlungen der Propheten', *ZAW* 64, 1952, pp. 101–20, also BZAW 99, 1967, pp. 92–112

— 'Remarks on Modern Interpretation of the Prophets', *JBL* 80, 1961, pp. 309–19

— *Introduction to the Old Testament*, Heidelberg 1965, ET London 1970

— 'Prophetie und Magie', *ZAW* 78, 1966, pp. 25–47, also BZAW 99, 1967, pp. 242–64

— *Die symbolischen Handlungen der Propheten*, 2nd edition, Zürich 1968

— *History of Israelite Religion*, Berlin 1969, ET London 1973

Fokkelman, J.P., *Narrative Art and Poetry in the Books of Samuel*, vols.I and II, Assen-Van Gorcum 1982 and 1986

Foster, R.S., *The Restoration of Israel*, London 1970

Frankfort, H., *Kingship and the Gods*, Chicago 1948

Fraser, E.R., 'Symbolic Acts of the Prophets', *StBTh* 4, 1974, pp. 45–53

Frazer, J.G., *The Golden Bough*, abridged edition, London 1923

Freehof, S.B., *The Book of Jeremiah*, The Jewish Commentary for Bible Readers, New York 1977

Frick, F.S., 'The Rechabites Reconsidered', JBL 90, 1971, pp. 279–87

Fuller, R.C. et al. (eds), *New Catholic Commentary on Holy Scripture*, London 1969

Gadd, C.J., 'Babylonian Myth and Ritual', *Myth and Ritual*, ed. S.H. Hooke, Oxford and London 1933, pp. 40–67

Gammie, J.E. et al. (eds), *Israelite Wisdom: Theological and Literary Essays in Honor of Samuel Terrien*, New York 1978

Gaster, T.H., *Myth, Legend and Custom in the Old Testament*, London 1969

— *Thespis: Ritual, Myth and Drama in the Ancient Near East*, 2nd edition, New York 1961

Ginsberg, H.L., *The Supernatural in the Prophets*, New York 1979

Godbey, A.H., 'The Hebrew Masal', *AJSL*, 39, 1922, pp. 89–108

Goldman, S., *Samuel*, The Soncino Books of the Bible, Hindhead 1951

Gottwald, N.K., *The Tribes of Yahweh*, Maryknoll, N.Y. 1979

Gottwald, N.K. and Wire, A.C. (eds), *The Bible and Liberation: Political and Social Hermeneutics*, Maryknoll, N.Y. 1976

Gray, G.B., *Sacrifice in the Old Testament*, Oxford 1925

— *Isaiah 1–27*, ICC, Edinburgh 1912

Gray, J., *The Canaanites*, London 1964

— *I and II Kings*, OTL, 2nd edition, London 1970

Greenberg, M., *Ezekiel 1–20*, AB, New York 1983

— 'On Ezekiel's Dumbness', *JBL* 77, 1958, pp. 101–5

Groenman, A.W., *Het Karakter van de Symbolische Handelingen der Oud-Testamentische Profeten*, Haarlem 1942

Guillaume, A., *Prophecy and Divination among the Hebrews and Other Semites*, London 1938

Gunkel, H., 'The Prophets as Writers and Poets', *Prophecy in Israel*, ed. David L. Petersen, Philadelphia and London 1987, pp. 22–73

Gunn, David M., *The Fate of King Saul: An interpretation of a Biblical Story*, Sheffield 1980

Guthrie, H.H., *Wisdom and Canon: Meanings of the Law and the Prophets*, Evanston, Illinois 1966

Hahn, H.F., *The Old Testament in Modern Research*, London 1956

Haldar, A., *Associations of Cult Prophets among the Ancient Semites*, Uppsala 1945

— *Studies in the Book of Nahum*, Uppsala 1946

Hammershaimb, E., *Some Aspects of Old Testament Prophecy from Isaiah to Malachi*, Copenhagen 1966

Hannay, T., 'The Temple', *SJT* 3, 1950, pp. 278–87

Harper, W.R., *Amos and Hosea*, ICC, Edinburgh 1905

Harrison, R.K., *Introduction to the Old Testament*, London 1970

— *Jeremiah*, TC, London 1973

Haupt, P., 'Hosea's Erring Spouse', *JBL* 34, 1915, pp. 41–53

Hayes, J.H., *The Oracles against the Nations in the Old Testament*, 1965

Hayes, J.H. and Irvine, S.A., *Isaiah, the Eighth-century Prophet: His Times and his Preaching*, Nashville 1987

Heaton, E.W., *The Old Testament Prophets*, 2nd edition, Harmondsworth, Middx., 1961

Herbert, A.S., 'The "Parable" (MASAL) in the Old Testament', *SJT* 7, 1954, pp. 180–96

— *Worship in Ancient Israel*, London 1959

Hertzberg, H.W., *I and II Samuel*, Göttingen 1960, ET OTL, London 1964

Hester, D.C., *Authority Claims in Jeremiah*, 1982

Hillers, D.R., *Micah*, Hermeneia, Philadelphia 1984

Hobbs, T.R., *2 Kings*, WBC, Waco, Texas 1985

— 'The Search for Prophetic Consciousness: Comments on Method', *BTB* 15, 1985, pp. 136–40

Holladay, William L., *Jeremiah: Spokesman out of Time*, Philadelphia 1974

— 'The Identification of the Two Scrolls of Jeremiah', *VT* 30, 1980, pp. 452–67

— 'The Years of Jeremiah's Preaching', *Int* 39, 1983, pp. 146–59

— *Jeremiah 1–25*, Hermeneia, Philadelphia 1986

Hölscher, G., *Die Profeten: Untersuchungen zur Religionsgeshichte Israels*, Leipzig 1914

Hooke, S.H. (ed.), *Myth and Ritual*, Oxford and London 1933

— 'The Myth and Ritual Pattern of the Ancient Near East', *Myth and Ritual*, Oxford and London 1933, pp. 1–4
— (ed.), *The Labyrinth*, London 1935
— *The Siege Perilous*, London 1956
— (ed.), *Myth, Ritual and Kingship*, Oxford and London 1958
— 'Myth and Ritual: Past and Present', *Myth, Ritual and Kingship*, Oxford and London 1958, pp. 1–21
Humbert, P., 'Mahēr Šālal Ḥaš Baz', *ZAW* 50, 1932, pp. 90–2
— *Problèmes du livre d'Habacuc*, Neuchâtel 1944
Hunter, A.V., *Seek the Lord*, Baltimore 1982
Hyatt, J.P., 'Jeremiah', *IB* vol. 5, New York and Nashville 1956
Jacob, E., *Theology of the Old Testament*, Neuchâtel 1955, ET London 1958
— 'Mourning', *IDB* vol.3, New York and Nashville 1962, pp. 452–4
James, E.O., *Myth and Ritual in the Ancient Near East*, London 1958
James, F., *Personalities of the Old Testament*, London 1963
Jensen, Joseph, 'The Age of Immanuel', *CBQ* 41, 1979, pp. 220–39
— *Isaiah 1–39*, Wilmington, Delaware 1984
Jevons, F.B., 'Magic and Religion', *Folklore* 28, 1917, pp. 259–78
Johnson, A.R., 'The Rôle of the King in the Jerusalem Cultus', *The Labyrinth*, ed. S.H. Hooke, London 1935, pp. 71–111
— 'The Prophet in Israel's Worship', *ExpTim* 47, 1935, pp. 312–19
— *The One and the Many in the Israelite Conception of God*, Cardiff 1942
— *The Vitality of the Individual in the Thought of Ancient Israel*, Cardiff 1949, 2nd edition 1964
— 'The Psalms', *The Old Testament and Modern Study*, ed. H.H. Rowley, London 1951
— *Sacral Kingship in Ancient Israel*, Cardiff 1955, cited from 2nd edition, 1967
— מָשָׁל , *Wisdom in Israel and in the Ancient Near East*, ed. M. Noth and D.W. Thomas, *VT* Supplement 3, Leiden 1960, pp. 162–9
— 'Hebrew Conceptions of Kingship', *Myth, Ritual and Kingship*, ed. S.H. Hooke, Oxford and London 1958, pp. 204–35
— *The Cultic Prophet in Ancient Israel*, Cardiff 1944, cited from 2nd edition, 1962
Jones, D.R., *Haggai, Zechariah and Malachi*, TBC, London 1962
Jones, Gwilym H., *I and II Kings*, NCB, London 1984
Josephus: see Whiston
Jung, C.G., *Man and his Symbols*, London 1964

Kaiser, O., *Introduction to the Old Testament: a Presentation of its Results and its Problems*, 1969, ET Oxford 1975

— *Isaiah 1–12*, Göttingen 1963, ET OTL London 1972

— *Isaiah 13–39*, Göttingen 1973, ET OTL, London 1974

Kapelrud, A.S., *Joel Studies*, Uppsala 1948

— 'Cult and Prophetic Words', *StTh* 4, 1951, pp. 5–15

— 'Shamanistic Features in the Old Testament', *Studies in Shamanism*, ed. C.M. Edsman, Stockholm 1962, pp. 90–96

Kaufmann, Y., *The Religion of Israel from its Beginnings to the Babylonian Exile*, Tel Aviv 1937–56, abridged edition, ET London 1961

Keil, C.F. and Delitzsch, F., *The Books of Kings*, 2nd edition, Edinburgh 1872

Keller, C.A., *Das Wort OTH als 'Offenbarungszeichen Gottes'*, Basel 1946

Kelso, J.L., 'Ezekiel's Parable of the Corroded Copper Cauldron', *JBL* 64, 1945, pp. 391–3

Kennett, R.H., *Ancient Hebrew Social Life and Custom as indicated in Law, Narrative and Metaphor*, London 1933

Kessler, M., 'The Significance of Jer. 36', *ZAW* 81, 1969, pp. 381–3

Kirkpatrick, A.F., *The Book of Psalms*, CBSC, Cambridge 1910

Kissane, E.J., *The Book of Isaiah*, 2 vols., Dublin 1941

— *The Book of Psalms*, 2 vols., Dublin 1953–4

Klein, R.W., *I Samuel*, WBC, Waco, Texas 1983

Knight, H., *The Hebrew Prophetic Consciousness*, London 1947

Koch, Klaus, *The Prophets: Volume One, The Assyrian Period*, Stuttgart 1978, ET London 1982

— *The Prophets: Volume Two, The Babylonian and Persian Periods*, Stuttgart 1980, ET London 1983

Koehler, L., *Old Testament Theology*, Tübingen 1935, ET London 1957

Kraeling, E.G., 'The Immanuel Prophecy', *JBL* 50, 1931, pp. 277–97

Kraus, H.-J., *Worship in Israel*, Munich 1962, ET Oxford 1966

Kselman, John S., 'The Social World of the Israelite Prophets: A Review Article', *RelSRev* 11, 1985, pp. 120–9

Kuhl, C., *The Prophets of Israel*, Edinburgh and London 1960

Lang, Bernhard, *Monotheism and the Prophetic Minority*, Sheffield 1983

— 'Old Testament and Anthropology: a Preliminary Bibliography',

Biblische Notizen: Beiträge zur exegetischen Diskussion 20, Bamberg 1983, pp. 37–46

— (ed.), *Anthropological Approaches to the Old Testament*, Philadelphia and London 1985

— 'Street Theater, Raising the Dead and the Zoroastrian Connection in Ezekiel's Prophecy', *Ezekiel and His Book*, ed. J. Lust, Leuven 1986, pp. 297–316

Leeuw, G. van der, *Religion in Essence and Manifestation*, Tübingen 1933, ET London 1937

— *Sacred and Profane Beauty*, ET London 1963

Leslie, E.A., *The Psalms*, New York 1949

Lévi-Strauss, C., *La Pensée Sauvage*, Paris 1963, ET *The Savage Mind*, London 1966

— 'The Structural Study of Myth', *Science and Literature*, ed. E.M. Jennings, New York 1970

Lévy-Bruhl, L., *La Mentalité Primitive*, Paris 1922, ET *Primitive Mentality*, London and New York 1925

— *Les Fonctions Mentales dans les Sociétés Inférieures*, Paris 1910, ET *How Natives Think*, New York 1926

— *L'Âme Primitive*, Paris 1927, ET *The 'Soul' of the Primitive*, London 1928

Lewis, Ioan M., 'Prophets and their Publics', *Semeia* 21, SBL, Chico, California 1982, pp. 113–7

Lienhardt, G., *Divinity and Experience: The Religion of the Dinka*, Oxford 1961

Lindblom, J., *Prophecy in Ancient Israel*, Oxford 1962

Ling, T., *A History of Religion East and West*, London 1968

Lipiński, E., 'Le שאר ישוב D'Isaïe VII 3', *VT* 23, 1972, pp. 245f.

— 'Recherches sur le livre de Zacharie', *VT* 20, 1970, pp. 25–55

Lods, A., 'Le Rôle des Idées Magiques dans la Mentalité Israélite', *Old Testament Essays*, ed. D.C. Simpson, London 1927, pp. 55–76

— 'Review of D. Buzy, "Les Symboles de l'Ancien Testament", 1923 and H.W. Robinson, "Prophetic Symbolism" in *Old Testament Essays*, 1927', *RHPR*, 1929, pp. 170–5

— *Israel from its Beginnings to the Middle of the Eighth Century*, London 1932

— *The Prophets and the Rise of Judaism*, ET London 1937

Lofthouse, W.F., *Ezekiel*, CB, London 1907

— 'Thus hath Jahveh Said', *AJSL* 40, 1924, pp. 231–51

Long, Burke O., 'The Social Setting for Prophetic Miracle Stories', *Semeia* 3, 1975, pp. 46–63

— 'Reports of Visions among the Prophets', *JBL* 95, 1976, pp. 353–65

— 'Prophetic Authority as Social Reality', *Canon and Authority*, ed. G.W. Coats and Burke O. Long, Philadelphia 1977

— 'Social Dimensions of Prophetic Conflict', *Semeia* 21, SBL, Chico California 1981, pp. 31–53

— *I Kings with an introduction to Historical Literature: The Forms of Old Testament Literature* 9, Grand Rapids, Michigan and Exeter 1984

Lowth, R., *Isaiah*, London 1807

Lumby, J.R., *I Kings*, CBSC, Cambridge 1886

— *II Kings*, CBSC, Cambridge 1887

Maimonides, *The Guide of the Perplexed*, ET by M. Friedlander, London 1875

Malinowski, B., 'Magic, Science and Religion', *Science, Religion and Reality*, ed. J. Needham, London 1926

Manson, T.W., *The Teaching of Jesus*, Cambridge 1931

Marett, R.R., 'Magic', *ERE* vol. 8, Edinburgh 1915, pp. 245–52

Marsh, J., *The Fulness of Time*, London 1952

Martin-Achard, R., *From Death to Life*, Edinburgh 1960

Matheney, M.P. and Honeycutt, R.L., *I and II Kings*, BBC vol.3, London 1971

Matthews, I.G., *Ezekiel*, Philadelphia 1939

Mauchline, J., 'Hosea' *IB* vol. 6, New York and Nashville 1956

— 'I and II Kings', *PC*, London and Edinburgh 1963

— *I and II Samuel*, NCB, London 1971

Mauss, M., *A General Theory of Magic*, 1950, ET London 1972

May, H.G., 'Ezekiel', *IB* vol. 6, New York and Nashville 1956

— 'An Interpretation of the Names of Hosea's Children', *JBL* 55, 1936

Mays, J.L., *Amos*, OTL, London 1969

— *Hosea*, OTL, London 1969

McCasland, S.V., 'Signs and Wonders', *JBL* 76, 1957, pp. 149–52

McConville, J.G., 'The Place of Ritual in Old Testament Religion', *IBS* 3, 1981, pp. 120–33

McKane, W., *I and II Samuel*, TBC, London 1963

— 'The Interpretation of Is. 7.14–25', *VT* 17, 1967, pp. 208–19

— 'Poison, Trial by Ordeal and the Cup of Wrath', *VT* 30, 1980, pp. 474–92

— *Jeremiah 1–25*, ICC, Edinburgh 1986

McKenzie, J.L., *Isaiah*, AB, New York 1968

Meek, T.J., *Hebrew Origins*, revised edition, New York 1950

Merrill, A.L. and Overholt, Thomas W., *Scripture in History and Theology*, Pittsburgh 1977

Meyers, Carol L. and Eric M., *Haggai, Zechariah 1–8*, AB, New York 1987

Miller, P.D. and Roberts, J.J.M., *The Hand of the Lord: A Reassessment of the 'Ark Narrative' of I Samuel*, Baltimore and London 1977

Mishnah, see Danby

Montgomery, J.A., *The Books of Kings*, ICC, Edinburgh 1951

Mottu, H., 'Jeremiah vs. Hananiah: Ideology and Truth in Old Testament Prophecy', *The Bible and Liberation: Political and Social Hermeneutics*, ed. N.K. Gottwald and A.C. Wire, Maryknoll, N.Y. 1976

Motyer, J.A., 'Prophecy, Prophets', *NBD*, London 1962

Mowinckel, S., *Psalmenstudien*, 6 vols., Christiana 1921–4

— *Prophecy and Tradition*, Oslo 1946

— *He that Cometh*, Copenhagen 1951, ET New York and Nashville 1954

— *The Psalms in Israel's Worship*, 2 vols., Oslo 1951, ET Oxford 1961

Muilenburg, J., 'Ezekiel', *PC*, London and Edinburgh 1963

Munz, P., *Problems of Religious Knowledge*, London 1959

Myers, J.M., *Chronicles*, 2 vols., AB, New York 1965

Napier, B.D., *Prophets in Perspective*, New York 1963

Neher, A., *The Prophetic Existence*, Paris 1955, ET South Brunswick 1969

Nicholson, E.W., *Preaching to the Exiles: A Study of the Prose Traditions in the Book of Jeremiah*, Oxford and New York 1970

— *The Book of the Prophet Jeremiah*, 2 vols., CBC, Cambridge 1973 and 1975

Nicol, T., 'Mourning', *HDB* vol. 3, Edinburgh 1905

Niditch, S., *The Symbolic Vision in Biblical Tradition*, Chico, California 1983

Norbeck, E., *Religion in Primitive Society*, New York 1961

North, C.R., *The Old Testament Interpretation of History*, London 1946

Noth, M., *Das System der Zwölf Stämme Israels*, Darmstadt 1930

— *The Deuteronomistic History*, Stuttgart 1943, ET Sheffield 1981

— *The History of Israel*, Göttingen 1960, ET 2nd edition, London 1960

Noth, M., *Exodus*, Göttingen 1959, ET OTL, London 1961

— 'The Laws in the Pentateuch: Their Assumptions and Meaning', 'Jerusalem and the Israelite Tradition', and 'God, King, and Nation', *The Laws in the Pentateuch and Other Essays*, ET Edinburgh and London 1966, pp. 1–107, 132–44, 145–78

— *Numbers*, Göttingen 1966, ET OTL, London 1968

Oesterley, W.O.E. *The Sacred Dance*, Cambridge 1923

— 'Early Hebrew Festival Rituals', *Myth and Ritual*, ed. S.H. Hooke, Oxford and London 1933, pp. 111–46

— *Sacrifice in Ancient Israel*, London 1937

Oesterley, W.O.E. and Robinson, T.H., *A History of Israel*, 2 vols., Oxford and London 1932

— *Hebrew Religion: Its Origin and Development*, London 1952

Orelli, C. von, *The Prophecies of Jeremiah*, Edinburgh 1889

Oswalt, J.N., *Isaiah 1–39*, NIC, Grand Rapids, Michigan 1987

Otto, R., *The Idea of the Holy*, Gotha 1919, ET London 1923

Overholt, Thomas W., *The Threat of Falsehood: A Study in the Theology of the Book of Jeremiah*, SBT 2.16, London 1970

— 'Jeremiah and the Nature of the Prophetic Process', *Scripture in History and Theology*, ed. A.L. Merrill and T.W. Overholt, Pittsburgh 1977

— 'Seeing is Believing: the Social Setting of Prophetic Acts of Power', *JSOT* 23, 1982, pp. 3–31

— 'Prophecy: The Problem of Cross-Cultural Comparison', *Semeia* 21, Chico, California 1982, pp. 55–78, also in *Anthropological Approaches to the Old Testament*, ed. Bernhard Lang, Philadelphia and London 1985

— *Prophecy in Cross-Cultural Perspective*, Atlanta, Georgia 1986

Patai, R., 'The "Control of Rain" in Ancient Palestine', *HUCA* 14, 1939, pp. 251–86

Paterson, J., 'Jeremiah', *PC*, London and Edinburgh 1963

Paterson, Robert M., 'Reinterpretation in the Book of Jeremiah', *JSOT* 28, 1984, pp. 37–46

Pedersen, J., *Israel, its Life and Culture*, 2 vols., I (I–II) and II (III–IV), Copenhagen and London 1926 and 1940

— 'The Rôle Played by Inspired Persons among the Israelites and the Arabs', *Studies in Old Testament Prophecy*, ed. H.H. Rowley, Edinburgh 1950, pp. 127–42

Petersen, D.L., *The Roles of Israel's Prophets*, JSOTS 17, Sheffield 1981

— 'The Prophetic Process Reconsidered', *TIR* 40–41, 1983–4, pp. 13–19
— *Haggai and Zechariah 1–8*, OTL, London 1984
— (ed.), *Prophecy in Israel*, Philadelphia and London 1987
Pfeiffer, R.H., *Introduction to the Old Testament*, London 1952
Phythian-Adams, W.J., *The Call of Israel*, Oxford and London 1934
Podechard, E., *Le Psautier I*, Lyon 1949
Polk, T., 'Paradigms, Parables, and Mesalim: on Reading the Masal in Scripture', *CBQ* 45, 1983, pp. 564–83
— *The Prophetic Persona*, JSOTS 32, Sheffield 1984
Porteous, N.W., 'Prophet and Priest in Israel', *ExpTim* 62, 1950–1, pp. 4–9
Porter, J.R., 'II Samuel vi and Psalm cxxxii', *JTS* 5, 1954, pp. 161–73
— 'The Legal Aspects of "corporate personality" in the Old Testament', *VT* 15, 1965, pp. 361–80
— *The Extended Family in the Old Testament*, London 1967
Pritchard, J.B., *Ancient Near Eastern Texts relating to the Old Testament (ANET)*, Princeton 1950
— *The Ancient Near East in Pictures (ANEP)*, Princeton 1954
Quick, O.C., *The Christian Sacraments*, London 1927
Rad, G. von, *Genesis*, Göttingen 1956, ET OTL, London 1961
— *Old Testament Theology*, 2 vols., Munich 1957 and 1960, ET Edinburgh and London 1962 and 1965
— *Deuteronomy*, Göttingen 1964, ET OTL, London 1966
— 'The Form-Critical Problem of the Hexateuch' and 'The Promised Land and Yahweh's Land in the Hexateuch', *The Problem of the Hexateuch and Other Essays*, 1958, ET Edinburgh and London 1966, pp. 1–78, 79–93
— *The Message of the Prophets*, London 1972
Radin, P., *Primitive Religion: its Nature and Origin*, London 1957
— *Primitive Man as Philosopher*, New York 1927, 2nd edition 1958
Regnier, A., 'Le Réalisme dans les Symboles des Prophètes', *RB* 32, 1923, pp. 383–408
Renan, E., *History of the People of Israel*, Paris 1887–93, ET Boston 1892–6
Renaud, B., 'Osée 1–3: Analyse Diachronique et lecture Synchronique, Problème de méthode', *RevScRel* 57, 1983, pp. 249–60
Rengstorf, K.H., Article on σημεῖον etc., *TWNT* vol.7, Stuttgart 1964, ET Grand Rapids, Michigan 1971

Rice, Gene, 'The Interpretation of Isaiah 7.15–7', *JBL* 96, 1977, pp. 363–9

— 'A Neglected Interpretation of the Immanuel Prophecy', *ZAW* 90, 1978, pp. 220–7

Ridderbos, J., *Isaiah*, ET Bible Student's Commentary, Grand Rapids, Michigan, 1985

Rimbach, James A., 'Prophets in Conflict: Who Speaks for God?' *CurrTM* 9, 1982, pp. 174–7

Ringgren, H., *The Faith of the Psalmists*, ET London 1963

— *Israelite Religion*, ET London 1966

Robinson, H.W., *The Christian Doctrine of Man*, Edinburgh 1911

— 'Hebrew Psychology', *The People and the Book*, ed. A.S. Peake, Oxford 1925

— 'Prophetic Symbolism', *Old Testament Essays*, ed. D.C. Simpson, London 1927, pp. 1–17

— 'Hebrew Sacrifice and Prophetic Symbolism', *JTS* 43, 1942, pp. 129–39

— *Redemption and Revelation*, London 1942

— *Inspiration and Revelation*, Oxford 1946

— *Two Hebrew Prophets*, London 1948

— *Corporate Personality in Ancient Israel*, revised edition, Edinburgh 1981

Robinson, J., *The First Book of Kings*, CBC, Cambridge 1972

— *The Second Book of Kings*, CBC, Cambridge 1976

Rodd, Cyril S., 'On Applying a Sociological Theory to Biblical Studies', *JSOT* 19, 1981, pp. 95–106

Rogerson, J.W., 'The Hebrew Conception of Corporate Personality: a Re-Examination', *JTS* 21, 1970, pp. 1–16

— *Anthropology and the Old Testament*, Oxford 1978

Rowley, H.H., *The Re-Discovery of the Old Testament*, London 1945

— 'The Nature of Prophecy in the Light of Recent Study', *HTR* 38, 1945, pp. 1–38

— 'The Meaning of Sacrifice in the Old Testament', *BJRL* 33, 1950–1, pp. 74–110, reprinted in *From Moses to Qumran*, London 1963, pp. 67–107 (quoted from *BJRL*)

— (ed.), *Studies in Old Testament Prophecy*, Edinburgh 1950

— *The Unity of the Bible*, London 1953

— 'The Book of Ezekiel in Modern Study', *BJRL* 36, 1953, pp. 146–90, reprinted in *Men of God*, London and Edinburgh 1963, pp. 169–210

— *The Faith of Israel*, London 1956
— 'The Marriage of Hosea', *BJRL* 39, 1956-7, pp. 200–33, reprinted in *Men of God*, London and Edinburgh 1963, pp. 66–97
— 'Ritual and the Hebrew Prophets', *Myth, Ritual and Kingship* ed. S.H. Hooke, Oxford and London 1958, pp. 236–60, reprinted in *From Moses to Qumran*, London 1963, pp. 111–38
— 'Elijah on Mount Carmel', *BJRL* 43, 1960, pp. 190–219, reprinted in *Men of God*, London and Edinburgh 1963, pp. 37–65
— *Worship in Ancient Israel*, London 1967
Sanday, W., *Inspiration*, London 1894
Sansom, M.C., 'Laying on of Hands in the Old Testament', *ExpTim* 94, 1982-3, pp. 323–6
Sawyer, John F.A., *Isaiah*, vol. 1, DSB, Edinburgh 1984
— *Prophecy and the Prophets of the Old Testament*, Oxford 1987
Schmidt, K.W., 'Prophetic Delegation: A Form-Critical Enquiry', *Bib* 63, 1982, pp. 206–18
Scott, R.B.Y., *The Relevance of the Prophets*, New York 1944
— 'Isaiah', *IB* vol.5, New York and Nashville 1956
Segal, J.B. *The Hebrew Passover from Earliest Times to A.D. 70*, London 1963
Seilhammer, F.H., *Prophets and Prophecy*, 1977
Sellers, O.R., 'Hosea's Motives', *AJSL* 41, 1925, pp. 243–7
Shedd, R.P., *Man in Community*, London 1958
Sherlock, Charles, 'Ezekiel's Dumbness', *ExpTim* 94, 1982-3, pp. 296–8
Siegmann, E.F., *The False Prophets of the Old Testament*, Washington 1939
Silver, Morris, *Prophets and Markets*, Boston and London 1983
Skinner, J., *Prophecy and Religion: Studies in the Life of Jeremiah*, Cambridge 1922
— *Isaiah 1–39*, CBSC, revised edition, Cambridge 1951
Skorupski, John, *Symbol and Theory: a Philosophical Study of Theories of Religion in Social Anthropology*, Cambridge 1976
Slotki, I.W., *Kings*, London 1950
Smith, C.R., *The Bible Doctrine of Man*, London 1951
Smith, H.P., *The Books of Samuel*, ICC, Edinburgh 1912
Smith, Ralph L., *Micah-Malachi*, WBC, Waco, Texas 1984
— *Hosea-Jonah*, WBC, Waco, Texas 1987
Smith, W.R., *The Religion of the Semites*, 2nd edition, London 1907
Snaith, N.H., *The Distinctive Ideas of the Old Testament*, London 1944

— *Mercy and Sacrifice: a Study of the Book of Hosea*, London 1953
— 'I and II Kings', *IB* vol.3, New York and Nashville 1954
— 'Time in the Old Testament', *Promise and Fulfilment*, ed. F.F. Bruce, Edinburgh 1963, pp. 175–86
Southwood, C.H., 'The Spoiling of Jeremiah's Girdle (Jer. 13.1–11)', *VT* 29, 1979, pp. 231–7
Stacey, W.D., *The Pauline View of Man*, London 1956
— 'A Pre-battle Rite in Ancient Israel', *Studia Evangelica*, vol.VII. ed. Elizabeth A. Livingstone, TU 126, Berlin 1982, pp. 471–3
Stalker, D.M.G., *Ezekiel*, TBC, London 1968
Streane, A.W., *Jeremiah and Lamentations*, CBSC, Cambridge 1913
Taylor, John B., *Ezekiel*, TC, London 1969
TeStroete, G.A., 'Ezekiel 24.15–27: The Meaning of a Symbolic Act', *BTFT* 38, 1977, pp. 163–75
Thiselton, A.C., 'The Supposed Power of Words in the Biblical Writings', *JTS* 25, 1974, pp. 283–99
Thomas, D. Winton, 'Zechariah', *IB* vol. 6, New York and Nashville 1956
— (ed.), *Documents from Old Testament Times*, London 1958
Thompson, J.A., *The Book of Jeremiah*, NIC, Grand Rapids, Michigan 1980
Thompson, M.E.W., *Situation and Theology: Old Testament Interpretations of the Syro-Ephraimite War*, Sheffield 1982
— 'Isaiah's Sign of Immanuel', *ExpTim* 95, 1983–4, pp. 67–71
Thompson, R.C., *Semitic Magic: Its Origin and Development*, London 1908
Tillich, P., *The Protestant Era*, London 1951
— 'The Religious Symbol', *Myth and Symbol*, ed. F.W. Dillistone, London 1966, pp. 15–34
Torczyner, H., *Lachish I*, London 1938
Toy, C.H., 'Note on Hosea 1–3', *JBL* 32, 1913, pp. 75–9
Tromp, N.J., 'Water and Fire on Mount Carmel: a Conciliatory Suggestion', *Bib* 56, 1975, pp. 480–502
Tucker, Gene M., 'The Role of the Prophets and the Role of the Church', *Prophecy in Israel*, ed. David L. Petersen, Philadelphia and London 1987, pp. 159–74
Turner, V.W., *The Forest of Symbols: Aspects of Ndembu Ritual*, Ithaca, N.Y. 1967
— *The Drums of Affliction*, Oxford 1968
— *The Ritual Process: Structure and Anti-Structure*, London 1969

— 'Introduction', *Forms of Symbolic Action*, ed. R. Spencer, Seattle 1969

— *Dramas, Fields and Metaphors: Symbolic Action in Human Society*, Ithaca, N.Y. 1974

Turro, J.C., 'I Samuel', *JBC*, London 1968

Uehlinger C., ' "Zeichne eine Stadt . . . und belagere sie!" Bild und Wort in einer Zeichenhandlung Ezechiels gegen Jerusalem (Ez. 4f)', *Jerusalem: Texte-Bilder-Steine* ed. Max Küchler and Christoph Uehlinger, Göttingen 1987, pp. 111–200

Vaux, R. de, *Ancient Israel: Its Life and Institutions*, Paris 1957, ET London 1961

— *Studies in Old Testament Sacrifice*, Cardiff 1964

Vawter, B., *The Conscience of Israel*, London 1961

— *Amos, Hosea and Micah*, Wilmington, Delaware 1981

— 'Were the Prophets nabî's?' *Bib* 66, 1985, pp. 206–20

Vogels, Walter, ' "Osée-Gomer" car et comme "Yahwe-Israel" ', *NRT* 103, 1981, pp. 711–27

— 'Hosea's Gift to Gomer (Hos. 3.2)', *Bib* 69, 1988, pp. 412–21

Vries, Simon de, *Prophet Against Prophet*, Grand Rapids, Michigan 1978

— *I Kings*, WBC, Waco, Texas 1985

Vriezen, T.C., *An Outline of Old Testament Theology*, Wageningen 1949, ET Oxford 1958

Wade, G.W., *The Book of the Prophet Isaiah*, London 1911

Ward, J.M., *Hosea*, New York 1966

— *The Prophets*, Nashville 1982

Watson-Franke, Maria-Barbara and Watson, Lawrence C., 'Understanding Anthropology: a Philosophical Reminder', *Current Anthropology* 16, Chicago 1975, pp. 247–62

Watts, John D.W., *Isaiah 1–33*, WBC, Waco, Texas 1985

Wax, Murray and Rosalie, 'The Notion of Magic', *Current Anthropology* 4, Chicago 1963, pp. 495–518

Weiser, A., *Introduction to the Old Testament*, 4th edition, Göttingen 1957, ET London 1961

— *Psalms*, Göttingen 1959, ET OTL, London 1962

Westermann, C., *Basic Forms of Prophetic Speech*, ET London 1967

— *The Praise of God in the Psalms*, ET London 1966

Wevers, J.W., 'A Study in Form Criticism of Individual Complaint Psalms', *VT* 6, 1956, pp. 80–96

— *Ezekiel*, NCB, London 1969

Whiston, William, *The Works of Flavius Josephus*, London 1860

Whitehouse, O.C., *Isaiah 1–39*, CB, Edinburgh 1905

Whitley, C.F., *The Prophetic Achievement*, London 1963

Widengren, G., *Literary and Psychological Aspects of the Hebrew Prophets*, Uppsala 1948

— 'Early Hebrew Myths and Their Interpretation', *Myth, Ritual and Kingship*, ed. S.H. Hooke, Oxford and London 1958, pp. 149–203

Willis, J.T., 'The Meaning of Is. 7.14 and its Application to Mt. 1.23', *ResQ* 21, 1978, pp. 1–18

Wilson, Robert R., 'An Interpretation of Ezekiel's Dumbness', *VT* 22, 1974, pp. 91–104

— 'Prophecy and Ecstasy: a Re-examination', *JBL* 98, 1979, pp. 321–37

— *Prophecy and Society in Ancient Israel*, Philadelphia 1980

— *Sociological Approaches to the Study of the Old Testament*, Philadelphia 1984

Winward, S.F., *A Guide to the Prophets*, London 1968

Wolfe, R.E., 'Micah', *IB* vol. 6, New York and Nashville 1956

Wolff, H.W., *Anthropology of the Old Testament*, Munich 1973, ET London 1974

— *Hosea*, 1961, ET Hermeneia, Philadelphia 1974

— *Joel and Amos*, 1969, ET Hermeneia, Philadelphia 1977

— *Micah the Prophet*, München 1978, ET Philadelphia 1981

— *Confrontations with the Prophets*, München 1982, ET Philadelphia 1983

— 'Prophets and Institutions in the Old Testament', *CurrTM* 13, 1986, pp. 5–12

Wright, G.E., 'The Temple in Palestine-Syria', Part III of 'The Significance on the Temple in the Ancient Near East', *BA* 7, 1944, pp. 65–77

— *The Old Testament against its Environment*, SBT 2, London 1950

— *The Biblical Doctrine of Man in Society*, London 1954

— *Biblical Archaeology*, London 1957

Yalman, Nur, Article on 'Magic', *International Encyclopedia of the Social Sciences*, vol. 9, ed. David L. Sills, New York 1968, p. 525

Young, E.J., *The Book of Isaiah*, 3 vols., Grand Rapids, Michigan 1969

Zimmerli, W., *Ezekiel*, 2 vols., 1969, ET Hermeneia, Philadelphia 1979 and 1983

Index of Modern Authors

Index of Biblical References